A SEMANTIC AND STRUCTURAL ANALYSIS OF COLOSSIANS

SEMANTIC AND STRUCTURAL ANALYSIS SERIES

JOHN BANKER, GENERAL EDITOR

A SEMANTIC AND STRUCTURAL ANALYSIS OF COLOSSIANS

Second edition

John Callow

SIL International

Second edition

© 2002 by SIL International

ISBN: 155671-130-1

Library of Congress Control Number: 2002105349

First edition 1983
Printed in the United States of America

All Rights Reserved

No part of this publication may be reproduced, stored in a retrieval system, or transmitted in any form or by any means—electronic, mechanical, photocopy, recording, or otherwise—without the express permission of SIL International, with the exception of brief excerpts in journal articles or reviews.

Copies of this and other publications of SIL International may be obtained from

International Academic Bookstore
7500 West Camp Wisdom Road
Dallas, TX 75236, USA

Voice: 972-708-7404
Fax: 972-708-7363
E-mail: academic_books@sil.org
Internet: http://www.sil.org

CONTENTS

Preface vii
Abbreviations viii
General Introduction: The Theory and Presentation of Semantic and Structural Analyses ix
    Communication Relations Chart xiii
Introduction to the Semantic Structure of Colossians 1
    Overview: The Constituent Organization of Colossians... 3
    Overview: The Semantic Units and Their Theme Statements 3
The Presentation and Discussion of the Semantic Units of Colossians 7
Colossians 1:1–4:18 (Epistle)... 7
    Epistle Constituent 1:1–2 (Paragraph) 8
    Epistle Constituent 1:3–4:6 (Part) 11
        Part Constituent 1:3–12 (Section) 13
            Section Constituent 1:3–8 (Paragraph) 15
            Section Constituent 1:9–12 (Paragraph) 23
        Part Constituent 1:13–3:17 (Sub-part) 32
            Sub-part Constituent 1:13–2:5 (Division) 34
                Division Constituent 1:13–23 (Section) 36
                    Section Constituent 1:13–20 (Paragraph) 37
                    Section Constituent 1:21–23 (Paragraph) 53
                Division Constituent 1:24–2:5 (Section) 58
                    Section Constituent 1:24–29 (Paragraph) 60
                    Section Constituent 2:1–5 (Paragraph) 70
            Sub-part Constituent 2:6–3:17 (Division) 79
                Division Constituent 2:6–7 (Paragraph)... 81
                Division Constituent 2:8–23 (Section)... 86
                    Section Constituent 2:8–15 (Paragraph) 87
                    Section Constituent 2:16–19 (Paragraph) 101
                    Section Constituent 2:20–23 (Paragraph) 108
                Division Constituent 3:1–16 (Section)... 113
                    Section Constituent 3:1–4 (Paragraph) 114
                    Section Constituent 3:5–11 (Paragraph) 118
                    Section Constituent 3:12–14 (Paragraph) 125
                    Section Constituent 3:15–16 (Paragraph) 130
                Division Constituent 3:17 (Propositional Cluster) 136
        Part Constituent 3:18–4:6 (Division)... 138
            Division Constituent 3:18–4:1 (Section) 139
                Section Constituent 3:18–19 (Paragraph) 141
                Section Constituent 3:20–21 (Paragraph) 143
                Section Constituent 3:22–4:1 (Paragraph) 145
            Division Constituent 4:2–6 (Section) 150
                Section Constituent 4:2–4 (Paragraph 151
                Section Constituent 4:5–6 (Paragraph) 154
    Epistle Constituent 4:7–18 (Section) 156
        Section Constituent 4:7–9 (Paragraph)... 157
        Section Constituent 4:10–14 (Paragraph) 161
        Section Constituent 4:15–17 (Paragraph) 166
        Section Constituent 4:18 (Paragraph) 169
Bibliography 171

PREFACE

Since 1983, there has been considerable refinement of the SSA format, so that when the first edition of *A Semantic Structure Analysis of Colossians* was no longer in print, yet still in demand, a new edition was called for. However, this second edition does not utilize all of the most recent SSA terminology; the 1983 analysis and notes remain essentially the same, though I have made some minor changes. (The most notable difference between this and the other SSAs published since 1994 is that this one does not discuss "paragraph patterns.")

I want to express sincere gratitude for the many hours of work on this second edition given by Alan Thomas, who keyboarded the entire book, copying the first edition so that a second edition could be a computerized revision; by Dick Blight, who formatted the displays and shepherded the book through the editorial process; and by copyeditor Betty Eastman, who did the final edit of the manuscript.

John Banker, general editor
March, 2002

PREFACE TO FIRST EDITION

In the summer of 1973, John Beekman, who was at that time the International Translation Coordinator for Wycliffe Bible Translators and the Summer Institute of Linguistics, gathered together a group of translation consultants at the International Linguistics Center in Dallas, Texas, with the expressed purpose of preparing a technical semantically-oriented analysis of the Epistle to the Colossians. They worked as a team, reviewing one another's work, and some weeks later had prepared an initial analysis of Colossians, together with notes on all their decisions. The following spring, John Beekman, with two of those consultants, reviewed and edited the analysis, notes, and displays. The end result was circulated for comment and feedback to selected persons in the different countries in which the Summer Institute of Linguistics was working. It was known then as a "Literary-Semantic Analysis" and is referred to a number of times in this revision as "the earlier analysis (Beekman 1974)."

About two years later, John Callow was asked to do a thorough revision of the analysis, taking into account the various comments that had been received, developments in the theory of semantic structure, new ideas concerning the formats to be used for the displays, etc. This work was undertaken in the course of the following three years. But even that revision involved lengthy discussions with Greek scholars Dr. Harold Greenlee and Dr. John Werner, as well as many discussions with John Beekman. Finally, in 1982, the work was subjected to a detailed review by myself and John Callow, paying particular attention to recent developments in the underlying theory and further experience in publishing what are now known as Semantic Structure Analyses (SSAs).

Consequently, although one author's name appears in connection with this work, and he is responsible for its final form, this has been very much a team-effort from the start, and the author is very much aware that he has made extensive use of the contributions of others, which he very readily and gladly acknowledges.

Both I, as editor, and John Callow are aware that there are still a number of places in this analysis of Colossians where we are by no means sure what the best understanding of the original is. More light is still needed, but it is hoped that with further theoretical developments and with continued research into New Testament Greek, the number of places where there is still uncertainty can be steadily reduced.

We want to express sincere gratitude to Elaine Beekman, Bonnie Kopesec, Jennifer Kopesec, and Ida Wells for the numerous hours they gave to the preparation of the manuscript for publication.

Michael F. Kopesec
September, 1982

ABBREVIATIONS

Versions

JB	Jerusalem Bible
KJV	King James Version
LB	Living Bible
NAB	New American Bible
NEB	New English Bible
NIV	New International Version
RSV	Revised Standard Version
TEV	Today's English Version (*Good News Bible,* 1976 edition, unless otherwise stated)

Abbreviations Used in Displays

(exc)	exclusive
[HEN]	hendiadys
[HYP]	hyperbole
(inc)	inclusive (all unmarked first person plural pronouns are also inclusive)
[MET]	metaphor
[MTY]	metonymy
[PRS]	personification
(pl)	plural (all unmarked second person pronouns are also plural)
(sg)	singular
[SYN]	synecdoche

Other Abbreviations

UBS	United Bible Societies

GENERAL INTRODUCTION: THE THEORY AND PRESENTATION OF SEMANTIC AND STRUCTURAL ANALYSES

The theory on which a semantic and structural analysis is based

This volume is an analytical commentary on Paul's letter to the church in Colosse. It is based on the theory of semantic structure set forth in "The Semantic Structure of Written Communication" (Beekman, Callow, and Kopesec) and has been prepared with the particular needs of Bible translators in view. Like other commentaries, it aims to arrive at the meaning that the original writer intended to communicate to the original recipients. It differs from most other commentaries, however, in that it is consciously based on a theory of the structure of meaning. Consequently, a consistent and comprehensive approach to the analysis of the meaning is applied to the total document, whether that meaning is conveyed by the smallest segments of the written communication (i.e., morphemes or words) or by the largest segments (i.e., the major constituents of the document or the whole document itself).

The title *A Semantic and Structural Analysis of Colossians* has been carefully chosen. By "structural" is meant that the letter is composed of a coherent grouping of constituent parts. Each of the major constituents, in turn, consists of coherent groupings of yet smaller constituents, and so on. These constituents, of whatever size or complexity, are identified and then described as to their role, or function, within the total structure and as to their relationship to other constituents. As a structural analysis, the focus is also on the most important (i.e., the prominent) information being communicated by the document as a whole and by each of its constituent parts and on its overall organization. "Semantic" highlights the concern of this approach with meaning, since, in a system of communication, meaning has priority over the forms used to convey it. This correlates well with the concern of Bible translators and expositors to determine the meaning intended by the original writers and to convey that meaning to an audience of a time, place, culture, and language other than those of the original addressees.

The theory on which this approach is based has two main emphases: (1) discourses are arranged hierarchically; and (2) every semantic unit, large or small, can be analyzed in terms of certain inherent features. These two points are summarized in the next two sections.

Semantic units in a hierarchical system

Any well-structured written communication such as the books of the New Testament are, consists of *semantic units* arranged in a *hierarchical system*. That is to say, the smaller semantic units are combined into larger semantic units, which in turn are combined into yet larger units, and so on, as in the constituent organization chart on page 3.

A written discourse consists of three basic semantic units: the discourse concept, the proposition, and the propositional configuration. The *discourse concept* corresponds roughly to what in grammar is a word or a phrase. It is, typically, a coherent grouping of lexical concepts that refers to a thing, an event, an attribute, or a relation in the world that is being referred to in the document. (Lexical concepts are the concepts commonly found as entries in a dictionary. A writer may use them singly or in combination in the discourse.) A discourse concept will also have an expressive, or emotive, component of meaning, commonly referred to as its connotation. A discourse concept characteristically functions as a constituent of a proposition.

The *proposition* corresponds roughly to a clause. However, in Koine Greek other grammatical forms are often used to express a proposition. For example, nouns and adjectives may represent event propositions (e.g., 'salvation' and 'saving'). Similarly, phrases may represent propositions (e.g., 'into the knowledge of God', representing the proposition 'in order that people may know God'). The proposition is, typically, a coherent grouping of discourse concepts that communicates an event (e.g., 'Jesus overturned the tables') or a state (e.g., 'Zacchaeus was a small man'). Broadly speaking, the proposition carries one of three communication, or illocutionary, functions: it states, questions, or commands the event or state that it refers to. The constituents of a proposition (typically discourse concepts) are linked together by a system of relations called "case roles." (For more on case roles, see Beekman, Callow, and Kopesec, chap. 6.)

The *propositional configuration* is a coherent grouping of propositions and/or other propositional configurations related to each other by a system of "communication relations" (see Beekman, Callow, and Kopesec, chapter 8). The extent of development of a particular discourse, combined with the human tendency to "package" or group things for more effective conceptual or cognitive control, has given rise to a number of typical groupings of propositional configurations. For narrative material, a typical hierarchy of propositional configurations is: propositional cluster, paragraph, episode, scene, act, and part (ranging from small to large). In nonnarrative literature (such as the Epistles), the more typical configurations encountered are: propositional cluster, paragraph, section, division, and part.

Each type of configuration is defined in terms of its composition. That is, a division is a propositional configuration consisting of two or more constituents, at least one of which is a section; a section is a propositional configuration consisting of two or more constituents, at least one of which is a paragraph; etc. The classification of the propositional configurations into paragraph, section, etc., is sensitive to other considerations as well. The general size and complexity of the unit is one of the main considerations. Often the classification can be made on this basis alone. However, there are times when the size and complexity of the unit does not unequivocally decide the issue. In such cases, another factor comes into play—the distribution of the unit in the overall organization of the discourse. For example, two units of about the same complexity and size may be classified differently, because the one is functioning at a level in the overall structure that is characteristic of propositions, whereas the other is functioning at a level that is characteristic of paragraphs or larger units. The first could be regarded as a propositional cluster and the second as a paragraph.

The features of a semantic unit

The second main point of the theory that is especially relevant to a semantic and structural analysis is that each semantic unit, no matter how small or how large, is characterized by six features, three being "analytical features" and three "holistic features."

Analytical features	Constituency	(Internal) Coherence	Prominence
Holistic features	Classification	(External) Coherence	Thematic content

The three *analytical* features enable the analyst to identify the semantic units in a written document so as to distinguish one unit from another; to relate the units to each other; and to pick out the most important information that is communicated by each unit. (The discussions below the displays of each semantic unit will describe these particular features in detail.) The three *holistic* features come into play in the overall characterization of a unit as shown by the unit title and theme statement as well as in the discussion of the unit's purpose.

Since the analytical features are more overtly involved in the process of analysis, they are discussed here in more detail. The feature of *constituency* refers to the fact that each semantic unit is made up of other semantic units. The feature of *coherence* has to do with how the constituent units combine with each other. They have to be referentially coherent; in other words, there is repetition of reference in the unit, whether by identical repetition, the use of synonyms or "pro" forms, or structural devices such as parallelism, chiasmus, or "sandwich structure." They have to be situationally coherent, meaning that the time frame should be acceptable in the world being talked about and that there should be expressive, or connotational, consistency, as well as overall illocutionary consistency. And they should also be organizationally coherent; that is, the relations between any two constituents should be compatible with the contents of those constituents (again, in the world being talked about by the writer).

The third analytical feature, *prominence*, has to do with the relative importance of information in a semantic unit. (Note that the determination of relative importance is not from a theological perspective, nor from an overall biblical perspective, but from the perspective of the organization of the particular unit being analyzed.) The most significant thing to be pointed out about the feature of prominence is the distinction between natural and marked (or special) prominence. *Natural prominence* has to do with the relational structure: In many binary pairs of the communication relations, one of the two relations is naturally more prominent. For example, an exhortation is more prominent than the grounds it is paired with, and a means is more prominent than the purpose. *Marked prominence*, on the other hand, is prominence that is shown by special linguistic devices in the particular language.

In Koine Greek, for example, at the propositional cluster level, marked prominence is generally shown by an atypical ordering of the clauses, or by a propositional cluster of lesser natural prominence being given the form that would be expected of a naturally prominent cluster. At the propositional level, placement of material in front of the verb is a frequent prominence-marking device. Marked prominence is used in a discourse for a variety of reasons, for example, topic identification and maintenance, contrast, and intensification.

The parts of the SSA

The communication situation

Every written discourse is produced by someone in a particular place, time, and set of circumstances, and is directed toward someone in a particular place, time, and set of circumstances. There is also, generally, a specific aspect of this "situational context" that motivates the writer to address the reader. The nature of the physical, cultural, and psychological setting, the relationship between the writer and the intended reader(s), and the particular details of the motivating factors have a very obvious influence on the shape that the written communication takes. Those factors in the communication situation which are regarded as particularly significant for the adequate understanding of the document being analyzed are presented in this part of the SSA.

The overview

An SSA overview provides readers with a bird's-eye view of the whole discourse. It enables them, as they work with a particular portion, to keep track of that portion's place in the whole discourse. The overview consists simply of a constituent organization chart and a thematic outline of the semantic units. The former is a graphic presentation of the constituents of the discourse hierarchically arranged with respect to one another, but without a statement of the contents or semantic roles of the constituents. The latter presents the semantic units in an outline format. The role that each unit plays in the configuration of which it is a part is identified in the unit title, and following each title the unit's theme statement appears. In other words, not only are the units seen in their respective relationships to other units, but also the most important information of each one is summarized. The thematic outline is, then, something of a "condensed version" of the entire discourse. (The overview of the Epistle to the Colossians appears at the end of the "Introduction to the Semantic Structure of Colossians.")

The presentation and discussion of the units

The semantic units of a discourse are described in the order indicated by the following diagram:

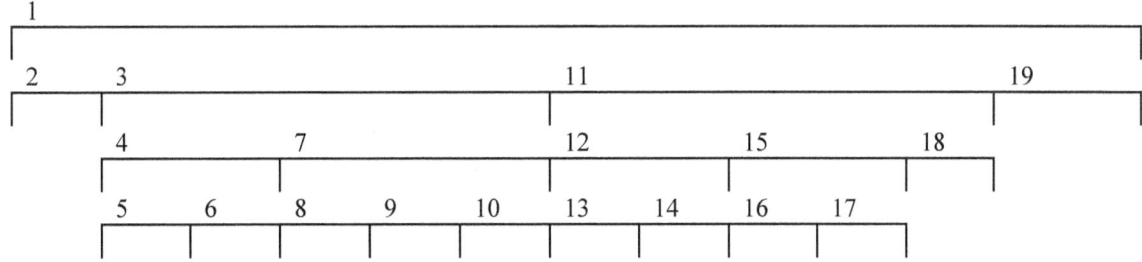

Such an order accomplishes two things. First, it allows each unit to be discussed in terms of the higher-level framework into which it fits. Second, it allows the units to be discussed in the order in which they occur. In other words, the order of discussion is sensitive both to the hierarchical and the linear aspects of the contents.

The unit titles appear at the top of the respective displays. They are designed to provide the user with a good deal of information. Take, for example, a title such as "division constituent 2:6–7 (Paragraph: Nucleus of 2:6–3:17)." In this example, "division constituent" indicates that the unit is an immediate constituent of a configuration which, by its composition, is a division. In the parenthesis, "Paragraph" tells the user that the unit being discussed is, by its composition, a paragraph. This is followed by an indication of that paragraph's role in the relational structure of the division in which it is functioning. In this example, paragraph 2:6–7 is said to serve as the nucleus of 2:6–3:17, a constituent of the division that also includes 2:8–23, 3:1–16, and 3:17. This particular title illustrates an important fact. Note that the 2:6–7 unit is compositionally a paragraph, and yet it is said to be a principal constituent of a division. A paragraph is more commonly a principal constituent of a section, and a section is more commonly a principal constituent of a division. A strict hierarchical approach would require that every principal constituent of a division be labeled a section; but the approach used in the SSA establishes the class of a unit (paragraph, section, etc.) primarily on the basis of its composition, and not primarily on the basis of the organizational level on which the unit is functioning. A higher-level unit, viewed compositionally, consists of a configuration of two or more principal constituents, one of which must be a unit of the next lower compositional level, while the other constituent(s) may be of any level lower than the configuration itself. For example, a division must consist of at least two principal constituents, one of which must be a section, while the others may be sections, paragraphs, propositional clusters, or propositions. More commonly, the principal constituents of a division are sections and paragraphs, but occasionally a propositional cluster functions as a principal constituent of a division, and very rarely, a proposition does.

The unit themes appear following the title of each unit. The theme is an expression of the most prominent information in the unit. This generally consists of the theme statement of the most prominent proposition, propositional cluster, or constituent in the relational structure, along with any other constituent or portion of a constituent (e.g., a thematic motif) that is marked by special devices as prominent. (Of course, theme statements are not necessarily given in the strict propositional form used in the right-hand column of the displays.)

The unit displays are divided into two columns. The left-hand column, entitled "Relational Structure," shows how the constituents are grouped together and related to one another. The relational labels come from Beekman and Callow's *Translating the Word of God* (chap. 18) and Beekman, Callow, and Kopesec's "The Semantic Structure of Written Communication" (chap. 8). This system, with some further refinements and modifications, appears in the chart on the next page, "Relations of Communication Units."

Many of the displays are multi-layered, which illustrates the fact that the constituents of a communication unit are so structured that they group together in a variety of configurations and patterns. Groupings of constituents as well as single constituents may function as the highest-level (or principal) constituents of the unit. Then each of those groupings may be broken down into either single constituents or groupings, and in turn these lower-level groupings into single constituents or groupings, and so on. The leftmost set of relational labels in a display shows the way the unit divides into its principal constituents. The next layer to the right shows how some or all of those principal constituents divide further into smaller ones, and the next layer after that shows how some or all of those may divide still further.

The number of levels or layers used to display a given unit is largely a matter of the analyst's judgment as to what is useful for communicating the unit's organizational development. Obviously, the more that can be shown with a single display without rendering the chart unwieldy or overly atomistic, the better. At the finer levels of delicacy, the decision as to whether to separate the constituents and display the relationship between them is based on a number of factors:

1. The complexity of a constituent may require several layers of relations to display its organization, whereas another constituent may require only one or two layers because it is so briefly stated. For example, in the relational structure display for Col. 1:24–29 NUCLEUS$_1$, NUCLEUS$_3$, and NUCLEUS$_4$ each have two layers, but NUCLEUS$_2$ has no less than five layers.

Relations of Communication Units[1]

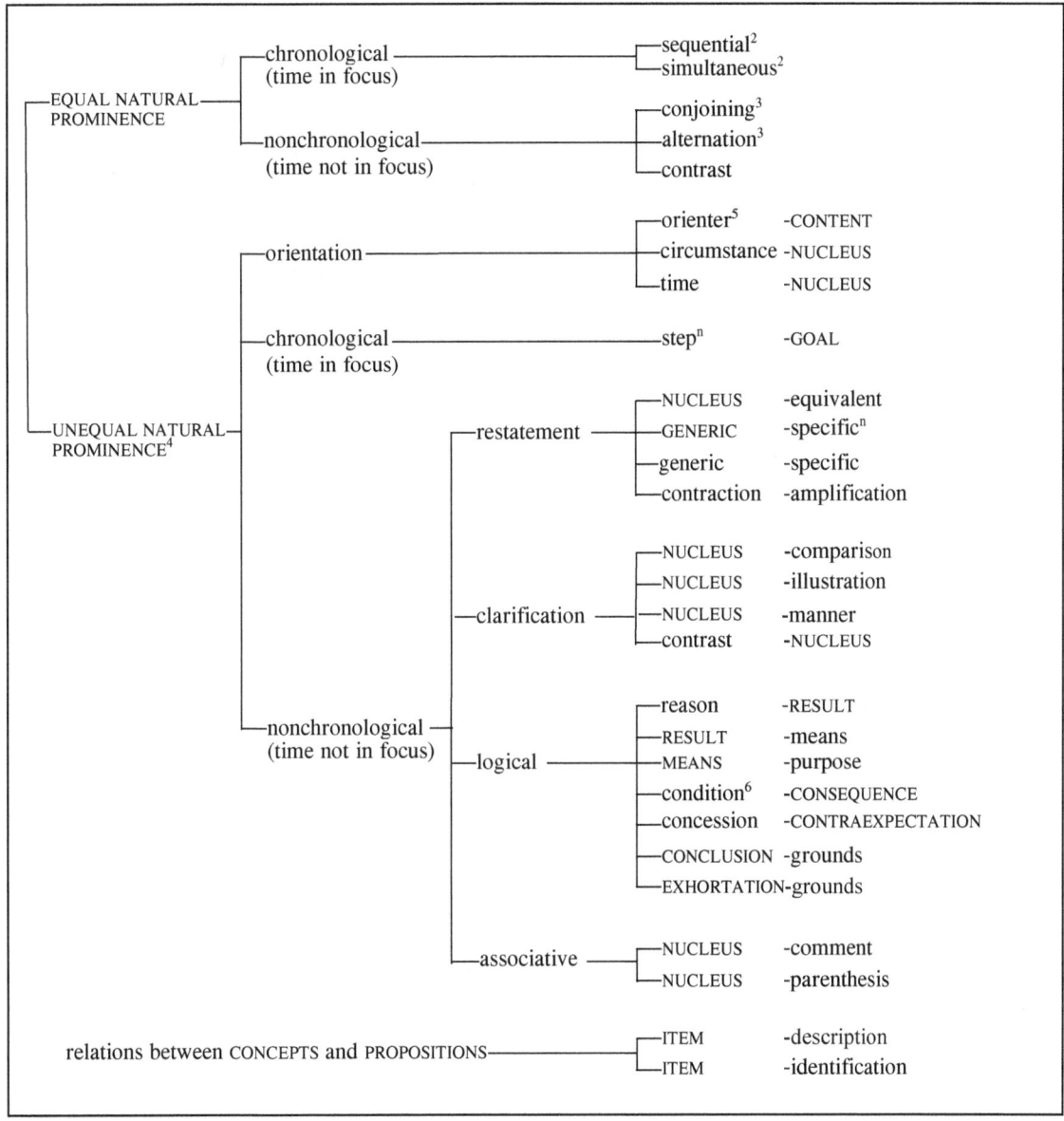

Notes:

[1] A communication unit (CU) is a proposition or propositional configuration that functions as a unit. As a larger configuration is analyzed into its constituent CUs, each constituent will be found to be in some relation with at least one other constituent in that configuration, and each will have with respect to the other a role corresponding with that relation.

[2] In a display, the labels "sequential" and "simultaneous" are used in conjunction with the label "NUCLEUS" (e.g., sequential NUCLEUS$_1$–sequential NUCLEUS$_2$ or simultaneous NUCLEUS$_1$–simultaneous NUCLEUS$_2$).

[3] The labels "conjoining" and "alternation" are not normally used in a display. Rather, a conjoining relation is shown by subscript numbers following each label of the conjoined units (e.g., NUCLEUS$_1$-NUCLEUS$_2$, etc., or reason$_1$-reason$_2$, etc.). If alternation is involved, the units are labeled as follows: alternate NUCLEUS$_1$–alternate NUCLEUS$_2$, etc., or alternate reason$_1$–alternate reason$_2$, etc. Where "conjoined" is used in lowercase letters in a display, it signifies that the constituent is less prominent than one or more of the other constituents it is conjoined with.

[4] For a given pair of labels, the role of the CU with greater natural prominence is shown in uppercase letters, and the role of the CU with lesser prominence is shown in lowercase. The role labels for each pair are shown in the order in which the units more frequently occur in New Testament Greek texts.

[5] "Orienter" types are speech, perceptual, emotional, cognitive, volitional, evaluative, and prominence.

[6] "Condition" may be subdivided into three types: contrary to fact, general potential fact, and particular potential fact.

2. Closely related to point 1 is the relative significance of the different relations. Often another layer is added in order to display a logical relationship, but not a restatement, a clarification, or an orientation relationship. Usually, addition relations at the lower levels of delicacy are not sufficient cause for adding layers. This principle is illustrated by Col. 1:21–23. Notice that the 1:21 concession constituent has been further analyzed into CONCLUSION (1:21a–b) and grounds (1:21c–d), whereas the relations between the constituents of 1:23a–e are not displayed, even though the two constituents are more or less equivalent in size. In part, this is due to the generic-specific relation between the main constituents of 1:23a–e, which is a restatement relation.

3. The organizational level on which a particular element is functioning often enters into the decision. For example, quite frequently an orienter-content relation is not elaborated in the display's relational structure. Thus, in the display of Col. 1:3–8 the 1:8a orienter 'He told us(exc)' is not separated from what he told us (i.e., its content in 1:8b). However, in 1:9–12 the orienter *is* separate, primarily because it is functioning in the introduction to the body, and also because the content would make an unduly large undifferentiated unit. (This is avoided whenever possible.) In other cases of an orienter, it may be necessary to show it as a separate constituent in the display so as to avoid giving a false representation of the structure, particularly the grouping. For example, if the content introduced by an orienter is grouped with two nuclear propositions that are conjoined, one of which is developed at some length and the other not, the developed one will be displayed to several layers. This requires its being presented as a separate grouping in the display, which means that the orienter and the undeveloped proposition will also have to be displayed as separate (small) groupings. A somewhat complex example of this is in the display of 2:1–5, where the orienter (2:1a) introduces a (prominent) means and two conjoined purpose constituents (2:2a–c and 2:2d–3). Because these constituents are developed somewhat, they are displayed separately, as is the orienter.

The following notational conventions are used in the *left-hand side* of the displays:

1. The relational label of a higher layer (a label to the left) is aligned horizontally with the label of the prominent element of the next lower layer, as in the diagram below.

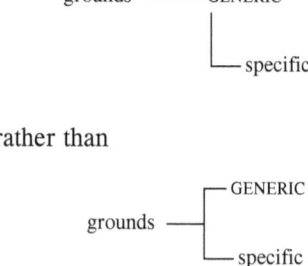

rather than

Although this violates the symmetry that a standard tree diagram would display, it is a particularly useful visual convention. By aligning the labels in this manner, the user can quickly determine all of the relationships that any given constituent has. The user should follow the horizontal line leftward from a specific constituent in the right-hand side of the display, observing the relational labels as they are encountered. For example, in the display of Col. 1:24–29, notice that by following the horizontal line leftward from constituent 1:27c, three relational labels are encountered. The first one is REASON, which indicates that 1:27c is supported by 1:27d (being a result of what is said in 1:27c). The second label encountered along that line is SPECIFIC. This label indicates that the grouping 1:27c–d is supported by 1:26a–27b, which supports the prominent specific constituent (1:27c–d) with a generic constituent. Then, continuing to the left along the horizontal line, one encounters the label "description of 'message'." This indicates that the whole grouping from 1:26a to 1:27d provides a description of the discourse concept 'the whole message from/about God' in 1:25, of which 'message' is the organizational center.

2. The relational labels are spelled with either all uppercase or all lowercase letters, a graphic device for contrasting the prominent elements with the support elements in a given set of related constituents. The prominent relation in the set is labeled in uppercase letters, and the support relation in lowercase letters. Occasionally, the support element in a set of related units has "marked" prominence in the Greek. In such cases both labels are in uppercase letters. An example of this is in the display of Col. 2:1–5. The purpose label for 2:4–5 would normally be in lowercase letters because it is a support element; but here the purpose constituent has marked prominence in the Greek surface structure. Therefore, it is considered of equal prominence with the naturally prominent means constituent (2:1–3).

3. A grouping of related constituents at any given layer of delicacy consists of a minimum of two units, at least one of which must be prominent. Quite commonly, two or more support constituents relate to the same prominent constituent. An example of this can be seen in the display of 1:21–23, where the NUCLEUS is supported by a (preceding) concession, and by a (following) means and purpose. This means that the NUCLEUS in this paragraph is functioning as the contra-expectation to the concession, the result of the means, and the means of the purpose. In other words, when a nuclear constituent occurs on the same line with supportive constituents, the direct relationship is always the one between the nuclear constituent and the individual supportive constituents.

4. Subscript numbers are used to indicate units related by addition. The addition relationship of conjoining is illustrated in the relational structure display for Col. 1:9–12. There it can be seen that 1:10d, 10e, 11a–d, and 12a–d are labeled specific$_1$, specific$_2$, specific$_3$, specific$_4$, respectively, indicating that they are conjoined specifics in support of the 1:10a–c prominent GENERIC nucleus. The addition relationship of alternation does not occur in Colossians, but would be handled by labeling the alternate items as, for example, alternate purpose$_1$ and alternate purpose$_2$.

As to the *right-hand side* of the displays, the "Contents," its purpose is to represent the unit's semantic content as unambiguously and as completely as possible. If the unit under discussion is compositionally larger than one paragraph (i.e., section, division, etc.), then the contents consists of the theme statements for the unit's constituents as in, for example, the display of 1:13–2:5. However, if the unit under discussion is a paragraph or propositional cluster, then the contents consist of a propositionalized representation of the semantic information contained in the Greek text of the unit.

A word needs to be said concerning the nature and representation of propositions and also the general principles for the propositionalization of the contents of a unit. Technically, a proposition is a *semantic* entity; it underlies, or is signaled by, the surface-structure form. It is a grouping of discourse concepts, one of which expresses the state or event notion to which the others are related by the case relations. The proposition has one of the three basic illocutionary or communicative functions: statement, question, or command. Since the proposition is not a surface-structure (i.e., grammatical and phonological) entity, it cannot properly be equated with any specific surface-structure form. However, for practical purposes, it has been necessary to work out a means of representing the propositions and their interrelationships in a way that is as complete and unambiguous as possible and with the least distortion of the underlying semantic content as possible. The following principles underlie this type of representation:

1. The grammatical form of the representation should match as closely as possible the class of the semantic units (Beekman and Callow, p. 282). This means that "events," as defined in semantic theory, are represented consistently by verbs and not by nouns (e.g., *salvation*, grammatically a noun, is represented by some form of the verb *to save*). "Things" (animate beings and inanimate objects) are consistently represented by nouns. "Attributes" of things, such as size and color, are consistently represented by adjectives (e.g., *big, green*); attributes of events, by adverbs (e.g., *quickly*); and attributes of attributes, by adverbs such as *very* (e.g., *very hot*). Semantic relations—those between discourse concepts (the case relations)

and those between propositions, paragraphs, etc. (the communication relations)—are represented by surface-structure devices that signal how one unit is related to another. These often are conjunctions (e.g., *because* indicating a reason relationship and *in order that* indicating a purpose relationship). Most often the relationship signaled by the particular relator will be self-evident. However, when there is ambiguity, the relational structure on the left side of the display disambiguates the conjunction by indicating the relation explicitly. Frequently, it is necessary to represent the relation with a relator word plus the repetition of previously given information that indicates the relationship between the units concerned.

2. Passive forms are avoided in the propositionalized contents, except when they are used to maintain the identity of the topic of the unit. Whenever a passive form *is* used, the doer of the action is supplied in italics; thus, 'you were saved' may be propositionalized as 'you were saved *by God*'.

3. Implicit information is supplied in the propositions of the displays in italics, for instance, '*by God*' in the preceding example. Languages differ considerably as to what information must be signaled explicitly and what can be left implicit; so, to aid translators in languages with different requirements, the implicit information is given in the propositions, but in italics to distinguish it from what is explicit in the Greek text. One of the main functions of words in italics is to supply the case frame of event propositions, that is to say, the case roles that are focal or necessary for a proper understanding of that event. For example, the abstract noun 'salvation' could be represented propositionally as '*God* saves *people*'. Only 'saves' is not in italics, since the only referent explicit in the text is the event concept of the proposition; both 'God' and 'people' are in italics because the event 'to save' has a case frame of agent (here 'God') and patient (here 'people'). Also in italics is information that is repeated for linking purposes; information that disambiguates pronominal references; and information that clarifies obscurities due to the presuppositions and cultural knowledge of the original audience. For example, in the display of Col. 1:1–2, constituent 1:2a supplies 'town' after 'Colosse', because that would have been clear to the original audience concerning the place named Colosse.

4. Figures of speech such as dead metaphor, metonymy, synecdoche, litotes, and hyperbole, are propositionalized by explicating the figure nonfiguratively. The propositionalizations of live metaphors generally retain the image as well as the nonfigurative content communicated by the figure. Rhetorical questions are expressed straightforwardly as statements or commands, depending on their communication function. In cases where there is a significant difference in form between the figure and its nonfigurative equivalent, or where the figure carries considerable emotional overtones, then the figure is identified by capital letters in brackets after its propositional representation; see, for example, "[HYP]" for hyperbole, in 1:3a and 1:9a.

5. Propositionalization requires, among other things, the expression of relative prominence. One way to express this is with conjunctions and other relation-marking devices, which serve not only to indicate the relation of one proposition (or propositional configuration) to another, but also to indicate relative natural prominence. Such things as topic, focus, and the highlighting of information or motifs also need to be represented. Generally, standard English prominence-marking devices are used to represent this aspect of meaning. However, some features of prominence in the Greek text cannot be easily represented in English; where these occur, they are discussed in the notes.

6. Wherever a pronoun in the Greek text is ambiguous as to its referent, the noun referent is given instead of the pronoun (e.g., 'God's Son' instead of 'he' in 1:15a).

7. First person plural inclusive pronouns are followed by "(inc)" except for places where their nature is very obvious. First person plural exclusive pronouns are *always* followed by "(exc)." The second person pronoun is to be taken as plural unless followed by "(sg)," in which case it is singular.

In the right-hand side of the displays each constituent appears following its chapter and verse number(s). For a verse composed of two or more constituents, lowercase letters follow the verse number to indicate the subdivision (e.g., 1:12a, 1:12b, 1:12c, etc.). There are some cases where, for clarity of presentation, the order of the constituents in the display differs from their order of occurrence in the Greek surface structure. (The identifying relational labels in the display's left-hand side always conform to the order of the propositions in the right-hand side.) Where several propositions are grouped together to form a single constituent in the display, the identification at the beginning will refer to all of the propositions, for example, 3:5c-f (see the display of 3:5-11). Subsequent propositions within that constituent are identified in parentheses without repeating the chapter number, as, in this case, "(5d)," "(5e)," and "(5f)."

The discussions following each display center around (1) evidence for the identification of the unit; (2) evidence for the theme (and purpose) of the unit; and (3) decisions concerning the relational structure and propositionalization of the contents. The first of these is discussed under "Boundaries and Coherence" and describes the features that establish the unit as a distinct and discrete whole, setting the unit apart from contiguous ones. The second is discussed under "Prominence and Theme" and has to do with the derivation of the theme statement. The unit's relational structure as it relates to natural prominence is considered as well as other features that mark special prominence. Elements in the theme statement which derive from constituents other than the naturally prominent one(s) are justified. In some cases, a unit's purpose will also be discussed. This is more likely in the case of higher-level units, but is also occasionally done for some paragraphs. Since, in epistle material, purpose is closely related to a unit's theme, a discussion of purpose is combined with discussion of theme.

The third area of discussion comes under "Notes." There are two types: notes on the relational structure of the unit, and decisions on meanings and renderings. In a unit's relational structure there often are points that need explanation, justification, or the presentation of alternative possibilities. The other notes have to do with the meaning of the text and the manner of expressing that meaning in propositional form. Commentators may differ quite markedly about the intended meaning; yet, for the display one option has to be chosen. The basis for such a decision is presented in the notes. When there *is* no conclusive evidence that can clear up a particular exegetical ambiguity, the option that appears to the analyst to be the most likely one is presented in the display, and the alternative interpretations are discussed in the notes. Occasionally, equally good alternatives are both given in the display.

Each note begins with a quotation of the part(s) of the proposition to be discussed. This appears in bold type. Readers will find it helpful to follow along in a Geek text.

The bibliography lists materials that were helpful to the analyst in determining the exegetical choices and factors to be weighed in reaching an exegetical decision. In many cases, the information derived from the source materials had to be reworked and reworded by the analyst(s) to conform to the general linguistic orientation of an SSA. Hence, detailed acknowledgment of individual sources for every piece of information that was helpful is generally not practicable. Generally, sources are cited only where a minority or unusual decision is under discussion. In citing a source, only the author's name is given except where more than one work by the same author is listed in the bibliography; in that case the date is given as well. A page number is cited only for works that are not commentaries or Bible versions; in the commentaries and versions the quotation can be found at the particular verse under discussion. To learn the title and facts of publication of a cited work the reader needs to refer to the bibliography.

Using an SSA

The question arises as to how a technical commentary of this nature should be used, and how it relates to other available aids. A cursory comparison of the standard exegetical or critical commentaries will reveal a wide variety of alternative interpretations at numerous points in the text. In contrast, an SSA attempts to arrive at one specific interpretation, taking into account all the factors considered to be relevant—the words used, the grammatical constructions involved, the relational structure, the theme of the units, the overall purpose of the document, etc. An SSA represents the fruit of careful reasoning by a number of scholars. Consequently, it is recommended to the translator as a special type of commentary, one in which the translator's needs have been uppermost in the minds of those preparing it. It should, however, be used along with other commentaries and versions. Where there is obvious agreement, the translator can move ahead with confidence. But where the display appears to depart from the versions or commentaries, or where a number of alternatives occur, then the relevant discussion should be carefully studied to see what led to the decision represented in the display. The users should then be in a good position to form their own informed judgment as to the best interpretation.

Although the needs of translators are the primary motivation in the production of this sort of commentary, it is certainly hoped that others would find them useful, too. Pastors and teachers who desire to expound the Scriptures faithfully and to base their messages on a careful exposition of the text should find an SSA a real help as they wrestle with the meaning of God's Word. In addition to arguments for and against differing interpretations they will also find various types of information not generally found in other commentaries, for example, the relationships of statements to each other and which statements are the most important in a specific context. The overall analysis of a whole Bible book is of considerable help, too.

And what is of help to a pastor or teacher is also of help to any serious Bible student. Bible college and seminary professors will find the approach and its underlying theory stimulating to interact with. Bible college or seminary students, or anyone who leads a Bible study aimed at discovering the meaning of the text, will likewise find an SSA helpful.

All who are involved in the many hours of work required to produce an SSA use every means at their disposal—the standard reference works, the commentaries, the insights of linguistics, the theory of semantic structure—so as to arrive at as accurate an understanding of the Scripture as is possible in our present state of knowledge. For all who share this same concern, this commentary should prove useful.

INTRODUCTION TO THE SEMANTIC STRUCTURE OF COLOSSIANS

The communication situation: Identification and status of the participants

It is clear from Paul's explicit statements in Col. 1:1, 1:23, and 4:18 that he himself, the apostle to the Gentiles, wrote the letter to the Colossians. In 4:18 the phrase τῇ ἐμῇ χειρί 'by my (own) hand' indicates that Paul penned that part of the letter with the intention of guaranteeing the letter's authenticity. He was in prison at the time of writing. This is clear from 4:3, where he refers to being bound, and from 4:18, where he also refers to his bonds. Both references are presented in the context of his requesting prayer for himself. His lack of mobility also underlies the statement in 2:5 that, although he was not present physically at Colosse, he was certainly with the Colossians in spirit.

Colosse was in Asia Minor about a hundred miles inland, to the east of Ephesus, where Paul had spent a considerable time when establishing the church there. It seems probable, in the light of statements in this letter, that the church at Colosse arose as a result of the ministry of Epaphras rather than of Paul. Thus in 1:7, Paul, having referred to the spread of the gospel to Colosse and to his addressees' having become believers, now says 'just as you learned from Epaphras'. Again, in 2:6–7, verses which contain the main command in the epistle, 'walk in Christ', he repeats the idea 'just as you were taught'; coupled with the earlier reference, it seems reasonable to conclude that this also refers to the ministry of Epaphras. Moreover, the expression 'one of yourselves' in 4:12 indicates that Epaphras came from Colosse. (Epaphras's deep concern for the believers in the nearby towns of Laodicea and Hierapolis is also mentioned, so he may well have played a major part in founding those churches as well.)

If Epaphras was the founder, under God, of the church at Colosse, and not Paul, this would explain why Paul is at considerable pains (in 2:1) to make clear to the Colossians and Laodiceans that his not being personally known to them in no way diminished his keen interest in their spiritual welfare, and his concern for their faithfulness to the gospel message they had received. Indeed, the whole 2:1–5 paragraph makes this clear. It probably also explains why he devotes another paragraph, 1:24–29, to describing in some detail his commission to make known the mystery—the now-revealed truth of God—to all men, in particular, to Gentiles such as the Colossian believers predominantly were.

The communication situation: Occasion and purpose of the letter

Paul is writing from prison to the believers in Colosse after having heard the report that Epaphras brought him on the situation at Colosse (1:8). Basically, the report was an encouraging one. In the introduction to the main part of the epistle, 1:3–8, Paul says that he has heard of their faith in the Lord Jesus and their love for all God's people—he says this both in 1:4 and in 1:8. Again, in 2:5, he comments on their good order and the steadfastness of their faith in Christ. The form of 2:7, with its perfect participle and present participles, indicates that he is urging them to continue rooted in Christ, advancing in Christian growth and steadfastness. In the light of these commendations, it seems best, in 1:2, to interpret πιστοῖς ἀδελφοῖς as meaning 'faithful brothers'. The gospel had come to them, and they had held firmly to its truths and to the Savior it proclaimed. Paul is obviously happy (2:5) to have had these facts reported to him.

But it is also clear from the statement 'I am saying this so that no one may deceive you by fine-sounding arguments' (2:4) that some form of false teaching was being presented to the Colossian believers, and that Paul (as well as Epaphras) was concerned for the Colossians lest they be persuaded by it.

There is considerable discussion in many commentaries as to whether or not this teaching was Gnosticism, perhaps in an early form. All that is known about it for certain, however, is what can be deduced from statements made in Colossians. These points may be summed up as asceticism and ritualism:

1. It emphasized abstinence from certain foods and some types of drink (2:16, 22).
2. It required the observance of various feasts, at different intervals (2:16).

3. It stressed self-abasement or a false humility of some sort (2:18, 23), probably in connection with private or public worship.
4. It inculcated the worship of the angels (2:18).
5. It taught the need for ἐθελοθρησκία (2:23), a compound word which may been invented by Paul. While its meaning is not entirely clear, it probably refers to a type of worship which was of human origin, perhaps deriving from the originator of the false teaching.
6. It praised the value of treating the body severely (2:23).

Since a writer's purpose determines what he chooses to include and what he stresses as important, it seems reasonable to deduce the following additional descriptions of this false teaching:

1. It demoted Christ from his supreme place. This is deduced from the frequent references to Christ in Paul's letter, twenty-six in all, and from the fact that the letter contains one of the most extended treatments in the New Testament of Christ's supremacy over all creation and the church, and of his central part in God's reconciling work (1:13–20). Twice the statement is made that all the fullness of God dwells in him (1:19; 2:9). But since there is no direct statement concerning the view of Christ held by this particular false teaching, various explanations are given as to why Paul so stressed the supremacy of Christ. Many suggest that in view of the several references to angelic beings of various degrees of power and authority (1:16; 2:10, 15), it may have been that angels were given the place, at least to some extent, that Christ should have had.
2. This false teaching claimed to promote a higher spirituality. When Paul starts to warn the Colossians against the false teaching, he stresses that they are spiritually complete in Christ (2:10), and he goes on to expound in some detail their position in Christ. Again, as he closes his warnings (2:23), he states clearly that following the rules and regulations of this religious system only promotes the satisfaction or indulgence of the flesh, the exact opposite of what it claimed to do.
3. This false teaching may have emphasized the importance of circumcision, since Paul stresses the fact that the Colossians had already undergone a spiritual circumcision (2:11).
4. Less certainly, there may have been some stress on a death-burial-resurrection motif. Perhaps they practiced such a ritual. This would explain why Paul reminds the Colossians that they had died and risen with Christ (2:12; cf. also 2:13, 20; 3:1, 5).
5. Possibly, too, the false teaching may have cast some doubt on the completeness or certainty of forgiveness, as not only is forgiveness referred to three times (1:14; 2:13; 3:13), but a vivid description of forgiveness is given (2:14).

While such deductions are reasonable, and may be correct, it has to be borne in mind that Paul may have had other reasons for stressing such matters. But since 2:8–23 is overtly directed against this teaching, it is not unreasonable to take that passage as being directed, explicitly or implicitly, against various strands or implications of this false religious philosophy.

It seems likely, then, that the report Epaphras brought to Paul was of a teaching that claimed to promote true spirituality but did so by means of rules and regulations that concerned food and drink, festivals, and forms of worship, and in some way undermined the supremacy of Christ. Paul makes it very clear that this type of teaching was of human origin, not divine; was essentially elementary, not to be compared with the full flower of the Christian message; and failed entirely to fulfill its claims. In short, not only did it demote the Christ of the gospel, but it had nothing to offer believers who were already spiritually complete in Christ.

Thus, the purpose of the epistle was to confirm the Colossians in their adherence to the gospel and the Lord Jesus Christ, and to warn them against the spurious claims of this new false teaching. It is perhaps worth pointing out that explicit warnings against the false teaching are found only in 2:4 and 2:8–23—seventeen verses, less than a fifth of the total epistle. Paul, therefore, is as much concerned with stressing the truth as with exposing error in this particular letter, but it seems very likely that the truths stressed were such as would help the believers at Colosse to see through and hence reject the false teaching.

INTRODUCTION 3

OVERVIEW: THE CONSTITUENT ORGANIZATION OF COLOSSIANS

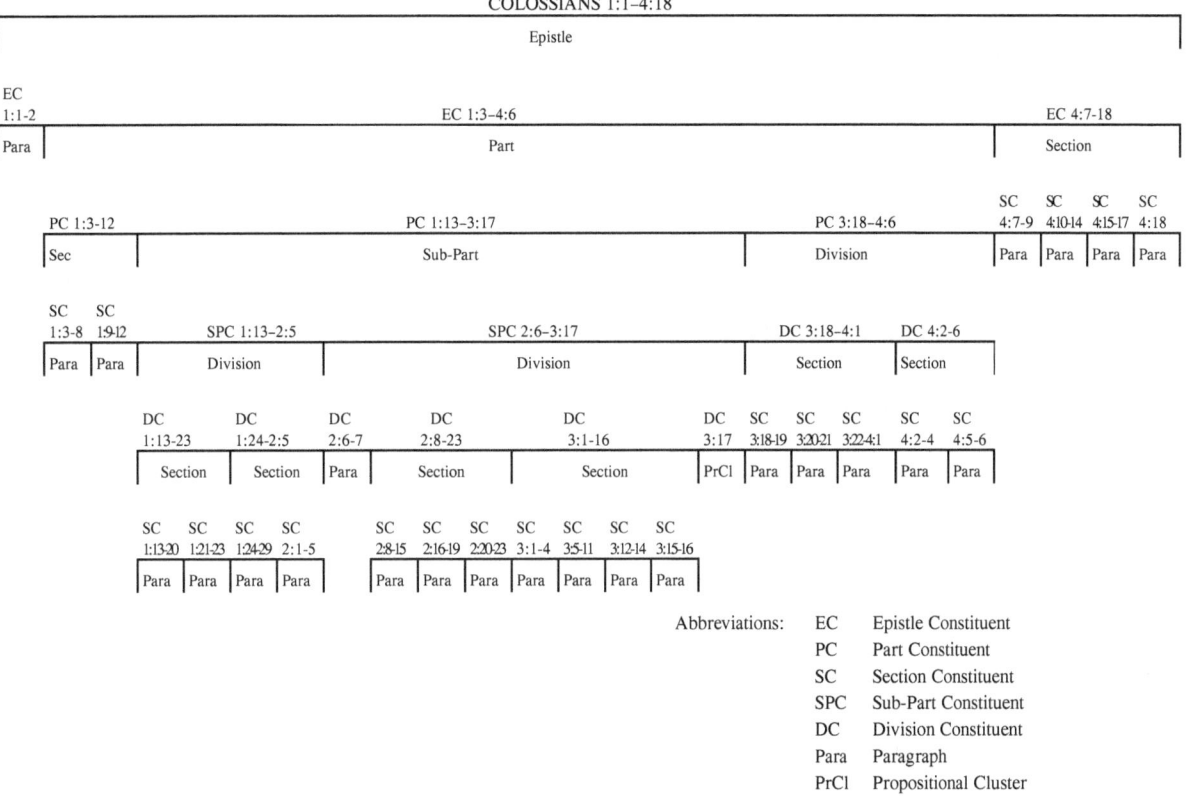

OVERVIEW: THE SEMANTIC UNITS AND THEIR THEME STATEMENTS

COLOSSIANS 1:1–4:18 (Epistle)
THEME: Conduct yourselves as those should who are united to Christ Jesus our Lord, who ranks above everything that has been created. In particular, make sure that no one makes you become his disciples by teaching you a false religious philosophy; rather, be constantly wanting what is associated with heaven.

EPISTLE CONSTITUENT 1:1–2 (Paragraph: Opening of the Epistle)
THEME: I, Paul, am sending this letter to you, who are God's people in Colosse. We pray that God will bless you.

EPISTLE CONSTITUENT 1:3–4:6 (Part: Body of the Epistle)
THEME: Conduct yourselves as those should who are united to Christ Jesus our Lord, who ranks above everything that has been created. In particular, make sure that no one makes you become his disciples by teaching you a false religious philosophy; rather, be constantly wanting what is associated with heaven.

PART CONSTITUENT 1:3–12 (Section: Introduction to 1:13–4:6)
THEME: We thank God very often that you believe in Christ Jesus and that you love all God's people. We have also been praying to God for you very often that you will come to know truly all that he wants you to do, in order that you will conduct yourselves as the Lord's people should.

SECTION CONSTITUENT 1:3–8 (Paragraph: Nucleus$_1$ of 1:3–12)
THEME: We thank God for you very often that you believe in Christ Jesus and that you love all God's people.

SECTION CONSTITUENT 1:9–12 (Paragraph: Nucleus₂ of 1:3–12)

THEME: We have also been praying to God for you very often that you will know truly all that he wants you to do, in order that you will conduct yourselves as the Lord's people should.

PART CONSTITUENT 1:13–3:17 (Sub-Part: Nucleus (primary matters) of 1:3–4:6)

THEME: Conduct yourselves as those should who are united to Christ Jesus our Lord, who ranks above everything that has been created. In particular, make sure that no one makes you become his disciples by teaching you a false religious philosophy; rather, be constantly wanting what is associated with heaven.

SUB-PART CONSTITUENT 1:13–2:5 (Division: Grounds of 2:6–3:17)

THEME: God our Father has reconciled you to himself and he has caused you to be ruled by his Son, who ranks above everything that has been created. I, Paul, am exerting myself very greatly on your behalf in order that you might truly know the secret-message about Christ, in order that no one may delude you.

DIVISION CONSTITUENT 1:13–23 (Section: Nucleus₁ of 1:13–2:5)

THEME: God our Father has reconciled you to himself and he has caused you to be ruled by his Son, who ranks above everything that has been created.

SECTION CONSTITUENT 1:13–20 (Paragraph: Nucleus₁ of 1:13–23)

THEME: God our Father has caused us to be ruled by his Son, who ranks above everything that has been created.

SECTION CONSTITUENT 1:21–23 (Paragraph: Nucleus₂ of 1:13–23)

THEME: As for you, God our Father has now reconciled you to himself.

DIVISION CONSTITUENT 1:24–2:5 (Section: Nucleus₂ of 1:13–2:15)

THEME: I, Paul, am exerting myself very greatly on your behalf in order that you might truly know the secret-message about Christ, in order that no one might delude you.

SECTION CONSTITUENT 1:24–29 (Paragraph: Generic of 2:1–5)

THEME: I am completing that which Christ appointed, that I should suffer physically for the benefit of the church. And I proclaim the secret-message about Christ to every class of persons.

SECTION CONSTITUENT 2:1–5 (Paragraph: Specific nucleus of 1:24–2:5)

THEME: I am exerting myself very greatly on your behalf in order that you might truly know the secret-message about Christ, in order that no one might delude you.

SUB-PART CONSTITUENT 2:6–3:17 (Division: Hortatory nucleus of 1:13–3:17)

THEME: Conduct yourselves as those should who are united to such a one as Christ Jesus our Lord. In particular, make sure that no one makes you become his disciples by teaching you a false religious philosophy; rather, be constantly wanting what is associated with heaven.

DIVISION CONSTITUENT 2:6–7 (Paragraph: Nucleus of 2:6–3:17)

THEME: Conduct yourselves as those should who are united to such a one as Christ Jesus our Lord is.

DIVISION CONSTITUENT 2:8–23 (Section: Specific₁ of 2:6–7)

THEME: Make sure that no one makes you become his disciples by teaching you a false religious philosophy, since you are spiritually complete because you are united to Christ.

SECTION CONSTITUENT 2:8–15 (Paragraph: Generic nucleus of 2:8–23)

THEME: Make sure that no one makes you become his disciples by teaching you a false religious philosophy, since you are spiritually complete because you are united to Christ.

SECTION CONSTITUENT 2:16–19 (Paragraph: Specific₁ of 2:8–15)

THEME: Disregard anyone who condemns you because you do not obey certain regulations and because you do not worship God as he insists you should.

SECTION CONSTITUENT 2:20–23 (Paragraph: Specific₂ of 2:8–15)

THEME: Do not submit to elementary regulations, which are concerned merely with what is external.

DIVISION CONSTITUENT 3:1–16 (Section: Specific₂ of 2:6–7)

THEME: Be constantly wanting what is associated with heaven.

SECTION CONSTITUENT 3:1-4 (Paragraph: Generic nucleus of 3:5-16)

THEME: Be constantly wanting what is associated with heaven.

SECTION CONSTITUENT 3:5-11 (Paragraph: Specific$_1$ of 3:1-4)

THEME: Do not do what is evil.

SECTION CONSTITUENT 3:12-14 (Paragraph: Specific$_2$ of 3:1-4)

THEME: Do what is good; in particular, love one another.

SECTION CONSTITUENT 3:15-16 (Paragraph: Specific$_3$ of 3:1-4)

THEME: Continue to be at peace with one another, be constantly thanking God, and continue getting to thoroughly know the message about Christ.

DIVISION CONSTITUENT 3:17 (Propositional Cluster: Equivalent of 2:6-7)

THEME: Do everything in the manner that those should do who are the people of the Lord Jesus.

PART CONSTITUENT 3:18-4:6 (Division: Conjoined (secondary matters) to 1:13-3:17)

THEME: Act as believers should toward those of their household. Pray persistently, and act wisely toward unbelievers.

DIVISION CONSTITUENT 3:18-4:1 (Section: Nucleus$_1$ of 3:18-4:6)

THEME: Be subject to those in authority at home; and if you have authority, exercise it as those who believe in the Lord Jesus should do.

SECTION CONSTITUENT 3:18-19 (Paragraph: Nucleus$_1$ of 3:18-4:1)

THEME: Wives, be subject to your husbands; husbands, love your wives.

SECTION CONSTITUENT 3:20-21 (Paragraph: Nucleus$_2$ of 3:18-4:1)

THEME: Children, obey your parents in every circumstance; parents, do not overcorrect your children.

SECTION CONSTITUENT 3:22-4:1 (Paragraph: Nucleus$_3$ of 3:18-4:1)

THEME: Slaves, obey your masters in every circumstance sincerely and wholeheartedly; masters, provide for your slaves justly and fairly.

DIVISION CONSTITUENT 4:2-6 (Section: Nucleus$_2$ of 3:18-4:6)

THEME: Pray to God persistently and pray for me. Also, always speak wisely and graciously toward those who do not believe in the Lord Jesus.

SECTION CONSTITUENT 4:2-4 (Paragraph: Nucleus$_1$ of 4:2-6)

THEME: Pray to God persistently. And pray that God will give me opportunities to declare the secret-message about Christ.

SECTION CONSTITUENT 4:5-6 (Paragraph: Nucleus$_2$ of 4:2-6)

THEME: Always speak wisely and graciously to those who do not believe in the Lord Jesus.

EPISTLE CONSTITUENT 4:7-18 (Section: Closing of the Epistle)

THEME: As for all that has been happening to me Tychicus will tell you. My fellow workers here greet you. Obey these instructions. I, Paul, am penning this final greeting myself in order that you may know that this letter was truly sent by me. Remember to pray about the fact that I am in prison.

SECTION CONSTITUENT 4:7-9 (Paragraph: Nucleus$_1$ of 4:7-18)

THEME: As for all that has been happening to me Tychicus will tell you.

SECTION CONSTITUENT 4:10-14 (Paragraph: Nucleus$_2$ of 4:7-18)

THEME: My fellow workers here greet you.

SECTION CONSTITUENT 4:15-17 (Paragraph: Nucleus$_3$ of 4:7-18)

THEME: Obey these instructions.

SECTION CONSTITUENT 4:18 (Paragraph: Nucleus$_4$ of 4:7-18)

THEME: I, Paul, am penning this final greeting myself in order that you may know that this letter was sent by me. Remember to pray about the fact that I am in prison

THE PRESENTATION AND DISCUSSION OF THE SEMANTIC UNITS OF COLOSSIANS

COLOSSIANS 1:1–4:18 (Epistle)

THEME: Conduct yourselves as those should who are united to Christ Jesus our Lord, who ranks above everything that has been created. In particular, make sure that no one makes you become his disciples by teaching you a false religious philosophy; rather, be constantly wanting what is associated with heaven.

RELATIONAL STRUCTURE	CONTENTS
opening	1:1–2 I, Paul, am sending this letter to you, who are God's people in Colosse. We pray that God will bless you.
BODY	1:3–4:6 Conduct yourselves as those should who are united to Christ Jesus our Lord, who ranks above everything that has been created. In particular, make sure that no one makes you become his disciples by teaching you a false religious philosophy; rather, be constantly wanting what is associated with heaven.
closing	4:7–18 As for all that has been happening to me Tychicus will tell you My fellow workers here greet you. Obey these instructions. I, Paul, am penning this final greeting myself in order that you may know that this letter was truly sent by me. Remember to pray about the fact that I am in prison.

COHERENCE

Paul's epistle to the Colossians follows the established pattern of Greek letters—opening, body, and closing. It is this formal structure of the total discourse that constitutes its organizational (or structural) coherence.

For the epistle as a whole, the situational coherence is particularly significant. The situation is that Paul is writing a letter to the believers at Colosse, so the whole epistle is characterized by first person forms referring to or including Paul, and by second person plural forms referring to the believers at Colosse. Further, in this situation, Paul is an apostle, and so stands in a position of authority with respect to the Colossian believers, and the letter is coherent with respect to that relationship—Paul does not write at any point as one who is, for example, under the authority of the Colossians.

PROMINENCE AND THEME

Of the three constituent parts of the epistle, the body is clearly the most prominent one. Thus the most prominent information of the body is also the theme of the epistle. This being so, the question of the theme for the whole discourse is most naturally discussed in connection with the prominence and theme of the body itself (1:3–4:6).

EPISTLE CONSTITUENT 1:1–2 (Paragraph: Opening of the Epistle)

THEME: I, Paul, am sending this letter to you, who are God's people in Colosse. We pray that God will bless you.

RELATIONAL STRUCTURE	CONTENTS
NUCLEUS₁ — NUCLEUS₁ — NUCLEUS	1:1a *I, Paul, together with Timothy, who is our(inc) brother, am sending this letter to you.*
description of 'Paul'	1:1b *I am an apostle who represents Christ Jesus,* (1c) because God chose *me in order that I should be an apostle.*
NUCLEUS₂	1:2a-c *I am sending this letter to you* who are in Colosse *town* (2b) *and* who are God's people and our(inc) faithful brothers (2c) *and* who are united to Christ.
NUCLEUS₂ — NUCLEUS₁	1:2d *We(exc) pray that* God our(inc) Father [and our(inc) Lord Jesus Christ] *will act graciously towards you*
NUCLEUS₂	1:2e and *that* God our Father [and our Lord Jesus Christ] *will cause you to have peace.*

BOUNDARIES AND COHERENCE

The boundaries of the 1:1–2 unit are very clearly marked by the transition from nonverbal material in 1:1–2 to the first verb in 1:3. In addition, the contents mark these two verses as the opening of a letter in normal Greek style, since they identify the senders and the recipients, and express a somewhat formalized wish for the recipients' welfare.

There are, therefore, three distinct parts to this constituent of the epistle—the identification of the senders with any further descriptions of them, using the nominative case; the identification of the recipients and any further descriptions of them, using the dative case; and, in this case, a wish that God might bless the recipients, expressed without a verb. (This is typical of Paul's letters. Peter's two letters and Jude's *do* use a verb.) While there is no formal connection between these three parts, the first two parts are linked together in the display to form a unit, leaving the third to form a separate unit. The reason for this is that the first two parts, though not connected together by a formal conjunction of any sort, are linked by the use of the two cases, the nominative and the dative. Thus they can be considered as the two halves of a nonverbal clause in Greek, the verb 'to write' or 'to send' being omitted in the opening's frozen forms.

In view of the semantic theory presented in the introduction, the question arises as to which unit in the semantic hierarchy the opening salutation is. Compositionally, it consists of two propositional clusters, the first identifying the senders and recipients, the second expressing the blessing. It, therefore, has the structure of a short paragraph. From the organizational perspective, it is one of the three constituents of the epistle—the opening, the body, and the closing. The opening is, thus, an epistle constituent, manifested compositionally in this particular case by a (compound) paragraph, that is, a paragraph consisting of two or more propositional clusters related by conjoining.

It might not appear that there would be much obvious coherence in a formal epistle opening such as this, but there are lexical and relational aspects of coherence present. The reciprocal nature of the senders and the recipients is one aspect of coherence here. There are references to the Godhead throughout—Christ Jesus and God in Greek text 1:1a, Christ in 1:2a, God the Father (and the Lord Jesus Christ, depending on the text followed) in 1:2b. There are a number of lexical items drawn from the semantic domain of the Christian faith—'apostle', 'brother', 'saints', 'grace', 'peace'. Also, in the final verbless blessing there is explicit reference to 'you(pl)' and to 'we'—the 'you(pl)' referring back to 1:2a and the 'we' embracing both the first person references (Paul and Timothy) and the second person references (the Colossians). Thus, 1:1 and 1:2 are bound into a unity, even if the data is a little unusual compared with that found in the body of the letter.

PROMINENCE AND THEME

As already pointed out, the epistle's opening consists of two propositional clusters in a conjoining relation. There is no obvious evidence that one of the propositional clusters is more prominent than the other, so the theme is drawn from both halves, which are diverse in content. The second cluster does not have any support propositions, so its content is stated in the more generic form: 'we pray that God will bless you'. 'God' refers to the Godhead, not just the Father, and 'bless' is generic, including both grace and peace. In the first cluster, 'Paul' is more prominent than 'Timothy', since Paul is mentioned first and described as an apostle and Timothy is simply a Christian brother. Hence, the theme statement does not refer to Timothy.

NOTES

1:1a *I*, Paul, together with Timothy, who is *our(inc)* brother, *am sending this letter to you*. The names 'Paul' and 'Timothy' are in the nominative case; they identify the senders of this letter. There are two questions in connection with these names. The first is that since no verb is used anywhere in these first two verses, what verb is implied? It might be thought that, since the names are of the senders of the letter, the implied verb is 'to write'. But this immediately brings into focus the second question. Since the two names are joined by καί 'and', in what sense is Timothy involved in the writing of the letter? Timothy is not the author; clearly Paul is, as the 'I' passages (e.g., 1:24–2:5) attest and as Paul's name at the end, in his own handwriting (4:18) further attest. Yet Timothy is associated with Paul in the 'we' passages (e.g., 1:3–12). In other words, Paul is the author of the letter, but Timothy is, as it were, identified with the contents and is included in a number of the statements made in the letter. In view of all this, the opening proposition reads '*I, Paul, together with Timothy, am sending this letter*', the use of the singular verb making it clear that Paul is the author, even though Timothy is involved, and 'send' being used instead of 'write' to avoid the impression that the letter was co-authored. Also, Paul did not literally pen the letter (see 4:18). The verb 'send' is intended to mean that Paul was responsible for composing the letter, dictating its contents, and seeing that it was safely transmitted to the Christians in Colosse.

All are agreed that ὁ ἀδελφός 'the brother' means a Christian brother (not a fellow apostle). This is a figure: the word is not used in the biological sense. It refers to one with whom there are ties of love, who is a member of the same spiritual family and to whom one has various spiritual responsibilities. It is used throughout the letter in this special Christian sense.

The implicit 'our(inclusive)' is supplied because Paul was addressing Christians and Timothy was their brother as well as his.

1:1b–c *I am an apostle who represents Christ Jesus*, because God chose *me in order that I should be an apostle*. Having given his name, Paul then goes on to describe himself as an apostle. He doubtless intended to draw attention to his authority to write to a church that he had not founded himself, particularly since one of the main issues in the letter was heretical teaching.

The terms ἀπόστολος 'apostle' and Χριστοῦ Ἰησοῦ 'Christ Jesus' are linked in a genitive construction. The semantic relation between the terms is generally considered to be that Paul was acting *on behalf of* Christ Jesus. The most common analogy used in the commentaries is that of an ambassador acting on behalf of a king. The most natural English equivalent for this is 'represents'. If a given receptor language does not have such a word, then it would be acceptable to use 'appointed by', 'commissioned by', or 'authorized by'; however, the reason for his being an apostle is stated in the following proposition, so 'represents' is preferable in this particular context.

The phrase διὰ θελήματος θεοῦ 'by God's will' means that it was God's will that Paul should act as an apostle. This is semantically equivalent to 'God chose me that I should be an apostle', implying both God's decision and God's corresponding action.

It should be pointed out that the words Χριστός 'Christ' and Ἰησοῦς 'Jesus', when they occur together, appear in the display in the same order as in the Greek text. However, there does not appear to be any semantic distinction signaled by the two different orders. If the receptor language requires that the names be translated always in the same order, this can be done without fear that some semantic distinction has been lost as a result. In this particular case, some of the manuscripts have the order 'Jesus Christ', so it is not altogether certain what the original order was at this point.

1:2a–c *I am sending this letter to you* who are in Colosse *town and* who are God's people and our(inc) faithful brothers *and* who are united to Christ. The use of the dative case here (τοῖς, ἁγίοις, etc.) indicates that Paul is now referring to the recipients of the letter. Just as Paul and Timothy were identified by name, so the recipients of the letter are identified by the name of the town in which they were living. The implicit information that Colosse was a town is supplied in the display. The verb form 'are' is used rather than 'live' since the verb 'to be' is explicit in this type of context in a number of Paul's letters (Romans, 1 and 2 Corinthians, Ephesus, Philippians).

There are several interrelated exegetical questions here: (1) Is ἁγίοις functioning as a noun, 'saints', or as an adjective, 'holy'? (2) Does πιστοῖς mean 'faithful' or 'believing'? (3) To what part(s) of this construction is ἐν Χριστῷ 'in Christ' attached?

These are answered as follows:

1. In the openings of the letters to the Romans (1:7), the Corinthians (2 Cor.1:1), and the Philippians (1:1), Paul uses the word ἅγιοι unambiguously as a noun; so it seems reasonable to assume, along with most commentators, that it is used in the same way here. Those who take it to mean 'holy' and to modify the noun ἀδελφοῖς 'brothers' point out that there is only one article (τοῖς) in this compound noun phrase, concluding therefore that both ἁγίοις and πιστοῖς are adjectives. But the grammars point out that the article is often omitted when both nouns have the same number and gender (as here) and when only one group of people is being referred to (as here). Hence, the interpretation 'saints' is preferred. But this term is not used in the display because the primary meaning of that word in English has an entirely different sense. Instead, it is rendered as 'God's people', the Greek 'saint' being understood to mean 'the people set apart for and belonging to God'.

2. As is clear from the letter as a whole, the Colossian church was being threatened by a heresy and Paul was much concerned that the Colossians not be led astray by it. The contents of the letter, however, suggest that they had not yet gone astray (see "The communication situation" in "The Introduction to the Semantic Structure of Colossians"). Hence, Paul uses the encouraging and tactful πιστοῖς here to show that he realized that they were still faithful to the truth that they had been taught. The rendering 'faithful' is contextually more suitable than 'believing'. (Some commentators point out that 'believing brothers' would be a strange expression to use, since 'brother' in this context means 'one who believes in Christ'.)

3. As to what ἐν Χριστῷ is attached to, one possibility is that it is attached to πιστοῖς, but only if πιστοῖς be taken to mean 'believing', which is widely rejected on collocational grounds (see the arguments under point 2). The better view is to take ἐν Χριστῷ with the whole phrase since ἐν Χριστῷ stands outside the noun phrase boundaries of τοῖς and ἀδελφοῖς and since it refers to one group of people. This view is supported by the fact that 'brothers' is never modified by 'in Christ' in the New Testament, so ἐν Χριστῷ could be collocated only with the first half of the phrase, yet its final position is against that analysis. Thus, it is viewed as a further description of the recipients, a separate proposition (1:2c). It is very widely agreed that in this context this phrase means 'incorporated into Christ' or 'united to Christ'; hence in the display it is rendered 'who are united to Christ'.

1:2d–e *We(exc) pray that* **God our(inc) Father [and our(inc) Lord Jesus Christ]** *will* **act graciously towards you and** *that* **God our Father [and our Lord Jesus Christ]** *will* **cause you to have peace.** The manuscripts are divided concerning whether the phrase 'and from the Lord Jesus Christ' is included following 'God our Father'. One's conclusions in such matters depend on one's theory of which manuscripts are considered the most reliable, how the various errors are accounted for, and which factors affecting transmission are to be weighed the most heavily. Since the translator is faced with rival and irreconcilable theories here, all that can be said is that the translator will have to choose for himself or herself until it is possible to regard one theory as substantially correct. (Other considerations, such as the text used in a national version, may, of course, affect the choice.)

The word χάρις 'grace' is represented as a verb in the display, 'act graciously'. This is a term used in the New Testament in a special Christian sense; it is an event or action on the part of God (and the Lord Jesus) toward sinful mankind. But since there is no English verb that is the counterpart of the noun 'grace', 'act graciously' is used here.

The word εἰρήνη 'peace' is even more difficult. It is generally agreed among the commentators that peace is the state enjoyed by the recipients of God's grace and that it is similar in meaning to the Hebrew word *shalom* (often translated by εἰρήνη in the Septuagint). The Hebrew word, however, means more than internal peacefulness or outward freedom from war and strife. It corresponds more nearly to the English word *well-being*, a state of blessedness or prosperity of body and soul. How far the ideas associated with the Hebrew word carried over into the Greek εἰρήνη is hard to say, especially when used in a conventional salutation of a letter.

Another problem, from the point of view of semantics, is that whereas 'grace' clearly comes from the Godhead, 'peace' is man's experience, so that the Greek preposition meaning 'from' has the meaning 'cause to come to pass'. This is the basis for 'cause you to have peace' in the display. An alternate would be 'cause that you be peaceful', 'peace(ful)' being understood in the sense just mentioned for *shalom*.

EPISTLE CONSTITUENT 1:3–4:6 (Part: Body of the Epistle)

THEME: Conduct yourselves as those should who are united to Christ Jesus our Lord, who ranks above everything that has been created. In particular, make sure that no one makes you become his disciples by teaching you a false religious philosophy; rather, be constantly wanting what is associated with heaven.

RELATIONAL STRUCTURE	CONTENTS
introduction	1:3–12 We thank God very often that you believe in Christ Jesus and that you love all God's people. We have also been praying to God for you very often that you will come to know truly all that he wants you to do, in order that you will conduct yourselves as the Lord's people should.
NUCLEUS (primary matters)	1:13–3:17 Conduct yourselves as those should who are united to Christ Jesus our Lord, who ranks above everything that has been created. In particular, make sure that no one makes you become his disciples by teaching you a false religious philosophy; rather, be constantly wanting what is associated with heaven.
conjoined (secondary matters)	3:18–4:6 Act as believers should toward those of their household. Pray persistently, and act wisely toward unbelievers.

BOUNDARIES AND COHERENCE

The initial boundary of the body is clearly marked by a change, though without a formal marker (asyndeton), from the formalized opening, with its absence of verb forms, to the first verb form εὐχαριστοῦμεν 'we thank'. The closing boundary of the body is marked by the end of the hortatory material at 4:6, followed by personal information concerning Paul and his associates. The change in genre is shown by the switch from finite verbs in the imperative mood to verbs in the indicative mood. The announcement of the topic τὰ κατ' ἐμὲ πάντα 'all the things about me' is another boundary marker.

The body is characterized by features that distinguish it from the opening and the closing of the epistle. These particular features distinguish it from the bodies of other epistles as well. There are three such features:

1. The occurrence of a group of words having to do with the semantic area of knowledge. Listed in alphabetical order and with the number of occurrences, these are:

   ἐπιγινώσκω 'to know truly' (1)
   ἐπίγνωσις 'true knowledge' (4)
   γνῶσις 'knowledge' (1)
   σοφία 'wisdom' (6)
   σύνεσις 'insight, understanding, discernment' (2)

   The first occurrence of one of these words is in 1:6, where ἐπιγινώσκω is used; the last is in 4:5, where σοφία is used.

2. The frequency of πᾶς/πᾶσα/πᾶν 'all, every'. This adjective is found no less than thirty-five times in the body, the first occurrence being in

1:4 ('*all* the saints') and the last being in 3:22 ('slaves, obey your earthly masters in *every* respect').
3. The distribution of χάρις 'grace' and its cognate forms εὐχαριστέω, εὐχαριστία, and εὐχάριστος 'to thank', 'thanks', and 'thankful'. Reference to thanksgiving is found in 1:3 in the introduction to the body (εὐχαριστοῦμεν 'we thank') and in 1:12 (εὐχαριστοῦντες 'thanking'). There are two more references in the last few verses of the nucleus of the body, in 3:15 (εὐχάριστοι 'thankful') and in 3:17 (εὐχαριστοῦντες 'thanking'). Further, there is a reference to thanksgiving in 2:7 (εὐχαριστίᾳ 'thanksgiving'), where it is attached to the central command of the whole epistle; another is in 4:2, in the secondary matters dealt with by Paul (εὐχαριστίᾳ 'thanksgiving'). This means that a reference to thanksgiving in some form closes both the introduction to the body and the head of the body.

In addition, χάρις 'grace' occurs between the two references to thanksgiving in the introduction to the body, in 1:6, and also between the two references to thanksgiving that close the nucleus of the body, in 3:16. The body is, therefore, characterized by a distinctive patterning of references to 'grace' and 'thanksgiving'.

These features take on greater significance when they are compared with what is found in similar epistles, such as Ephesians and Philippians. In Colossians a member of the group of words having to do with knowledge occurs about every six and one half verses, but in Ephesians, a somewhat similar epistle, the overall frequency of this same group of words is only about once in every twenty verses. Similarly, the adjective πᾶς/πᾶσα/πᾶν 'all, every' is somewhat more frequent in Colossians than in the other two epistles. And references to thanksgiving are about three times more frequent than in the other two epistles.

The body of Colossians, then, is characterized by emphases on true spiritual knowledge, grace, and thankfulness. These are aspects of the referential coherence of the body.

Situational coherence is particularly evident in the body. Indeed, it is only from the information provided in the nucleus of the body that anything at all is known of the situation that occasioned Paul's writing of this letter: a false φιλοσοφία 'philosophy' had arisen in Colosse and there was a danger that the Colossian believers would be attracted to it. Not only does Paul point out the human origin of this φιλοσοφία and its tendency to promote the flesh rather than the spirit (in 2:8-23), but in what he says in 1:13-2:5, he paves the way for his exposure of the false teaching by emphasizing the unique supremacy of Christ over everything in creation, including angelic powers, and his own responsibility to make known the 'mystery' which God had now revealed to his people, including those who were Gentiles.

Structural (or organizational) coherence is reflected in the structure's consisting of an introduction, with its orienters 'we thank God' and 'we pray'; a nucleus in which the major matter of the false teaching is dealt with; and then some secondary matters (exhortations), which Paul evidently wished to pass on to the Colossian believers but which did not have an immediate connection with the exposure of the false teaching.

PROMINENCE AND THEME

Of the three constituents of the 1:3-4:6 body, 1:13-3:17 is the prominent one; 1:3-12 simply introduces it, and 3:18-4:6 adds some secondary matters to it. The theme of the body is, therefore, identical with the theme of 1:13-3:17.

PART CONSTITUENT 1:3–12 (Section: Introduction to 1:13–4:6)

THEME: We thank God very often that you believe in Christ Jesus and that you love all God's people. We have also been praying to God for you very often that you will come to know truly all that he wants you to do, in order that you will conduct yourselves as the Lord's people should.

RELATIONAL STRUCTURE	CONTENTS
NUCLEUS₁	1:3–8 We thank God for you very often that you believe in Christ Jesus and that you love all God's people.
NUCLEUS₂	1:9–12 We have also been praying to God for you very often that you will know truly all that he wants you to do, in order that you will conduct yourselves as the Lord's people should.

BOUNDARIES AND COHERENCE

The beginning of the 1:3–12 unit is clearly marked by the formal switch from the epistle opening's verbless clauses to the first finite verb, the first word in 1:3. Where the unit ends is, however, much more disputed. Of twenty-eight versions consulted, eight make a paragraph break at the end of 1:12, but not at the end of 1:14; ten make a paragraph break at the end of 1:14, but not at 1:12; two make a break at both points; six make no break at either point; and the remaining two make different breaks altogether (at 1:11 and 1:13). Of fourteen commentaries consulted, all but one had a major or minor break at 1:14, but only four at 1:12.

Nevertheless, as will be argued, there *is* a major break at 1:12 (for the exact location of the boundary, see the discussion of the boundaries of 1:9–12). There are four major grounds for so arguing:

1. The *rhetorical bracketing*, or sandwich structure, of 1:3 and 1:12. In both verses thanks are given to God the Father, but there is no other mention of thanks within this span of verses, nor again until 2:7.
2. The number of *parallelisms* between 1:3–8 and 1:9–12. They indicate a close connection between these two paragraphs, and a separation from the material that follows:
   a. Both paragraphs begin with a performative verb with the same subject, 'we'.
   b. Both refer to Paul and Timothy's praying for the Colossians (1:3, 9) and both draw attention to the frequency of the thanksgiving and the praying—'always', in the one case, 'without ceasing', in the other.
   c. Both refer to the reports about the Colossians having been *heard* (1:4, 9).
   d. Both use the phrase ἀφ' ἧς ἡμέρας 'since the day' (1:6, 9), and both use the expression 'bearing fruit and growing' (1:6, 10).
   e. Both use the stem ἐπιγνω- 'to know (truly)', in the verb form in 1:6 and in the noun form in 1:9 and 10—and not again until 2:2.
3. The features of *lexical coherence* shared by these verses, but not by those immediately following.
   a. These verses are characterized by second person plural verbs, dependent participles, and pronouns, but such forms do not occur after 1:12 until 1:21.
   b. The first person plural forms (verbs and pronouns), and the participles dependent on them, are all interpreted as exclusive, referring to Paul and Timothy. The switch to the inclusive comes either in the second half of 1:12, or in 1:13, depending upon which text is followed. (The only exception is 'we' in 1:3a, where Paul speaks of 'our Lord Jesus Christ', interpreted as inclusive.)
4. The complex structure of the next unit, 1:13–20. Verses 1:13–14 are in a chiastic relation with 1:20, so that a break is needed both at 1:12 (the start of the chiasmus) and at 1:14 (a boundary within the chiasmus). For further discussion, see the analysis of 1:13–20.

This combined evidence provides a very strong case for treating 1:3–12 as a semantic unit in Colossians. The many parallelisms between 1:3–8 and 1:9–12 (along with other evidence which will be given in detail later) indicate that there are two paragraphs and that the two-paragraph unit is compositionally a section. In addition, within the structure of the body of the epistle, these two paragraphs function as an introduction to the body.

In John Lee White's monograph *The Form and Function of the Body of the Greek Letter*, he suggests that the body of the Greek letter consists of an opening, middle, and closure, and that the opening "posits the basis of mutuality" (p. 39). Based on this, it seems very likely that 1:3–12 is the body opening, and that Paul's primary purpose in writing it is to establish a suitable relationship between himself and the Colossians for what he has to say in the rest of the letter. There are subsidiary purposes, such as giving his apostolic backing to Epaphras, but the primary one is to establish a "basis of mutuality" with a group of believers whom he has not personally met.

Hence, 1:3–12, which is a section consisting of two paragraphs, is taken to be the body's introduction, one of its three constituents. This is supported by the considerable agreement that either 1:3–12 or 1:3–14 forms a type of introductory unit—only the boundary is in dispute. A couple of versions (Beck and the Twentieth Century) treat 1:3–12 as a unit of thanksgiving and prayer; TEV, Saint Joseph, NIV, JB, NAB, and Kleist and Lilly treat 1:3–14 similarly.

PROMINENCE AND THEME

Since 1:3–8 and 1:9–12 are conjoined and of equal prominence, a section theme has to be either abstracted from them jointly or the two themes conjoined. Here, the two themes are conjoined.

SECTION CONSTITUENT 1:3–8 (Paragraph: Nucleus₁ of 1:3–12)

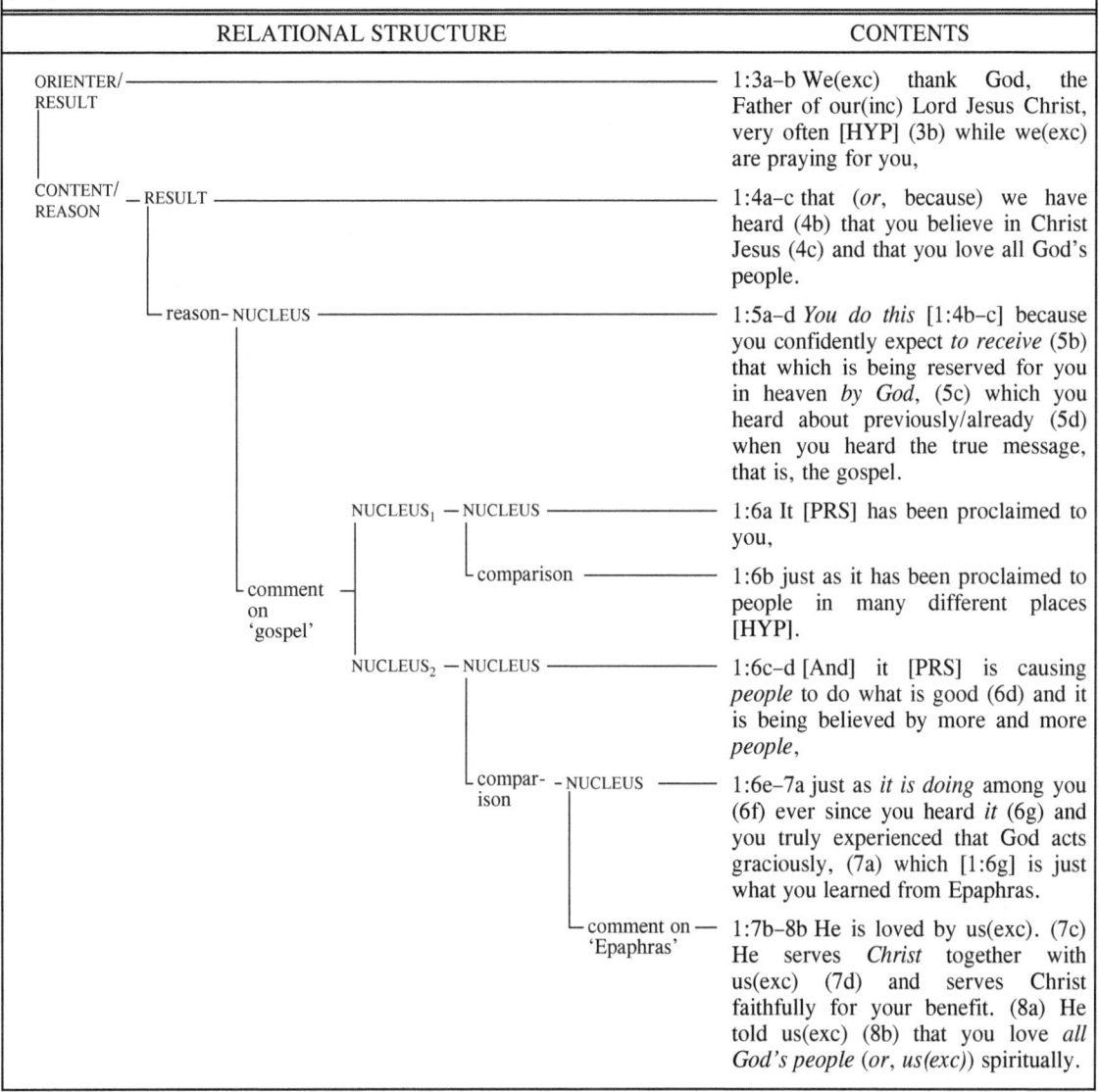

THEME: We thank God for you very often that you believe in Christ Jesus and that you love all God's people.

BOUNDARIES AND COHERENCE

The initial boundary of the 1:3–8 unit is clear: The formal opening of the letter ends at the end of 1:2; and εὐχαριστοῦμεν 'we thank', the first finite verb, opens the body of the letter. The closing boundary is equally clear: At 1:9 a new paragraph is signaled by the connector phrase διὰ τοῦτο 'for this reason', the free subject ἡμεῖς 'we', and a switch to the theme of prayer from that of thanks.

Two features mark vv. 1:3–8 as a semantic unit: the rhetorical bracketing (sandwich structure) and the unit's coherence. The rhetorical bracketing involves (1) the use of 'we'-oriented forms in 1:3–4a and again in 1:7b and 8; (2) the reference to the Colossians' love in 1:4 and in 1:8; and (3) the reference to the verbal report brought to Paul and Timothy, expressed by ἀκούσαντες '(we) having heard' in 1:4 and ὁ καὶ δηλώσας ἡμῖν 'who has also told us' in 1:8, the latter being the semantic reciprocal of the former.

The paragraph's coherence is shown by (1) the eleven pronoun or verb references to the Colossians themselves; (2) the use of the indicative mood throughout; and (3) the fact that these verses are one long sentence in Greek (or possibly two).

Although this paragraph starts with thanksgiving to God, it also contains extended comments on the gospel and Epaphras. This raises two questions: Where are the inner boundaries that separate these three parts, and what is the status of the cluster of propositions of which each part consists?

There are two places at which the first of these inner boundaries could be drawn, and two places at which the second could be drawn; from a grammatical point of view, the choice depends on the same criteria. Both at the end of 1:5 carrying over to the beginning of 1:6 and in 1:7, the topic noun, 'gospel' in the first case, 'Epaphras' in the second, is followed immediately by an article + participle/adjective construction. In the first case, the topic is followed by τοῦ παρόντος εἰς ὑμᾶς '(which) is present with you'; and in the second, the topic is followed by τοῦ ἀγαπητοῦ συνδούλου ἡμῶν '(who is) the beloved fellow-slave of us'. The question, then, is whether these two phrases should be grouped with the preceding constituent or the following one. On the one hand, it can be argued that once the (sub)topics of the gospel and Epaphras have been introduced by the use of the noun, the following constituent develops that topic. On the other hand, it can be argued that the use of the article + participle/adjective construction ties this information closely to the noun, whereas the subsequent constructions are somewhat more detached. In 1:7, it makes little difference. In 1:6, however, the decision is tied up with the further decision on how to handle the sequence καθώς . . . καθώς 'just as . . . just as'. It is considered that the better interpretation is to separate the two occurrences of καθώς. Where the same problem arises again in 1:12 in the following paragraph, it makes for a simpler overall analysis to make the division *after* the article + participle construction rather than before. In the present case, however, it is simpler to make the division immediately after the proposition in which the topic noun ('gospel', 'Epaphras') is referred to.

The paragraph is therefore regarded as consisting of a main or independent constituent (1:3-5), together with two embedded constituents (1:6a-7a and 1:7b-8). They are regarded as embedded because, semantically, they are both comments on a "thing," in one case the gospel, in the other, Epaphras. An alternative analysis would be to analyze 1:3-8 as consisting of three separate paragraphs with tail-head links. But the strong evidence for the unity of 1:3-8 and the close grammatical links militate against this alternative.

PROMINENCE AND THEME

In 1:3a 'we thank' is a performative, a paragraph orienter represented by the opening independent clause. In 1:4a is another orienter, 'we have heard', which introduces the content of what has been heard. In fact, the flow of thought would not be affected by its omission: 'We thank God that you believe . . . '. The content of what had been heard is important, however, as it constitutes either the reason or the content for the thanks. (With the verb 'to thank' as orienter, the distinction between reason and content appears to be neutralized.) The theme includes the paragraph orienter because of the fact that this paragraph is part of the body introduction and orienters such as 'we thank' and 'we pray' establish the genre and are thereby thematic (cf. 'we command' in hortatory genre). The embedded paragraphs do not contribute information to the nuclear thanksgiving theme of the paragraph and so are not represented in the theme statement.

NOTES

1:3a We(exc) thank God, the Father of our(inc) Lord Jesus Christ, very often The first problem in εὐχαριστοῦμεν τῷ θεῷ 'we thank God' is the referent of 'we'. One solution is to say, following Martin (1973), "Paul's custom is to oscillate between 'I' and 'we', with no apparent change of meaning." The other, following other commentators, is to look for some rationale in the 'I' and 'we' occurrences.

Of Paul's thirteen letters, two (Galatians and Titus) are without an expression of thanks; two (2 Corinthians and Ephesians) give thanks in the form of a doxology, hence without a performative; and in the other nine, the situation is as follows:

1. In Romans and 1 and 2 Timothy no one is associated with Paul in the salutation; thus the subject of the verb 'to thank' is 'I'.
2. In 1 Corinthians, Philippians, and Philemon, others *are* associated with Paul in the salutation, but the subject of 'to thank' is 'I'.
3. In Colossians and 1 and 2 Thessalonians, others are associated with Paul in the salutation and the subject of 'to thank' is 'we'.

From this we may conclude that the use of the first person singular or plural is deliberate rather than random. Perhaps the singular is used in 1 Corinthians, Philippians, and Philemon because of the more personal nature of what is said in those letters, whereas in Colossians and 1 and 2 Thessalonians, where the plural is used, the contents are not so personal. Therefore, 'we' in Colossians is interpreted as referring to Paul and Timothy (i.e., first person dual exclusive). This applies to this paragraph and the following one. From 1:23 on, however, Paul uses 'I' when speaking of his apostolic ministry to the Gentiles, which tends to confirm the view that 'we' in the initial paragraphs refers to Paul and Timothy.

Another problem here is where the boundary is between the first two clauses in the Greek. Since 'we thank God the Father of our Lord Jesus Christ' obviously belongs to the first clause, the question centers on the words πάντοτε περὶ ὑμῶν 'always for you'. There is very little on which to base a judgment—both 'always' and 'for you' can occur collocated with 'thank' and both can occur with 'pray'. Also 'always' can occur clause initially, medially, or finally. All that can be said is that when the giving of thanks is mentioned alone (1 Cor. 1:4; 2 Thess. 1:3; 2:13), it occurs only in this position, and when both thanks and prayer are mentioned (as in Phil. 1:3–4; 1 Thess. 1:2; Philem. 4), the same ambiguity arises as here. Hence, there seems a slight reason to favor putting 'always' with the main verb, following the unambiguous cases.

The question also arises as to whether περὶ ὑμῶν 'for you' closes the first clause or opens the second one (assuming that 'always' belongs to the first clause). Both verbs occur elsewhere collocated with περί 'for', so there is no preference on that basis. However, 1:4 makes clear who the persons are for whom Paul and Timothy are thanking God, so there seems a slight reason to take 'for you' with 'praying'.

Another problem here is the textual variants: 'God Father' versus 'God and Father' (i.e., with or without καί 'and'). But, so far as I can ascertain, it makes no difference to the meaning. With καί, the καί is understood to be "epexegetical," equivalent to 'that is'; without καί, 'Father' is appositional. In either case 'God' is further identified as that God who is the Father of the Lord Jesus.

1:3b while we(exc) are praying for you, Since εὐχαριστοῦμεν 'we thank' and προσευχόμενοι 'praying' are simultaneous, the praying is treated as being in the relation of circumstance to the thanksgiving. This is supported by the fact that a finite verb expresses the thanking, whereas a present participle expresses the praying.

1:4a that (*or,* because) we have heard The 1:4a proposition is linked to the preceding material by the relation of reason, a common use of the aorist participle. It could be purely temporal, but the fact that it is the present state of the Colossians which moved Paul and Timothy to thank God and pray for them points to a logical rather than temporal connection. Also, in 1:9, when Paul draws attention to the temporal factor, he uses ἀφ' ἧς ἡμέρας 'since the day'.

1:4b–c that you believe in Christ Jesus and that you love all God's people. The question here is whether the preposition ἐν 'in' indicates that the faith is placed in Christ Jesus, or refers to the sphere in which faith is operative. Although ἐν is not common with the verb πιστεύω 'to believe', it is as common as any other preposition with the noun πίστις 'faith'. (Other good examples will be found in Gal. 3:26, Eph. 1:15, 1 Tim. 3:13, and 2 Tim. 3:15.) Also, there is a formal parallel with the following statement where the preposition εἰς 'toward' certainly indicates the persons to whom the love is directed. Thus it is likely that ἐν indicates the person to whom the faith is directed. If this view is not followed, then there is no statement of the object of the Colossians' faith, and it tends to make 'in Christ Jesus' a third reason for the thanksgiving, which is in conflict with the symmetry of the construction centered around 'and'.

The abstract nouns and the present tense of the verb ἔχετε 'you have' indicate that Paul and Timothy are giving thanks for the *present* state of the Colossian Christians and not some earlier state.

1:5a *You do this [1:4b–c]* because you confidently expect *to receive* Commentators devote much space to the logical connection of the statement 'because of the hope'. They suggest three alternatives: (1) that it is a (further) reason for the thanksgiving; (2) that it is the reason for the faith and love; and (3) that it is the reason for the love only.

The main arguments against connecting this statement with the thanksgiving are as follows:

1. In other epistles, the content/reason connected with Paul's giving of thanks in the body introduction is the spiritual state of those to whom the epistle is written, not something like the Christian hope, which is true regardless of the spiritual state of those addressed.
2. The verb εὐχαριστέω 'to thank' is nowhere else in the New Testament collocated with the preposition διά 'because of'. A possible exception is in 1 Thess. 2:13, but there it is in the phrase διὰ τοῦτο 'because of this', referring forward (probably) to the ὅτι clause that is the reason/content of the thanksgiving. No διά + accusative phrase, as such, is the content of a thanksgiving in the New Testament.
3. The phrase occurs quite a distance from the main verb.

The reason why it has been suggested that 'because of the hope' is a reason/content for the thanksgiving is that some commentators find it difficult to conceive of a reason for either Christian faith or love. Hendriksen meets this problem as follows: "Christian mental and moral attitudes and activities such as believing, hoping, and loving, always react upon each other. In general, the more there is of the one, the more there will be of the other. This holds too with respect to hope. . . . It is a living and sanctifying force (1 Pet. 1:3; 1 John 3:3)."

As to whether it should be linked only to 'the love' or also to 'the faith', it is much harder to say. Meyer and Alford regard the different construction used with 'the love' ('which you have') as singling it out, and they point to 1:8, where love is mentioned again as confirmation of this. They would, therefore, argue for its referring back only to 'the love'. It is not an important issue, but the arguments of Meyer and Alford give some support to linking 'the hope' only to 'the love', in spite of their being joined by καί 'and'. Proposition 1:5a is thus either the reason for 1:4c (slight preference), or for 1:4b–c. However, in view of this uncertainty, 1:5a–d is linked in the display to both 1:4b and 1:4c as the compound nucleus.

1:5b that which is being reserved for you in heaven *by God*, This proposition introduces the first of many figures in Colossians. The hope is described as ἀποκειμένην 'put away, stored up' (Arndt and Gingrich), as if it were an object put to one side or stored away carefully in heaven. This is regarded as a dead figure in the absence of any of the evidences for its being a live one; it has the sense of either 'kept safe' or else 'reserved for' (which is the sense of this verb when used impersonally, according to Arndt and Gingrich). The latter meaning seems more appropriate in this general context, which has no mention of any threat to the hope or threat to the Colossian believers. Commentators call it the "objective" hope, what we are looking forward to, rather than the activity of hoping. However, the activity and the goal of that activity are very closely linked. Simply to say 'you . . . love all the saints because of what is reserved for you in heaven', without mentioning the activity of looking forward to it, seems strange. Hence, the noun ἐλπίς 'hope' is represented in the display by both an event and a thing. And because 'what you hope for' carries the idea of uncertainty in modern English, 'confidently expect' is used rather than 'hope'.

In the Greek this is a passive construction. The passive is retained in the display in order that the proposition's topic might be 'the hope', and 'by God' is supplied, giving the agent of the event.

1:5c which you heard about previously/already The verb here means that they *heard* about the hope *before* some other event. The following are suggested for what this event was: (1) before the realization of the hope; (2) before Paul's writing of the letter; and (3) a general 'beforehand, previously' (i.e., referring to information already known to them). This last view seems preferable contextually, since one of Paul's purposes in this opening paragraph is to give his apostolic approval both to the message they believed and to the messenger (Epaphras) who brought it; it also includes the other two views. Further, 1:5d makes it clear that they had heard about the hope when they heard the gospel itself. Hence, the alternative propositionalization 'which you heard about already'. In either case, both 'already' and 'previously' refer to a time before Paul sent this letter.

1:5d when you heard the true message, that is, the gospel. The first question here is the meaning of ἣν προηκούσατε ἐν τῷ λόγῳ 'which you heard about previously in the message'. Presumably it means that the message conveyed information to them concerning the hope to which Paul has just referred. This is best represented by 'when you heard the message', repeating the main verb 'you heard'.

The second question is the meaning of the double genitive construction τῆς ἀληθείας τοῦ εὐαγγελίου 'of-the truth of-the gospel'. There are two main views on this: either treat the expression as a sequence of genitives, or treat 'the gospel' as appositional to 'the message of the truth'. The former would mean 'the message that conveyed the truth associated with the gospel, the message of gospel-truth'. The latter would mean 'the message that conveyed the truth, that is, the gospel'. There is not a great deal of difference, but the second is preferred because the next few statements are on the topic of the gospel.

The phrase ἡ ἀλήθεια 'the truth' is rather difficult propositionally, since 'true' is an attribute relating to some thing or event. In this case, the thing is taken to be the message, so it is expressed propositionally as 'the true message'. Again, Paul is giving his approval to what they had heard, saying it was true and was the gospel.

1:6a–7a As discussed under the coherence of this paragraph, 1:6a–7a are considered an embedded constituent that comments on the topic of the gospel. In terms of its composition, it could be regarded as either a paragraph or a propositional cluster, but since it is a constituent of a paragraph, the second of these alternatives is preferred.

As to the reason for an embedded comment on the gospel here, commentators are generally agreed that it has the twofold purpose of drawing attention to the universality of the gospel and encouraging the Colossians to continue believing it. Both points are made against the background of the false teaching that had arrived at Colosse, which was not universal truth but a localized heresy, and they were not to abandon the gospel for it.

1:6a–e It has been proclaimed to you, just as it has been proclaimed to people in many different places. [And] it is causing *people* to do what is good and it is being believed by more and more *people*, just as *it is doing* among you The Greek underlying these propositions combines the double problem of unusual grammar and a textual variant, namely 'and' at the beginning of 6c (shown in brackets). With the shorter text, in which καί 'and' is omitted, the question is whether Paul is making one or two comparisons; with the longer text, there would be two.

The double comparison would be:

> the gospel has come to you, just as it has come to all the world; and
> the gospel is bearing fruit and growing, just as it is among you.

The following points can be made concerning this interpretation.

1. In the first comparison, the switch from the preposition εἰς 'to' (1:6a) to ἐν 'in' (1:6b) makes a somewhat irregular comparison. However, semantically, παρόντος εἰς 'present with' is equivalent to 'has arrived at and is still present in' and this latter idea would collocate well with the ἐν used in the second half of the comparison.
2. An ellipsis of 'it has come' in the second half of the first comparison would have to be assumed, but it is common to have an ellipsis in the second half of a comparison, as here in the second half of the second comparison.
3. With the double comparison, there is a chiastic reference to 'you' and 'the world'. That is, they occur in the sequence 'you', 'the world', 'the world', 'you', but the second reference to 'the world' is implicit, not explicit.
4. If καί 'and' is present here, it would join the two comparisons formally. Without it, conjoining could still be assumed.
5. If the double-comparison view is followed, it means that 1:6a would be grouped with 1:6b–c rather than with 1:5.

The main problem with the single-comparison view is that it has to assume a unique double use of καθώς 'as', and no other such example is to be found in the New Testament. The normal pattern has οὕτως καί 'thus also' introducing the second part of the comparison, as in 3:13, or else simply καί. There would be no need to assume an ellipsis other than the obvious one in 1:6d.

The double-comparison view, which poses fewer and less serious problems, is the one shown in the display. The single comparison would be:

> (6a) This gospel has been proclaimed to you.
> (6b) Just as this gospel is causing *people* everywhere to do what is good
> (6c) and just as it is being believed by more and more people *everywhere*,
> (6d) so also this [6b–c] is happening among you.

1:6a It has been proclaimed to you, In the Greek the gospel is personified—it is said to be 'present'.

It was not the gospel that was present, however, but Epaphras who had made it known to them. In the display this is stated nonfiguratively, 'has been proclaimed to you', rather than 'is present with you', with the topic still the gospel and no focus on who brought it. If this information has to be supplied, then 'by Epaphras' would be best.

1:6b just as it has been proclaimed to people in many different places. Here the gospel is described as operative 'in all the world' (ἐν παντὶ τῷ κόσμῳ), which is hyperbole. This is represented in the display with the expression 'in many different places'.

1:6c–d [And] it is causing *people* to do what is good and it is being believed by more and more *people*, There is another figure here. The gospel is spoken of as if it were a living plant or tree: καρποφορούμενον 'bearing fruit' and αὐξανόμενον 'growing'. In spite of the use of two terms, which might indicate a live metaphor, it is taken as a dead metaphor, since each word is used elsewhere in contexts where it would be difficult to prove that they are acting as live metaphors rather than dead ones (see, for instance, Rom. 7:5 and Acts 7:17). It is generally agreed among the commentators that 'bearing fruit' refers to the gospel's effects in the lives of the Christians, and 'growing' to its spread to more and more people. In the display 'the gospel' has been kept as the topic of the propositions, even though this is a somewhat figurative rendering, saying that the gospel is causing people to do something, as if it were a living agent.

1:6e just as *it is doing* among you There is no verb in the Greek, so the generic verb 'doing' is supplied. It represents the two specific events 'causing to do what is good' and 'being believed'.

1:6f ever since you heard *it* In the Greek the verb 'you heard' has no explicit object, but since there has already been a reference to their hearing the gospel, and since 'the gospel' is the topic of this embedded constituent, this is assumed to be the object here. Alternatively, the object of 'heard' could be the same as the object of 'came to know' in the following proposition, namely, 'the grace of God'.

1:6g and you truly experienced that God acts graciously, The Greek is καὶ ἐπέγνωτε τὴν χάριν τοῦ θεοῦ ἐν ἀληθείᾳ 'and you came-to-know the grace of God in truth'. The question is whether the compound form of the verb (ἐπί + γινώσκω) is to be contrasted with the simple form here, and if so, what the contrast is. For this context, Arndt and Gingrich say "with the preposition making its influence felt—a. *know exactly, completely, through and through.*" This sounds fine until you realize that the object of the verb is 'the grace of God'. Under the corresponding noun ἐπίγνωσις, Arndt and Gingrich say "in our lit. limited to relig. and moral things." Could it be that the compound form of the verb covers the idea of experience as well as understanding? It has also been suggested that the compound form can mean 'to know truly', 'to have a true knowledge of' (Greenlee). This would tie in well with Arndt and Gingrich's observation and is followed throughout (in 1:9, 10; 2:2; 3:10), wherever the noun ἐπίγνωσις is used.

There are two problems with the phrase τὴν χάριν τοῦ θεοῦ ἐν ἀληθείᾳ 'the grace of God in truth'. The first problem is the semantic class of 'grace', whether it is a thing, event, attribute, or relation? Clearly, it is not a thing or a relation. That leaves event or attribute. Perhaps, as it relates to God, it is both—a quality of character that expresses itself in action. But since the Colossians are spoken of as having experienced it, event seems preferable here. Yet English has no verb form for 'grace' in this sense, so it is rendered 'acts graciously' with the understanding that this is a technical religious term.

The second problem relates to ἐν ἀληθείᾳ 'in truth', which represents an attribute, as ἐν + an abstract noun often does. But of what is it an attribute, the 'knowing/experiencing' or the 'grace'? Commentators are divided between the two. The only reason advanced is the overall context: Paul is supporting their past knowledge as opposed to what the false teacher would like them to believe now. The collocation of 'true' and 'grace' seems rather unusual, although it is nicely rendered by Lightfoot as "in its genuine simplicity, without adulteration" and by Martin (1973) as "the message of God's grace 'as it truly is'." Or it could be taken in the sense that the heresy being propagated was a false understanding of grace. Since, however, Paul has already said that they had heard the true message, it seems better to take the view that he is saying that their experience of that true message was also true. This view also relates better to the earlier statement that the gospel was bearing fruit among them. This would mean that ἐν ἀληθείᾳ 'truly' was an attribute reinforcing the component 'truly' in ἐπιγινώσκω 'to know truly'.

1:7a which is just what you learned from Epaphras. This is a formal comparison, comparing what they had experienced with what Epaphras had taught them.

1:7b–8b The remaining statements in this paragraph constitute a second embedded constituent elaborating the topic of Epaphras introduced in 1:7a. It was Epaphras who had taken the gospel to Colosse in the first place, and it was Epaphras who had brought the recent report of the state of the Colossian church to Paul. So Paul commends this servant of God for his faithfulness, lest the Colossians fall into the error of thinking that the new (false) teacher was to be preferred to the old (faithful) teacher.

1:7b–c He is loved by us(exc). He serves *Christ* together with us(exc) The adjective ἀγαπητοῦ 'beloved' expresses an event, to love, and the following ἡμῶν 'of-us' makes it clear who the agent of the event is. Thus the proposition in its basic form is 'we(exc) love Epaphras'. However, the passive form is used in the display to retain Epaphras as the subject-topic.

The noun συνδούλου 'fellow-slave' is more difficult to handle. It represents two state propositions: 'we are slaves' and 'Epaphras is also a slave'. These propositions express role relations, but they are also figurative—'slave' is not used in its literal sense. Nor is it stated with respect to whom the role of slave is sustained. This last question is the most easily dealt with. Of seven cases in which Paul speaks of himself or others as slaves of either God or Christ, in only one is it of God (Tit. 1:1); in all the others the role of slave is with respect to Christ. Furthermore, the whole epistle has much to say about Christ; and he is specifically referred to in the next proposition as the one served.

But what is the nonfigurative significance of Epaphras's being a slave of Christ? It probably covers both the idea of belonging to him and of obeying or serving him. The latter is then specifically commented on in 7d, so it seems likely that this is the aspect that Paul has primarily in mind; therefore it is expressed in the display as an event proposition, 'and serves *Christ* together with us(exc)'.

1:7d and serves Christ faithfully for your benefit. The main question here is the text, the two alternatives being 'you' and 'us'. Metzger (p. 620) says that "a majority of the [UBS text] Committee [were] impressed by the widespread currency of ὑμῶν in versional and patristic witnesses." If the variant ὑμῶν is accepted, as here, there are two possible interpretations:

1. The meaning of ὑπὲρ ὑμῶν 'for you' is that Epaphras was acting on behalf of the Colossians in going to Paul and Timothy. This interpretation runs counter to the whole thrust of the paragraph.

2. The meaning of ὑπὲρ ὑμῶν is 'for your benefit'. That is to say, Epaphras had been serving Christ and it was the Colossians who had benefited from that faithful ministry. This fits in much better with the context in which Paul is giving his apostolic support to Epaphras's ministry to the Colossians. The rendering in the display is based on this interpretation.

But even if the variant ἡμῶν 'us' is preferred, its meaning is much the same as in the second interpretation of ὑπὲρ ὑμῶν. The difference is that it states explicitly that Epaphras was acting on behalf of Paul and Timothy and only implies that it was the Colossians who benefited from his ministry.

The phrase 'servant of Christ' means 'serves Christ'. (This rendering would be valid with the variant ἡμῶν as well: 'serves Christ for our benefit'.)

The words διάκονος 'servant' (here in 1:7d) and δοῦλος 'slave' (in 1:7c) cannot be easily distinguished with verbal equivalents in English—'to serve' has to be used for both. It is likely that δοῦλος draws attention to the role relation, διάκονος to the type of work done.

1:8a–b He told us(exc) that you love *all God's people (or, us(exc))* spiritually. Here καί probably means 'in addition to': in addition to preaching to them (see 1:7a) he had also reported back to Paul on how things were going.

In regard to τὴν ὑμῶν ἀγάπην ἐν πνεύματι 'the love of-you in spirit', there are two questions:

1. The construction τὴν ὑμῶν ἀγάπην 'the love of you' means 'you love', but whom did the Colossians love? Three suggestions have been made: Paul himself (or Paul and Timothy, since 'we' is still being used in 1:8a); Epaphras; or 'all the saints', as in 1:4. While each of these

alternatives makes good sense and would be true in the overall context of the letter, the last is chosen for two reasons. (1) It has been explicitly stated in 1:4, where it was part of the reason for the thanksgiving (the other alternatives are implicit). And (2) it is the more generic, covering the other two by implication. (When there is an ellipsis of this sort, the more generic alternative is normally to be preferred.) Even so, the first alternative, Paul and Timothy, is also given in the display because of the frequent reference to 'us(we)' in 1:7b–8a.

2. What does ἐν πνεύματι 'in spirit' mean? Since it modifies the love just referred to, it is taken to be spiritual love that Paul is speaking of, not natural affection or any other sort of love. Such love, like all things spiritual, comes from the Spirit— 'the fruit of the Spirit is love . . .' (Gal. 5:22). Should the proposition, then, describe the effect or should it refer to the cause? Though there seems to be no basis for choosing, the former, the effect, is chosen, since a choice has to be made. That is, Paul is referring (again) to their present state, and that is one of showing spiritual love.

In some receptor languages, however, the only way to express the concept 'spiritually' may require explicit reference to the Holy Spirit. In that case, 'by means of the *Holy* Spirit *enabling you*' would convey what is meant.

SECTION CONSTITUENT 1:9–12 (Paragraph: Nucleus₂ of 1:3–12)

THEME: We have also been praying to God for you very often that you will know truly all that he wants you to do, in order that you will conduct yourselves as the Lord's people should.

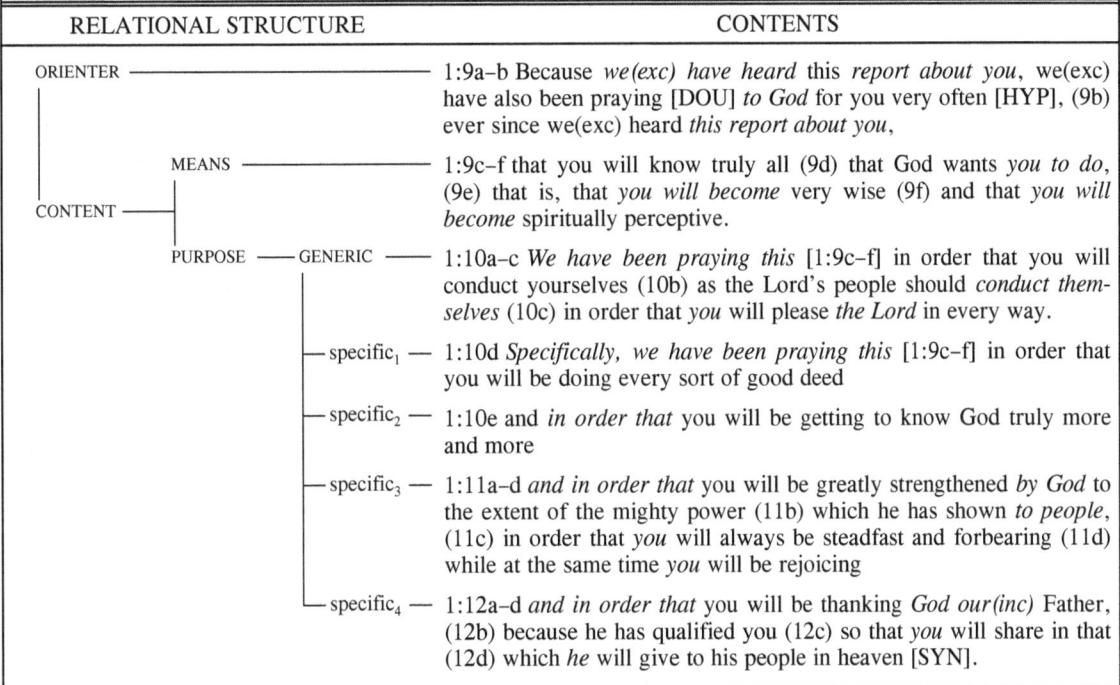

BOUNDARIES AND COHERENCE

The evidence for the initial boundary of the 1:9–12 unit has already been given in connection with the discussion of the boundaries of 1:3–8.

As to the closing boundary, it was stated in the discussion of the boundaries of 1:3–12 (of which 1:9–12 is the second constituent) that the 1:3–12 section ended either with 1:12 or somewhere within that verse. We will now look at this difficult decision in more detail.

It should first be noted that either decision will cut across the grammar: the sentence that begins with 1:9 runs on through 1:12 and 13 to 1:16 by means of relative clauses. The clause at the end of 1:12 begins with the article in the dative case in agreement with τῷ πατρί 'the Father'; the clause at the beginning of 1:13 begins with the relative pronoun in the nominative case, because it is the subject of the following finite verb and also refers back to 'the Father'.

In favor of starting the next paragraph with 1:13 are the following points:

1. The relative pronoun is more independent of what precedes it than an article is.
2. Finite verbs occur in 1:13 but not in 1:12.
3. The latter part of 1:12 is the reason for the 1:12a thanksgiving and so belongs to the preceding paragraph. (However, the same can be argued for including 1:13–14 with the preceding verses.)
4. Verse 1:15 is the beginning of a unit with the topic of the Son, and it, too, begins with a relative pronoun in the nominative case, so this strengthens the case for seeing 1:13 similarly.

The following points argue for starting the next paragraph immediately after τῷ πατρί 'the Father':

1. This is semantically logical: τῷ πατρί is the new topic, so what follows it is then the development of that topic. (This is how the same question was handled in the preceding paragraph in reference to 'the gospel' at the end of 1:5 and 'Epaphras' in 1:7.)
2. In the note on 1:12a are some further arguments, suggesting that the use of 'the Father' signals a return to the use of 'we(inc)' after two paragraphs of 'we(exc)', thus marking the boundary.
3. There is a shift from present tense participles to an aorist tense participle (ἱκανώσαντι 'having made-worthy').

There is little basis on which to make this decision, but the arguments in favor of treating all of verse 1:12 as belonging to the same paragraph seem better, so this is the view reflected in the display.

The paragraph's unity is shown in the same three ways as the preceding paragraph's unity was shown:

1. There is repeated reference to the Colossians themselves, by pronoun, finite verb, and dependent verb forms (eight altogether).
2. The indicative mood is used throughout, apart from one subjunctive verb dependent on ἵνα (1:9).
3. These verses are all part of one closely linked sentence in Greek. (The fact that the sentence continues beyond 1:12 does not weaken this argument.)

PROMINENCE AND THEME

Here in 1:9–12, there is a verbal phrase in the Greek that is semantically equivalent to a first person plural performative orienter, 'we pray' (see note on 1:9a). This orienter introduces the paragraph just as the performative 'we thank' introduced 1:3–8. The content of the prayer is introduced by ἵνα '(in order) that' and is divided between a means, 'that you might be filled with the knowledge of God's will' (9), and its purpose, 'to walk worthy of the Lord' (10–12). The relation of means is considered to be naturally more prominent than the purpose it is intended to achieve. However, in this case, the purpose is considered to be equally prominent with the means, for the following reasons:

1. It is very similar in content to the command in 2:6, which is the most prominent information in the epistle: ἐν αὐτῷ περιπατεῖτε 'in him [Christ Jesus, the Lord] walk'. Verse 1:10 has περιπατῆσαι ἀξίως τοῦ κυρίου 'to walk worthily of the Lord'.
2. It is extensively developed by means of four specifics.
3. Paul's concern for their conduct is almost certainly in response to the behavioral implications of the false teaching that had come to Colosse. (Paul was always concerned for the behavior of believers, but this general apostolic concern is strengthened by his awareness of another—and unacceptable—pattern of behavior being presented to the Colossian believers. That is to say, his concern is closely connected with the situation in which the letter was written.)

It is also worth pointing out that the cluster of 'knowledge' words used in the means—ἐπίγνωσις 'true knowledge', σοφία 'wisdom', and σύνεσις πνευματική 'spiritual insight'—supports the prominence of the means. In fact, this cluster can be considered a motif in this epistle (cf. 2:2–3, also the negative and positive uses of σοφία 'wisdom' in 2:23 and 3:16).

The theme, then, of 1:9–12 consists of the orienter, the means, and the purpose, since these last two are both prominent within the context. It should be noted that προσευχόμενοι 'praying' and αἰτούμενοι 'asking' are a generic-specific pair of verbs (see note on 1:9c) and that normally the specific, 'asking', would be the more prominent. But here 'praying' is regarded as more prominent, since the verb 'to ask' (αἰτέω) is not collocated in the New Testament with ἵνα 'that', whereas 'to pray' (προσεύχομαι) is.

NOTES

1:9a Because *we(exc) have heard* **this** *report about you,* **we(exc) have also been praying** *to God* **for you very often,** The phrase διὰ τοῦτο 'because of this' overtly indicates the relation between this performative and what precedes. All the commentators consulted agree that it was the good news of the Colossians' faith and love that moved Paul and Timothy to pray for them. This would point to the relation of reason-result, just as with the thanks, which also arose from the good report. However, there is also the phrase καὶ ἡμεῖς 'also we'. This use of a free pronoun signals a return to Paul and Timothy as agents after the embedded paragraphs on the gospel and Epaphras. The occurrence of καί 'also' signals that they were doing something else besides thanking God for them—they were praying for them also. There is no mention of anyone else praying, so that the possible meaning of 'we also pray, as well as others' is ruled out by the context.

This analysis implies that paragraphs 1:3–8 and 1:9–12 are conjoined, but, even so, this does not conflict with the statement above about the relation of reason-result: Although both the thanksgiving and the prayer were the result of hearing Epaphras's report, they are themselves coordinate with one another. The following diagram shows the triangle of relations:

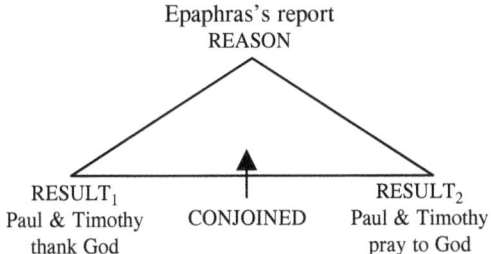

In the Greek, οὐ παυόμεθα ... προσευχόμενοι 'we do not cease praying', there is a litotes and also a mismatch between the surface form and the meaning. The double negative οὐ παυόμεθα '(we) do not cease' is equivalent to '(we) very frequently (do)', meaning something they had done many times and regularly (but not continuously). The event is to pray, but expressed as a dependent participial form in the Greek, while the main verb is 'cease'. In propositional form the verb is 'pray'; 'we do not cease' is rendered as an intensified attribute, 'very often'. The mismatch in the Greek is probably what makes the attribute prominent—Paul is emphasizing how constantly he and Timothy had been praying for them. This statement parallels 'give thanks always' in 1:3.

Beekman in his earlier analysis suggested quite a different interpretation of διὰ τοῦτο 'because of this' (also Hale, p. 3). He takes the viewpoint that διὰ τοῦτο does not refer back to what has been said, but refers forward to the ἵνα 'that' clause that expresses the content of the prayer. The arguments presented are as follows:

1. In Greek, the demonstratives 'this' and 'that' can refer either backwards or forwards.
2. In particular, the phrase διὰ τοῦτο refers forward unambiguously in 1 Thess. 2:13, 3:5, and Philem. 15. (Hale gives eleven examples altogether, but his comments make it clear that not all of these are unambiguous.) It is Philem. 15 that is the closest in formal structure to Col. 1:9a, since διὰ τοῦτο refers forward to a ἵνα clause there.
3. Paul wished to draw attention to the content of his prayer (introduced by ἵνα) and the initial διὰ τοῦτο, as a type of prominence device, serves that purpose. His use of ἐπίγνωσις 'true knowledge' in the ἵνα clause shows the importance of the content:

he uses ἐπίγνωσις or the corresponding verb ἐπιγινώσκω 'fully know' five times in Colossians.
4. In Eph. 1:15-17 there is a parallel usage. The opening διὰ τοῦτο (1:15) refers forward to the ἵνα clause of 1:17, which introduces the content of Paul's prayer.

I am not convinced by these arguments. While points 1 and 2 are correct observations, they mean simply that, in any given context, it must be decided whether διὰ τοῦτο is best understood as referring backwards or forwards. As to point 3, it is doubtful. The use of οὐ παυόμεθα 'we do not cease', the phrase ἀφ' ἧς ἡμέρας ἠκούσαμεν 'from which day we heard', and the generic-specific doublet προσευχόμενοι καὶ αἰτούμενοι 'praying and asking' (and perhaps also the use of ἡμεῖς 'we') seems to me to emphasize the *constancy* of Paul's prayers for the Colossians, rather than the content.

On point 4, it is doubtful exegetically how the initial διὰ τοῦτο in Eph. 1:15 is to be taken. There are three possibilities. It could (1) refer back to what Paul has just said, and mean 'in the light of all God's blessings, I thank God and pray for you'; or (2) refer forward to the immediately following clause as the content/reason of his thanksgiving and prayer, making Eph. 1:15-17 a sort of condensed parallel to Col. 1:3-4 and 9-12; or (3) refer forward to the content of the prayer.

In nine of the eleven examples cited by Hale, διὰ τοῦτο refers forward to a purpose (expressed by ἵνα with the subjunctive or εἰς with the infinitive). Only in the disputed Eph. 1:15-17 does the ἵνα introduce the content of a prayer. (In 1 Thess. 2:13 ὅτι is used, explaining what τοῦτο refers to.) I would argue, therefore, that διὰ τοῦτο be considered as possibly referring forward only when a purpose follows, not the content of a prayer.

The words καὶ αἰτούμενοι 'and asking' appear not to be represented in the display. This is because 'praying and asking' are here considered a doublet and both rendered with only 'praying'. Even though it is widely stated by the commentators that 'praying' is a generic term and 'asking' a specific term referring to a type of prayer, and even though Moore does not list it as a doublet, nevertheless they *could* be understood as a doublet, two lexical items referring to the same event. The basis for this view is that the following ἵνα does not collocate well with αἰτέω 'to ask' but it does with προσεύχομαι 'to pray'. Also, it could be argued that praying is a specific type of asking—namely, asking God. Since the generic-specific relationship is thus reversible, depending on perspective, it seems better to regard the two words as a doublet, drawing attention to the intense activity of prayer.

1:9b ever since we(exc) heard *this report about you,* Here a specific term, ἡμέρας 'day', is used for the more generic 'the time', though in English neither term is needed with *ever since*. What Paul and Timothy heard is not stated explicitly, but since there have already been two references to hearing in 1:4 and 8, the reference is clearly to the report of the Colossians' faith and love brought by Epaphras.

1:9c that you will know truly all Here ἵνα 'that' introduces what Paul and Timothy were asking, the content of their prayer. Again, there is a mismatch between the semantic structure and the surface structure, as in 9a. An attribute is expressed by a finite verb, and an event by a compound abstract noun. A matched form would be 'that you will know truly all', 'all' being the best nonfigurative equivalent of the figurative 'filled with'.

1:9d that God wants *you to do,* A genitive construction, 'the will of him', follows the phrase τὴν ἐπίγνωσιν 'the true knowledge' in 1:9c. It states what it is that is to be known, the will of God, the one to whom the prayer is addressed. While it would be possible to express this propositionally as 'what God wills', it is probably better understood as more directly related to the Colossians. The generic 'what God wills' covers many things the Colossians need not know and could not know. Hence, in the display it is expressed more specifically as 'what God wants you to do', since the following verses explain at some length what God's will for their behavior is.

1:9e-f that is, that *you will become* **very wise and that** *you will become* **spiritually perceptive.** Phrases introduced by ἐν 'in' in Greek are often difficult to interpret, since ἐν has a wide range of senses. The question here is, How does this compound phrase relate to what has just been said?

Three main views are given in the commentaries: (1) It is *by means of* becoming wise and understanding that the Colossians would know fully. (2) The phrase 'wisdom and understanding' restate the meaning of 'to know fully'. (3) Knowledge *is to be accompanied by* wisdom and understanding.

It is difficult to find criteria on which to base a choice of one of these views. Beekman argued that means was unsatisfactory, because it seems equally valid to say that you come to know by being wise and understanding, or that you become wise and understanding by coming to know. The reversibility of the statement is not typical of a means-result relation, nor of a circumstance relation, which is implied by view 3. This leaves the second view as most likely, that is, Paul defines what he means by ἐπίγνωσις 'true knowledge' by adding the compound ἐν phrase.

However, there are other questions that also need answering:

1. Do the adjectives πάσῃ 'all' and πνευματικῇ 'spiritual' apply to both nouns, or only to the one with which they are contiguous?
2. How is 'spiritual' to be interpreted—as an attribute, or as referring to the Holy Spirit, the one who gives the wisdom and understanding? (See the similar problem in 1:8.)
3. Are σοφία 'wisdom' and συνέσει 'understanding' to be distinguished in this context, or are they a doublet with a prominence function of some sort?

To answer question 1, three observations may be helpful: (1) the word 'all' is collocated with 'wisdom' elsewhere in the New Testament (Acts 7:22 and Eph. 1:8 and in Colossians itself, 1:28 and 3:16); (2) the word 'all' is not collocated with 'understanding' elsewhere in the New Testament; (3) the word 'spiritual' is not elsewhere collocated with either 'wisdom' or 'understanding'. This evidence would indicate that 'all' goes with 'wisdom', and 'spiritual' goes with 'understanding'. The symmetry of the surface form, adj-N and N-adj, supports this view. Based on this symmetry either both adjectives go with both nouns or else each adjective goes only with its contiguous noun. The observations about the collocations support this second alternative.

To answer question 2 is to choose between the effect, spiritual understanding, or the agent of that understanding, the Spirit. Since Paul is referring to the effect or the result when he writes of knowledge, wisdom, and understanding, it seems better to retain this reference by taking 'spiritual' as an attribute, as was done in 1:8b.

So far as question 3 is concerned, Arndt and Gingrich give "wisdom" as the gloss for σοφία, and "the faculty of comprehension, intelligence, acuteness, shrewdness" for sense 1 of σύνεσις. They give "*insight, understanding* in the religio-ethical realm" as sense 2, and as sense 3 "the wisdom of the creator" (but the examples they cite in this last case are extrabiblical). This evidence would not support the view that 'wisdom and understanding' form a doublet, nor can I find any other New Testament use of this pair. (There is, however, an Old Testament quotation in 1 Cor. 1:19 in which σοφία and σύνεσις together with σοφοί and συνετοί are used as a doublet.)

To represent σύνεσις here, 'perceptive' is chosen since commentators agree that it refers to the faculty of being able to "see through" differing theories. In the larger context of the false teaching, seeing what its implications were would certainly be something Paul would pray for on behalf of the Colossians.

1:10a We have been praying this *[1:9c-f]* in order that you will conduct yourselves The literal Greek is 'to walk' or 'walk about', a dead metaphor with the meaning 'to conduct oneself'. It is a generic term referring to how one behaves, what one's ethical behavior is like. It is used again in 2:6 when the hortatory material is introduced.

The aorist infinitive can have the relation of result or purpose. In the context of prayer, an expression of one's longings and desires to God for what is necessarily future, the relation of purpose seems preferable. Paul's desire is that the behavior of the Colossians might be worthy of their professed faith in the Lord Jesus, and he prays to that end, for that purpose.

1:10b as the Lord's people should *conduct themselves* The Greek is an adverbial phrase: ἀξίως τοῦ κυρίου 'worthily of the Lord'. Propositionally, it is expressed as a comparison. The manner of the believers' walk is to be appropriate to their relation to the Lord. The phrase 'the Lord' is widely taken to refer specifically to Christ, rather than to God the Father. (Several commentators maintain that in Paul's writings 'Lord' always refers to Christ.)

1:10c in order that *you* will please *the Lord* in every way. The abstract noun ἀρεσκείαν 'pleasing' represents the event to please (someone). No explicit statement is made as to who is pleasing whom. However, 'you' is the implicit subject of the infinitive περιπατῆσαι 'to walk' and thus can be assumed as the subject of 'pleasing'. Commentators are divided about who is to be pleased, since in literature outside the Scriptures ἀρεσκεία often refers to pleasing God. But it seems better to take it as referring to 'the Lord', mentioned earlier in the same clause.

Like the aorist infinitive, the preposition εἰς 'to' can signal the relation of either result or purpose (Arndt and Gingrich on εἰς, 4e, f). Again, it is not easy to make a choice, but probably purpose is slightly better. In other words, Paul has in mind two purposes of their knowing God's will for them fully, the nearer one of their behaving worthily of the Lord, the further one of their pleasing him by that behavior. A sequence of purposes is not uncommon in the Pauline writings, the last one often being the glory of Christ, and expressed by εἰς as here.

1:10d–12d The rest of this paragraph is built round four participles, all of which are nominative plural and present tense. These participial phrases express four specifics of the general reference to conduct, and they are related to one another by conjoining. In the Greek, the first two are joined by καί 'and'; the other two are simply added without connectives. This pattern has led some commentators to say that there are really three specifics, 'bearing fruit and growing' being only one. Meyer takes this further by pointing out that, if this threefold analysis is correct, then each clause has an opening prepositional phrase and is also followed by one or more phrases. It is not clear to me whether the threefold or fourfold approach is preferable, nor how to assess the linking of the first two participles by καί. Nor am I sure what the significance is of the chiastic arrangement of the first two clauses: modifying phrase + verb + verb + modifying phrase.

1:10d *Specifically, we have been praying this [1:9c-f]* in order that you will be doing every sort of good deed The same dead figure that was used in 1:6c is used here: καρποφοροῦντες 'bearing fruit'. In 6c it was given the nonfigurative meaning 'to do good'. The additional phrase ἐν παντὶ ἔργῳ ἀγαθῷ 'in every good work' that is here in 10d probably intensifies the meaning of the verb.

1:10e and *in order that* you will be getting to know God truly more and more There is another dead figure here, αὐξανόμενοι 'growing', which was also used in 1:6, where it referred to the numerical spread of the gospel. Here it refers to an increase in something. The older commentators took τῇ ἐπιγνώσει τοῦ θεοῦ 'the knowledge of God' as the means of the growth; but modern commentators, versions, and Arndt and Gingrich take 'the knowledge of God' to be what is increasing. The abstract noun 'knowledge' represents the event 'to know', and 'growing' represents an attribute such as 'increasingly' or 'more and more'.

This is the third time in these two paragraphs that Paul uses either the verb ἐπιγινώσκω or the noun ἐπίγνωσις (see 1:6 and 9). Again, the sense of the compound form is taken to be the true, experiential knowledge of God.

1:11a–b *and in order that* you will be greatly strengthened *by God* to the extent of the mighty power which he has shown *to people,* Concerning the prepositional phrase ἐν πάσῃ δυνάμει 'in all strength', commentators are divided between two views: (1) that it states the means by which they were to be strengthened or (2) that it refers to that aspect of their lives in which they were to be strengthened.

In the former view the strength comes from God; in the latter view the strength is that of the Colossians. In support of the second view it is suggested that the phrases attached to the two previous participles, 'in every good work' and 'with respect to knowledge', both refer to the Colossians themselves, not to God. It is argued, therefore, that the same is true in connection with this third participle. (It could be said that the same is true of 'with joy', if it is considered as attached to the fourth participle.) However, it seems somewhat forced to refer to the Colossians' strength since believers are more commonly spoken of in the New Testament as being weak, not strong. Hence the first view is preferable.

The use of a cognate in the same expression is a type of emphatic doublet; thus 'strengthened with all strength' is equivalent to 'strengthened greatly'. The same construction occurs in Matt. 2:10, 'they rejoiced with very great joy (accusative)'; in John 3:29, 'rejoices with joy (dative)'; and in 1 Thess. 3:9, 'because of all the joy with which (dative) we rejoice'. Although none of these examples uses ἐν 'in' with the dative, the simple dative is often used in ways parallel to the dative governed by ἐν (cf. Col. 1:10d, where 'bearing fruit in (ἐν) every good work' shows the same sort of redundancy, since 'bearing fruit' means 'doing good works'.) This view is similar to the first of the two views mentioned before, in that it is implied the strength comes from God, but takes the prepositional phrase as manner, not instrument. This is the view followed here.

The word αὐτοῦ 'of-him' in the phrase κατὰ τὸ κράτος τῆς δόξης αὐτοῦ 'according to the might of-the glory of-him' refers to God, who is also referred to explicitly in the preceding clause. There are two main questions in connection with this phrase:

1. What relation does κατά 'according-to' signal?
2. How is τῆς δόξης 'the glory' to be related to the other parts of this genitive construction?

Commentators generally explain κατά as meaning 'corresponding to'. That is to say, the standard by which their being strengthened is to be measured is the divine might. There is a type of comparison involved. Put somewhat differently, it could be said that the limit of the strengthening is set by God's might; in other words, there is no measurable limit—it could be expressed 'to the extent of the . . .'. However, this does not involve a new event, so 'to the extent of the mighty power' becomes part of 11a.

Based on this interpretation τῆς δόξης αὐτοῦ 'the glory of-him' defines 'mighty power' as belonging to God essentially, not to any other being. It seems that δόξα 'glory' refers either to the sum-total of God's perfect attributes, his wisdom, holiness, omnipresence—of which 'mighty power' is one attribute; or to God's revelation of himself to men. His 'glory' is what he has shown of himself to man, both in the creation and sustaining of the universe and in his mighty deeds throughout history. There does not seem to be anything in the context to choose, and, in any case, there is little real difference since man knows nothing of God except what God has chosen to reveal, and what God reveals always corresponds to his attributes.

In the New Testament, κράτος, rendered here as 'mighty power', is used to refer only to God and the devil; it is the power exercised by supernatural beings. It is never said that man possesses or exercises κράτος.

1:11c–d in order that *you* will always be steadfast and forbearing while at the same time *you* will be rejoicing The prepositional phrase beginning with εἰς is again interpreted as indicating the purpose of their being strengthened.

But there is a question concerning ὑπομονὴν καὶ μακροθυμίαν 'endurance and patience' (the usual English translation), whether or not it forms a doublet in this context. Arndt and Gingrich translate ὑπομονή as "*patience, endurance, fortitude, steadfastness, perseverance* ... esp. as they are shown in the enduring of toil and suffering." They translate μακροθυμία as "*patience, steadfastness, endurance*" and "*forbearance, patience toward others.*" This would certainly point to a doublet (see Moore, p. 24). However, apart from two lists in 2 Cor. 6:4–6 and 2 Tim. 3:10, the words are found together only in James 5:10–11, where it seems likely, but by no means certain, that James is using them interchangeably. If they are regarded as abstract nouns representing events, then 'all' is an attribute modifying the events, either 'always' or 'in every circumstance'. The distinction most commonly drawn by the commentators is that ὑπομονή relates to the trials and difficulties themselves whereas μακροθυμία is patience or forbearance exercised towards those who actively persecute. If this is correct, then ὑπομονή is probably best rendered by 'steadfastness', and μακροθυμία by 'forbearance' or 'self-restraint'. Since it is by no means certain that these two nouns are intended as synonyms here, they are represented separately in the display.

There is considerable discussion as to whether the phrase μετὰ χαρᾶς 'with joy' belongs to 11 or 12a. In favor of its belonging with 11 is the fact that in the New Testament 'joy' occurs in a context that mentions trials and difficulties (e.g., Matt. 5:11–12, Jas. 1:2, and 1 Pet. 1:6), but there are *no* examples that I can find of 'thanksgiving' collocated with 'joy'.

Against putting 'with joy' with 11 (with the third participle) is that to do so would leave the final participle without an associated prepositional phrase, unlike each of the preceding ones. A good case could be made for a symmetrical structure here. If 'p' is used to represent prepositional phrase, and 'P' to represent participle, then the pattern of these four participles could be diagrammed as follows:

$$p - P_1 - καί - P_2 - p, \; p - P_3 - p, \; p - P_4$$

The first pair of participles are in a type of chiastic arrangement, and the second pair are broadly parallel with each other. The symmetry of this arrangement would support taking 'joy' with 'thanksgiving'.

There is also the unusual pattern of three prepositional phrases following a verb form, which would be the case if 'joy' goes with the third participle in 11c–d. A final question, which cannot be answered at this stage, is whether the preposition μετά 'with' ever occurs after εἰς 'to' in the same clause when εἰς is signaling purpose/result. Intuitively, it seems unlikely, but considerable research would be needed to find out.

Yet, in spite of these possibly good reasons for linking 'with joy' to 'thanksgiving', in the display it is linked to 11c because that is a known collocation. However, an acceptable alternative would be to place 1:11d after the end of 1:12a.

1:12a *and in order that* you will be thanking *God our(inc)* Father, The first question here regards the textual variants. A glance at the UBS apparatus on τῷ πατρί 'the Father' shows that many (relatively minor) variants of this phrase are found in the manuscripts. All of them represent some form of expansion on the simple phrase that appears in the UBS text. It is rare in Paul's letters to find the simple, unqualified phrase 'the Father'. Commentators who discuss the text agree that the longer variants represent attempts to make an unusual phrase more normal. In any case, there is no difference in meaning, except to specify who 'the Father' is. Since the shorter form is also well supported by the manuscripts, it is the one given in the display as explicit.

Another problem is the inadequacy of simply 'the Father' with no pronoun showing relationship. This problem is closely connected with the question of where the paragraph boundary is to be drawn, whether at the end of v. 12, or immediately after τῷ πατρί 'to-the Father' (see the discussion of the boundaries of this paragraph). It is also closely connected with a choice that has to be made between textual variants in 1:12b: between ἡμᾶς 'us' and ὑμᾶς 'you'. If the paragraph break is made at the end of 1:12, then the verse is best considered 'you' oriented, with 'you' giving thanks to the Father, who has made 'you' worthy. In that case, 'your Father' would be contextually appropriate, but, so far as I am aware, this is never said in the Epistles.

If the break is made after τῷ πατρί 'the Father', the 'you'-orientation comes to an end with 'giving thanks': 'the Father' is the transition point from the 'you' orientation to 'we(inc)' orientation, 'we(inc)' being the normal modifier of 'Father' and the pronoun in the display. Nevertheless, the paragraph is regarded as ending after v. 12, not in the middle of it.

1:12b because he has qualified you This is the first statement about what the Father has done for us. There is considerable doubt over whether 'you' or 'us' is the original reading. Since in the 1:13 statements about what the Father has done 'we' is the object, this reading could be followed in 1:12b also. However, this is not done in the display since 1:12b-d is taken as the final statement of the preceding paragraph, giving a reason for the thanksgiving of 1:12a, and, since the whole of that paragraph is 'you' oriented, the reading 'you' fits the context better. (This is a good example of where more certainty over the original text could well help with difficult decisions concerning paragraph boundaries.)

As to the meaning of ἱκανώσαντι 'qualified', it is not clear from the commentators or Arndt and Gingrich whether 'qualified' refers to status (justified, forgiven, redeemed, etc.) or to character. Doubtless both are true in general, but the aorist tense of ἱκανώσαντι, together with the aorist tense of the following two verbs, both describing what the Father has done, points to qualification by status rather than character in this context.

1:12c-d so that *you* will share in that which *he* will give to his people in heaven. These two propositions are taken together since they express one long complex genitive construction together with a final prepositional phrase. The initial εἰς 'to' introduces the result of being qualified—without such qualification there would be no part in the inheritance. Alternatively, εἰς could signify purpose, but that would leave unstated whether or not the intention was fulfilled. Here there is no doubt, so result is preferred. Then comes a string of terms pointing to an implicit comparison with the Israelites' possession of allotted portions of the promised land. The comparison can be drawn as follows:

> the allotted portion of the inheritance of the Israelites in Canaan
> the allotted portion of the inheritance of the saints in the light

In other words, the Old Testament people of God were each given a portion of land 'in Canaan'; similarly, the New Testament people of God will each receive their part of the spiritual inheritance 'in the light'.

This brings up the question of what κλῆρος 'lot' means. Strictly speaking, it refers to a lot, and then to what is received as a result of the casting of a lot. Hence, some commentators take μερίς 'share' and κλῆρος 'lot' as referring to the same entity—a part of the whole allotted to them. However, others argue that it is simpler to take μερίς as part and κλῆρος as the whole, the promised inheritance. It is this view that is followed here.

While Arndt and Gingrich give "portion, share" as the meaning of κλῆρος, they render it "inheritance" in this verse. Foerster states that κλῆρος is "the portion allotted to someone" (p. 763). In this particular verse, κλῆρος and μερίς are regarded as a doublet, and equal to 'portion', so that the idea of 'inheritance', or 'what God gives', is fused with that of 'portion'.

As to τῶν ἁγίων, it is taken to refer to the saints. The fact that this is its common sense in the New Testament, along with the comparison to the Old Testament people of God, is adequate reason for taking ἅγιοι in this sense here. A few commentators take it as referring to the angels, but others maintain that ἅγιοι is used in the New Testament to refer only to the saints. Arndt and Gingrich suggest that ἅγιοι means 'angels' in 1 Thess. 3:13 and 2 Thess. 1:10 (that could be disputed in both cases). The reason given for assuming the sense of 'angels' here is the reference to 'the light', where it is said the angels dwell. But interpreting 'in the light' is difficult in itself.

Two closely related questions arise in connection with ἐν τῷ φωτί 'in the light':

1. How does it relate to the material that precedes it?
2. What does it actually refer to?

The fact that there is a comparison here with the Old Testament inheritance of God's people helps answer question 1: 'in the light' corresponds to 'in Canaan' and describes where the inheritance is located. And the contrast with σκότος 'darkness' (v. 13), the domain from which God has rescued us, helps answer question 2.

One final question is whether sharing in the inheritance is, in this context, a present reality or a future one. A decision on this will affect the decision on how 'light' is to be understood. A number of references to the inheritance are clearly future (e.g., Mat. 25:34; 1 Cor. 15:50; Eph. 1:14; Heb. 1:14); and none of the others using κληρονομέω 'to inherit', κληρονομία 'inheritance', κληρονόμος 'heir', or κλῆρος 'lot, inheritance' refer unambiguously to the present. Thus it is my impression that when these terms are used, it is the future that is referred to, rather than the present. Foerster, on this verse (p. 763), says that 'inheritance' means "the eschatological portion assigned to man," implying that it is still future. Assuming that is so, then 'light' should be regarded as a synecdoche meaning 'heaven', an (important) attribute being used for the whole. This view maintains the parallel with the Old Testament 'inheritance'. (In 1:5 is a somewhat similar reference to what God has ready for his people in heaven.)

PART CONSTITUENT 1:13–3:17
(Sub-part: Nucleus (primary matters) of 1:3–4:6)

THEME: Conduct yourselves as those should who are united to Christ Jesus our Lord, who ranks above everything that has been created. In particular, make sure that no one makes you become his disciples by teaching you a false religious philosophy; rather, be constantly wanting what is associated with heaven.

RELATIONAL STRUCTURE	CONTENTS
GROUNDS	1:13–2:5 God our Father has reconciled you to himself and he has caused you to be ruled by his Son, who ranks above everything that has been created. I, Paul, am exerting myself very greatly on your behalf in order that you might truly know the secret-message about Christ, in order that no one may delude you.
HORTATORY NUCLEUS	2:6–3:17 Conduct yourselves as those should who are united to such a one as Christ Jesus our Lord. In particular, make sure that no one makes you become his disciples by teaching you a false religious philosophy; rather, be constantly wanting what is associated with heaven.

BOUNDARIES AND COHERENCE

As has already been discussed in connection with the body (1:3–4:6), the introduction closes with 1:12, and the main part of the body starts with 1:13. This main part of the body consists of two major groupings, the primary matters (1:13–3:17) and the secondary matters (3:18–4:6).

The reasons for this analysis are as follows: First, there are two major breaks within 1:13–4:6: between 2:5 and 2:6 and then again between 3:17 and 3:18. At the first break Paul changes from expository genre, marked by indicatives and occasional subjunctives, to hortatory genre, where the main statements are imperative. In addition, in 2:6, where the hortatory material starts, there is the first occurrence of οὖν 'therefore'—this particle is found only in the (hortatory) span 2:6–3:17.

In 3:17, just before the second major break, there is a generic command, matching the opening generic command in 2:6. Although there are exhortations in 3:18–4:6, there are no further occurrences of οὖν.

These two major breaks could be considered as evidence of three comparable constituents of the span 1:13–4:6. However, there are two pieces of evidence indicating that 1:13–2:5 and 2:6–3:17 are linked together in a way that is not true of 3:18–4:6.

The first piece of evidence is the already-mentioned opening οὖν in 2:6 and its further occurrences only in 2:6–3:17. While it could be argued that οὖν simply marks the hortatory material as over against the expository material, it is more in accord with the functions of οὖν elsewhere in the New Testament to take it as indicating that the exhortations which it marks are based on the preceding material as grounds. Similarly, the absence of οὖν from 3:18–4:6 can be taken to indicate that the exhortations contained in that span are not closely linked to the material in 1:13–2:5.

The second piece of evidence is a certain amount of overlap of the content of 1:13–2:5 and 2:6–3:17. The six most significant examples of such overlap follow.

1. In 2:6a are grounds for the command that immediately follows it: ὡς παρελάβετε τὸν Χριστὸν Ἰησοῦν τὸν κύριον 'as you received Christ Jesus, the Lord'. The verb παραλαμβάνω 'to receive' refers to the teaching that had been transmitted to them, not to the initial act of their believing in the Lord. (The context strongly supports this sense.) Paul has been at considerable pains to remind them what that message was in 1:13–20, one of the most elaborate statements of Christ's supremacy over creation and the church found in the New Testament. So, while Paul may have had more in mind than what he himself had just said earlier in the letter, there is no reason to exclude reference to that material. Hence, the summary statement in 2:6a is considered to refer back to 1:13–20.

2. In 2:8 there is overlap with 2:4. In 2:8 Paul warns the Colossians against being 'captured' by a useless, deceptive φιλοσοφία 'religious philosophy'. In 2:4 he had expressly stated that he had written 2:1–3 so that they would not be deceived by plausible arguments. The two statements both refer to the impressive and

elaborate system of false teaching that had evidently appeared at Colosse, and against which Paul was warning them.

3. In 2:9 there is overlap with 1:19. In 1:19 Paul states that 'all the fullness was pleased to dwell in him [the Son]', and in 2:9 he makes an almost identical statement as part of the grounds for his warning in 2:8: 'all the fullness of the Godhead dwells bodily in him, Christ'.

4. In 2:10b there is overlap with 1:16. As part of his teaching that everything was created by the Son, Paul specifically mentions ἀρχαὶ εἴτε ἐξουσίαι 'rulers and authorities' (1:16). In 2:10b he says that Christ is 'the head' of πάσης ἀρχῆς καὶ ἐξουσίας 'all rule and authority', using the same two words.

5. In 2:19 there is overlap with 1:18. In describing the Son's supremacy over the church, Paul in 1:18 calls him ἡ κεφαλὴ τοῦ σώματος 'the head of the body'; and in 2:19 he speaks of Christ as τὴν κεφαλήν, ἐξ οὗ πᾶν τὸ σῶμα . . . αὔξει 'the head, from whom the whole body . . . grows', using the same terms for the Son and the church. (Paul uses this same terminology elsewhere in his epistles, but it is the matching between 1:13-2:5 and 2:6-3:17 that is in focus here.)

6. In 3:10 there is overlap with 1:15-16. In 3:10 Paul describes the 'new man' that the Colossians had now put on as being renewed 'according to the image of the one who created him'. Both εἰκών 'image' and the verb κτίζω 'to create' are the same words as were used of Christ in 1:15-16, where he is described as 'the image of the invisible God' and as the mediate agent in creation.

It will be seen that, except for the last one, the examples of overlap quoted are all from 2:6-23, the span that is directed against the false teaching. This would indicate that in 1:13-2:5 Paul was writing with this heresy primarily in mind. However, 3:1-17, which deals with the sort of behavior Paul was expecting from the Colossians, has many links with statements made in 2:8-23. A number of the grounds used in 2:8-15 are taken up again in 3:1-17 as grounds for the exhortations there. In other words, just as 2:6-23 is closely linked with 1:13-2:5, so 3:1-17 is closely linked with 2:8-23.

From this evidence it is concluded that 1:13-3:17 constitutes a unit within the epistle. It is titled "the primary matters" of the body, being the main things that Paul wanted to say to the Colossians. Similarly, 3:18-4:6 also constitutes a unit within the body, and is titled "the secondary matters," being matters of lesser importance and not overtly connected with the opening expository material. Put somewhat differently, it is clear that the primary matters were written because of the false teaching that had come to Colosse; but, so far as we know, the secondary matters could have been written to any of the churches, and, in fact, there are quite a few parallels in Ephesians. Peter, too, in his first epistle, deals with much the same issues.

PROMINENCE AND THEME

The two constituents of 1:13-3:17 are 1:13-2:5 and 2:6-3:17. The first, which is expository, functions as grounds for the second, which is hortatory, as indicated in the display.

Only the prominent, the most important, information is included in a theme. In trying to decide what is the most important information communicated in *this* unit, two issues have to be resolved. First, should the theme draw only on the hortatory nucleus and not the grounds? (In other words, is there marked prominence in the grounds?) And second, what particular information is most prominent in the nucleus (and the grounds, if included)?

An exhortation has greater natural prominence than the grounds on which it is based. In this case, however, the grounds have marked prominence in that they precede the hortatory nucleus (the reverse of the usual order). Moreover, they are not subordinated formally to the nucleus (it is the nucleus that is marked by οὖν); also, they are fully developed. Hence, the theme is drawn from both the grounds and the hortatory nucleus.

However, not all of the information in the grounds (1:13-2:5) is equally important. The overlap of content between the grounds and the exhortation shows this; it is only 1:13-23 that is echoed in the exhortation (apart from Paul's statement of purpose in 2:4). This would seem to indicate that what Paul has to say about his own ministry in 1:24-2:5 is less significant as grounds.

A second indication that some information in the grounds is more significant than the rest is that in the main command itself, there is the summary statement 'as those should who are united to such a one as Christ Jesus our Lord is'. This summarizes what Paul had already communicated to them about Christ Jesus; 'united to Christ Jesus' is a generic expression including their being reconciled to God and ruled by his Son, which is what is specifically stated in the grounds.

Based on these two arguments, the statement from the grounds '(Christ) ranks above everything that has been created' is included in the theme. But there is still the question as to whether the two specifics given in the nucleus of the primary matters should be included in the theme. Normally, when there are several specifics, a theme statement is drawn only from the generic nucleus. However, here the theme of the primary matters is the theme of the whole epistle, and the epistle deals with these specific problems and issues. Hence, these specifics, along with the generic statement, are prominent. They are what reflect the situation that gave rise to the epistle. Without them, the theme would be so general that it could have been written to any of the churches.

The theme, then, is the same as the theme of the primary hortatory material plus the statement about the supremacy of Christ from the grounds.

SUB-PART CONSTITUENT 1:13–2:5 (Division: Grounds of 2:6–3:17)

THEME: God our Father has reconciled you to himself and he has caused you to be ruled by his Son, who ranks above everything that has been created. I, Paul, am exerting myself very greatly on your behalf in order that you might truly know the secret-message about Christ, in order that no one may delude you.

RELATIONAL STRUCTURE	CONTENTS
NUCLEUS₁	1:13–23 God our Father has reconciled you to himself and he has caused you to be ruled by his Son, who ranks above everything that has been created.
NUCLEUS₂	1:24–2:5 I, Paul, am exerting myself very greatly on your behalf in order that you might truly know the secret-message about Christ, in order that no one might delude you.

BOUNDARIES AND COHERENCE

The material between 1:13 and 2:5 is clearly bounded: The body introduction, which ended with 1:12, was organized around the two performatives 'we(exc) thank God for you' and 'we(exc) pray to God for you'. The next marked change in the discourse structure occurs at 2:6, where the discourse genre changes from expository to hortatory. This is shown by the occurrence of the first verb in the epistle in the imperative mood, and also by the first occurrence of οὖν 'therefore', a conjunction found only in hortatory material in this epistle.

As for a *major* internal boundary within 1:13–2:5, there is no evidence for one. The boundaries that are perceived are more readily ascribed to lower-ranking units, such as paragraphs and sections. Moreover, all the information between the opening and closing boundaries of 1:13–2:5 shares two main characteristics:

1. The paragraphs in this part of the epistle are linked together by tail-head lexical links, and this is the case across section boundaries also. This method of paragraph linkage contrasts with the parallelisms of the body introduction as well as with the parallelisms that are also characteristic of the rest of the body. In other words, tail-head linkages are characteristic of this division and this division only. For example, 1:12 refers to the Father; 1:13–14 has the Father as topic. Verse 1:13 refers to the Son; 1:15–19 has the Son as topic. Verse 1:20 uses the verb 'to reconcile' in the aorist tense; 1:22 does likewise in the main clause. Verse 1:23 reintroduces Paul; 1:24–29 has his ministry as the topic. Verse 1:29 uses the verb ἀγωνίζομαι 'to strive' of Paul's ministry; 2:1 uses the cognate noun ἀγών 'struggle', also about Paul's ministry.

2. The finite verbs in this unit are almost all indicative in mood—out of thirty-six finite verbs

used, only four are in the subjunctive mood (1:18, 28; 2:2, 4) and none are imperative.

This division is considerably more diverse than the other divisions as to the persons referred to, often as topics. There is information about the work of God the Father, about the person and work of God the Son, and also about Paul's ministry. As a result, along with this diversity, there are parts of paragraphs, and also whole paragraphs, which do not refer to the Colossians at all. This is not the case with the rest of the epistle body.

The 1:13–2:5 unit is a division, consisting of two sections, 1:13–23 and 1:24–2:5. These, in turn, each consist of two paragraphs.

PROMINENCE AND THEME

The two sections of the 1:13–2:5 division are considered to be conjoined and of equal prominence, so the question arises as to whether a theme should be abstracted or the two lower-level themes compounded. The diversity of content between the two section themes precludes the former. In considering a compound theme, however, it is noted that there are six propositions in the two theme statements. How many of them should be included in the division theme, and in what form? In reaching a decision, the following factors have been considered:

1. Constituent 1:13–2:5 is related to 2:6–7 in a grounds-exhortation relationship; that is, the first constituent provides the springboard for the commands in the second, a pattern found in Paul's epistles. The thematic command in the second constituent is 'walk in him' (2:6), 'him' referring to Christ. Therefore, information related to Christ in the section themes should be seriously considered for inclusion in the division theme. (The second and third propositions of the theme of 1:13–23 refer to Christ.)

2. Since the command 'walk in him' is addressed to the Colossian Christians, it seems reasonable that reference to 'you' be included in the grounds attached to the command. The first two propositions of section 1:13–23 and all three of the propositions in the theme of section 1:24–2:5 refer to 'you'.

3. Although the theme of 2:6–7 is, essentially, based on 'walk in him', this is an abbreviated way of saying 'I command you: walk in him', where 'I command you' is a performative. The suggestion has been made that section 1:24–2:5 provides grounds for this performative. That is, Paul is saying: Since I am the apostle to the Gentiles (a ministry that involves both suffering and exertion), you, who are Gentiles, should pay careful attention to what I urge you to do.

These arguments support the theme's consisting of the conjoined themes of the two constituent sections.

DIVISION CONSTITUENT 1:13–23 (Section: Nucleus₁ of 1:13–2:5)

THEME: God our Father has reconciled you to himself and he has caused you to be ruled by his Son, who ranks above everything that has been created.

RELATIONAL STRUCTURE	CONTENTS
NUCLEUS₁ ———————	1:13–20 God our Father has caused us to be ruled by his Son, who ranks above everything that has been created.
NUCLEUS₂ ———————	1:21–23 As for you, God our Father has now reconciled you to himself.

BOUNDARIES AND COHERENCE

The evidence for a new unit at 1:13 has already been discussed in connection with the boundaries of 1:3–12.

The principal evidence for the closing boundary of the 1:13–23 section is the change in the pattern of referents. In this section, reference is made to 'we(inc)' in 1:13–14, and to 'you' in 1:21–23, but there is no reference to either 'I' or 'we(exc)' throughout this section, except for the last clause of 1:23, where Paul introduces a clear reference to himself, ἐγὼ Παῦλος, 'I, Paul'. This serves as part of a tail-head link, indicating a shift from the 'you'-oriented material of 1:21–23 to the 'I'-oriented material of the next section. The switch of principal referents plus the tail-head device indicates a boundary.

This evidence is reinforced by a marked change of theme. Section 1:13–23 is concerned with the redemptive and reconciling work of the Father, the preeminence of the Son, and then a specific 0application of that redemptive and reconciling work to the Colossians themselves. The following section (1:24–2:5) has for its theme the apostolic ministry of Paul to the Gentiles, among whom the Colossians were included.

The evidence for the internal unity of this section is rather unusual. It consists of two paragraphs, the first of which is highly structured; it opens and closes with reference to the Father's saving work through the Son. In particular, the end of this first paragraph refers to the Father having reconciled *everything* through the Son. From this generic statement, the second paragraph develops a specific application to the Colossians—the Father has reconciled *you* in particular. It could also be added that, apart from one ἵνα 'in order that' clause (1:18), the whole section is characterized by the indicative mood.

PROMINENCE AND THEME

The 1:13–23 section consists of two paragraphs, 1:13–20 and 1:21–23. The themes of these two constituents are regarded as conjoined. In considering a theme statement for the section, it can be seen there is a certain overlap in content between the two themes: in both of them 'God our(inc) Father' is the agent and 'us(inc)' includes 'you'. However, since 'you' represents those to whom the letter is written, 'you' is given situational prominence over 'us(inc)'. The two paragraph themes are combined in a way that eliminates this overlap; and, since reconciliation is logically prior to being ruled by God's Son, the theme of 1:21–23 is placed first in the theme of the section.

SECTION CONSTITUENT 1:13–20 (Paragraph: Nucleus₁ of 1:13–23)

THEME: God our Father has caused us to be ruled by his Son, who ranks above everything that has been created.

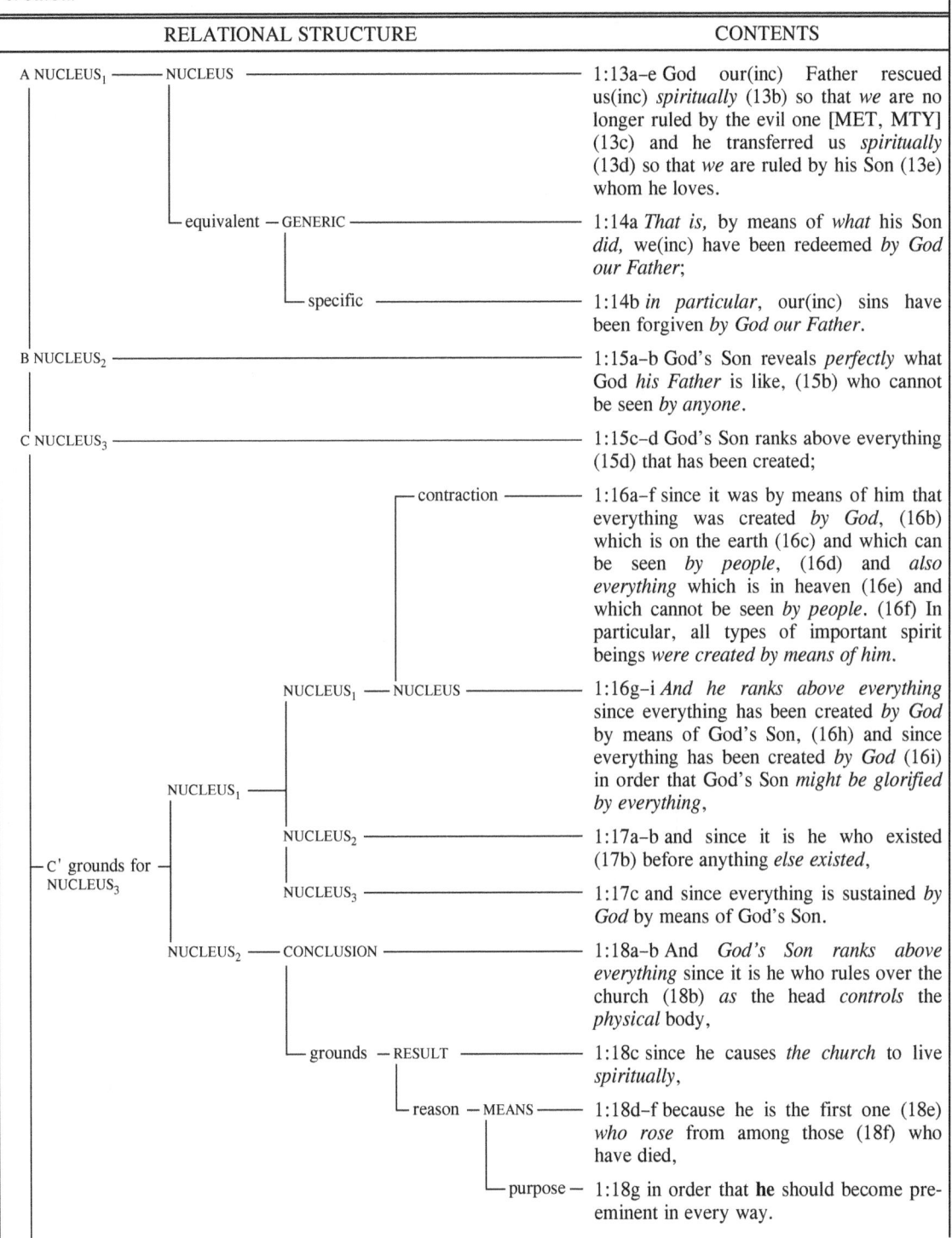

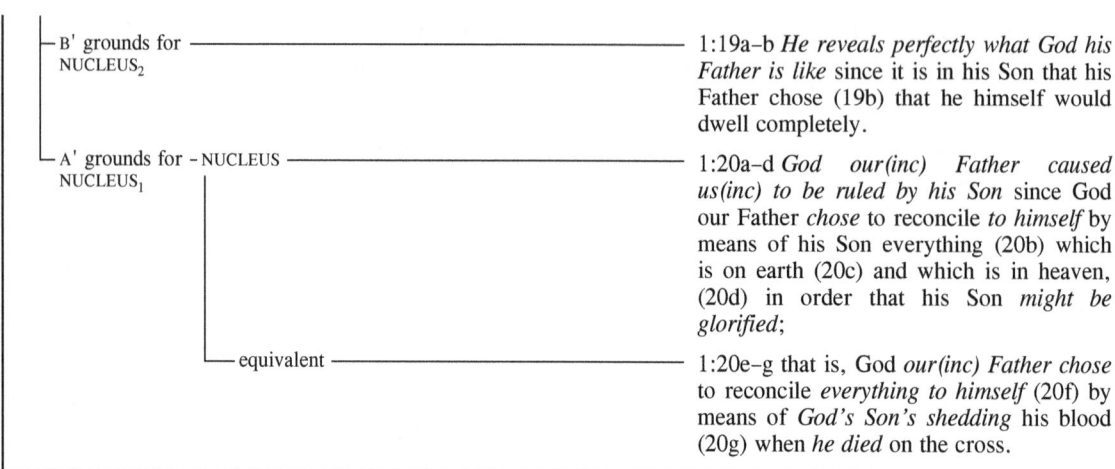

In the following alternative display the chiastic material is rearranged so that directly related propositional clusters are juxtaposed.

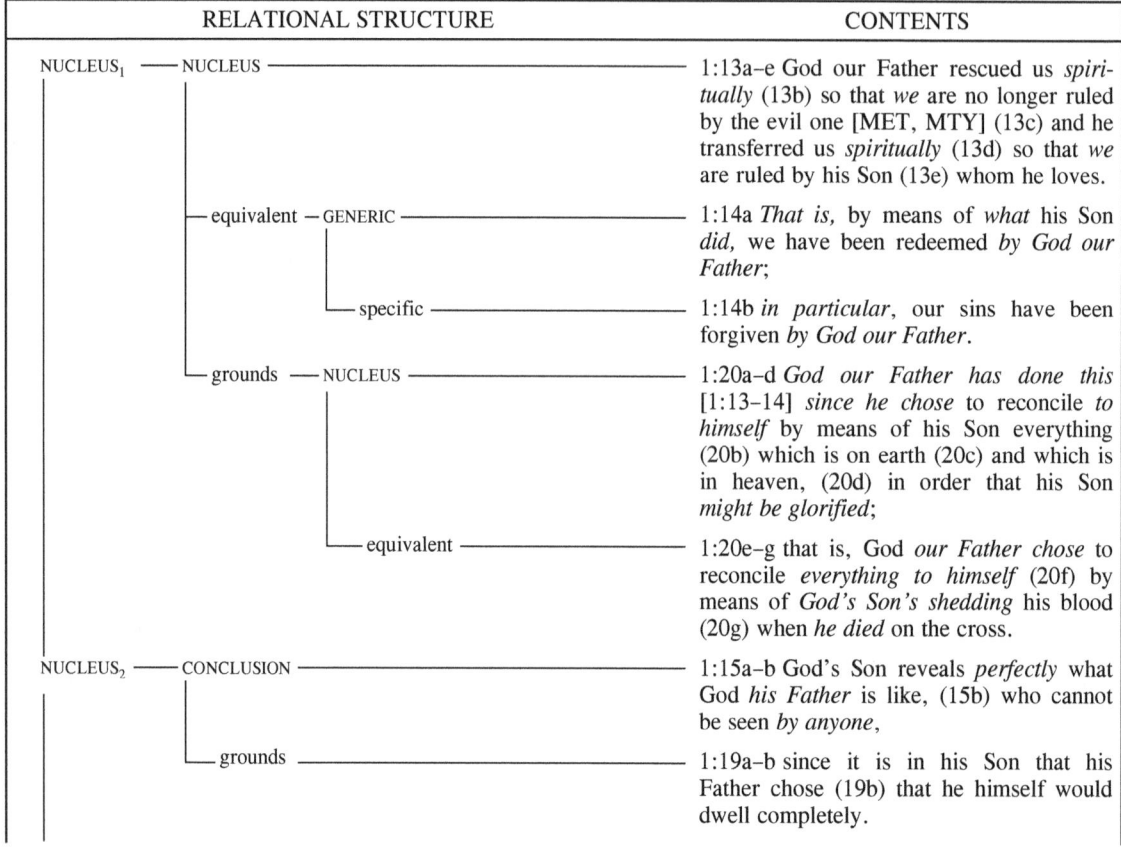

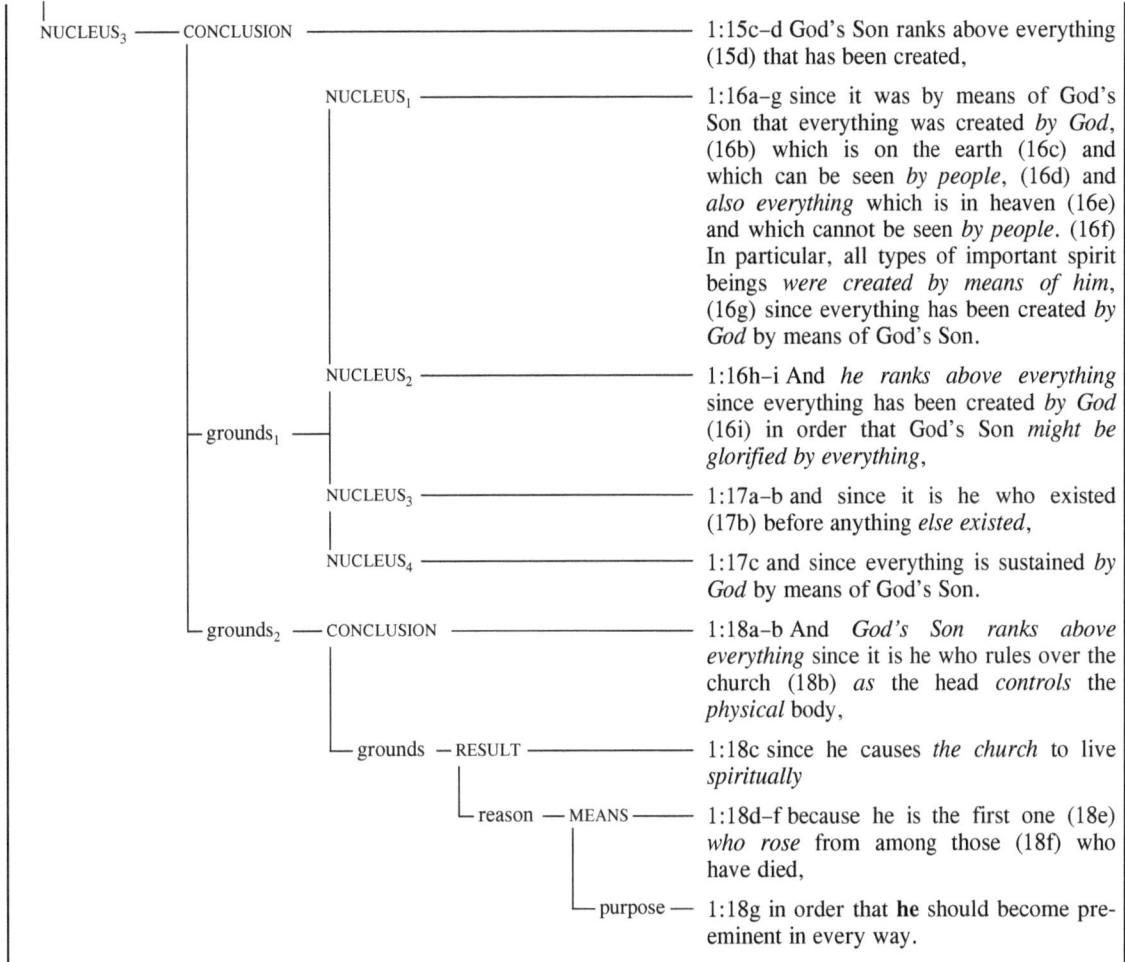

BOUNDARIES AND COHERENCE

The initial boundary of the 1:13–20 paragraph coincides with that of the 1:13–23 section and of the 1:13–2:5 division (see the earlier discussions).

As for the closing boundary, the principal arguments for ending this paragraph with 1:20 are as follows:

1. *The 'you' references* end with 1:12, are entirely absent from 1:13–20, and are re-introduced in 1:21.
2. There is *logical structure* in that 1:16–20 presents grounds for preceding statements, whereas 1:21 is related to a following independent statement in 1:22.
3. There is *rhetorical structure* in that 1:13 and 1:20 have a rhetorical bracketing function. In both verses the subject/agent is 'God the Father' (the referent of the pronoun); in both his saving work is mentioned using the aorist tense; and in both it is clear that this saving work is achieved by means of the Son. For these reasons, 1:13–20 is treated as a single paragraph, even though the majority of versions and commentaries make a paragraph break between v. 14 and v. 15.

The 1:13–20 paragraph, though considered a single paragraph, is nonetheless highly complex. In particular, 1:15–20 has a marked formal structure in the Greek, so much so that a number of modern commentators suggest that these verses represent an early Christian hymn or rhythmic statement of doctrine adapted by Paul to his own particular purposes. Such theories of origin are not of immediate concern to the translator; what does concern the translator is the correlation or lack of it between the semantic analysis and formal analysis of these verses. This is an important issue for this paragraph.

The formal parallelisms in 1:15–20 can be summarized as follows:

1. In vv. 15-16 the following Greek words occur and in this order: ὅς ἐστιν 'who is', πρωτότοκος 'firstborn', ὅτι ἐν αὐτῷ 'because in him'. It is the same in vv. 18 and 19.
2. Verse 17 starts with καὶ αὐτός ἐστιν 'and he is'. So does verse 18.
3. The first ὅτι ἐν αὐτῷ clause (v. 16) is followed by a clause in which δι' αὐτοῦ 'through him' and εἰς αὐτόν 'for/to him' occur in that order. Similarly, the second ὅτι ἐν αὐτῷ clause (v. 19) is followed by a clause with the same words and in the same order.

These observations can be diagrammed as follows:

A ὅς ἐστιν ... (15a)
   πρωτότοκος ... (15b)
   ὅτι ἐν αὐτῷ ... (16a)
   ... δι' αὐτοῦ ... εἰς αὐτόν ... (16b)

B καὶ αὐτός ἐστιν ... (17a)
B' καὶ αὐτός ἐστιν ... (18a)

A' ὅς ἐστιν ... (18b)
   πρωτότοκος ... (18c)
   ὅτι ἐν αὐτῷ ... (19)
   ... δι' αὐτοῦ ... εἰς αὐτόν (20a)

From this it is obvious that the formal parallelisms point to either a threefold structure in which B + B' is treated as a single unit, or a fourfold unit in which B and B' are separated to give A-B-B'-A'. Some commentators have sought for a semantic analysis which would match one or the other of these formal patterns. This is very difficult to do, however, since, from the point of view of the content, 17a is closely tied to 16a and b and 18a to 18b and c.

The most common semantic approach, therefore, is to divide 1:15-20 into two parts, with vv. 15-17 relating the Son to the universe and vv. 18-20 relating him to the church. But there are difficulties with this approach also, especially because in vv. 19 and 20 Paul returns to τὰ πάντα 'all things' after references to the church in v. 18.

My analysis of 1:13-20 (presented in the display) is different from any of the analyses referred to above. It is chiastic in structure and is based on the following considerations:

1. Verses 13 and 20 form a rhetorical bracket. But v. 20 is joined to v. 19 by καί 'and' and v. 19 is introduced by ὅτι 'because'. This points to the possibility that v. 20 is related to v. 13 (and also v. 14, which is closely linked to v. 13 both grammatically and semantically) by means of ὅτι, as well as its similarity in content. Consequently, the paragraph is considered to start with v. 13, not v. 15, with its beginning and end linked, as is typical of chiasmus.
2. Verse 18 ends with a purpose clause introduced by ἵνα 'in order that', and v. 19 opens with a grounds clause introduced by ὅτι. Many commentators regard the ἵνα clause as a statement of the theme of this paragraph, 'in order that he might be preeminent in everything'. This suggests that the ὅτι clauses are separated from the material they are related to, with the ἵνα clause marking a terminal point of some sort in the argument.
3. Two statements in this material relate the Son to the Father only, and not to the created universe or to the church. These are in 15a, 'he is the image of the invisible God', and in 19, 'because all the fullness was pleased to dwell in him'. This points to the plausibility of linking these two statements together in some way.

Based on these considerations, the following analysis is proposed for 1:13-20.

A The Father has redeemed us through his Son (13-14)
  B The Son is the image of God the Father (15a)
    C The Son is supreme over every creature (15b)
    C' Grounds for C (16-18)
  B' Grounds for B (19)
A' Grounds for A (20)

The second half of the chiasmus provides grounds (signaled by ὅτι in vv. 16 and 19) for the statements in the first half. But note that the semantic structure is out of step with the formal structure in this analysis, as it is in the more traditional twofold analysis. However, this is not a problem: it is an integral part of the semantic theory on which this analysis is based that it is not unusual for the formal structure to lack direct correspondence with the semantic structure. While it is more satisfying when the two directly correspond, the lack of such a correspondence does not prove that the semantic analysis is thereby erroneous.

PROMINENCE AND THEME

Paragraph 1:13-20 consists of six constituents, three of which are nuclei and three of which are supporting grounds. The main propositions for the second and third nuclei are readily identified:

God's Son reveals *perfectly* what God is like (1:15a)
God's Son ranks above everything (1:15c)

It is not so immediately obvious what the main proposition is in the first nucleus, 1:13-14. It can be seen from the display that 1:14 is regarded as restating the content of 1:13 in a more abbreviated form, making it a less prominent equivalent of 1:13. But 1:13 itself consists basically of two conjoined statements, 'the Father rescued us' and 'the Father transferred us' in which the latter is regarded as more prominent than the former due to the step-goal sequence involved—the rescue preceded the transfer and was a necessary means to achieving that result. It is more prominent also because of the explicit reference to the Son (in 13d-e), about whom this paragraph has so much to say.

Hence, the main information in the propositional cluster 1:13-14 is considered to be 'God our Father transferred us so that we are ruled by his Son'. However, since 'transferred' implies 'from somewhere', the information is slightly modified to 'God our Father caused us to be ruled by his Son'.

These three main propositions are related to each other by conjoining. But since the first and third are developed in considerably more detail than the second, they are considered to be of greater semantic prominence. Further, in a chiasmus with an even number of constituents, as here, it is the outside pair of constituents that is prominent. These two considerations would indicate that the main proposition of 1:13-14 is the theme of this paragraph. However, the third main proposition (1:15c) has marked prominence, by virtue of (1) the double use of πρωτότοκος, which is propositionalized as 'ranks above'; (2) the restatement of Christ's preeminence in the 1:18g purpose proposition; and (3) the extensive grounds supporting 1:15c-d.

NOTES

1:13a-d God our(inc) Father rescued us(inc) *spiritually* **so that** *we* **are no longer ruled by the evil one and he transferred us** *spiritually* **so that** *we* **are ruled by his Son** The first four propositions in 1:13 are considered together here, since the two clauses of which the verse consists are closely parallel:

1:13a-b	1:13c-d
ὃ ἐρρύσατο ἡμᾶς	καὶ μετέστησεν
who rescued us	and he transferred *us*
ἐκ τῆς ἐξουσίας	εἰς τὴν βασιλείαν
from the authority	into the kingdom
τοῦ σκότους	τοῦ υἱοῦ
of the darkness	of the Son

This verse with its sequence of metaphorical terms ('rescued', 'transferred') involves a live metaphor. The primary sense of 'rescued' is physical rescue from danger or bad circumstances, but here the rescue is from spiritual captivity and bondage. Likewise, 'transferred' primarily speaks of the physical realm but here of the spiritual.

Opinions differ among the commentators as to the degree of figurativeness of τὸ σκότος 'the darkness'. Some take ἐξουσία 'authority' to refer to the region over which the authority is exercised, a view with which Arndt and Gingrich agree (see ἐξουσία, 4b). With this view, the genitive τοῦ σκότους 'of the darkness' is understood as describing this region: it is an evil one, since τὸ σκότος 'the darkness' is figurative for 'evil'. Other commentators go further, and take it as a personification referring to 'the evil one', a parallel with 'the Son'. This view is followed here, since the parallelism does strongly suggest reference to two kingdoms ruled over by two authorities, with a transference being made from the one to the other. In the display, therefore, the phrases τῆς ἐξουσίας 'of the authority' and τὴν βασιλείαν 'the kingdom' are both represented by 'ruled by'. (It is generally agreed that ἐξουσία does not mean simply power, but rather authority exercised over others. [The word for 'power' is δύναμις.] Whether it is a legitimate or usurped authority is not in focus in the word ἐξουσία.)

Since this is a live figure, some indication of the point of similarity needs to be given in the display. In this case, this is very difficult. To preface the propositions with 'it is like' gives the impression that the rescue and removal are not real. The best solution seems to be to add 'spiritually' to the two verbs; an alternate would be to describe the two kingdoms as 'spiritual'.

1:13e whom he loves. The phrase τῆς ἀγάπης αὐτοῦ 'of-the love of-him' is unique in form as a way of referring to the Father's love for the Son. The commentators discuss whether it is semantically equivalent to 'his beloved Son', or whether there is a difference. Moule (1957) and also Turner (1963:214) say they are equivalent. Some commentators say, however, that the surface form gives prominence to 'love'. From a semantic point of view, ἀγάπης represents the event 'to love', and the only way this could be made prominent would be by using an intensifier. This is not done in the display because it is too uncertain whether the Greek surface form really signals prominence on 'love'. (The view of those who say that it means that the Son was begotten by the Father's love, or that the Son fully reveals that love, are generally rejected as incompatible with the surface form of the Greek and modes of expression used elsewhere in the New Testament.)

1:14a *That is,* **by means of** *what* **his Son** *did,* **we(inc) have been redeemed** *by* **God our Father;** The subject in Greek is 'we', not 'God the Father'; and the tense is present, not aorist. This verse is thus drawing attention to our present state, rather than to what great acts God has done for us.

One problem here is the noun ἀπολύτρωσιν 'redemption'. It is an abstract noun representing the event 'to redeem' or 'to ransom'. But the use of the present tense and the verb ἔχω 'to have' show that the reference is to a present *state*. The surface form, which is formally active, represents a deep-structure passive: we did not redeem ourselves—someone else redeemed us. To keep the shift of subject which the Greek passive verb entails, and yet convey something of the state focus, it seems best to refer to a past act with present benefits: 'we have been redeemed'.

A second problem is how to understand ἐν ᾧ 'in whom'. Its most common meaning elsewhere in the New Testament is 'in union with Christ'. It is possible, however, to argue for the sense of agent:

1. An analysis as agent here has support elsewhere in Scripture. In Titus 2:14 it is explicitly stated that Christ redeemed us: he is the agent of redemption.
2. Some verses later, in 1:16a and 17b, ἐν αὐτῷ 'in him', referring to Christ, is used, and the best interpretation of those references is that they refer to Christ as the (mediate) agent in the creation and sustaining of the universe. Certainly, the union of Christ and believers is not in the context. This creates a stronger case for Christ's being spoken of in the same way here in v. 14. (In 1:16a and 17b the surface structure is passive in form, but as has already been argued, 1:14a is passive in meaning, though not in form.)
3. The agency of the Son in reconciliation is made quite explicit in 1:20: δι' αὐτοῦ 'by means of him' and διὰ τοῦ αἵματος τοῦ σταυροῦ αὐτοῦ 'by means of the blood of his cross'.

So we can conclude that though it is possible to see ἐν ᾧ 'in whom' as referring to union with Christ, the emphasis on his agency throughout this paragraph points to the meaning of agent as the preferable interpretation.

Beekman also argued that the initial ἐν ᾧ shows focus on the agency of the Son. But if the agency of the Son is expressed by ἐν + dative instead of by being the subject of the verb, then there are three alternative surface forms:

1. ἐν ᾧ ἔχομεν τὴν ἀπολύτρωσιν (the form in the text) 'in whom we have redemption'
2. ἔχομεν τὴν ἀπολύτρωσιν ἐν αὐτῷ (normal unemphatic order) 'we have redemption in him'
3. ἐν αὐτῷ ἔχομεν τὴν ἀπολύτρωσιν (emphatic order) 'in **him** we have redemption'

The last two forms would have meant starting a new sentence, or at least making a major break. Paul avoided this by using a relative clause, a device commonly used by him in this epistle to maintain grammatical coherence. But since in a relative clause the relative pronoun must come first, there is no prominence given to ἐν ᾧ 'in whom'.

The final question in this connection is, Is the agency spoken of as a mediate agency (i.e., someone else was ultimately responsible) or a nonmediate agency (the Son was ultimately responsible)? Two factors favor the former view.

1. The previous verse (v. 13) has spoken of what the Father has done; this one (v. 14), then, indicates the agent through whom the Father effected our redemption. Hendriksen says that

1:13b and 14 describe "the redemptive work accomplished by means of the Son."

2. In 1:16a and 17b ἐν αὐτῷ 'in him' refers to the Son's mediate agency. The δι' αὐτοῦ 'through him' of 1:16b can also be considered to be a restatement of ἐν αὐτῷ in 1:16a, thus strengthening the case, since διά 'through' much more clearly signals means, or mediate agent. The same argument applies to the use of διά in 1:20.

The propositionalization of this interpretation is: 'by means of *what* his Son *did* we have been redeemed *by God our Father*'.

1:14b *in particular,* our(inc) sins have been forgiven *by God our Father*. In the Greek text the phrase τὴν ἄφεσιν τῶν ἁμαρτιῶν 'the forgiveness of sins' is in apposition to ἀπολύτρωσιν 'redemption', as is shown by its being in the accusative case. Expressed fully as a clause, it would be ἔχομεν τὴν ἄφεσιν τῶν ἁμαρτιῶν 'we have the forgiveness of sins'. So proposition 14b is expressed in the passive with the perfect tense in order to parallel 14a.

What is the relationship of proposition 14b to 14a? The appositional construction in the surface form points to a relation of equivalence or generic-specific. The latter alternative seems preferable, since redemption is generally considered to include more than forgiveness. (In some contexts it is more or less synonymous with 'to save'.) The linking phrase 'in particular' is used to show that it was this particular aspect of redemption Paul was drawing attention to, rather than to other specifics.

1:15a-b God's Son reveals *perfectly* what God *his Father* is like, who cannot be seen *by anyone*. The main question here concerns εἰκών 'image'. But two minor grammatical points should be noted first:

1. The absence of an article with εἰκών 'image' is normal when the complement follows the verb 'to be' (so Ellicott; Alford by implication). Its absence does not suggest the English indefinite article ('an image'), but is more like a title, 'he is image'.

2. The article occurs both before and after 'God', the second one preceding 'invisible'. This repetition gives some prominence to the concept of invisibility.

There is general agreement that εἰκών 'image' in this verse has three components of meaning. Lightfoot spells them out as follows:

1. *Similarity, likeness*—the image is *like* what it is compared to. However, the point of similarity has to be derived from a consideration of the two things compared and from the context.

2. *Representation*—the likeness is not fortuitous, as the likeness of two eggs is; it is designed. The Emperor's head on a coin is an image, and man as first created. The existence of an image presupposes a prototype.

3. *Manifestation*—in this context, the εἰκών has the function of revealing, or making manifest, that which is inherently invisible. This aspect of the meaning is not inherent in the word εἰκών, it is implied by the prominence given to 'invisible'.

Notice that *perfect* is not included in the preceding list. The word εἰκών does not in itself imply a perfect image, but the teaching of the Scriptures elsewhere makes it unambiguously clear that the Son is the perfect image of the Father. The word 'perfectly', therefore, is supplied in the display.

The meaning of ἀοράτου 'invisible' may seem obvious, but in fact many commentaries say that it means not only 'physically invisible', but also 'unknowable' since God cannot be known by any created being unless he chooses to reveal himself. I am inclined, however, to agree with Findlay that the primary meaning here is 'physically invisible' in view of what follows about the creation. He says,

> This title [Image of God] the apostle had before conferred on Christ in 2 Cor. iv. 4. There it is in the moral and redemptional attributes of the Godhead ... that ... the incarnate Redeemer appears as 'the Image of God': here the title is put upon him as representing the invisible God in all that pertains to nature and creation. The Colossian error rested on a philosophical dualism. It assumed an absolute separation between the infinite God and the finite, material world. ...

Romans 1:20 is very similar: 'Ever since the creation of the world, his invisible nature, namely, his eternal power and deity, has been clearly perceived in the things that have been made'.

1:15c-d God's Son ranks above everything that has been created; The primary meaning of the word πρωτότοκος 'firstborn' is oldest son. The oldest son had various privileges as a result of being born first. The story of Jacob and Esau illustrates this vividly: Jacob was prepared to go to considerable lengths to obtain the privileges which were not his by birth. The question in this context is whether Paul is using the word in its primary sense or as a metonymy for the firstborn's privileges. Commentators are divided, but there is good evidence that both senses were used in the Old Testament, and that the word was not always used in its primary sense. There are three possible views concerning its meaning in this particular context:

1. It refers to both priority in time and ranking above creation.
2. It refers only to rank, not to time.
3. It refers to time, not to rank.

Verse 1:16, which is introduced by ὅτι 'because', evidently gives logical support for the description of the Son as πρωτότοκος. Any of these views is compatible with v. 16, because priority in time is required if the Son is to be seen as the agent of creation and, as agent, he ranks above the creation, for the creator is more important than what he creates. In 1:17a, however, Paul says explicitly that he existed before everything; in other words, he had priority in time. Hence, the πρωτότοκος phrase could be taken as in view 1, with 1:16 dealing specifically with rank and 1:17a with time. Or it could be taken as referring to rank, with 1:16 and 1:17 giving reasons for that rank. This latter view seems preferable for three reasons:

1. It would be very unusual for ὅτι 'because' to connect specifics to a generic term; direct apposition seems a more likely relation.
2. Both 1:17a and b are introduced by καί 'and' and should, if possible, be interpreted in a parallel manner. In view 2 they are taken as two further grounds for calling the Son πρωτότοκος, implying that πρωτότοκος is a generic term for supremacy over the creation.
3. In the LXX rendering of Ps. 89:27 πρωτότοκος is used with reference to rank: 'And I will make him the firstborn, the highest of the kings of the earth'. The term did, in fact, become a messianic title, and that may be why Paul uses it here.

Turner (1965:122-24) gives a somewhat different understanding of πρωτότοκος. He keeps the primary sense of 'born first', but interprets πρωτότοκος as identifying the Son closely with "the family of which he is head, i.e. the whole of creation which looks eagerly for redemption" (p. 124). He renders it "archetype" and refers to Romans 5, where Christ is described as the new Adam. The family with which the Son is identified is that of believers, and, as the new Adam, he is the head of that family. However, the terms of 1:16, which logically supports the statement about the πρωτότοκος, are clearly universal in scope and cover all of creation, not just the family of the redeemed. This weakens the support for Turner's view. Moreover, Turner fails to show that πρωτότοκος can carry the sense of 'identification with'.

Commentators discuss whether πάσης κτίσεως is to be understood collectively as 'all creation', or individually as 'every creature'. But as Hendriksen says, it makes little difference. The arguments from the presence or the absence of the article with κτίσις 'creation' seem inconclusive. However, the fact that the Son is individual and that different created entities are elaborated upon in 1:16 would point to the individual sense. Christ ranks above every created thing, no matter where it is to be found (in heaven or on earth) and no matter what it is (rulers, authorities, etc.).

1:16a since it was by means of him that everything was created *by God*, The Greek is ὅτι ἐν αὐτῷ ἐκτίσθη τὰ πάντα 'because in him were created all things'. The conjunction ὅτι 'because' shows that this statement (and the following ones that support it) give grounds for why the Son is asserted to be the πρωτότοκος, the one ranking above everything in creation. He is the creator and therefore stands apart from and far above that which is created, no matter how powerful or wonderful. The aorist tense of ἐκτίσθη 'were created' points to the historical fact of creation; τὰ πάντα is all-inclusive—everything that has been created.

The main question here is the sense of the prepositional phrase ἐν αὐτῷ 'in him'. Its common Pauline sense is union with Christ, but the problem here is that it is not the church that is in view. The question is twofold: First we should ask if ἐν αὐτῷ here is the same as δι' αὐτοῦ 'through him' in the last clause of this verse? Then, if it is not, what *does* it mean?

The more or less universal answer to the first question is no; the answer to the second question is very hard to understand. Its meaning is variously suggested to be 'resting in Him' and 'depending on Him' (Ellicott; cf. Peake [*Expositor's Greek Testament*]), "the conditional element" (Alford; cf.

Abbott), "the 'sphere' within which the work of creation takes place" (Bruce 1957), "with reference to" or "in relation to" (Hendriksen), "Its ground and raison d'être" (Findlay). Turner (1963:253) suggests "because of." What is common to all of these is the sense of causality: the Son caused the act of creation.

It is quite widely noted that the final clause of this verse is essentially a restatement or recapitulation of the rest of the verse. This observation would support the view that no distinction is necessarily intended by the change from ἐν 'in' to διά 'through'. Paul does vary his prepositions (as well as distinguish them) as in Rom. 3:30, where ἐκ 'out of' and διά 'through' are used interchangeably. The best solution may be indicated by Meyer's statement that "the causal relation which was previously denoted by ἐν is now more precisely indicated as a relation of *mediate agency*"; Barclay is similar in that he translates both prepositions by "he is the agent."

The position of ἐν αὐτῷ is emphatic, since it precedes the verb. To express this most clearly in the display, through the medium of English, it is necessary to use the cleft construction 'it was by him that . . .', but the translator should remember that this is an English surface-structure device and use the appropriate prominence device of the receptor language.

1:16b–e which is on the earth and which can be seen *by people,* **and** *also everything* **which is in heaven and which cannot be seen** *by people.* In the Greek are two prepositional phrases that serve to emphasize the all-inclusiveness of 'everything' by specifically naming the two principal locations where 'everything' is found.

There are two different views of the final phrase τὰ ὁρατὰ καὶ τὰ ἀόρατα 'the seen-things and the unseen-things'. Those who hold the first view take them as a different cross-classification of τὰ πάντα 'everything' from that in 16b and 16d; those who hold the second view take them as referring to the same things, but expressed in terms of visibility rather than location. Those who favor the first view say that 'seen things' include such objects as the sun, moon, and stars, which are in the heavens, and 'unseen things' include the soul, which is on earth. Those who favor the second view say that this is an example of chiastic structure, so that both 'things in the heavens' and 'the unseen things' have the same referent (i.e., the world of spirit beings) and 'things on the earth' and 'the seen things' are similarly synonymous, referring to the world of human beings and their environment. Since the next proposition refers to angelic beings, and since Paul was concerned to refute the honor paid to angelic beings in the false teaching, the chiastic view is preferred, especially since the outer elements of an even chiastic structure are given more prominence than the inner ones. Since the display is intended to represent the deep structure, the chiastic structure is not replicated in the display; rather, the related phrases are juxtaposed and, as a result, the order of the propositions does not match the Greek order.

1:16f In particular, all types of important spirit beings *were created by means of him.* It is generally agreed that this list is a further, more detailed, specification of 'things in heaven' and 'things unseen' and that it refers to angelic beings. It is also generally agreed that this list is not intended to be a precise formulation of an angelic hierarchy, but that if any distinctions of rank *were* intended, they are not known now. It is clear from the context that the intended sense of the list is 'no matter who they are or what titles they may have'. Ellicott quotes from Pearson, as follows: "He nameth those which are of greatest eminence, and in them comprehendeth the rest." This seems the best view to take—Paul uses the names given to leading groups of angelic beings, since that would include all lesser ones.

The question has been raised as to whether these are good angels or fallen ones. It seems very unlikely that the false teacher was inculcating the worship of demons, so good angels would be referred to. The comprehensiveness of 'everything' would include demons, but this specific fourfold list would not include demons. It should also be borne in mind that it is clear from the Scriptures that the demons are such because they fell, not because they were created that way.

This list poses problems for the translator. Should an attempt be made to reproduce the list, or would a generic statement be better? Since it is generally agreed that precise distinctions were probably not intended, and that, if they were, they are no longer known, it is very difficult to translate the list as it stands. Hence, in the display, a more generic statement is given.

1:16g–i *And he ranks above everything* **since everything has been created** *by God* **by means of God's Son, and since everything has been**

created *by God* in order that God's Son *might be glorified by everything,* The clause here is a restatement of 1:16a. To some extent, it has already been discussed in connection with that proposition. However, there are the following differences:

1. The phrase δι' αὐτοῦ 'through him' expresses mediate agency unambiguously. The somewhat artificial 'by means of him' is equivalent semantically to 'God the Father caused him to create'. The reason it is not expressed this way in the display is in order to keep 'everything' as the topic as in the Greek. For a given receptor language, however, the translator may prefer the overtly causative form.

2. Here ἔκτισται 'has been created' is in the perfect tense whereas the Greek underlying 1:16a is in the aorist tense (ἐκτίσθη). Turner (1963:70) says that "any subtle distinction here is doubtful," and says that while there *are* clear examples in the New Testament where the distinction is maintained, in other examples any distinction is doubtful. By the fourth century A.D., the perfect tense had been eclipsed as a distinct tense. Hence, the variation here may be purely for stylistic reasons, to avoid unacceptable repetitiousness. If a distinction is intended, then it would be that the perfect tense of ἔκτισται draws attention to the present existence of the creation as well as to the historic act of creation. It would correspond more or less to the English *was brought into existence and continues to exist*.

3. A further concept, εἰς αὐτόν 'unto him', is added to what is expressed in 1:16a. Commentators agree that it has a meaning such as "the aim and end" (Meyer; cf. Martin, 1972:50) or the "ultimate goal" (Lightfoot, cf. Bruce 1957). Few commentators get beyond such expressions as those quoted, but Meyer also says "to serve His will," Findlay "to serve His kingdom," and Hendriksen "must contribute glory to him and serve his purpose." Because of the very generic context, the sense 'to bring glory to him' seems better, because that includes the idea of serving his purposes.

4. The Greek word order here is different from that of 1:16a. The significance of the word order may be understood in one of two ways. First, since everything in the clause precedes the verb, all the phrases may be considered emphatic—the subject and the two prepositional phrases. Or it may be that prominence is not signaled by the order at all, but rather the end of the first (and expanded) ground stating why the Son is the πρωτότοκος 'firstborn'—namely, because he is the creator of everything. This second view is based on some evidence that an alternative word order is sometimes used in final positions (sentence final, paragraph final, major breaks within a sentence) with the verb being transposed to clause-final position, as in this case (cf. also 1:17b). Since it is very unusual to have every part of a clause emphatic (although not impossible), and since in 1:16a only 'in him' is emphatic, the latter view is followed in the display. However, the translator is at liberty to follow the former.

1:17a–b and since it is he who existed before anything *else existed,* It is widely agreed that the use of αὐτός 'he' in this clause is emphatic, and is intended as a contrast with 'everything' in the previous clause. There is also general agreement that πρό means 'before (in time)'.

1:17c and since everything is sustained *by God* by means of God's Son. The use of the prepositional phrase ἐν αὐτῷ 'in/by him' raises the same question as was raised in connection with 1:16a. Since it is still τὰ πάντα 'all things' (the whole created universe) that is being spoken of, it is contextually preferable to treat ἐν αὐτῷ in the same way as in v. 16, that is, as indicating 'by means of him'.

There is also the question of just what συνέστηκεν means. Arndt and Gingrich have "continue, endure, exist," though they say that this sense may be blended with the sense "*be composed* or *compounded, consist . . .* of." Most English versions have "holds together," but the TEV has "all things have their proper place." Versions also vary between active and passive. If ἐν αὐτῷ is taken to signal the (mediate) agent, then the sense of the verb is essentially passive, so that the sense is 'is held together' or 'is maintained' (Bruce 1957) or 'is sustained' (Bruce 1957, cf. Martin, 1972:50). The idea appears to be that the universe is dependent on the Son both for its continued existence and for its orderliness.

The same question of order arises here as in connection with the Greek clause underlying 16g–i. Hence, there are the same two alternative interpretations here as are described under point 4 in the 1:16g–i note. As previously, the second of these two alternatives is preferred, since this is the last statement relating the Son to creation. The next proposition goes on to relate the Son to the church.

What is the relationship of these two coordinate clauses with the preceding material? Since they all explicitly relate the Son to τὰ πάντα 'all things', and since they are linked by καί 'and', the most straightforward interpretation is to interpret them as giving further grounds for the nucleus assertion 'God's Son ranks above everything' (1:15c).

1:18a–b And *God's Son ranks above everything* **since it is he who rules over the church** *as the head* **controls** *the physical body,* With this verse a new aspect of the main theme is taken up. Paul leaves off describing the relationship between the Son and creation and turns to the relationship between the Son and the church, the *new* creation. It seems reasonable to suppose, as do some of the commentators, that the false teaching was, in some way, undermining the doctrine of Christ's supreme rule with respect to the church, probably by giving angels too much significance, perhaps as mediators in some way.

A few points should be noted:

1. Almost all commentators agree that here the pronoun αὐτός 'he' is used emphatically or, rather, contrastively: he, the Son, not τὰ πάντα 'all things', is the subject. This may well be so, though Turner (1963:40–41) will say no more than "probably the pronoun has some emphasis" (see the note on 17a–b, where the Greek is the same).

2. It is also widely agreed that the final two words of the clause, τῆς ἐκκλησίας 'the church', are in apposition to τοῦ σώματος 'the body', and are not a continuation of the genitive construction. They serve to identify what the body is.

3. The phrase 'the head of the body' is metaphorical, but it is not easy to decide whether it is a live or dead metaphor. With this uncertainty, the point of similarity is given in the display.

As to how these two propositions are related to the preceding ones, we see that, formally, they are linked to what precedes by καί 'and' and their form is parallel to the form underlying 17a and b. This would point to a continuation of the grounds for 15c and d. However, there is the change of reference from τὰ πάντα 'all things' to τῆς ἐκκλησίας 'the church', which separates 18a and b from the preceding propositions. Both of these factors have been taken account of in the display, by taking 18a–b as further grounds for 15c–d, but at the same time taking them as the first propositions in a separate grounds cluster.

One implication of this analysis should be spelled out clearly, since it departs from the views of most commentators: The new creation, the church, not just the universe and its inhabitants, are included in 15c–d, which reads 'God's Son ranks above everything that has been created'. Most commentators contrast the Son's supremacy over the old and the new creations, rather than uniting them under the πρωτότοκος 'firstborn' statement in 1:15, as is done here.

1:18c–f since he causes *the church* **to live** *spiritually,* **because he is the first one** *who rose from among those who have died,* It is necessary to consider these two phrases together because it is generally agreed that the second phrase delimits the sense of ἀρχή 'beginning', which is generic. As Abbott puts it, these words "express the aspect in which ἀρχή is here viewed."

The word ἀρχή has the general sense of 'beginning', with the more specific senses of 'origin', and, in philosophy, 'the first cause'. Normally, it is followed by some further description to indicate that it is the beginning of some sequence of historical events. (This seems the commonest sense.) Hence, it is generally taken here to mean 'the source/origin of the new creation, the church, or the church's life'. The last of these alternatives seems preferable in the context, since it is resurrection life that the church has. According to Abbott, "πρωτότοκος implies that other νεκροί follow; ἀρχή, that He it was who made possible that others should follow."

There is no article with ἀρχή, just as there is no article with εἰκών 'image' in 1:15; in both places the noun is used somewhat like a title (in fact, "Beginning" is capitalized in Phillips and the JB). From a propositional standpoint, the sense is causative. It is expressed in the display as 'he causes *the church* to live', both in the present, spiritually, and in the future resurrection of the body.

It would be much more satisfactory if πρωτότοκος could be taken in the same sense here as in 15d. The majority of the commentators, however, take it to refer to priority in time, and this is the sense that best suits the sequence of thought. The phrase ἐκ τῶν νεκρῶν 'out of the dead' is so commonly collocated with some form of the verb ἐγείρω 'to rise (from the dead)' that all the commentators take the whole phrase as meaning 'the first to rise from the dead'.

Again, there is the question of the semantic relation with what precedes. Interestingly enough, several of the older commentators (Alford, Ellicott, Abbott, Peake) say that ὅς ἐστιν 'who is' has an argumentative force—that it is logically connected with the preceding statement—rather than simply a description of the Son, as in the surface grammar. This would give the relation of grounds, the conclusion being in proposition 18a. This parallels the statements in 1:16 and 17 fairly closely (that the Son is above creation because he caused it to come into existence).

It is generally agreed that the phrase πρωτότοκος ἐκ τῶν νεκρῶν 'firstborn from the dead' "defines" ἀρχή 'beginning, first one', but what does this mean in particular? The relation that seems to fit best is that of reason—he is the source of the church's life because he has triumphed over death by rising from it.

1:18g in order that he should become preeminent in every way. This clause expresses the purpose of the preceding statement(s) (see last paragraph of this note). Several points here are noteworthy:

1. The use of the aorist γένηται 'he might become' points to the historical fact of the resurrection, the purpose of which was that he should become preeminent in the church. It should not be translated as if it were the verb 'to be'.
2. The phrase ἐν πᾶσιν 'in all things' is understood adverbially: 'in every respect, in every way'. It does not refer back to τὰ πάντα 'all things'. It emphasizes that Christ's preeminence has no limitations of any sort. Its position in the clause is emphatic also.
3. Like the commentators, I take the view that in this clause αὐτός 'he' is emphatic. This is because there has been no change of subject from the preceding ὅς 'who' and αὐτός 'he'.
4. The verb πρωτεύω 'to be preeminent', which is not used elsewhere in the New Testament, has the meaning of 'rank over/above, be preeminent'. Turner (1963:89) takes the combination of γένηται and πρωτεύων as a periphrasis for the future, so that, to coin a word, the verb could be translated 'so that he will preeminate in every way'. However, the combination of an aorist (γένηται) and a present (πρωτεύων) is very unusual. It was the resurrection that brought Christ into the (continuous) state of unrestricted preeminence with respect to both the old and new creations (cf. Michaelis, p. 882).

To what in particular does this purpose relate? To 18d–f only, or also to the nucleus, 18a–b? The force of the argument seems to be that Christ already ranks above the created universe because he is the agent of creation, and that God raised him from the dead first so that he might also rank above all those who, in turn, will rise from the dead. Hence, it seems bests to attach it directly to 18d–f and only indirectly to 18a–b. The content of the purpose, however, is very similar to that of 1:15c, and serves to reinforce 15c and signal the end of the material running from 1:15c to 18g. It is an example of rhetorical bracketing within a paragraph, defining the bounds of the central constituents of the chiasmus.

1:19a–b *He reveals perfectly what God his Father is like* since it is in his Son that his Father chose that he himself would dwell completely. The Greek is ὅτι ἐν αὐτῷ εὐδόκησεν πᾶν τὸ πλήρωμα κατοικῆσαι 'because in him was pleased all the fullness to dwell'. The verse bristles with problems; most of the commentators devote considerable space to discussing it. The issues are as follows:

1. The main problem arises from a morphological ambiguity: neuter nominals in Greek do not differentiate between the nominative and accusative cases. Since τὸ πλήρωμα 'the fullness', is a neuter noun, it could be either the subject or the object of the verb εὐδόκησεν 'was pleased'. But if it is not the subject, that would mean there is no explicit subject in the clause and the only other possibility for the subject is either an implicit 'the Father' or 'the Son'. There are thus three choices of subject for the main verb. The choice is not an easy one, and there are long and complex arguments in favor of all three views. The discussion can be summarized as follows:
    a. From a *grammatical* point of view, 'God the Father' is the poorest choice. Its last occurrence is at the beginning of this paragraph

(in 1:13-14). Either 'the Son' or 'all the fullness' would be quite acceptable grammatically, since 'the Son' is the subject of the preceding clause and 'all the fullness' is explicit. However, the opening (emphatic) ἐν αὐτῷ 'in him' refers to the Son (no one questions this reference), so the sense would be 'the Son was pleased that *in himself* all the fullness should dwell'. This seems unlikely, even apart from the fact the Greek is ἐν αὐτῷ 'in him', not ἐν ἑαυτῷ 'in himself'. (The same problem would be repeated with the δι' αὐτοῦ 'through him' in the next verse, which also refers to the Son.) Further, when using the verb εὐδοκέω followed by an infinitive elsewhere in his letters, Paul always states the third person subject explicitly, in a noun phrase or subordinate clause. The grammatical evidence, then, points strongly to the subject's being the explicit πᾶν τὸ πλήρωμα 'all the fullness'.

b. In terms of a *natural collocation*, the evidence favors the subject's being 'God the Father'. If a divine person is the subject of εὐδοκέω 'to please', it is always God the Father in the New Testament, never the Son. Further, whoever is the referent of the subject of the main verb here, it is the same for the subject of the dependent infinitive, ἀποκαταλλάξαι 'to reconcile', in the next verse. In the active uses of the simpler form of the verb, καταλλάσσω, 'God the Father' is the subject (2 Cor. 5:18-19), but in Eph. 2:16 the compound form ἀποκαταλλάσσω occurs with Christ as subject. However, in Ephesians, Christ is reconciling Jew and Gentile to each other, so that the references in 2 Corinthians parallel the use here in Colossians more closely. So the evidence all supports 'God the Father' as the appropriate choice to collocate with εὐδόκησεν 'he was pleased', as well as with the following ἀποκαταλλάξαι 'to reconcile'.

c. Most commentators consider that the collocational evidence outweighs the grammatical evidence, and choose 'God the Father' as subject. They also point out that if πᾶν τὸ πλήρωμα 'all the fullness' were the subject, then πᾶν τὸ πλήρωμα would involve personification: 'be pleased', 'to dwell', and 'to reconcile'. This, it is said, is quite un-Pauline, and more like the language of the second century. In answer to this, however, it can be pointed out that Paul uses it unambiguously as a personification in 2:9 of this same epistle, where πᾶν τὸ πλήρωμα is collocated with 'to dwell'.

My solution here is that πᾶν τὸ πλήρωμα is the subject, that it is personified, and since it is the subject of the verb εὐδόκησεν 'to please', it refers to 'God the Father'. Paul may have chosen this form of expression because of the false teaching he was combating. He clearly states that all that can be said of the Father as God is also true of the Son, the only difference being their role relation of father-son.

2. The second problem is the meaning of πᾶν τὸ πλήρωμα. One view is that it refers to all the fullness of God, the "entire plenitude of nature and of power" (Findlay), "the totality of the Divine powers and attributes" (Lightfoot), "all the attributes and activities of God" (Bruce 1957). This is the majority view. However, one or two commentators draw attention to the fact that all of the verb forms in 1:19-20 are aorist, and so argue that they refer to the relationship between the Son and the church, which is rooted in the historic events of his incarnation, death, resurrection, and ascension. Meyer argues that εὐδόκησεν refers to the sending of the Son, and Findlay that it refers to the ascension. Meyer then favors a more restricted understanding of πᾶν τὸ πλήρωμα, which he expresses as "the whole *charismatic riches of God*, His whole *gracious fullness* of εὐλογία πνευματική ['spiritual blessing']," and he cites Eph. 1:3, John 1:16, and Eph. 4:13 as support. One possible view, taking the aorist verbs as historical in reference, would be to refer the main verb, εὐδόκησεν 'was pleased', to Jesus' baptism, when he was equipped with all the fullness of the Holy Spirit for his public Messianic ministry, including, of course, his reconciling death, which is referred to in the following verse.

3. Semantically, ἐν αὐτῷ 'in him' is related to κατοικῆσαι 'to dwell', but it is put at the beginning of the clause for emphasis.

4. It is generally agreed that, since the infinitive κατοικῆσαι 'to dwell' is in the aorist tense, it marks the (temporal) beginning of the

indwelling. Meyer, for example, translates it "to take up its abode." This particular verb expresses settledness, relative permanence; the idea of transitory or temporary dwelling is conveyed by a different verb, παροικέω.

5. Another question is the logical connection of this verse. The conjunction ὅτι shows it is reason or grounds. But the question is, For which of the previous statements is it a reason or grounds? According to the commentators, it is either a grounds backing up the purpose just stated (18g) or a grounds for the assertion that the Son is head of the church (18a). It is not at all easy to decide between these alternative interpretations. I can find only two insights in the commentaries that are helpful:

   a. Grounds for Christ's being the head of the church have already been given in 18c–f, so it seems unlikely that 1:19 continues those grounds.
   b. The sequence of clauses introduced by ὅτι in 1:16 gave grounds for the πρωτότοκος phrase (1:15), so the same pattern might reasonably be expected here (but, in fact, the commentator took this to mean an argument in support of his being head of the church).

Point a is certainly true. Moreover, a purpose clause generally comes last in a sequence, so that a grounds following it is likely to refer back to some earlier assertions. The arguments already given point to v. 19's relating to statements preceding v. 18. But vv. 16 and 17 are grounds for 15c–d, which deal with the Son's supremacy over all creation; and since there is no reference to τὰ πάντα 'all things' in v. 19, it seems unlikely that it is giving further grounds for 15c–d. It also seems unlikely that the grounds for supremacy over creation would be resumed after stating the Son's supremacy over the church. Thus, in the display, proposition 19 is shown as relating back to propositions 15a–b. This analysis is confirmed by the content of both groups of propositions—they contain no reference to either the creation or the church, but rather make statements about the relation between the Father and the Son.

Two objections have been raised to relating 1:19 to the first half of 1:15:

1. There is too much distance between them. In defense of this the chiastic arrangement can be pointed out, the noncentral parts of a chiasmus are necessarily separated by other material. Moreover, occasional examples of such separations occur even apart from chiastic structures. In the semantic analysis of 1 Timothy it is suggested that γάρ in 3:13 relates that verse to 3:1 and γάρ in 5:15 relates that verse to 5:11.
2. Meyer rejects the relation shown in the display on the grounds that 15a–b are essentially timeless ('he is the Image of God'), whereas the verb in v. 19 is aorist, thus time related. However, there is a mixture of aorists and (timeless) presents in this paragraph elsewhere (see, for example, the note on 18g), so such a mixture is not atypical of the context. The implication of the mixture of tenses may be that the statement 'he is the Image of God' is not necessarily timeless, but describes Christ's present state as the God-man who reveals God to man, and that that state as God-man had its origins in time, or at least in a particular decision of the Father (the time of εὐδόκησεν 'he was pleased' is not, after all, stated). Again, Paul may well be focusing on issues raised by the false teaching as it relates to Jesus as mediator, rather than Jesus as Son apart from his mediatorial functions.

In the display εὐδόκησεν is represented by 'he chose'. Arndt and Gingrich give its glosses as "consider good, consent, determine, resolve." This verb refers to the action of the divine will. The aorist tense of the infinitive 'to dwell' is not specifically represented in the display. The phrase 'all the fullness', which is understood as referring emphatically to the Father, is represented by 'he himself'.

1:20a, d *God our(inc) Father caused us(inc) to be ruled by his Son* since God our Father *chose* to reconcile *to himself* by means of his Son everything . . . in order that his Son *might be glorified;* Verse 20 receives a lot of attention in the commentaries, but such discussions do not affect its translation. All agree that τὰ πάντα 'all things' is to be given the same unlimited scope here as in 1:15–17 (i.e., 'everything that has been created'). The phrases 'whether on earth or in heaven' at the end of this verse confirm this interpretation. The focus of discussion is what 'to reconcile everything' can mean theologically, especially since it includes 'things in heaven', but so far as the translator is concerned the meaning is 'to reconcile everything'. The following points are noteworthy:

1. The initial καί 'and' links the aorist infinitive ἀποκαταλλάξαι 'to reconcile' with the main verb εὐδόκησεν 'he was pleased' and the introductory ὅτι 'because'. Hence, this statement is a further coordinate grounds with 1:19.
2. The phrase δι' αὐτοῦ 'through him' is in emphatic position, paralleling ἐν αὐτῷ 'in him' in 1:19. The preposition διά indicates the mediate agent (the one by whom it was done), the ultimate agent being the subject of the verb 'to reconcile', namely 'God the Father'. In the display, it is expressed as 'by means of his Son, as it was in 1:16g.
3. Some of the commentators discuss whether the form of the verb ἀποκαταλλάσσω 'reconcile', with the initial ἀπο-, is different in sense from the form without it, καταλλάσσω, which is the form Paul uses in epistles other than Colossians and Ephesians. Two meanings are suggested for ἀποκαταλλάσσω: (a) "to take *back* into favour" (Findlay) and (b) an intensive sense (Bruce 1957, quoting Morris). The former seems unlikely, since it implies a previous state of reconciliation. While such a state did prevail before the entrance of sin into creation, there is nothing in the context to suggest this idea. The latter therefore seems more plausible, if by *intensive* is meant 'completely' (Peake), an intensification directed against the false teaching that implied or directly taught that Christ's reconciling work needed to be supplemented by angelic intermediaries. However, 'completely' is not used in the display since it is not certain that this component is in fact present.
4. The final phrase of 1:20a is εἰς αὐτόν 'to him'. The issue is who the referent of this pronoun is, God the Father or God the Son. In favor of the Father, it is argued that elsewhere in the New Testament it is the Father who is referred to in connection with reconciliation (see Rom. 5:10; 2 Cor. 5:18, 19, 20). Of course, with 'God the Father' the subject of the clause (as represented by πᾶν τὸ πλήρωμα), the reflexive form εἰς ἑαυτόν 'to himself' would be expected here; yet it is εἰς αὐτόν 'to him'. Those in favor of the Father as referent handle this difficulty by maintaining that, when unemphatic, εἰς αὐτόν is equivalent to εἰς ἑαυτόν or that it should be spelled εἰς αὑτόν. (The only difference is a diacritic, and diacritics were not used with capital letters, in which many of the manuscripts were written.)

In favor of the Son as referent, it is argued that the three pronouns in these two verses (ἐν αὐτῷ, δι' αὐτοῦ, and εἰς αὐτόν) all have the same referent, the Son—there is nothing to indicate otherwise. This argument is sometimes backed up by pointing out that in 1:16 the same three prepositional phrases are found, and in the same order, all referring to the Son—a striking parallel certainly. Moreover, in the passages referred to above (and in 1 Cor. 7:11 where husband and wife are in view) the verb καταλλάσσω 'to reconcile' always couples with the simple dative for the person to whom reconciliation is made. The εἰς + accusative construction is found only here.

The arguments for the pronoun's referent being the Son seem to be the better ones. However, that still leaves the question of the meaning of εἰς αὐτόν in this context. One suggestion is "*the end for which* rather than *the person to whom*" (Findlay). This is a common meaning for εἰς; however, it refers to a person here, rather than to an end. The idea is parallel to that of proposition 16i, where the same thing is said of creation—that the ultimate purpose of God's creating everything through his Son is to glorify the Son. It is the same with reconciliation. The whole thrust of this passage about the Son is that everything in the old and new creation is ultimately for his glory; hence the words '*might be glorified*' are supplied in 1:20d.

1:20b–c which is on earth and which is in heaven, As in 1:16, the two phrases introduced by τά 'the' highlight τὰ πάντα 'all things' by specifying location, making it unambiguously clear that τὰ πάντα is universal in scope.

There is a textual question here as to whether δι' αὐτοῦ 'through him' should be included or not. The UBS textual apparatus rated it "D," which is defined as "a very high degree of doubt concerning the reading selected for the text" (Metzger, p. xxviii). It is generally assumed that it got omitted from some of the texts because the transcriber felt the Greek read more smoothly without it. The majority of the commentators regard it as genuine and, according to Metzger (p. 621), so did a majority of the UBS text committee. For the display it is treated as part of the text.

Another problem is that in the display it is very awkward for two descriptive propositions to be so far removed from the thing described. One solution would be to repeat the whole of 20a and attach the descriptive propositions to it. It is clearer, however, to attach them to 20a directly, even though this is not the order of the Greek. The repeated δι' αὐτοῦ functions to maintain the prominence of δι' αὐτοῦ in the main clause and also to show that the two τά phrases relate back to τὰ πάντα in that main clause, and not to the participle 'having made peace'. Both of these functions are realized by placing the corresponding propositions immediately after 20a.

1:20e–g that is, God *our(inc)* **Father chose to reconcile** *everything to himself* **by means of** *God's Son shedding* **his blood when** *he died* **on the cross.** The compound verb εἰρηνοποιήσας 'having made peace' is another way of speaking of reconciliation. As in 16g and 20a, διά + genitive indicates the means. In 16g and 20a, however, the means was a mediate agent; here it is an event, that of shedding blood on the cross.

While 'blood' is a metonymy for the event of a violent death in which blood was shed, it constitutes a symbol of considerable theological importance, being found throughout the whole Bible. It should, therefore, be retained in translation and not simply be replaced with 'by his death' or 'by means of his dying'.

SECTION CONSTITUENT 1:21–23 (Paragraph: Nucleus₂ of 1:13–23)

THEME: *As for you, God our Father has now reconciled you to himself.*

RELATIONAL STRUCTURE	CONTENTS
┌─ concession - CONCLUSION	1:21a–b As for you, although you were formerly alienated *from God* (21b) and although you were formerly hostile *to God*,
│ └─ grounds (evidential)	1:21c–d since *you* thought *evilly* (21d) and since you acted evilly,
NUCLEUS ───	1:22a nevertheless, God *our(inc) Father* has now reconciled you *to himself*.
├─ means	1:22b He did this [1:22a] by means of his Son's dying physically.
└─ purpose ── CONSEQUENCE	1:22c–d He did this [1:22a] in order that you should be completely holy (22d) when he brings you into his presence,
└─ condition - CONCLUSION	1:23a–e provided that you continue to believe *the gospel*; (23b) *specifically*, provided that you continue to be stable (23c) and you continue to confidently expect that (23d) which you heard about (23e) *when you heard* the gospel,
└─ grounds	1:23f–h *since* this gospel has been proclaimed *to people* in very many places [HYP], (23g) *and since* I, Paul, have become one (23h) who makes it known *to people*.

BOUNDARIES AND COHERENCE

The start of the 1:21–23 paragraph is marked by the switch to the topic of 'you(pl)' signaled by a forefronted καὶ ὑμᾶς 'and you(pl)'. The end of the paragraph is signaled by a tail-head link: the final clause announces the topic of Paul's ministry, which is taken up in the two succeeding paragraphs.

Grammatically, 1:21–23 is a single sentence, centered on the main finite verb in 1:22a, ἀποκατήλλαξεν 'he reconciled'. The verb is preceded by a dependent participial construction and followed by an infinitive, two 'if' clauses, and three relative clauses.

There is considerable referential coherence: 'you(pl)' references occur throughout the paragraph—in every clause, in fact, until the last two relative clauses. In addition, various parts of the paragraph are tied together lexically. In vv. 21 and 22 there is a set of three initial contrasts: 'alienated' and 'enemies' in contrast with 'reconciled'; 'evil' in contrast with 'holy, blameless, and irreproachable'; and 'formerly' in contrast with 'now'. In v. 23, there is a set of three near-synonymous terms—'established' and 'firm' and 'not shifting'. Also, the last three clauses in v. 23 all refer back to 'the gospel', mentioned earlier in the same verse.

PROMINENCE AND THEME

In 22a is a clear central statement, the contra-expectation of the concession expressed in v. 21, and also the result of the means expressed in 22b and the means of the purpose expressed in 22c–23h. It contains the only finite verb in an independent clause in this paragraph. (Of the two other finite verbs, one is in an 'if' clause, the other in a relative clause.)

Within this theme statement, the object, ὑμᾶς 'you(pl)', is topicalized. This is indicated in English by 'As for you' in initial position.

NOTES

1:21a As for you, although you were formerly alienated *from God* The front-shifting of ὑμᾶς 'you' is a topicalizing device, here rendered 'as for you'. The use of the present participle ὄντας 'being' and the perfect participle ἀπηλλοτριωμένους 'being alienated' emphasizes a state; ποτέ 'formerly' marks it as a former state. The passive form of the perfect participle puts out of focus any agent of the alienation. In other words, it is not stated whether it was God who alienated them because of their sin or whether they alienated themselves by their sin. But it is clear from the context that it is from God that they are alienated, not from others, such as the Jews. This is made clear in the following statements describing their state, as well as in the statement of reconciliation—

reconciliation to God being implied (see 1:20 and 1:22).

The contrastive lexical items and the use of the particle δέ in 1:22 point to the relation of contrast or concession-contraexpectation between this proposition and the main one in 1:22. Several commentators suggest the latter, and it is preferred, since there is the element of unexpectedness present, as well as contrast. It is inherently unexpected that a holy God would reconcile evil sinners to himself.

1:21b and although you were formerly hostile *to God,* The words καὶ ἐχθρούς 'and enemies' give a further description of the Colossians' former estate. Although some commentators, most notably Meyer, take the enmity as God's enmity to sinners, it is more generally argued that the two following phrases, which are in the dative case and refer to the Colossians' thinking and activities, support the sense of the Colossians' hostility to God. The other sense, it is also argued, would require διά with the accusative case, meaning 'because of', whereas the dative, both with and without ἐν, describes those aspects of their personality and behavior in which the hostility showed itself.

1:21c–d since *you* **thought** *evilly* **and since you acted evilly,** The abstract noun διάνοια 'mind' expresses the event of thinking. Here it is in the dative case, so that its semantic relationship to the attribute 'hostile' is not precisely defined. The same is true of the following phrase, 'in evil deeds'. The abstract noun ἔργοις 'deeds' expresses the event 'to act/behave', and the preposition ἐν 'in' that governs it can signal a number of different relations.

Along with the problem of semantic relation there is also the question of which of these two modifying phrases relates to which of the two nucleus statements. Most commentators appear to regard both of the modifying phrases as descriptive of both of the two main phrases. This approach is reflected in the display: 21a and 21b are equally ranked, and 21c and 21d equally support both 21a and 21b.

Beekman saw four possible semantic relations here: reason, grounds, circumstance, and specific. The first would mean they were alienated from God and hostile to him *because of* their thinking and evil deeds. This is rejected by the commentators; they suggest that 'because of' would have to be expressed explicitly by a preposition. The second would mean that *the evidence for* the statements that they were alienated and hostile was to be found in their thinking and evil deeds. The third would mean that at the same time as being alienated and hostile *they were also* evil in thinking and deed (but this seems to make the semantic link too weak for the lexical items being used). The last would mean that their general alienation and hostility were shown *specifically* in evil thinking and deeds. All of these relations make acceptable sense here, and it is difficult to suggest any clear arguments for and against. Like Beekman, I prefer the relation of evidential grounds here. Alienation and hostility can be regarded as theological statements of their (wrong) relation to God; the evidential proof of this wrong relation was to be found in their former way of thinking and outward behavior. This also contrasts well with what Paul goes on to say about the evidence that should demonstrate the reality of their new reconciled state in 1:22.

An alternative analysis is to assume a chiastic structure here, so that evil deeds are the evidence for the alienation, and evil thinking for the hostility. This would be propositionalized as follows:

(21a) Although you were formerly alienated *from God*
    (21d) since you acted/behaved evilly [grounds for 21a]
(21b) and although you were formerly hostile *to God*
    (21c) since you thought *evilly* [grounds for 21b]

1:22a nevertheless, God *our(inc) Father* **has now reconciled you** *to himself.* The major issue here is textual. Is the best text the active form ἀποκατήλλαξεν 'he reconciled' or the passive form ἀποκατηλλάγητε 'you were reconciled'? (The latter occurs as a participle in some of the manuscripts, but this gives rise to a very elaborate syntax which seems much less satisfactory than either ἀποκατήλλαξεν or ἀποκατηλλάγητε.)

The arguments can be summarized as follows:
1. Both readings have good support, though the active is generally better supported. Metzger (p. 622–23) says of the active that "the reading ἀποκατήλλαξεν is well supported" and it has "the preponderance of external testimony." Of the passive he says "attested by diversified and early witnesses."
2. If the active form is original, then it is difficult to see how the passive would have arisen since it involves introducing a grammatical clash,

whereas the active could have been substituted for the passive to give better syntax.
3. If the active form is original, then there is a minor grammatical problem in that one half of the (formal) contrast is in participial form, the other in finite form. But since the same mismatch of the two halves of a contrast is found in 1:26, this need not be seen as a great problem. On the other hand, if the passive is original, there is a marked grammatical clash: the opening words, καὶ ὑμᾶς 'and you', are accusative and would normally be expected to be the object of the following main verb. (This type of construction is found later in 2:13.) If, however, the main verb is passive, then 'you' would be the subject of that verb and would be in the nominative case: καὶ ὑμεῖς 'and you'. Hence, if the passive is original, there is a marked mismatch of case, and it has to be assumed that Paul (a native speaker!) made a mistake.
4. The infinitive that follows the main verb is παραστῆσαι 'to present'; it is followed by its own object phrase, ὑμᾶς ἁγίους καί . . . 'you holy and' (meaning 'to present you holy and . . . '). If the original is passive, then there is a switch to a new subject for the infinitive, unless it is taken to mean 'in order that you present yourselves', which seems rather far-fetched.
5. The verb 'to reconcile' was used in 1:20, with 'God the Father' as the subject and τὰ πάντα 'all things' as the object. Because καὶ ὑμᾶς 'and you' is in the same (accusative) case and is linked by καί 'and', it is most naturally considered to be a subgroup of the referents of τὰ πάντα. If this is so, then it seems more likely that the active form of the verb would be used in 1:22, just as it was in 1:20. Against this is the possibility that Paul, having focused on 'you' with the opening words, went on to maintain this focus by using a passive verb. But this is much less likely in Greek than it appears in English because of the different cases involved.

The commentators are more or less evenly divided on this question. It is point 2 that persuades those who favor the passive—the apparent impossibility of seeing how a passive variant could ever have arisen. However, if the passive was original, then Paul certainly produced a marked grammatical clash. On the whole, it seems more likely that a scribe introduced the grammatical clash than that Paul did. The arguments in favor or the active form seem much better, so that is the basis for the rendering in the display.

With the active form, the question arises as to what the subject is. Since the verb is a repeat of the same verb in 1:20, and since 'God the Father' was the subject there, it is taken to be the subject here also. No change of subject has been signaled. (That the subject is 'God the Father' probably explains why there is no reference to what or whom the Colossians are alienated from. This is explicitly stated in the only other two uses of this verb, in Eph. 2:12 and 4:18.)

1:22b *He did this [1:22a]* **by means of his Son's dying physically.** As in 1:20, the means by which reconciliation was achieved is said to be the death of the Son. It is very widely argued that the phrase τῆς σαρκὸς αὐτοῦ 'of the flesh of him' is added to give prominence to its being a *physical* death, an actual bodily death. It is thought that Paul stressed this point in opposition to the emphasis that the false teaching gave to angelic intermediaries. (Docetism, a heresy that denied the reality of Christ's body, is considered not to have arisen until after this time.) In effect, Paul is saying that since the angels do not have bodies and die, they cannot contribute to reconciliation.

1:22c–d *He did this [1:22a]* **in order that you should be completely holy when he brings you into his presence,** The aorist infinitive παραστῆσαι 'to present' is widely considered to express the purpose of the reconciliation mentioned in 1:22a. (A result relation is excluded by the following 'if' statements.) Beekman, however, raised this question: Is the purpose the presentation in God's presence as such, or the state ('holy, blameless, and irreproachable') in which the Colossians would be at the time of that presentation? Beekman took the latter view, which makes good sense in the context. Previously, the Colossians were both alienated and evil in practice; now they are reconciled and are to become holy in practice. Moreover, their state, being highlighted by this threefold statement, is considered prominent. Hence, it is their state of holiness that is deemed to be the purpose; the presentation is the *time* when that purpose will be fulfilled. (The presentation is generally regarded as taking place at the Lord's return, which is implicit here.)

There is no essential distinction between the three terms: ἁγίους 'holy' states the concept positively; ἀμώμους 'blameless' and ἀνεγκλήτους 'irreproachable' are a double negation. In other words, the positive term is followed by two negated antonyms forming a doublet. (Moore, p. 25, classifies 'blameless' and 'irreproachable' here as a synonymous doublet.) Thus there is only one strongly emphasized concept, 'holy'. It is rendered 'completely holy' in the display, although in translating, of course, the appropriate receptor language intensification devices should be used.

Finally, the subject of the infinitive παραστῆσαι 'to present' and the referent of αὐτοῦ 'his' need to be decided. Elsewhere in the New Testament, it is Paul that presents (2 Cor. 11:2; Col. 1:28), God the Father that presents (2 Cor. 4:14), or Christ that presents (Eph. 5:27). Here, 'the Father' would be the expected subject, since a dependent infinitive generally has the same subject as the verb to which it is related unless a change of subject is signaled. On the other hand, the last personal pronoun preceding the infinitive refers to the Son, and it would be quite natural for 'the Son' to be the subject of the infinitive. Therefore, from a grammatical point of view, *either* 'God the Father' or 'God the Son' could be the subject. In Eph. 5:27, Christ as presenter is in the special context of the husband-wife figure, which figure is absent from this context; so, while either is possible here, 'God the Father' is considered to be more likely. This is supported by the occurrences of κατενώπιον αὐτοῦ 'before him' elsewhere in the New Testament (2 Cor. 2:17; 12:19; Eph. 1:4; Jude 24), which are best interpreted as meaning 'before the Father' in each case. Hence, the subject of the verb παραστῆσαι 'to present' and the referent of αὐτοῦ are both taken to be the Father.

For κατενώπιον 'before' Robertson (1919: 644) has "in the presence of." Barclay renders the combination 'presented . . . before' as "brought you unto his own presence." This is probably the best way to express it in English and is used for the display.

1:23a provided that you continue to believe *the gospel;* There is a question here as to the force of the particle γέ in the clause εἴ γε ἐπιμένετε τῇ πίστει 'if you remain in the faith'. The verb that follows it is in the present indicative, so the condition is "thought of as real" (Arndt and Gingrich, εἰ, 1.a); that is, Paul is not expressing doubts about the Colossians' perseverance but rather stating a necessary condition for the purpose to be fulfilled. It may be that the particle γέ draws attention to this "necessary" aspect. According to Beekman "the emphasis falls . . . on the need of steadfast continuance in the future." NEB and TEV use "must." Certainly a simple 'if' does not convey this sense in English; the best equivalent in English may be "provided that" (RSV).

There is a mismatch in this clause between the surface form and the meaning. The finite verb ἐπιμένετε 'you remain' expresses an attribute, continuation; and the abstract noun πίστει 'faith' expresses an event, to believe. Probably the mismatch is a Greek device for giving prominence to the attribute.

As to what previous statement this condition is attached to, the choice is between the nuclear statement of the paragraph (22a), 'God has now reconciled you', and the purpose (22c), 'in order that you should be completely holy'. Clearly it should be related to the purpose. Reconciliation with God is not dependent on perseverance or stability on the part of Christians—it is received by faith. Holiness, on the other hand, is closely connected with steadfast continuance—abandoning hope and stability will bring about declension in holiness. (Hollenbach n.d., however, takes these conditions as subordinate to the nuclear statement, not to the purpose.) Meyer, Alford, and Hendriksen, and also Wilbur Pickering in his thesis (1977a), support the linking of the conditions with the purpose. Could there be an ordering of relations here, so that purpose closes those related directly to the theme (see the note on 1:18g)? If that is so, the conditions would have to relate to some statement subsequent to the theme.

There is some debate as to whether πίστει 'faith' refers to the event of believing or the content of what is believed. But since the context requires the event of believing, the choice is really between believing in the Lord Jesus and believing the gospel. The latter is given preference since the gospel is referred to explicitly later in this verse.

1:23b *specifically*, provided that you continue to be stable The terms θεμελιόω 'establish' and ἑδραῖος 'firm' are regarded as dead figures taken from the semantic domain of building. Arndt and Gingrich give a quotation from the first century B.C. in which θεμελιόω 'establish' is used figuratively; ἑδραῖος 'firm' was used of people long before that. The two terms are regarded as a doublet used to emphasize the concept of stability (Moore, p. 25, regards them as a "near synonymous doublet.") The concept is further emphasized by the negated antonym in the next proposition.

The question also arises as to how this proposition (and the following one) relates to 1:23a. Beekman took the relation to be a generic-specific, stability being a specific aspect of continuing to believe the gospel. This is a good analysis, since remaining stable is one aspect of continuing to believe and holding to the hope of the gospel is another aspect, hope being one of the central truths of the gospel.

1:23c-e and you continue to confidently expect that which you heard about *when you heard* the gospel, The use of μετακινέω 'to move away' is another dead figure—it seems to have been used in this way for some centuries. In combination with the negative it is synonymous with the concept of continuing; in other words, it is a litotes, a double negative used to draw attention to the positive.

The word 'hope' in the phrase τῆς ἐλπίδος τοῦ εὐαγγελίου 'the hope of the gospel' expresses an event. It is best rendered in English by 'confidently expect' rather than by 'hope', the modern sense of which most often implies uncertainty. In semantic terminology 'gospel' is a "thing," the content of the (apostolic) preaching. The connection between the two concepts, spelled out, is: 'continue to look forward to that which you heard about when you heard the gospel'. At the time that the gospel had been proclaimed to them, they had heard, as part of that gospel, about the future hope. (There is a very similar statement in 1:5.)

1:23f *since* this gospel has been proclaimed *to people* in very many places, The Greek is τοῦ κηρυχθέντος ἐν πάσῃ κτίσει τῇ ὑπὸ τὸν οὐρανόν 'having been proclaimed in all creation under the sky/heaven'. That this is hyperbole—an overstatement for the purpose of giving prominence to the nonhyperbolic concept— is generally agreed upon (cf. 1:6b for a very similar hyperbolic statement). It is also generally agreed that Paul is emphasizing the universality of the proclamation of the gospel as an encouragement to the Colossians not to abandon such a widely and publicly known message for a local heresy. Thus the semantic relation is not that of comment, but rather grounds supporting the condition. The particular subtype of grounds would be encouragement, possibly motivation.

There is some difference of opinion as to what ἐν signifies. In most versions 'proclaimed in' is considered equivalent to 'proclaimed to'. That is, they regard it (apparently) as a metonymy, the place where people are found being used for the people who are found there. It seems simpler to take ἐν as indicating location, 'people' (those to whom the proclamation is made) being implicit. The phrase πάσῃ κτίσει τῇ ὑπὸ τὸν οὐρανόν 'all creation under heaven' is simply an emphatic way of referring to this world.

The passive form is retained in the display to keep 'the gospel' in focus and the agents of the proclamation out of focus. If it has to be translated with the agents expressed, then it should be expressed in as generic a way as possible.

1:23g-h *and since* I, Paul, have become one who makes it known *to people*. This statement anticipates the theme of the next paragraph, the topic of which is Paul's ministry. However, some of the commentators suggest that it is also a further grounds for warning the Colossians not to abandon the gospel. Paul is backing up his warning with his own authority as one appointed to preach the gospel, hence, the emphatic 'I, Paul'. Consequently, in the display, the semantic relation is given as grounds, there being two conjoined grounds.

The use of 'I became', as opposed to 'I am', is probably intended to give prominence to the event of Paul's becoming an apostle, but at the same time, it divert attention from how, by whom, etc. It is the reciprocal of 'God appointed me'.

The meaning of the genitive construction οὗ . . . διάκονος 'a servant of which (the gospel)' is apparently 'to be active on behalf of the gospel'; that is to say, Paul was working to proclaim the gospel. In 1:25 the almost identical statement is followed by 'to fulfill the message of God, the mystery' where 'fulfill' probably covers the ideas of spreading widely and teaching the full contents of. The expression here, in 1:23, however, is generic. An adequate rendering is difficult to find, since it must be a generic concept that collocates with 'the gospel' and yet does not personify the gospel. A general expression, 'who makes the gospel known', has been used in the display.

DIVISION CONSTITUENT 1:24–2:5 (Section: Nucleus₂ of 1:13–2:5)

THEME: I, Paul, am exerting myself very greatly on your behalf in order that you might truly know the secret-message about Christ, in order that no one might delude you.

RELATIONAL STRUCTURE	CONTENTS
generic	1:24–29 I am completing that which Christ appointed, that I should suffer physically for the benefit of the church. And I proclaim the secret-message about Christ to every class of persons.
SPECIFIC	2:1–5 In particular, I am exerting myself very greatly on your behalf in order that you might truly know the secret-message about Christ, in order that no one might delude you.

BOUNDARIES AND COHERENCE

The principle evidence for the opening boundary of the 1:24–2:5 section has already been discussed in connection with 1:13–23. That evidence consists of the tail-head link of 1:23 with 1:24–25 and the shift of participants from 'God the Father' and 'you' to 'I' and 'you'.

The closing boundary of the 1:24–2:5 section coincides with the end of the 1:13–2:5 division. In addition to the evidence presented in the discussion of the closing boundary of 1:13–2:5 (primarily change of genre from expository to hortatory), there is the cessation of 'I' references at 2:5.

Referential coherence is shown by the following:

1. Paul's references to himself as agent and affectant throughout 1:24–2:5. Half of the eighteen finite verbs in this section have 'I' as subject, and there are also five uses of the free first person singular pronoun. The whole section is strongly 'I' oriented.
2. References to μυστήριον 'secret-message'. This term is introduced in 1:25, described in 1:26 and 27, and is referred to again in 2:2. Other than these occurrences, μυστήριον is absent except for one other occurrence in 4:3; in other words, all the references to μυστήριον in the primary matters of the body are in 1:24–2:5. Associated with μυστήριον are related lexical items such as 'hidden' (1:26; 2:3); a group of 'knowledge' words (γνωρίζω 'to make known' in 1:27, and in 2:2–3 γνῶσις 'knowledge', ἐπίγνωσις 'full knowledge', σοφία 'wisdom', and σύνεσις 'insight'); 'wealth/riches' (1:27; 2:2); and 'treasures' (2:3). Also associated with μυστήριον are explicit references to Christ (1:27; 2:2).
3. References to the Colossians, but never in an agent role. This contrasts with both the preceding and following sections.

PROMINENCE AND THEME

First, the semantic relation between the two constituent paragraphs (1:24–29 and 2:1–5) needs to be determined. It should be noted that in 1:24–29, Paul slides from 'you'-oriented statements to more general statements without reference to 'you'. (This is not reflected in the theme statement.) Thus, in 1:24, he speaks of his sufferings both for the Colossians and for the whole church; and in 1:25–27, after again speaking of the spiritual stewardship he had been given for the Colossians, he goes on to speak of the 'mystery', the secret-message, as being revealed to the saints and having to do with the Gentile nations. Then in 1:28–29 there are no references to 'you' at all, but only 'everyone' (πάντα ἄνθρωπον 'all mankind, every human being'). This, together with the 'you' orientation in 2:1–5 and the absence of universal references, points to the conclusion that what is in the forefront of Paul's mind in 1:24–29 is his God-given universal ministry (of which his ministry to the Colossians is therefore a part), whereas in 2:1–5 he is concerned with his ministry to the Colossians (and two nearby churches).

Further, the conjunction γάρ 'for' in the first sentence of 2:1–5 could be understood as meaning that the universal statements of 1:24–29 are paving the way for the 'you'-oriented statements in 2:1–5. Some commentators (e.g., Alford) suggest that 2:1–5 "exemplifies"; similarly, Abbott says that "the general statement κοπιῶ ἀγωνιζόμενος ['I toil struggling'] is supported by this special instance of his anxiety for the Colossian church." Even if γάρ does refer back only to 1:29, where Paul uses the verb ἀγωνίζομαι 'to struggle' in connection with his universal ministry (in 2:1 he uses the cognate noun ἀγών 'struggle'), it is still linking the specific 'you' back to the universal 'all'.

It is concluded, then, that the best choice for the relation between these two paragraphs is that of generic-specific. But the next question is which of the two is the more prominent. Two considerations favor the specific as the more important of the two:

1. When a generic statement is followed by a single specific statement, or a generic paragraph by a specific paragraph, it is the (single) specific that is the more prominent; the generic, as it were, provides a sort of introduction, or background, for the specific.
2. In Col. 1:24–2:5 the two constituent paragraphs are in a letter, not a theological tract or treatise. Hence, it is considered situationally (i.e., pragmatically) appropriate for the 'you'-oriented material to be what is prominent, rather than the more general material. Paul's statements about his general ministry he probably saw as necessary when writing to a church to whom he had not ministered personally. He no doubt intended them simply to provide the prelude to what he had to say about his ministry to the letter's readers/hearers.

The theme, then, of this section is the same as the theme of the 2:1–5 paragraph. However, it is probably worth raising the question as to whether the reference to Paul's suffering in 1:24 should be considered thematic for the section as a whole. I am inclined to say probably not, since the event 'exerting myself' (ἀγών) in 2:1 seems unlikely to refer to suffering, but rather such active ministries as proclaiming the message, praying, and writing letters.

SECTION CONSTITUENT 1:24–29 (Paragraph: Generic of 2:1–5)

THEME: I am completing that which Christ appointed, that I should suffer physically for the benefit of the church. And I proclaim the secret-message about Christ to every class of persons.

RELATIONAL STRUCTURE	CONTENTS
NUCLEUS₁ — CONTENT — orienter (attitudinal)	1:24a At the present time I am rejoicing
NUCLEUS — contraction	1:24b that I am suffering for your benefit;
NUCLEUS	1:24c that is, I am completing that which Christ *appointed* that I should suffer physically for the benefit of the church, which is *like* Christ's body.
NUCLEUS₂ — NUCLEUS — means — RESULT	1:25a I myself became one who serves the church,
reason	1:25b because I was appointed by God to be responsible toward you *who are Gentiles*.
NUCLEUS	1:25c *I became one who serves the church* in order that I should make known *to you Gentiles* the whole message from/about God.
description of 'message' — generic — NUCLEUS — contraction — NUCLEUS	1:26a *This message from/about God is* a secret-message;
contrast	1:26b that is, it was concealed *by God* from the people *who lived in all* the *previous* ages
NUCLEUS	1:26c but it has now been revealed *by God* to his people.
generic — NUCLEUS	1:27a-b *That is*, God chose to make known to them (27b) that this secret-message *declares that* the Gentiles *will be* very greatly blessed *by God*.
SPECIFIC — REASON	1:27c *Specifically, this secret-message declares that* Christ *will* live in you *who are Gentiles*
result	1:27d *with the result that you* confidently expect that *you will be* glorified.
NUCLEUS₃ — MEANS — GENERIC	1:28a We(exc)/I proclaim *the message about* Christ *to every class of persons*;
specific	1:28b-c *specifically*, we(exc)/I admonish every class of persons, (28c) and *specifically*, we(exc)/I teach every class of persons very wisely.
purpose	1:28d-e *We(exc) do this* [1:28a-c] in order that every person who is united to Christ may be perfect (28e) *when* we(exc)/I present them *to God/Christ*.
NUCLEUS₄ — MEANS — purpose	1:29a In order that *I might achieve* this [1:28],
NUCLEUS — contraction	1:29b I am also working hard;
NUCLEUS	1:29c-d that is, I am exerting myself (29d) *by* means of Christ's empowering me very greatly.

SECTION CONSTITUENT 1:24-29

BOUNDARIES AND COHERENCE

The beginning of the 1:24-29 paragraph has already been mentioned in connection with section 1:13-23. Further evidence for 1:24 as the initial boundary as well as the evidence for 1:29 as the closing boundary of a semantic paragraph is as follows:

1. *The presence of a sandwich structure*. The subject of the finite verbs in 1:24 is 'I' and the verbs are in the present tense: 'I am rejoicing' and 'I am completing'. In 1:29, the same is true, 'I am working hard'. This is not true of any other verse.
2. *Parallelism*. Verses 1:24 and 2:1 are also parallel—they are both first person singular orienters (1:24, 'I am rejoicing'; 2:1, 'I want'). The latter marks the start of a new semantic unit.

Like the preceding paragraphs, 1:24-29 consists of one long sentence in Greek. It is held together by no less than seven relative clauses together with an article and participle clause and two appositives.

Semantically, however, the coherence is less obvious. The paragraph deals with four topics in the following order: 'my sufferings' (1:24); 'my stewardship' (1:25-27); 'our(exc) proclaiming' (1:28); 'my striving' (1:29). Note that 'our(exc)' of 1:28 is equivalent semantically to 'I + others, but not you', making it clear that the topic of most of the paragraph is Paul's ministry. It is this that gives unity to the paragraph. In addition, there are a number of references to the fact that Paul's ministry has to do with the whole church, not just his fellow-Jews: he suffers for the church (1:24), he is a servant of the church (1:25), the message he proclaims is for God's saints (1:26), for the Gentiles (1:27), and his speaking ministry is to everyone (repeated three times in 1:28). The emphasis on the universality of his message is absent from the following paragraph, which is again 'you' oriented.

The relational structure of 1:24-29 is particularly difficult to establish because the surface forms are very largely relative clauses. There are seventeen clauses altogether, but only four conjunctions linking any of them: three instances of καί 'and' and one of ἵνα 'in order to'. The relations between propositions and clusters of propositions that I propose are seen in the above display and are discussed in the following notes.

PROMINENCE AND THEME

As has already been pointed out, the boundaries of this paragraph have been determined based partly on the contrast between what is said about Paul's ministry in these verses and what he goes on to say in 2:1-5. Because of this contrast, it is concluded that what is prominent are Paul's statements concerning the universality of his ministry (even though there are 'you'-oriented statements in 1:24-29).

The paragraph consists of four constituents, each (except the first) being introduced by a relative clause in which the relative pronoun is not the subject of the following verb. These constituents are 1:24, 1:25-27, 1:28, and 1:29. In each constituent except the second, the verb tense in the main proposition is the present tense. (The tense in the second is aorist.) Further, the contents of the second and third constituents are very similar, relating to Paul's speaking ministry. If the main propositions in the second and third constituents are combined, they yield the joint main proposition 'I proclaim the secret-message about Christ to every class of person'.

Are there any grounds for considering that one of the three main propositions is more prominent than the others? The three main propositions are:

I am completing that which Christ *appointed* that I should suffer physically for the benefit of the church

I proclaim the secret-message about Christ to every class of person

I am exerting myself in order that I might achieve this (the second main proposition)

It can be seen that the third main proposition is a means to the end of the second one; that is, Paul is exerting himself in order to proclaim this message to every class and condition of person. Hence, the third main proposition can be considered to be supporting the second one. However, there seems to be no reason for considering either of the first two main propositions more important than the other. Hence, the theme consists of these two statements in the relation of conjoining.

NOTES

1:24a At the present time I am rejoicing It is widely agreed that νῦν refers to the present time and is not used in an inferential sense; in fact, there is considerable doubt as to whether νῦν, on its own as here (i.e., without a preceding καί 'and'), has any other meaning than present time. Its use is generally seen as stressing Paul's present experience as compared with his past experience (just mentioned) of becoming a minister, and as tying in with his being a prisoner at the time of writing, actually undergoing suffering. Based on this interpretation of νῦν, the verb χαίρω 'I am rejoicing' is rendered as present continuous. Paul was rejoicing even as he wrote. The proposition serves as an attitudinal orienter to what follows.

1:24b that I am suffering for your benefit; The abstract noun παθήμασιν 'sufferings' represents the event 'to suffer'. The article τοῖς indicates both that the sufferings were Paul's own and that the Colossians knew about that. In other words, Paul is not informing them of his sufferings, but of his attitude ('I rejoice') and why his sufferings are spiritually worthwhile (see the next proposition). Thus, 'I am suffering', the topic of 1:24, is known information to the readers but new information in the discourse.

The sense of ὑπέρ is widely given as 'on behalf of', but in this context the more specific sense 'for the benefit of' is preferable (cf. Meyer) and has been so rendered here (i.e., 'you' has the role of beneficiary). If the translator cannot handle it in this way, it may be expressed in an expanded form such as 'I am rejoicing that I am suffering because I know that the fact that I am suffering will benefit you *spiritually*'.

1:24c that is, I am completing that which Christ *appointed* that I should suffer physically for the benefit of the church, which is *like* Christ's body. Commentators discuss this clause at considerable length in view of the problems:

1. What does the genitive phrase τῶν θλίψεων τοῦ Χριστοῦ 'the afflictions of Christ' mean?
2. In what sense could these afflictions be said to be ὑστερήματα 'lacking'?
3. What does the verb ἀνταναπληρόω mean? (Both ἀνα-πληρόω and προς-ανα-πληρόω are found in the New Testament collocated with ὑστερήματα, but the compound ἀντ(ι)-ανα-πληρόω is not found elsewhere in the New Testament, nor in the Septuagint.)

The first two questions are the most important ones, and they affect one another closely. In particular, 'the afflictions of Christ' has to be understood in a way that the concept of 'lacking something' can be applied to it. In addition to the restriction on the possible range of meanings that this collocation imposes, it is noted by the commentaries that the noun θλῖψις 'affliction' is never used of Christ elsewhere in the New Testament, though the noun πάθημα 'sufferings' is. It is also pointed out that θλῖψις linked with a genitive noun referring to a person always has the meaning of the affliction undergone by that person, rather than the affliction he brings upon others, a meaning possible in other collocations of the noun.

The various interpretations of this central genitive construction are well stated by Abbott. They can be summarized as follows:

1. The word 'afflictions' does not refer to Christ's vicarious sufferings, but to his exemplary sufferings. The weakness of this interpretation is that while it is true that Christ's attitudes and responses to suffering are held up as examples to us, the distinction is not supported elsewhere in Scripture. And even if it were, in what *sense* are his sufferings lacking? As Abbott says: "His work, including His sufferings, was absolutely complete."

2. The word 'afflictions' refers not to Christ's own personal sufferings while on earth, but to the sufferings of his body, the church, which are spoken of as his own because he really feels them—he suffers in his people's sufferings. Those who hold this view cite Acts 9:4 'Saul, Saul, why are you persecuting me?' Again, Abbott is well worth quoting: "The idea that the glorified Christ continues to suffer . . . is inconsistent with the scriptural representations of His exalted state. It is true that He sympathises with the afflictions of His people; but sympathy is not affliction. . . ." In addition, it is not at all clear that the church is ever referred to as Christ—Israel, yes, but not Christ.

3. The word 'afflictions' refers to Paul's own sufferings. Those who hold this view recognize that θλῖψις is never used of Christ, but often of Paul and Christians in general. Further, Paul's sufferings have just been mentioned in the

previous clause and no change of topic has been signaled. Also, later in the same clause, Paul uses the phrase 'in my flesh', referring to his physical sufferings.

So, there is strong contextual pressure to understand Paul to be referring to his own afflictions. Why, then, does he refer to them as 'the afflictions of Christ'? Abbott takes it to mean "the type of all those [afflictions] that are endured by His followers on behalf of the church," but this seems to require too much implicit information.

What other possibilities are there? In Matt. 20:23 the Lord says to two of his apostles, 'You will drink my cup'. In the context, this means, 'You will suffer as I am going to suffer'. If this thought is behind 'afflictions of Christ', the meaning would be 'sufferings like those Christ suffered' or, more literally, 'afflictions like those Christ underwent', the genitive construction linking the two parts of a comparison.

A third alternative is to take the genitive phrase here as parallel with 'a prisoner of Christ Jesus' in Philem. 1 and 9 (a prisoner because he serves Christ). This would give 'my afflictions because I serve Christ', which makes good contextual sense in a paragraph that deals with different aspects of Paul's apostolic ministry.

A fourth alternative is similar to the third. When Paul was converted, Ananias was instructed to tell him on behalf of the Lord, 'I will show him how much he must suffer for the sake of my name' (Acts 9:16). Extensive suffering was appointed to Paul, who himself had caused so much suffering to the church. (Note, too, the use of δεῖ 'must' in Acts 9:16.)

As to the sense of Paul's afflictions' lacking anything, Caird says, "It is almost as if he is thinking of a fixed quota of suffering to be endured." This is probably how it is to be understood. Not only did Paul know that he would suffer much affliction, but he knew that his sufferings were not yet over. (There may be the implication that they would be completed by his death as a martyr.)

This brings us to the question of the meaning of ἀνταναπληρόω. The simpler form ἀναπληρόω, when used with τὸ ὑστέρημα 'what is lacking' (1 Cor. 16:17; Phil. 2:30), has the sense of 'meeting the deficiency, fulfilling the lack, making up for some lack'. What, then, does ἀντι- contribute to the meaning? As a preposition compounded with a verb ἀντι- has three meanings: 'instead of'; 'opposed to'; and 'corresponding to'. It is the third of these that is most widely suggested as appropriate here; that is, Paul's sufferings matched up with the lack that remained. Abbott also says that "it is not, perhaps, an over-refinement to suggest that ἀνταναπληρόω is more unassuming than ἀναπληρόω, since part of the force of the word is thrown on the idea of correspondence." In other words, Paul is avoiding giving the impression that he was boasting. There was no superfluity in his sufferings.

The phrase ἐν τῇ σαρκί μου 'in my flesh' refers to Paul's affliction as physical ones. He mentions such sufferings in 2 Cor. 11:23-27, for example.

The phrase ὑπὲρ τοῦ σώματος αὐτοῦ 'on behalf of his body' identifies those who benefited from Paul's sufferings—the 'his' of 'his body' refers back to 'Christ'. (Whatever profit Paul himself derived from his sufferings is not in focus here.) It is the Colossians who in 1:24b were said to have benefited—now Paul extends the benefit to the whole church.

These various considerations give rise to the complex proposition 'I am completing that which Christ *appointed* that I should suffer physically for the benefit of the church'. Notice that in English 'afflict' is not used, but only the reciprocal 'suffer'. Also, the verb 'appointed' is supplied, in view of the original statement in Acts 9:16 where the modal 'must' (δεῖ) is used. (This rendering is based on the fourth interpretation.)

If the second interpretation is followed, it would give a rendering such as 'I am completing that which I am suffering, which resembles how Christ suffered, for the benefit of the church'. If the third interpretation is followed, it would give 'I am completing that which I am suffering because I am serving Christ, for the benefit of the church'.

Note that the nonfigurative term 'church' is used first instead of 'body', then the clarifying comparison in which 'like' is supplied: 'which is *like* Christ's body'. This is the reverse of the order in the Greek.

One question remains to be answered. What is the semantic relation between 1:24c and propositions 1:24a and b? Formally, they are connected by καί 'and'. However, a relation of simple addition to 1:24a–b seems unlikely since the content of 1:24c is very closely linked to that of 1:24b—they both deal with Paul's sufferings on behalf of others. The similarity between 1:24b and c in content would indicate the relation of either specific–generic or contraction–amplification. While 'for his body' is more generic than 'for you', basically 1:24c is adding further detail to 1:24b—the sufferings are physical, they are appointed by Christ, they are being completed, they are for the whole church. Hence, contraction-amplification seems the most appropriate relationship; this being the case, καί here is what the grammars call "epexegetical"; its function is to explain, clarify. It has already been argued that proposition 1:24c is more prominent in this paragraph, since it has the statement of the "universal" benefit of Paul's sufferings. This goes along with the general tendency found in Colossians that when two propositions are in the relation of contraction-amplification, it is the amplification that is prominent.

1:25a I myself became one who serves the church, Verse 25's opening pronoun, ἧς 'of which', refers back to the church—Paul is saying, 'I became a servant of the church'. This statement is very similar to that which underlies propositions 1:23g and h in the preceding paragraph. The use of the free pronoun ἐγώ 'I' draws attention to the fact that Paul himself had been appointed to serve the church, and hence, in particular, the Colossian believers. The term διάκονος 'servant' focuses on the activity of serving in contrast with δοῦλος 'slave' (used in 1:7), which focuses on a role relation with a master of some sort.

1:25b because I was appointed by God to be responsible toward you *who are Gentiles*. The word οἰκονομία 'stewardship' may refer to the role of administrator or supervisor, or it may be an abstract noun referring to the event of administrating or supervising, as the head steward in a large household would do. The latter sense is contextually preferable since the whole paragraph is about Paul's activities (suffering, proclaiming, toiling, etc.). However, the εἰς ὑμᾶς 'unto/toward you' at the end of this clause suggests that Paul is not so much saying that he is actively supervising the Colossians, as that he is engaged in an activity or role which has them as his goal or destination in the case-role sense (cf. Rom. 15:16, where he uses εἰς τὰ ἔθνη 'unto/toward the Gentiles'). This idea seems best expressed by taking οἰκονομία as an abstract noun representing the attribute 'responsible' associated with such tasks as administrating or supervising. What Paul is saying is that he is responsible for the Colossians—this is reflected in the rendering in the display. Underlying this statement is his consciousness of being the apostle to the Gentiles, which included the Colossians, a predominantly Gentile church. Thus 'you' carries the implication, understood by both writer and readers, 'you who are Gentiles'.

The genitive phrase τὴν οἰκονομίαν τοῦ θεοῦ 'stewardship of God' means that God was the source of the stewardship, and this is made explicit in the following participle δοθεῖσαν 'given'. The propositionalization of this statement is 'I was appointed by God to be responsible toward you(pl)'.

It is often difficult, when the preposition κατά is followed by the accusative case, to determine the semantic relation of the information that follows it to that which precedes it. The commonest uses of κατά are (1) comparison and (2) reason/grounds. In this epistle, examples of sense 1 are found in 1:11 and 3:10; examples of sense 2 in 2:8 and 2:22. In this context, sense 2 is the most appropriate. Paul's role as servant of the church was traceable to (=κατά) God's giving him this role. Hence, 1:25b is the reason for 1:25a.

1:25c *I became one who serves the church* in order that I should make known *to you Gentiles* the whole message from/about God. The main question here is the meaning of the verb πληρόω, which occurs here as the aorist active infinitive πληρῶσαι 'to complete, fulfill'. Specifically, what is the meaning of 'to complete the message of God'? (The only close parallel is in Rom. 15:19, where the same verb is used with 'the gospel of Christ' as its object.) There are two possibilities: πληρῶσαι, representing the attribute 'full', modifies either the message ('the whole message') or the proclamation of the message (meaning that the message was to be proclaimed fully, i.e., everywhere or to everyone). Both in Rom. 15:19 and here, either sense fits the context, and some commentators suggest both. But my preference is to take πληρόω as modifying the message ('make known the whole message') since Paul goes on immediately to describe the message in some detail.

The genitive phrase τὸν λόγον τοῦ θεοῦ 'the message of God' can mean either 'the message which has come from God' or 'the message which speaks about God'. Either is appropriate here, but since vv. 26 and 27 go on to describe how God has now revealed his purposes, especially for the

Gentiles, the first alternative is considered to be the more appropriate contextually. But both are given in the display, as both are acceptable.

Grammatically, it is possible for the infinitive πληρῶσαι ('to proclaim fully' in the sense of making known the whole message) to be attached either to the verb ἐγενόμην 'I became' or to the participle δοθεῖσαν 'given'. According to Hollenbach (n.d.), the infinitive should not be subordinate to a nominal phrase, in this case the κατά construction, so it relates back to the finite verb ἐγενόμην 'I became'. Its relation is purpose, the relation an aorist infinitive is widely considered to have.

With 1:25b the reason for 1:25a, and 1:25c its purpose, it would seem obvious that 1:25a should be the nucleus. However, in this paragraph, 1:25a is stating the topic 'my ministry' and 1:25c is a purpose commenting on the topic; therefore, 1:25c is regarded as the more prominent, as is supported by the detailed description of the message in 1:26–27 and a present tense restatement in 1:28a.

1:26a *This message from/about God is* a secret-message; This is the first time the word μυστήριον 'mystery' occurs in Colossians. It is used four times altogether: here, in 1:27, in 2:2, and in 4:3. All are agreed that when Paul uses μυστήριον (as he does twenty-one times in his letters) he is referring to truth known to God and which God has chosen to reveal to his people—as indeed 1:26 and 27 make quite clear. In other words, the equivalent of μυστήριον in modern English is, basically, 'a secret'—something known to a person, but which others know about only if it is shared. Abbott argues cogently that 'secret' was the primary meaning in Koine Greek. Hence, it is represented in the display by 'secret-message'. The idea of a mystery in the sense of something unknown which can (potentially, at least) be solved (as in detective stories) or explained (as in science) is not the meaning of μυστήριον. The translator needs to be aware that Paul is using the term in a technical Christian sense.

1:26b that is, it was concealed *by God* from the people *who lived in all* the *previous* ages This clause is seen as the first half of a contrast, the second half being introduced by the particle δέ in 1:26c. Recognizing this relationship helps resolve some of the problems of interpretation. Place the two halves together, and the contrasting concepts become clear:

(1) the one hidden (2) from the ages and (3) from the generations

(2) but now (1) has been revealed (3) to his saints

The first clause has three parts that contrast with three parts of the second clause (though in a different order). These contrasting parts are: events (hidden vs. revealed), time (the ages vs. now), and people (the former generations vs. his saints). Based on this, I interpret αἰώνων as referring to time, not to supernatural beings called "Aeons" (so Arndt and Gingrich under αἰών, 4), and I interpret γενεῶν 'generations' as referring to the people then living, not as forming a doublet with αἰώνων intended to emphasize the long period of time that passed before the mystery became known. (The repeated preposition ἀπό 'from' also speaks against considering αἰώνων and γενεῶν being a doublet.) When it refers to time, ἀπό usually means 'from the start of, since'; thus ἀπὸ τῶν γενεῶν is probably equivalent to 'ever since there were any ages', 'since the beginning of time'.

Hendriksen's comment is worth noting: "The mystery ... had been *hidden*; that is, ... it had not been historically realized. It was present, to be sure, in the *plan* of God and also in *prophecy*, but *not in actuality*." To this it could be added that God's purpose to save the Gentile nations was revealed in the Old Testament, but did not take effect till the proclamation of the gospel to the Gentiles.

1:26c but it has now been revealed *by God* to his people. As several commentators point out, there is a certain lopsidedness in the form of the 26b-c contrast. The verb form in the first part is a participle, whereas in the second part there is a finite verb. This, it is said, gives greater prominence to the second part. In any case, within the general theory of semantic relations, the positive side of the contrast has the greater natural prominence, so the second part (26c) is the more prominent of the two propositions on two counts.

1:27a *That is,* God chose to make known to them This proposition closely parallels the immediately preceding one, 26c:

26c the secret-message has now been revealed *by God* to his saints

27a God chose to make known to his saints the secret-message

In both 26c and 27a the same person (God) is undertaking the same event (reveal/make known) to the same people (his saints). All that 27a adds is that God did so of his own free choice—this is the significance of the addition of ἠθέλησεν 'he willed'. Hence, 27a is regarded as an amplified restatement of 26c.

1:27b that this secret-message *declares that* the Gentiles *will be* very greatly blessed *by God*. This clause states the content of what God chose to make known to his saints, but it is difficult to ascertain its exact meaning. The first problem here is the meaning of the genitive phrase τῆς δόξης τοῦ μυστηρίου τούτου 'the glory of this secret'. A close look at other phrases in which 'glory' is followed by a genitive noun does not reveal any obvious parallels to this one, for nowhere else does the genitive noun refer to a message or body of teaching. The reverse order is found in 'the gospel of the glory of Christ' (2 Cor. 4:4) and 'the gospel of the glory of God' (1 Tim. 1:11), but these do not really help. From the point of view of semantics there are two alternatives: either 'glory' modifies 'secret-message', with some such meaning as 'wonderful', or it modifies something else related to the secret-message. The commentators tend to take this latter approach. For example, Abbott's explanation of the 'glory of this mystery' is that "it is the glorious manifestation of God's dealings contained in this μυστήριον" (Lightfoot is similar); and Alford defines it as "the glory *of which the Gentiles are to become partakers* by the revelation of this mystery. . . . the mystery contains and reveals it as a portion of its contents." They take this approach because there do not seem to be any clear cases of 'glory' used to mean 'wonderful'. While Arndt and Gingrich give "*magnificence, splendor*, anything that catches the eye" as one of its senses, this has a physical reference.

In trying to decide what this genitive construction means, a significant contextual factor should be taken into account, namely that δόξα 'glory' occurs again later in this same verse: 'Christ in you' is said to be 'the hope of glory'. In this occurrence 'glory' is used in the eschatological sense of the future glory. While it is true that Paul can use the same word with different senses in the same context, yet an interpretation of the first use of δόξα that is obviously related to the second use should be given preference over some other unrelated interpretation. This suggests that δόξα might have a sense something like 'blessings'. Indeed, δόξα does occur in this sense in Rom. 2:7 and 10: 'Those who . . . seek for glory and honor and immortality' and 'glory and honor and peace for everyone who does good'. In these two verses 'glory' evidently refers to blessings conferred by God, along with honor, immortality, and peace. It might well have a similar sense here in Col. 1:27. Blessings conferred by God are part of the content of the secret message, and the eschatological glory referred to later in this same verse is the consummation of these blessings. Thus interpreted, the genitive phrase 'the glory of this secret' would mean 'the blessings revealed in this secret-message'.

The construction τί τὸ πλοῦτος 'what (is) the riches', which precedes 'the glory of the mystery', is in the form of an indirect exclamation, equivalent to the direct form 'how great . . . !' According to semantic theory, the exclamation form is a device used to give prominence to what is said. The phrase 'the riches (of)' draws attention to the abundance of the blessings; in other words, the τί construction represents attributes that modify the event 'to bless', intensifying the concept of greatness. In propositional form it is best rendered as 'very', thus avoiding a mismatch: 'the Gentiles *will be* very greatly blessed *by God*'.

Another problem is the prepositional phrase ἐν τοῖς ἔθνεσιν 'in the nations/Gentiles'. The sense 'Gentiles' is preferred to that of 'nations' here because the following phrase, 'Christ in you', refers to the Colossians, a particular group of Gentiles, but not a nation. Also the meaning of ἐν 'in' must be decided. There are two alternatives: '*among* the Gentiles' or '*for* (the benefit of) the Gentiles'. If δόξα is taken to mean something like blessings, then the most natural sequence following it would be 'conferred upon the Gentiles'—essentially a dative of advantage. (Turner [1963:264] implies that the senses 'among' and 'for' are often hard to distinguish when the preposition ἐν is used. Nor is there a great deal of difference in meaning in such a context as this.)

1:27c *Specifically, this secret-message declares that* Christ *will live* in you *who are Gentiles* The majority of texts have the masculine pronoun ὅς 'who' here; a minority have the neuter form, ὅ 'which'. There is no masculine form to refer back to, other than ὁ θεός 'God', which makes no sense, so if the masculine is correct, then its gender has been assimilated to the masculine noun Χριστός, a known feature of Greek grammar. The neuter pronoun would be an alternative grammatical form with the same meaning. Grammatically, there are three possible antecedents of the relative pronoun: πλοῦτος 'riches', a neuter noun; μυστήριον, another neuter noun; or the whole phrase 'the riches of the glory of this mystery'. The first is unlikely, as 'riches' is essentially an attribute relating to the head noun, μυστήριον. The second and third possibilities are equally good, but since 'the mystery' is the topic here, it is the one given the preference. According to Abbott, "the clause is not parenthetical, but carries on the description of the μυστήριον." In other words, 'Christ in you' is another way of stating the content of the 'secret-message'. Since the content of the 'secret-message' in 1:27b is expressed in a very generic way, 1:27c is considered to be a specific restatement of that content, referring to Christ and the Colossian Gentiles in particular. Thus 1:27c, a single specific attached to a generic, is regarded as more prominent than 1:27b and also as the nuclear constituent of the 1:26–27 cluster, which describes 'the message' referred to in 1:25c in considerable detail.

There is some difference of opinion as to the meaning of the preposition, whether it is '*in* you' or '*among* you'. The reason usually given for the second view is that it is to be interpreted in the same way as ἐν τοῖς ἔθνεσιν (1:27b), that is, '*among* the Gentiles'. However, the interpretation 'among the Gentiles' has not been adopted for 1:27b in the display; and, in any case, since 'Christ in you' is stated as the grounds for the hope of glory, 'in you' agrees much better with the general New Testament teaching on Christ's indwelling the believer.

Some verb needs to be supplied for the expression Χριστὸς ἐν ὑμῖν 'Christ in you'. Although 'is' is possible, either 'lives' or 'dwells' seems the best choice. This tends to give the statement a strongly physical sense, as if 'you' were a building of some sort and Christ was living there. Yet it is difficult to see how else it can be expressed without appearing to weaken the statement. At this point, the border between the literal and figurative senses of 'in' seems rather fuzzy.

1:27d *with the result that you* confidently expect *that you will be* glorified. Here δόξης 'glory' is collocated with ἐλπίς 'hope' in a genitive phrase, 'the hope of the glory'. For this reason δόξης is considered to refer to the future, "eschatological glory" (Hendriksen), "the future glory and blessedness in heaven" (Ellicott). As in 1:5 and 1:23, ἐλπίς 'hope' is translated 'confidently expect' to avoid the implications of uncertainty that the English *hope* often has. What is confidently expected is τῆς δόξης 'the glory'. The article probably indicates that it is the known glory, common knowledge among believers, though it could refer back to the earlier mention of glory. The noun 'glory' is regarded as representing an event here, hence is rendered '*you will be* glorified'.

As to the relation of this proposition to the previous one, commentators generally see 27c as the grounds for 27d—Christ's indwelling is the grounds on the basis of which we can look forward confidently to the coming glory. But in terms of the system of relations we are using, reason is the term to be preferred for this. Since the indwelling gives rise to a present expectation, 27c is the reason, and 27d the result.

1:28a We(exc)/I proclaim *the message about Christ to every class of persons;* The propositional cluster 1:28a–e is analyzed as a the third conjoined nucleus of the 1:24–29 paragraph. Within this 28a–e cluster, 1:28a is the prominent proposition, since it is supported by the others.

Paul uses 'we' here, and it is a question whether he is referring simply to himself (the editorial 'we') or also to others with himself. The use of 'I' elsewhere in this paragraph favors the view that 'we' is intended to have a plural reference. It probably refers to at least Timothy and Paul, and quite likely Epaphras also, who had preached to the Colossians. Lightfoot extends it more generally to "we preachers" and certainly what is said is very generally applicable. Alternatively, it could refer to "we apostles," perhaps with an implicit contrast (hence the use of the free pronoun ἡμεῖς) to whoever was attempting to mislead the Colossians with false teaching. However, it is possible that Paul is simply referring to himself by 'we' as he appears to do later (in 4:3). Consequently, 'I' is given as an alternative in the display, but 'we(exc)' is the preferred interpretation.

It is a little difficult to know how best to express ὃν ... καταγγέλλομεν 'whom ... we proclaim' in English. The word καταγγέλλω 'to proclaim' is used only by Luke (in Acts) and by Paul in some of his letters, but it does not seem to differ from κηρύσσω 'to proclaim', which is more widely used (in the Gospels, Acts, Pauline Epistles, 1 Peter, Revelation). Both καταγγέλλω and κηρύσσω appear to be generic terms meaning 'to proclaim publicly, announce, make known' and both are used generally of public preaching (e.g., Acts 15:36, 'Let us return and visit the brethren in every city where we proclaimed [καταγγέλλω] the word of the Lord'). In this clause, however, the formal object of καταγγέλλω is ὅν 'whom', referring back to Christ. From the point of view of semantics, proclaiming a person presumably means that many statements are made about that person, hence 'we proclaim *the message about* Christ'. The phrase 'to every class of persons' is supplied because καταγγέλλω is regarded as generic and the more specific verbs in the next two propositions have the explicit object 'everyone'. (For the meaning of πάντα ἄνθρωπον 'every person', see the note on 1:28b.)

1:28b *specifically,* **we(exc)/I admonish every class of persons,** There are two matters for comment here. One is the meaning of νουθετοῦντες 'warning'. It is widely agreed that νουθετέω is used when some wrongdoing is in view. Not that those addressed have necessarily done wrong; it may be that they simply are warned against doing it. Commenting on 1 Thess. 5:12, Leon Morris says, "There is often the notion of some tie between the admonisher and the admonished." Thus, in 1 Cor. 4:14 Paul speaks of admonishing the Corinthians as his beloved children. There seems to be no English word that adequately conveys these components, but 'admonish' matches the Greek components better than 'warn'.

The other matter for comment is πάντα ἄνθρωπον 'every person'. It is clear from the context, with its Gentile orientation, and also from Paul's apostolic principle of founding churches in strategic centers, that πάντα ἄνθρωπον is not to be understood to mean 'every individual person'. It is qualitative—every class and condition of person. No distinctions of any sort are made; the message about Christ is for all.

1:28c and *specifically,* **we(exc)/I teach every class of persons very wisely.** There is some difference of opinion over the prepositional phrase ἐν πάσῃ σοφίᾳ 'in all wisdom' at the end of this segment. Does it describe the manner of the teaching or its content? The content of what is taught is regularly expressed by the accusative case, not by an ἐν phrase; a common use of ἐν, on the other hand, is "to denote kind and manner, esp. in periphrasis for adverbs" (Arndt and Gingrich, ἐν, III.2). The examples that Arndt and Gingrich give are almost entirely cases of ἐν + an abstract noun, into which pattern the present example fits readily. Thus, it seems likely that 'in all wisdom' means that the preachers knew how to adapt a message, or rather its presentation, to the different audiences they addressed. The Areopagus Council, the superstitious pagans at Lystra, and the thoughtful Jews at Berea were very different indeed. Hence, in the display 'in all wisdom' is handled as a phrase of manner, 'very wisely'.

1:28d-e *We(exc) do this [1:28a-c]* **in order that every person who is united to Christ may be perfect** *when* **we(exc)/I present them** *to God/Christ.* The verb παρίστημι 'to present' has been discussed in the note on 1:22c-d. The form of the clause here is very similar, and it is handled here in the same way as in 1:22. The purpose of the speaking ministry is considered to be, not the presentation, as such, but the *state* of 'every person' at that presentation. The aim of Paul's ministry was that everyone should be τέλειον ἐν Χριστῷ 'perfect in Christ' at the time of presentation.

Since it is the presentation at the last day that is almost certainly in Paul's mind, the meaning 'perfect' rather than 'mature' is preferred for τέλειος. The prepositional phrase ἐν Χριστῷ 'in Christ' modifies τέλειον—it defines or describes the particular sort of perfection that was being aimed at. But it is difficult to know how best to render it for the display. The expression 'united to Christ' has been used since this is by far the commonest meaning of ἐν Χριστῷ in Paul's letters.

In 1:28e the implicit information is added that the presentation is to God (the Father) or to Christ himself.

1:29a In order that *I might achieve* **this [1:28],** The Greek underlying 29a is simply εἰς ὅ 'toward which'. There are two possible antecedents of ὅ. The first is the explicit purpose expressed in 1:28d-e; with this understanding of ὅ, Paul would be stating two means (both directed to the same end), the speaking ministry of 1:28a-c and the hard work and exertions of 1:29b-d. The second possibility as the antecedent of ὅ is the whole of 1:28 (and because of the emphasis in both on proclamation, 1:25-27 might also be considered); with this understanding of ὅ, Paul would be saying that the toil and effort went into the preaching, warning, and teaching. This second possibility is preferred because his public (and private) speaking ministries were the principal means to the end expressed in 1:28d-e, and the effort went into that principal means. This could be why Paul uses 'we' in 1:28, as this was true of all those involved in proclaiming Christ, whereas in 1:29 he reverts to 'I' again because he, of all the apostles and others, labored the hardest.

1:29b I am also working hard; Paul is not focusing upon himself here (that would require κἀγώ 'and I') so much as upon his toil to achieve this purpose. (Beekman's suggestion that καί here "brings back the focus upon himself and the extent of his own labors" is basically correct, but needs some slight modification.) As Alford says, "καί implies the addition of a new particular over and above the καταγγέλλειν, carrying it onwards even to this." Since this is a first person singular verb, like the verbs in 1:24 at the beginning of the paragraph, it is considered to be describing Paul's present activity. (The following verses confirm this.) Hence, in the display, καὶ κοπιῶ is rendered 'I am also working hard'.

1:29c-d that is, I am exerting myself by means of Christ's empowering me very greatly. The question here is whether κοπιῶ 'I toil' and ἀγωνιζόμενος 'striving' refer to different events or are a doublet aimed at intensifying the sense. (Beekman held the latter view.) Arndt and Gingrich give "work hard, toil, strive, struggle" as glosses for κοπιῶ (κοπιάω), and "fig. of any struggle" for ἀγωνίζομαι. These glosses show that this could be a doublet here. However, some commentators (Abbott, Alford) take ἀγωνιζόμενος 'striving' to refer to Paul's inward attitudes, especially his zealous spirit. Another factor is Paul's use of the noun ἀγών, cognate with ἀγωνιζόμενος, at the beginning of the next paragraph, and the connection is such that it is worth retaining the lexical link in the display, if this is possible. It has, therefore, been decided not to treat κοπιῶ and ἀγωνιζόμενος as synonymous. Rather, κοπιῶ is considered to refer to the actual hard work, and ἀγωνιζόμενος to the effort that produced the hard work. In the display, κοπιῶ is rendered by 'I am working hard', and ἀγωνιζόμενος by 'I am exerting myself', which covers the idea of effort and is collocationally suitable for 2:1.

Here the preposition κατά 'according to' again occurs with the accusative case. The commentaries are not much help in regard to the relation signaled; most versions render it 'with', based on an interpretation as means or instrument: it is by means of God's power at work in him that he is able to toil so hard. Arndt and Gingrich do not suggest means or instrument as a meaning of κατά, but under II.5.a, subsection δ, they do say "oft[en] the norm is at the same time the reason, so that *in accordance with* and *because of* are merged." Reason and means are very similar relations often hard to distinguish, so that some of the examples Arndt and Gingrich call reason could actually be means. In this particular context, means seems more appropriate; therefore the display has 'by means of'.

The abstract noun ἐνέργειαν 'inworking' and the participle ἐνεργουμένην 'inworking' refer to a single event, the double use probably serving to emphasize the event. Just as Paul's own toil is emphasized, so also is Christ's power at work in him. The final prepositional phrase ἐν δυνάμει 'in power' further modifies the event. It is not easy to know how best to render the verb ἐνεργέω in English: 'empower' has been used rather than the more popular 'work in' because the latter is somewhat figurative. To represent the intensification signaled by the cognate noun and the final prepositional phrase, 'very greatly' is used.

In order to identify which proposition in the 1:29a-d cluster is the prominent one, the relation between 29b and 29c-d must first be determined: in this analysis 29c-d is seen as an expansion of the statement in 29b, hence is more prominent than 29b. This is supported by the repetition of 'I am exerting' in the next verse (though in a different form in the Greek). It is proposed, then, that the prominent proposition in the 29a-d cluster is 'I am exerting myself', with 'on behalf of everyone' implied by 1:28.

SECTION CONSTITUENT 2:1–5 (Paragraph: Specific nucleus of 1:24–2:5)

THEME: I am exerting myself very greatly on your behalf in order that you might truly know the secret-message about Christ, in order that no one might delude you.

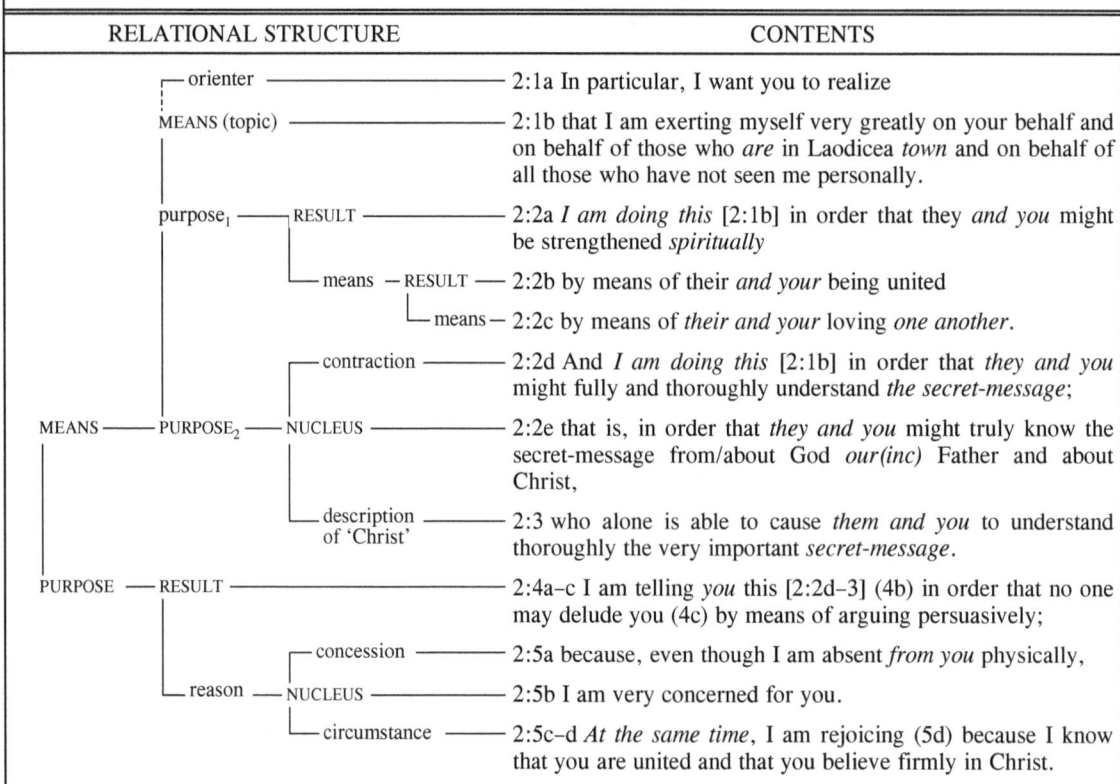

BOUNDARIES AND COHERENCE

The boundaries of the 2:1–5 paragraph are indicated by the following evidence:

1. *The rhetorical bracketing between 2:1 and 2:4–5.* All the first person singular verbs are found in 2:1 and 2:4–5. (There are also two present participles in 2:5 dependent on the last of the first person singular verbs.) All the second person plural pronouns are found in 2:1a and 2:4–5. Both 2:1 and 2:5 refer clearly to Paul's physical absence from those to whom he is writing, and in both places he refers to his physical absence with the term σάρξ 'flesh'. And both 2:1 and 5 refer to his strong interest in their spiritual welfare, even though he could not be present with them.
2. *The tail-head link.* In 1:29 Paul uses the participle ἀγωνιζόμενος 'striving' and in 2:1 he uses the cognate noun ἀγῶνα 'struggle'.
3. *The 'you' orientation.* In the last two verses of the previous paragraph, the emphasis is on universality, with πάντα ἄνθρωπον 'everyone' used three times in 1:28. In 2:1, there is a return to 'you', though this is extended to include others associated with the Colossians.
4. *End of a division.* As already discussed, 2:5 closes a division of the body and 2:6 opens a new division, which is hortatory, so there is a change of genre at this point.

Referential coherence is shown by the 'I' and 'you' references. Only in 2:2 and 2:3 are these absent, but even there the third person plural is best understood to mean 'they and you'. In addition, 2:2 and 2:3 are closely tied to each other lexically, with πλοῦτος 'riches' in 2:2 and θησαυροί 'treasures' in 2:3; συνέσεως 'understanding' and ἐπίγνωσιν 'true knowledge' in 2:2 and σοφίας 'wisdom' and γνώσεως 'knowledge' in 2:3; and μυστηρίου 'mystery' in 2:2 and ἀπόκρυφοι 'hidden' in 2:3.

The relational coherence is rather different from any previous paragraph. Grammatically, this paragraph consists of three sentences: 2:1–3, 2:4, and 2:5. This is probably one of the major reasons why many versions and commentaries divide 2:1-3 from 2:4 and 5. Verse 2:4 starts with the three words τοῦτο λέγω ἵνα 'this I say (in order) that'. This brings up two questions. What is the referent of τοῦτο 'this'—does it refer backwards or forwards?—and what is the function of ἵνα—does it introduce the purpose of λέγω 'I say' or does it introduce the content of it? The answers to these two questions are closely tied together.

Paul uses τοῦτο 'this' as the object of a verb about thirty times in his letters, and most of these are with a forward reference to something he is about to say. The forward reference, in such cases, is to the content of the orienter verb of which τοῦτο is the object. This content is usually introduced by ὅτι 'that', but sometimes there is no formal introduction, or an infinitive phrase may be used. Only once when τοῦτο is used is the content introduced by ἵνα, the form used here, and that is after the verb to pray (Phil. 1:9), ἵνα regularly being used to introduce the content of a prayer (as in 1:9 of this epistle).

However, Paul does use τοῦτο six times with a backward reference, this being indicated by the absence of any content to which it could refer forwards. In most cases, the backward-referring τοῦτο is accompanied by a purpose or manner clause.

While ἵνα commonly introduces the purpose associated with a verb, it can also introduce a command. (This is called the imperatival use of ἵνα.) There seems little doubt that ἵνα is used in this way in the New Testament, but apart from a small number of generally recognized examples, most possible examples meet with doubt. So far as Col. 2:4 is concerned, Arndt and Gingrich do not list it at all, and Turner, in his 1963 grammar (p. 95), lists its imperitival use here as "doubtful." Moule (1959:145), however, says, "Col. ii. 4 seems to be a further example [of the imperatival ἵνα]." Deer points out that Goodspeed's translation and the 1976 TEV also translate the ἵνα clause as a command. If τοῦτο is forward referring, then ἵνα would have to introduce the content of λέγω 'I say' (for τοῦτο to refer to it), and this would mean that ἵνα was introducing a command. This would result in some such translation as 'What I am saying is the following: Don't let anyone deceive you with beguiling speech'. Since this is not what Paul has been saying, but is what he is about to turn his attention to, such a statement would be expected to start a new semantic unit. But it has already been argued that there is good evidence for 2:1-5 to be seen as a paragraph without a major break after 2:3.

These arguments indicate that the backward-referring use of τοῦτο is to be preferred here, with ἵνα introducing the purpose of what Paul has been saying. In this case, τοῦτο provides a link between 2:4 and 2:1-3, grammatically enabling Paul to add an overall purpose to what has been said in 2:1-3.

Verse 2:5 is introduced by γάρ 'for'. This serves to link 2:5 with the preceding material, a natural link in view of v. 5's content being so similar to that of 2:1. Clearly, then, 2:1-5 is relationally coherent, with verses 2:4 and 2:5 linked to 2:1-3.

PROMINENCE AND THEME

Now we turn to consider what the most prominent information in this paragraph is. First it should be noted that 2:4 contains an independent finite verb, λέγω 'I say', which is linked to the preceding material by τοῦτο 'this', and any decision concerning the prominence of 2:4 is closely tied up with the decision concerning the reference of τοῦτο—just what is Paul referring back to? It is argued in the note on 2:4a that the singular form τοῦτο 'this' is much more limited in scope of reference than the corresponding plural form ταῦτα 'these'. This general observation fits the context here well, since the evidence showing that 2:1-5 is a semantic unit implies that τοῦτο is limited in scope to the preceding verses of the same paragraph, at the most. In fact, τοῦτο λέγω 'this I say' can be regarded as a grammatical device that enables Paul to add a purpose to all that has preceded it. That is to say, τοῦτο 'this' is regarded as referring to all of 2:1-3. This raises the question of the prominence of this purpose in 2:4. Normally, means is regarded as more prominent than purpose but, in this case, when the means is all of 2:1-3, and the purpose one that is relevant to a whole section of the epistle (2:8-23), the purpose is regarded as marked for prominence, and therefore thematic in this paragraph.

There is also the question of γάρ 'for', which links 2:5 to earlier information in the paragraph. The most straightforward explanation of its function is that it introduces a reason for 2:4. An alternative analysis of γάρ and the material it introduces is to link it back to the statements in 2:1. Having stated in 2:2-4 the *purposes* of his exertions on their behalf, Paul then gives, in 2:5, the *reason* for his exertions, namely, his concern for them all. Either analysis makes good sense, but the second alternative is given the preference for two reasons: (1) its independent form as a sentence would appear to indicate that it is not attached simply to what immediately precedes it but to the nucleus of the paragraph; and (2) it includes the first alternative, since 2:4 is analyzed as a purpose attached to 2:1–3.

The theme, then, is to be derived from 2:1–3 and 4. The main statement in 2:1 is the content of the orienter 'I want you to know': 'I am exerting myself very greatly on your behalf'. The reference to the Laodiceans and others who had not seen him is secondary compared to the references to the Colossians, the letter's recipients, so the former references are not considered to be thematic.

However, the question needs to be raised as to whether 'I am exerting myself very greatly on your behalf' is the only information in 2:1–3 that has thematic prominence. It seems somewhat implausible that this is the case, as this, in itself, without further explanation, hardly constituted a safeguard against being deceived by false teaching. Further, this proposition is analyzed as the topic of this paragraph, so one or more comments on it are needed for it to be a thematic statement.

It is therefore to be expected that one or more of the 2a–3 propositions should be considered thematic. But which? In the light of the extended description of 'the secret-message' in 1:26–27 and its being summarized as 'Christ in you', the statements in 2:2a–3 about the secret-message and about Christ should probably be considered the most prominent. These arguments point to 2e, which reads 'in order that *they and you* might truly know the secret-message from/about God our Father and about Christ'. For inclusion in the theme statement, references to 'you' are considered more prominent than references to 'they', and references to 'Christ' more prominent than to God the Father. Hence, the prominent information in 2a–3 is 'in order that you might truly know the secret-message about Christ'. Further, this content collocates well with Paul's being concerned with their not being deceived—knowing God's revealed truth about Christ was the best antidote to the teaching that was demoting Christ from his supreme position.

NOTES

2:1a In particular, I want you to realize This proposition functions as an orienter to the thematic topic in the next proposition. For comments on the significance of γάρ 'for', see the discussion of the prominence and theme of 1:24–2:5.

2:1b that I am exerting myself very greatly on your behalf The noun phrase ἡλίκον ἀγῶνα 'how great a struggle' is forefronted, which signals that it is the topic of this paragraph. Since ἀγών is an abstract noun representing an event, it means that the topic of this paragraph is a proposition in the semantic representation. This noun form corresponds to the participle ἀγωνιζόμενος 'striving' used in 1:29. (For the meaning of the root, see the note on 1:29c.) All that needs to be added here is that, since Paul was in prison when he wrote this, the primary reference of ἀγών is probably prayer, especially since in 4:12 Paul refers to Epaphras as 'striving in his prayers', and since 2:2 starts with ἵνα 'that', which normally introduces the content of a prayer. However, ἀγών could well include other activities, such as writing this letter to refute the false teaching that had arisen.

The form ἡλίκον 'how great' is that of an indirect question (Robertson 1919:733). Here it is essentially an indirect rhetorical question with an emphatic function (so Alford; also Turner [1963:50] on ἡλίκος). Hence, to avoid a mismatch, the form 'how great' is rendered 'very greatly' in the display.

and on behalf of those who *are* in Laodicea *town* and on behalf of all those who have not seen me personally. Paul's exertions are not confined to the benefit of the Colossians, but are for the Laodicean Christians as well. The ellipsed preposition ὑπέρ 'on behalf of' is understood here, as shown by the genitive case of the article τῶν. In the display text, this phrase is rendered as an identificational proposition, and the generic verb 'are' is supplied, as well as the information that Laodicea was a town.

There is a division of opinion as to how καὶ ὅσοι 'and such as' relates to the previous groups of people mentioned. While ὅσοι normally generalizes from what has been said—all those that are like those previously mentioned—it can, apparently, introduce the opposite category. Hence, a minority of commentators argue that Paul was known personally to the believers at Colosse and Laodicea. The majority, however, take the view that Paul was not known personally to the Colossian and Laodicean believers and is here expressing his apostolic interest in other believers in the area, who, like the Colossians and the Laodiceans, did not know him personally. Alford argues at some length on the matter, showing that if the minority view is followed there is a breakdown in the sequence of thought, and also pointing out that the switch from 'you' to 'they' to 'you' in 2:1–4 points to their being regarded as belonging to the same general category.

The arguments that Paul had visited Colosse and Laodicea and thus was known to many of the believers there are as follows:

1. Paul had traveled through Phrygia (Acts 18:23), in which area Colosse, Laodicea, and Hierapolis were situated, so he could have evangelized these cities on his way to Ephesus (Acts 19:1). But while this is possible, Acts 18:23 indicates that he was revisiting established churches before going to Ephesus ('traveled from place to place through the region of Galatia and Phrygia, strengthening all the disciples').
2. The letters to Philemon and the Colossians contain references to close friends in Colosse, making it likely that he had been there. This argument is not a strong one. The letter to Philemon refers to Apphia and Archippus only, apart from Philemon himself; the letter to the Colossians refers only to Archippus and Nympha. It is quite possible that he had met these believers in Ephesus, as travel was common. After all, Lydia was converted in Philippi, miles from her home in Thyatira, and Onesimus, the runaway slave, had traveled from Colosse to Rome, a distance of many hundreds of miles. Also, there is a long list of personal greetings at the end of the letter to the Romans (chap. 16), yet Paul had not visited Rome before he wrote the letter. How did he know them personally?
3. We read in his letter to them that Paul felt great affection and concern for the Colossians. However, his assurances of concern for them are very natural even if he had not actually visited them before, and there is no explicit statement concerning how the Colossians regarded him. Besides, if he *had* visited them earlier, he would have perhaps not felt such a need to emphasize his love and concern, for they would already have had personal knowledge of this.

These arguments that Paul had earlier visited Colosse and Laodicea do not seem convincing, certainly not convincing enough to overthrow the predominant sense of ὅσοι 'all such'. Hence, the majority view that Paul was not the one who had established the Colossian church is followed here.

2:2a *I am doing this [2:1b]* **in order that they** *and you* **might be strengthened** *spiritually* The third person pronoun αὐτῶν 'of them, their' is used here, following grammatically from the third person form ὅσοι in 2:1. But the context makes it clear that the Colossians are included in all that Paul says in 2:2; in fact, it is primarily to them that the paragraph is addressed, as 1a and 1b make clear, and the return to 'you' again in 2:4. Hence, the subject of the verb is taken to be 'they and you'.

The phrase αἱ καρδίαι 'the hearts' is a synecdoche signifying the people themselves, 'they and you'. However, many commentators tend not to take it as a synecdoche; their interpretation sees 'hearts' as referring to their inward spiritual life. In keeping with this view, 'spiritually' is supplied.

The passive form of the verb παρακαλέω occurs here. As is widely agreed, it does not here mean 'to be comforted', because sufferings are not in focus. What is in focus is the threat of a divisive heresy, so 'be strengthened', 'be encouraged', or 'be confirmed' would be appropriate—the opposite of becoming unsettled and confused by the false teaching. On the whole, 'strengthened' seems best, as 'encouraged' tends to imply that they were discouraged, and 'confirmed' is rather more doubtful as a meaning of παρακαλέω.

2:2b–c by means of their *and your* **being united by means of** *their and your* **loving one another.** The first question here is the meaning of συμβιβάζω. Its primary sense is 'physically joined together' as in 2:19 in reference to the joining of the body's ligaments. But it also has a cluster of related senses: 'conclude (from arguments or other evidence)' (Acts 16:10); 'prove (a conclusion, by reasoning)' (Acts 9:22); and, more generally, 'teach, advise' (although this sense seems to be confined to the Septuagint; see the quotation in 1 Cor. 2:16). The almost universal view of commentators and versions is that the first sense is used here, but intended figuratively, not literally. Beekman argued for the sense 'teach'. However, there is no focus on teaching in the immediate context (although there is a reference to teaching in 1:28c in the preceding paragraph and in 2:4 to false teaching). Moreover, the collocation of 'teaching' and 'in love' seems rather unusual. Later, in 3:14, where Paul says that love is the bond of perfection, the two ideas of love and being united are brought together again. This is the most convincing argument of all for the majority view, hence 'being united' in the display. (There may also be the implication that false teaching would bring divisions, since some would accept it and others would not.)

The next question is how the prepositional phrase ἐν ἀγάπῃ 'in love' is related to συμβιβασθέντες 'being united'. Beekman's suggestion that love is the means that brings about the unity fits well with the use of ἐν 'by' here. Hence, 2:2c is labeled as means of 2:2b (see the notes on 3:14a–b).

A more difficult question concerns how 2:2b and c relate to the preceding propositions. Beekman took 2b as the means of 2a; that is, by means of being united they would be strengthened. (In his display, however, the means was taken to be teaching.) This makes good sense here and is an established use of the aorist participle, so this is the view I take also. The NEB and TEV translate 2a and 2b as coordinate purposes. Turner (1963:343) states: "Paul also tends to make a participle coordinate with a finite verb." His examples are from 2 Corinthians only, but he does quote ten of them. Lightfoot, commenting on 3:16, takes a similar view: "the absolute participle . . . takes its colour from the general complexion of the sentence." It is possible, therefore, that 2b is a second purpose along with 2a rather than the means of 2a. (But see the notes on 2:2d and 2e, where it is concluded that the two occurrences of εἰς signal purposes; it seems unlikely, therefore, that the aorist participle signals yet another purpose.)

2:2d And *I am doing this [2:1b]* in order that *they and you* might fully and thoroughly understand *the secret-message;* The Greek here is a complex prepositional phrase: εἰς πᾶν πλοῦτος τῆς πληροφορίας τῆς συνέσεως 'to all wealth/riches of the full assurance of the understanding'. The noun 'riches' is used in a figurative sense; the imbedded double genitive construction is made up of two abstract nouns. As to the meaning of these terms, the older commentators agree that the abstract noun πληροφορία meant 'full assurance'; some more modern writers, such as Hendriksen, support this. Turner (1963:211) and also Caird propose 'conviction'. Arndt and Gingrich give both. However, the older commentators as well as Arndt and Gingrich mention that πληροφορία can *also* mean 'fullness'. If the meaning 'assurance/conviction' is taken, then this arises from 'the understanding', as a number of commentators maintain. Thus the main thrust of the statement is that the Colossians (and the Christians in the nearby towns) might have assurance arising from knowledge. But the overall structure of these phrases, as well as Paul's emphasis in the preceding chapter (e.g., 1:9 and 27; cf. also 3:16), points to knowledge as being the central focus of his message. If the rest of this verse and 2:3 are compared in literal English, the parallels are more obvious:

2d to **all riches** of the full-assurance of *the understanding*
2e to   *true-knowledge* of   the mystery
3a **all the treasures** of *wisdom and knowledge*   are hidden

Almost all of 2:2 is repeated in 2:3, using either near-synonyms or common collocates. In particular, in these two verses, Paul uses all of the words relating to the general area of knowing that he uses in this epistle: σύνεσις 'understanding', ἐπίγνωσις 'true-knowledge', σοφία 'wisdom', and γνῶσις 'knowledge'. Hence, an interpretation that makes 'knowledge' central is to be preferred to one that does not. For this reason, the sense 'fullness' for πληροφορία is preferred to that of 'assurance/conviction'.

With this sense of πληροφορία, the combination πᾶν πλοῦτος τῆς πληροφορίας 'all riches of the fullness' functions as an intensifier in which 'fullness' implies a considerable quantity and 'riches' intensifies the idea of quantity and adds the idea of 'valuable, worth having'. There is a great area of knowledge to be known, and Paul wants his readers to explore it to the highest possible degree.

To propositionalize this is not at all easy: it tends to sound rather flat after the richness of the Greek construction! To represent the attribute of fullness, 'fully' is used; and to represent the figurative 'all riches', 'thoroughly' is used. The abstract noun σύνεσις is regarded as expressing the event 'to understand'. Quite a few commentators and versions suggest 'insight', but there is no event word in English for 'insight', so 'understand' is used. There is no explicit statement as to *what* is understood, but this is readily supplied from the following phrase (2e), namely 'the secret-message'.

As to how this εἰς prepositional phrase relates to the preceding statements, commentators commonly relate it back to συμβιβασθέντες 'united', that is, to 2:2b, arguing that ἐν ἀγάπῃ 'in love' and εἰς πᾶν πλοῦτος 'to all riches' are linked by means of καί 'and' back to συμβιβασθέντες. Beekman suggested it could be the purpose of 2b or—less likely—the result. Of course, the preposition εἰς can signal either of these relations, so it is often hard to choose between them. But here, since 2:2-3, as a whole, expresses the goal of Paul's exertions on behalf of the Colossians, purpose is more contextually appropriate than result. And while Paul has a more immediate purpose in mind, their being strengthened and united in the face of false teaching, he also has an ultimate, or long-term, goal—their coming to a rich, full knowledge of God's mystery. For these reasons, Beekman considered 2d the purpose of 2b. However, there is one strong objection to such an analysis, and that is the presence of καί 'and'. If the two prepositional phrases were governed by the same preposition, καί would be quite normal. But to have two different prepositional phrases linked by καί is very unusual—they normally simply follow one another without conjunction. (See, for example, 1:11 in this epistle.) Rather, καὶ εἰς indicates a further purpose—the preceding purpose is stated in 2:2a. Hence, 2:2d is regarded as a second purpose attached to the topic proposition 2:1b. It can be asked, of course, why Paul did not use καὶ ἵνα 'and in order that', making an obvious addition to 2:2a. The answer to that question is not known, but it might be because no verb is expressed (ἵνα would require a verb), and because of the length of the grammatical construction. But these are only guesses.

2:2e that is, in order that *they and you* might truly know the secret-message from/about God *our(inc)* Father and about Christ, This is a second εἰς 'to' prepositional phrase immediately following the one in 2d. Grammatically, it is in apposition to the one in 2d. Commentators therefore take it as explaining the first εἰς phrase. Its relation to 2d is that of amplification, since it adds the content of what is known and its source or reference. The content of the true knowledge is the μυστήριον, the 'secret-message', introduced in 1:26 (see the note on 1:26a).

The words following μυστηρίου involve extensive textual variation. The various editions of the UBS Greek text have the shortest variant, τοῦ θεοῦ, Χριστοῦ 'of God, Christ', whereas the Majority Test has the longest variant, τοῦ θεοῦ καὶ πατρὸς καὶ τοῦ Χριστοῦ 'of God and of (the) Father and of the Christ'. The UBS apparatus lists no less than eleven textual variants. The UBS text follows the assumption (among others) that the longer forms of the text were explanatory expansions by scribes; advocates of the longer Majority Text would say that careless scribes omitted part of the original text. The Majority Text, even in this confused situation, does have the most numerous support, but it is relatively late; the UBS preferred text has early support, but there is only one papyrus, one uncial, and three early fathers in support.

Actually the meaning is not greatly affected by the textual choice. If the shorter UBS text is followed, then Χριστοῦ 'Christ' is most naturally taken as an appositive of μυστηρίου since they are both in the genitive case. This would imply that knowledge of the mystery is equated with knowledge of Christ. If the longer text is followed, then the mystery is said to come not only from God, or to be about God (to which 'the Father' is added), but also to come from Christ or to be about Christ. The previous paragraph summed up the 'secret-message' as 'Christ in you' and the message *from* God was contextually preferred. Here, however, the genitive construction seems more naturally understood as implying 'about'—the message is about God (i.e., the salvation he has made available to the Gentiles) and about Christ, who is as much a Savior for Gentiles as for Jews. But the interpretation 'from God' makes good sense here, too, and is quite acceptable; 'from Christ' is, contextually, however, an unlikely interpretation.

If the shorter text is preferred, then 2e along with an additional proposition 2f would read as follows:

> (2e) in order that *they and you* might know truly the secret-message about/from God,
> (2f) that is, *in order that they and you might truly know* Christ.

Proposition 2e would still be an amplification of 2d, and proposition 2f would be equivalent to 2e.

2:3 who alone is able to cause *them and you* to understand thoroughly the very important *secret-message.* As was pointed out in the notes on 2:2, many of the concepts referred to there are repeated here; but here they are related to Christ rather than the secret-message. This raises the question of the reference of the initial ἐν ᾧ 'in whom/which' in 2:3. Is it to 'Christ' or to 'the secret of God' in 2e? This form of the relative pronoun in Greek can be either masculine or neuter. If it is taken to be masculine, it refers to Christ; if neuter, to the mystery. The former seems much better because Χριστοῦ 'Christ' is the nearest noun to the relative pronoun, and also because this letter emphasizes the all-sufficiency of Christ in every way (cf. 1:19 and 2:9). Hence 3a is taken to be a description of Christ. It could, however, be analyzed as a reason for 2e: Paul wanted them to know what the secret-message revealed about Christ *because* Christ was able to give them all the knowledge and understanding they could possibly need or want.

In this context, σοφία 'wisdom' and γνῶσις 'knowledge' are taken to be a doublet used for emphasis. (Arndt and Gingrich say that "here γ[νῶσις] and σοφία are almost synonymous," under γνῶσις 2.) This is supported by use of the intensifying expression 'all the treasures' and the similar terms σύνεσις 'understanding' and ἐπίγνωσις 'true knowledge' that immediately precede v. 3. It is difficult to avoid the conclusion that Paul is giving this prominence to understanding because of the false teaching's rival claims to insight and knowledge. This conclusion is also supported by what Paul says in 2:4.

The last question here concerns the meaning of all this knowledge being 'hidden in Christ'. This is very difficult to restate as a proposition. But it helps to first recognize that ἀπόκρυφοι 'hidden' does not mean 'inaccessible', but quite the opposite. It is hidden only in the sense of not being indiscriminately available. This knowledge is compared "to valuable commodities locked away in a storehouse, accessible only to those who have access to the storehouse" (Beekman). The access is by faith in Christ, faith being specifically mentioned in 2:5.

Now, to express this propositionally, it must be decided whether to make a figurative or nonfigurative restatement. If a nonfigurative restatement of 'hidden in Christ' is attempted, then it seems necessary to say that Christ possesses this knowledge, and to obtain it we must therefore go to him. But does Christ's possessing this knowledge simply mean that he knows it or that he both knows it *and* imparts it? Beekman took the latter view. TEV is somewhat similar: "He is the key that opens all the hidden treasures." It is difficult to decide, but since Paul was deeply concerned that they would actually have this knowledge the second view is preferred.

In the display, therefore, the proposition takes the form 'he is able to cause *them and you* to understand thoroughly'. The word 'understand' is used to preserve the lexical links with 2:2 and because it is a better term in English than 'know'. (You can know things in English without understanding them.) The word 'thoroughly' represents πάντες οἱ θησαυροί 'all the treasures', just as in 2d it represents πᾶν πλοῦτος 'all the riches'. Since the verb 'understand' requires a grammatical object, this is provided by using 'secret-message' again, which collocates well with the ideas of 'hidden' and 'secret'.

2:4a–c I am telling *you* this [2:2d–3a] in order that no one may delude you by means of arguing persuasively; The significance of τοῦτο 'this' has already been discussed in connection with the paragraph's prominence and theme. It is taken here as referring back, not forward, mainly because of ἵνα 'in order that'. If τοῦτο referred to this ἵνα clause, the ἵνα clause would be the content of λέγω 'I say', not its purpose, and would be a command introducing a topic not mentioned at all as yet, namely the dangers inherent in the false teaching. If this were the correct analysis, 2:4 would introduce a new theme and a new paragraph; but the close links of 2:5 with 2:1 strongly suggest that 2:5 closes the paragraph that opens with 2:1. (The view taken in the display is a view held by some commentators; Caird and Lightfoot mention these reasons for this view.)

But that still leaves one question: What does τοῦτο actually refer back to? My research (Callow 1978) on τοῦτο leads me to think that it does not refer back far, unlike ταῦτα 'these things'. Since Paul states in 2:2 and 2:3 the purposes for which he is exerting himself so strenuously on their behalf, and since τοῦτο λέγω 'this I say' introduces a further purpose, τοῦτο could be regarded as referring to all of vv. 2 and 3. However, it is probably better to take it as referring primarily to the end of 2:2 and 2:3, since what Paul says there makes it clear that any knowledge or wisdom they might need was all to be found in Christ, thus refuting any claim on the part of the false teaching to new insights.

It is very widely agreed that παραλογίζομαι has the sense of 'to reason into error', 'deceive by argument', 'lead astray by false reasoning', and that πιθανολογία means 'a persuasive style of speaking', 'plausible arguments'. Caird gives the meaning of the clause as "a parade of rational ideas made plausible by specious but unsound argument." In the display is an attempt to express these meanings, treating the persuasive arguments as the means used to deceive or delude.

2:5a–b because, even though I am absent *from you* physically, I am very concerned for you. Propositions 5a and b are the two halves of a concession-contraexpectation pair. As Winer points out (p. 554), the sequence of εἰ καί . . . ἀλλά corresponds to 'though . . . yet'.

One question here is what γάρ 'for' relates 2:5 back to. This has already been discussed in connection with the paragraph's prominence and theme: it links 2:5 back to the main statement in 2:1, giving a reason in addition to the purposes given in 2:2–4.

Another question concerns the meaning of 'I am present with you in spirit'. Beekman expressed it as "I am thinking about you as much as if I were with you," supplying the implied "I am thinking about you." While this is the general area of meaning, a more forceful English equivalent is needed in the light of the strong statement in 2:1. Such expressions as 'very interested in' or 'very concerned for' are probably better. The latter is used in the display.

2:5c–d *At the same time*, I am rejoicing because I know that you are united and that you believe firmly in Christ. The meaning of the two participles χαίρων 'rejoicing' and βλέπων 'seeing' is clear, but what is not clear is how they are related to one another. There seem to be three main alternatives:

1. To take καί 'and' as coordinating. Paul was rejoicing and he was seeing, and the two are not more specifically connected.
2. To take καί as introducing the reason: Paul was rejoicing because of what he was seeing.
3. To take καί as indicating simultaneity in time, with βλέπων 'seeing' as more prominent than χαίρων 'rejoicing'. (See Winer, p. 588, who among several alternatives gives "seeing with delight," although it is not the alternative he prefers.)

This is a problem of semantic prominence—interpretation 1 ranks the two events equally, in 2 χαίρων 'rejoicing' is more prominent than βλέπων 'seeing', and in 3 βλέπων is more prominent than χαίρων. The main preferences are for 1 or 2, but I cannot find any objective reason for making a choice. Until more is known that would help to resolve this question, the second alternative is followed, so that βλέπων introduces the reason why Paul was rejoicing. (Arndt and Gingrich under καί I.1.e give "I am glad to see" and JB, NEB, NIV, and RSV are in the same vein, appearing to support this view.) Note that βλέπων does not refer to physically seeing, since Paul was not physically present, but to his awareness of the situation at Colosse. (Presumably Epaphras had told him.)

Another question here is how 'I am rejoicing' relates back to the main proposition 'I am very concerned for you'. The present participle, attached to a present tense verb, indicates simultaneity. Of the various possibilities that would fit the criterion of simultaneity, the best is circumstance. In other words, Paul's main point is his deep concern for them, but he lets them know that, at the same time, he is rejoicing because of their steadfast faith.

There is also a question whether the nouns τάξις 'order' and στερέωμα 'firmness' are military metaphors or not. Commentators as well as versions are divided. Those who consider them metaphors point to the fact that Paul was a prisoner in daily contact with soldiers and so military metaphors would spring readily to mind. This could well be so, but in any case there is no evidence that they are live metaphors in this context. Therefore it is the nonfigurative meaning that is in the display.

The word τάξις refers to their orderliness—the opposite of disarray and division. But it is not clear if this is in reference to their behavior or their unity. Beekman had "you act in an orderly manner," representing the first view; the TEV has "you stand together," representing the second view. The former is what is suggested by Arndt and Gingrich both here and for 1 Cor. 14:40. However, in this context 'united' seems more appropriate in view of the threat from a divisive heresy; moreover, the need for unity has already been referred to in 2b. The use of the abstract noun probably draws attention to their present state, so the display uses 'you are united'. The attribute 'firmly, steadfastly' is represented by στερέωμα. In other words, Paul is describing the unshaken state of the Colossian church. False teaching had arrived on the scene, but it had not yet produced obvious unsettledness in the congregation. In line with this, Paul urges them, in the next paragraph, to stay that way (see 2:7).

Note the overall chiastic surface structure of these two phrases: ὑμῶν τὴν τάξιν . . . τὸ στερέωμα . . . ὑμῶν 'your order // firmness your'. This form may well give some extra prominence to ὑμῶν 'your'. As Abbott says, "the apostle's interest was in them personally and in the τάξις only as belonging to them."

SUB-PART CONSTITUENT 2:6–3:17 (Division: Hortatory nucleus of 1:13–3:17)

THEME: Conduct yourselves as those should who are united to such a one as Christ Jesus our Lord. In particular, make sure that no one makes you become his disciples by teaching you a false religious philosophy; rather, be constantly wanting what is associated with heaven.

RELATIONAL STRUCTURE	CONTENTS
NUCLEUS	2:6–7 Conduct yourselves as those should who are united to such a one as Christ Jesus our Lord is.
SPECIFIC₁ (negative)	2:8–23 In particular, make sure that no one makes you become his disciples by teaching you a false religious philosophy, since you are spiritually complete because you are united to Christ.
SPECIFIC₂ (positive)	3:1–16 And in particular, be constantly wanting what is associated with heaven.
— equivalent	3:17 Do everything in the manner that those should do who are the people of the Lord Jesus.

BOUNDARIES AND COHERENCE

The beginning of a new unit is marked in 2:6 by the occurrence of the first verb in the imperative mood and the first occurrence of οὖν 'therefore', a conjunction restricted to hortatory material in Colossians. In fact, the five occurrences of οὖν in Colossians are all found in this division (in 2:6, 16; 3:1, 5, 12).

The end of the 2:6–3:17 division is clearly marked by rhetorical bracketing. The following parallels can be seen between the 2:6–7 and 3:17 units: (1) In both 2:6–7 and 3:17 very generic commands are expressed. In 2:6 the verb is περιπατέω 'walk' and in 3:17 it is ποιέω 'do', both referring to the whole range of Christian conduct. They are synonymous in this hortatory context. (2) In both the command is related to the Lord Jesus, ἐν αὐτῷ 'in him' in 2:6 and ἐν ὀνόματι κυρίου Ἰησοῦ 'in the name of the Lord Jesus' in 3:17. (3) In both there is thanksgiving. In 2:7 the Colossians were told to be 'abounding in thanksgiving'; in the closing words of 3:17 the Colossians were told to be 'giving thanks to God the Father through the Lord Jesus'.

There are certain characteristics of this division not shared by the previous division nor by the secondary matters. These are as follows:

1. The information in the 2:6–3:17 division is primarily of two sorts, commands addressed to the Colossians and grounds for these commands. In the main paragraphs and in the grounds information, reference is made to the Colossians' union with Christ, by means either of the preposition ἐν 'in' or of the preposition σύν 'with', this latter occurring both as a preposition and compounded with verbs that refer to both Christ and the Colossians. (There is only one occurrence of 'in Christ' in the previous division, in 1:28, and there it refers to the purpose of Paul's ministry, and not directly to the Colossians; and the secondary matters use the expression ἐν κυρίῳ 'in the Lord', not 'in Christ'. The σύν preposition is not used in either the previous division or the secondary matters.)

2. The 2:6–3:17 division is characterized by parallelisms. The first type is parallels between the two halves of a paragraph, that is to say, synonymous commands, usually using different lexical items:

   a. 'Don't let anyone judge you' (2:16)
      'Let no one decide against you' (2:18)

      'Seek the things above' (3:1)
      'Set your minds on the things above' (3:2)

      'Put to death . . '. (3:5)
      'Put off . . '. (3:8)

   b. The second type is parallels that are not synonymous. The clearest example of this is 2:20 and 3:1, 'since you died with Christ' and 'since you rose with Christ'. These statements begin two separate paragraphs, in different sections of this division. Another example is 3:15 and 3:16, 'let the peace of Christ rule in your hearts' and 'let the word of Christ/God dwell in you richly'.

It is interesting to note that though the previous division, 1:13–2:5, is also characterized by parallelisms, they are of a different sort from those here.

The 2:6–3:17 division consists of four major constituents. The first one, 2:6–7, is very short, only one paragraph long, but it is also very generic. The second constituent, 2:8–23, consists of three paragraphs that warn the Colossians against the false teaching. The third, 3:1–16, consists of four paragraphs that are exhortations relating to Christian behavior. The fourth, 3:17, is equivalent to the 2:6–7 nucleus.

PROMINENCE AND THEME

As indicated in the display, the second and third constituents of 2:6–3:17 are regarded as specifics of the first constituent, which is a command covering the whole of Christian behavior. However, these two specific constituents are regarded as thematic, along with the generic command, for two reasons: First, the situation of the letter requires it; that is to say, the particular specifics Paul chooses to refer to are those that are relevant to the Colossian believers. (Without such specifics, the highly generic command in 2:6 could be addressed to any group of believers anywhere.) And second, the two specific commands are considerably developed; each of them comprises a whole section.

The grounds statements in the theme of 2:8–23 are omitted from the higher-level theme. At this higher level, the support for the commands comes from 1:13–2:5, where the grounds are developed more fully, and to which the οὖν 'therefore' of 2:6 refers back.

DIVISION CONSTITUENT 2:6–7 (Paragraph: Nucleus of 2:6–3:17)

THEME: Conduct yourselves as those should who are united to such a one as Christ Jesus our Lord is.

RELATIONAL STRUCTURE	CONTENTS
┌─ comparison ───────────	2:6a In a way that is consistent with *the message* which you received/believed about Christ Jesus, *who is our(inc)* Lord,
NUCLEUS ──────────── (EXHORTATION)	2:6b-c conduct yourselves (6c) *as those should who are* united to *such a one as* he *is*.
│ ┌── NUCLEUS₁ ───────	2:7a Specifically, continue *believing and practicing* what you were first *taught* about Christ Jesus,
├─ specific₁ ─┤ (exhortation) └── NUCLEUS₂ ───────	2:7b and, specifically, continue to do this [2:7a] more and more;
├─ specific₂ ─── NUCLEUS ────── (exhortation)	2:7c and, specifically, continue to be convinced about the body of *true* teaching
│ └── comparison ──	2:7d just as you were taught *it by Epaphras*;
└─ specific₃ ─────────── (exhortation)	2:7e and, specifically, continue thanking *God our(inc) Father* very much.

BOUNDARIES AND COHERENCE

The initial boundary of the 2:6–7 paragraph coincides with the initial boundary of 2:6–3:17. Its closing boundary is indicated by the reference to thanksgiving at the end of 2:7. Apart from the opening paragraph of the body, which has 'we thank God' as its orienter (1:3), thanksgiving in a supporting role occurs two other times at the end of a semantic unit, in 1:12 and 3:17. The change to a new paragraph in 2:8 is also indicated by the change from the positive exhortation to Christian conduct in 2:6–7 to a warning against false teaching.

Another indication of the unity of 2:6–7 is that there is possibly a rhetorical bracketing here. The first clause in 2:6, 'as you received Christ Jesus the Lord', is interpreted to mean 'as you received the *teaching/message* about Christ Jesus our Lord' (see the note on 2:6a); this is similar in content to the penultimate clause in 2:7, 'just as you were *taught*'. Further, the clause in 2:6 starts with ὡς 'as' and that in 2:7 with καθώς, a compounded form of ὡς.

Grammatically, 2:6–7 is one sentence in Greek in which every finite verb form is second person plural and all the participles are nominative plural, referring to the same second person plural subject. There are also references to Christ in both verses, and the preposition ἐν 'in' is used in four or five of the seven clauses, depending on which text is followed. Relationally considered, there is a main statement, preceded by a comparison and followed by a series of specifics.

PROMINENCE AND THEME

The 2:6–7 paragraph is the first hortatory paragraph in Colossians. The main command 'walk in him' is an intransitive one, and in such cases, an intransitive command is considered to be the paragraph topic. The main comment is represented by the forefronted (and thereby highlighted) ἐν αὐτῷ 'in him', which is analyzed as a manner proposition in the form of a comparison (2:6c).

NOTES

2:6a In a way that is consistent with *the message* which you received/believed about Christ Jesus, *who is our(inc)* Lord, There are three difficult problems connected with this statement. The first is the meaning of παρελάβετε in this context. This is the second person plural aorist of the verb παραλαμβάνω 'to receive', and so refers to a past event in the experience of the Colossians. But what event? The problem arises because of a clash of criteria. In Paul's epistles παραλαμβάνω is used eleven times, and in nine of theses cases it is used of the reception of teaching, whether the teaching is spelled out (as in 1 Cor. 11:23, 15:3, Phil. 4:9, and 1 Thess. 4:1) or whether it is summed up in such terms as 'the gospel' (1 Cor. 15:1; Gal. 1:9, 12), 'the word' (1 Thess. 2:13) or 'the tradition' (2 Thess. 3:6). The two exceptions are both in Colossians—here in 2:6 and later in 4:17, where a 'ministry' is received. In other words, Col. 2:6 is the only example in which παραλαμβάνω occurs with a person as the object.

However, in the Gospels and Acts, παραλαμβάνω is very commonly collocated with persons, but it has the sense of 'to take', usually along with, or away. This is not appropriate here. The only close parallels appear to be in John's Gospel. In 1:11 John says, 'his own (people) did not receive him'; and in 19:16 it reads, 'they (the Jews) took Jesus', where 'took' translates the aorist of παραλαμβάνω.

Because of Paul's strong preference for the sense of 'receive what has been handed on/passed on', it seems best here to take the meaning to be "*accept* . . . the proclamation of him as Lord" (Arndt and Gingrich). The emphasis is not so much on personal faith in Christ, as on their having received (i.e., believed) a message about Christ. Hence, in the display, the verb παρελάβετε is rendered 'you received/believed the message about'. (Barclay has "The tradition you have received is.")

The second problem in this verse concerns the grammatical form of the verb's object, τὸν Χριστὸν Ἰησοῦν τὸν κύριον 'the Christ Jesus, the Lord'. The double use of the article in this phrase is unique in the New Testament. There are about seventy occurrences of 'Lord', 'Jesus', and 'Christ' together in the New Testament, and a study of these phrases suggests the following (tentative) conclusions:

1. The occurrence of κύριον 'Lord' at the end of the phrase probably indicates a certain emphasis on it, as opposed to the order 'Lord Jesus Christ', which appears to function as a title such as 'King Herod' or 'Governor Felix'.
2. The article occurs with 'Lord' because it is in apposition to a phrase with an article.
3. The initial article may possibly convey the sense 'the aforementioned, the one I have already spoken about', similar to its use in narrative. Paul has already said a good deal about God's Son in 1:13–20, 27, and 2:2–3.

The third problem in 6a is its relation to the command that follows it. Although the conjunction ὡς that formally introduces 6a usually signals a comparison of some sort, grounds is an alternative possibility. The use of the verb παραλαμβάνω here makes it very likely that this clause is broadly synonymous with the clause in 2:7, καθὼς ἐδιδάχθητε 'just as you were taught'. 'You were taught' and 'you received the message that was passed on to you' are very similar. The clause in 2:7 cannot be considered to be grounds, but a comparison, and this strengthens the likelihood that the initial ὡς in 2:6 also is intended to signal comparison rather than grounds. (It is also, at this state of knowledge, uncertain whether an initial ὡς can signal grounds. One or two examples of ὡς in Colossians do signal grounds (3:12 and possibly 4:4), but neither of these is initial—they both follow the command they support.) The relation between 6a and the command that follows it is therefore considered to be one of comparison.

But what exactly is the comparison? There are two clues to the answer:

1. The aorist tense of παρελάβετε 'you received' is in contrast with the present tense of περιπατεῖτε 'be-walking'. The verb παρελάβετε refers back to the Colossians' original reception of the gospel message, which they believed. The command περιπατεῖτε refers to their present, and continuing, conduct. A comparison, then, is being drawn between their initial acceptance of the gospel and their present behavior.
2. The noun phrase 'the Christ Jesus, the Lord' is the referent of 'him' in 'walk in him'.

What Paul is saying, apparently, is that the gospel they received centered on Christ Jesus the Lord, who, in chapter 1, is said to be the Image of God, in whom all the fullness dwells and the one through whom reconciliation to God has been effected. Further, he is indeed Lord—supreme over the whole of creation and the church as well. Having received the message about such a Savior, the Colossians are told that they should act accordingly. Put negatively, they should not now act in a way that is at variance with what they heard, and initially received. If they follow the prescriptions of the false teaching, that is what they will be doing. And so, in 2:8–20, Paul goes on to expose the errors and dangers of the false teaching.

This analysis is supported by parallel examples elsewhere in the New Testament. The two clearest examples are in the Gospel of Matthew. In Matt. 8:13, Jesus says to a centurion, 'Go! As you believed, let it be (like that) for you. And his servant was healed'. Clearly, 'as you believed' (ὡς ἐπίστευσας) refers to the content of the centurion's faith, namely, that Jesus could heal his servant, and so it is stated that what happened was in conformity with, or matched, the centurion's faith. In Matt.

15:28, Jesus says to the Syro-Phoenician woman, 'Let it happen as you want (ὡς θέλεις). And her daughter was healed'. Again, what happened matched the content of the woman's desire. Further examples in which ὡς refers to the content of an orienter such as 'to believe', 'to want', etc., are found in Gal. 1:9 and 1 John 2:27, as well as such passages as Luke 3:3-6 where ὡς γέγραπται 'as it is written' refers to the following quotation from Isaiah 40 and the matching events are from John the Baptist's ministry, described in Luke 3:3.

How best, then, can the opening clause of 6a be expressed propositionally? The particular sense of ὡς here seems best represented as it is in the display: 'In a way that is consistent with *the message* which you received/believed about Christ Jesus, *who is our(inc) Lord*'.

2:6b conduct yourselves The word περιπατεῖτε 'walk' is a dead metaphor for the sort of life one lives, one's conduct. The best nonfigurative equivalent in English seems to be 'conduct yourselves'. The present tense implies that they were already "walking" and should continue to do so.

2:6c *as those should who are* united to *such a one as* he *is*. Arndt and Gingrich point out that the figurative use of 'to walk' is always accompanied by a more exact definition of that walking. The phrase ἐν αὐτῷ 'in him', referring back to 'Christ Jesus', provides that more exact definition here. The most common Pauline meaning of 'in him', 'in Christ' is the believer's union with Christ; the same phrase is used a number of times with that sense in the following verses. Expressed propositionally, it is 'as those should who are united to him'. That is to say, ἐν αὐτῷ provides a description of the manner in which the believers were to conduct themselves. It makes use of an (implicit) comparison, as is often the case with manner.

The pre-verb position of the phrase 'in him' draws attention to it. The false teaching advocated certain types of behavior that Paul is about to discuss and reject. The Colossians' behavior was to be consistent with what they had been taught about Christ Jesus and with their union with him. This emphasis is shown in the propositionalization by 'such a one as he is'.

2:7a Specifically, continue *believing and practicing* what you were first *taught* about Christ Jesus, This is the first of four participial phrases that follow the command. The first three are joined by καί 'and', and the fourth is without a formal link. In the display, they are treated as being conjoined to each other. (An alternative analysis will be given at the end of 2:7, in which only the first three are related by conjoining.) The first is a perfect participle, the others are present participles.

As to the relationship of these participial phrases to the central command, the main alternatives appear to be that they are specifics of the command, grounds for the command, or circumstances accompanying it. It seems likely, however, that grounds would require aorist participles, leaving the choice between specifics and circumstances. This is not an easy choice. The main argument against specifics would be to suggest that 'being rooted', 'being built up', and 'being confirmed' are activities that are not covered by the generic concept of 'walk'. Rather, these are statements of things already true of the Colossians, providing a sort of descriptive background to the command. The fact that the last three participles are all present tense, while the first is a perfect participle, combined with their being attached to a present tense command, implies that these descriptions of the Colossians are the way they are to continue being—and that they have a responsibility to see that it is so. This last about their having a responsibility to see to this implies the main argument against circumstance as the relation, for once this idea is expressed propositionally the participial phrases emerge as *commands*, not simply accompanying circumstances. Hence, 'conduct yourselves' is considered to be a command generic enough to cover any command relating to Christian behavior, and the choice of specifics is given the preference.

The word ἐρριζωμένοι 'rooted', like περιπατεῖτε 'walk', is a dead metaphor; and, as is generally agreed, the phrase ἐν αὐτῷ 'in him' which follows the second participle applies equally to this first one. To express this figure in a nonfigurative propositional form is difficult. The basic idea, according to Arndt and Gingrich, is "be" or "become firmly rooted," or "fixed" when applied to such things as bridges and buildings (so also Lightfoot). The force of the perfect tense is that they were rooted in the past, and are still so, and its association with the present tense command implies that they are to continue in that state, despite the unsettling effect of the false teaching. Since the whole context of this paragraph is that of behavior consistent with what they were taught about the Lord Jesus, and since the false teaching would affect both behavior and beliefs, and since 'rooted' is both generic and looks back to when they first heard and believed, 2:7a is taken as referring to both belief and practice and also initial teaching.

2:7b and, specifically, continue to do this [2:7a] more and more; The second participle, ἐποικοδομούμενοι 'being built up', is yet another dead metaphor; it represents the general idea of developing, advancing, maturing. This participle is linked to ἐρριζωμένοι 'having been rooted' by καί 'and', and these two participles are both modified by ἐν αὐτῷ 'in him', which links them closely together. The first participle refers to laying the (initial) foundations, the second to building steadily on them. To spell it out nonfiguratively, they refer to beginning and continuing. Hence 2:7b is interpreted as urging the Colossians to continue doing what they had already started doing. Again, there is the implicit warning against switching allegiance to any new teaching.

2:7c and, specifically, continue to be convinced about the body of *true* teaching The third participle is βεβαιούμενοι 'being confirmed'. It is not figurative. The translator has to decide among its several similar senses—confirmed, convinced, established—and the decision could be affected by the choice of text here. The second edition of the UBS *Greek New Testament* (Aland et al.) has ἐν 'in' in brackets before τῇ πίστει and ἐν is omitted in the third edition altogether. Abbott, however, indicates that most of the manuscripts support the presence of ἐν. Those commentators who omit it assume it was inadvertently added by copying the preceding ἐν of ἐν αὐτῷ 'in him'; those who retain it assume it was omitted by carelessness, or was omitted because it was considered grammatically unnecessary. In fact, there are no examples of the verb βεβαιόω 'confirm' collocated with ἐν in the New Testament, and only one (in Heb. 13:9) with the dative.

A further question is whether πίστει 'faith' refers to their own faith, or to *the* faith, that is to say, to the body of Christian teaching communicated to them. In light of the meaning of παραλαμβάνω 'receive' in 6a, and in light also of the immediately following statement in 7d, 'just as you were taught', as well as the more general context of the false teaching, the second alternative is preferable contextually. This being so, 'convinced about the faith', 'confirmed in the faith', and 'established in the faith' are all virtually synonymous. Nor would the text without the preposition ἐν make any material difference: 'in the' would be replaced by 'with respect to the', but the meaning would be the same. In the display 'convinced about' is used, and 'the faith' is rendered as 'the body of *true* teaching', where 'body of' is intended to convey the idea that it is not specific truths that are referred to but a consistent whole. (Note that there is a metonymy here, in which the act of believing is put for what is believed.)

2:7d just as you were taught *it by Epaphras*; The Greek is a passive construction, καθὼς ἐδιδάχθητε 'as you were taught', which takes the focus off the agent. But since Epaphras is explicitly said to have been their instructor in the faith (1:6-7), 'by Epaphras' is supplied as the implicit agent.

As to which of the preceding propositions this one relates to, there are two possibilities. It may relate either to the single proposition 7c or to 7a–c. In favor of the first view, it can be argued that καί 'and' preceding βεβαιούμενοι 'being convinced' together with the new modifying phrase [ἐν] τῇ πίστει 'in the faith' separates the 7d clause from the earlier ones. Also in favor of the first view is that if 7d is another reference to 'the faith', it strengthens Paul's emphasis that they had been taught the truth and, by implication, should not depart from it. In favor of the second view is that the participles are linked to each other by καί 'and', but against the second view is that it implies that the Colossians had been taught the first three matters, but not taught to give thanks. The weight of this evidence is on the side of 7d's being related to 7c. To bring this out, the implicit object 'it' is supplied, which refers back to 'the body of *true* teaching'. The relation is one of comparison, more specifically equality. The 'body of teaching' Paul is urging them to be convinced about is the same as what was (previously) taught to them.

2:7e and, specifically, continue thanking *God our(inc) Father* very much. The choice of text at this point affects the analysis. The question is whether ἐν αὐτῇ 'in it' is included or not. Two different analyses are given here in full, one for each of the textual variants. It is the first analysis that the previous display is based upon.

First, if ἐν αὐτῇ is omitted, the proposition represented by this participial clause is analyzed as in the relation of conjoining to propositions 7a–c and is the final specific attached to the command in 6b. In 2:7e is another example of mismatch between the semantic structure and the grammatical structure. The verb form περισσεύοντες 'abounding' represents the attribute 'abundantly, very much', while the abstract noun εὐχαριστίᾳ 'thanksgiving' represents the event 'to thank'. Propositionally stated, it thus becomes 'continue thanking *God our Father* very much'. The one to be thanked can be supplied from the explicit statements in 1:3, 12, and 3:17. The mismatch probably gives some prominence to the attribute 'very much'.

Second, if ἐν αὐτῇ is included, the feminine pronoun αὐτῇ refers back to the last feminine noun, πίστει 'faith'. The meaning then would be 'abounding in faith with thanksgiving' (according to most commentators who comment on the longer text). In this case, it hardly makes sense to take 'faith' as referring to the apostolic body of truth, so both here and in 7c, 'faith' refers to the activity of believing, not to what is believed, and 7c would be rendered 'believing firmly, believing with confidence'. Also, if the longer text is used, 'thanksgiving' becomes the circumstance of 'abounding in faith'; and since 'abounding' (an attribute meaning 'very greatly' when used with 'believe') modifies the (same) event of believing in 7c, it is transferred there in the display. An alternative display based on the longer text with ἐν αὐτῇ is as follows:

(7c) and continue believing very firmly and very greatly
  (7d) just as you were taught *by Epaphras*,
  (7e) while you continue to thank *God our(inc) Father*.

Proposition 7c would be in a conjoining relation to 7a and 7b (just as in the display for the shorter text), and proposition 7d in a comparison relation with 7a–c, but proposition 7e would now be in the relation of circumstance to 7c, hence supporting it, not conjoined to it, as in the first analysis.

DIVISION CONSTITUENT 2:8–23 (Section: Specific₁ of 2:6–7)

THEME: Make sure that no one makes you become his disciples by teaching you a false religious philosophy, since you are spiritually complete because you are united to Christ.

RELATIONAL STRUCTURE	CONTENTS
GENERIC	2:8–15 Make sure that no one makes you become his disciples by teaching you a false religious philosophy, since you are spiritually complete because you are united to Christ.
specific₁	2:16–19 Disregard anyone who condemns you because you do not obey certain regulations and because you do not worship God as he insists you should.
specific₂	2:20–23 Do not submit to elementary regulations, which are concerned merely with what is external.

BOUNDARIES AND COHERENCE

The most obvious evidence that Col. 2:8–23 is a semantic unit (a section in this case) is that it deals with one topic: the false teaching that had arisen in the area of Colosse and was evidently making its appeal to the Colossian Christians. Each of the three paragraphs of which this section consists has for its theme a warning against the false teaching backed up by grounds as to why the warning should be heeded. Thus, many of the lexical items used are descriptive of the false teaching, terms such as φιλοσοφίας 'religious system' (2:8); κατὰ τὴν παράδοσιν τῶν ἀνθρώπων 'based on the traditions of men' (2:8); τὰ στοιχεῖα τοῦ κόσμου 'rudimentary external/physical regulations' (2:8); θρησκείᾳ 'outward worship' (2:18) and ἐθελοθρησκίᾳ 'outward will-worship' (2:23); ταπεινοφροσύνῃ 'a (false) humility' (2:18, 23); and ἀφειδίᾳ σώματος 'severity to the body' (2:23). There is also constant reference to Christ throughout this section. Thus, 2:8–23 clearly forms a well-marked, coherent unit.

In addition to its lexical coherence, three pieces of evidence point to the boundaries of this section:

1. The initial βλέπετε μή 'beware lest'. The 2:6–7 unit, which immediately precedes this command, deals generally with Christian behavior, and the following chapter likewise. Hence, βλέπετε μή signals the start of a series of commands that are warnings *against* something, rather than exhortations *to* a certain type of conduct.

2. Rhetorical bracketing. A good case can be made for a sandwich structure with parallels between the opening verse (2:8) and the closing paragraph (2:20–23):
   a. In 2:8 the false teaching is referred to as φιλοσοφία 'religious philosophy'; in 2:23 this teaching is said to give the impression of σοφία 'wisdom', σοφία being part of the compound word in 2:8.
   b. In the description of the false teaching in 2:8, the expression τὰ στοιχεῖα τοῦ κόσμου is used. This same expression is used in 2:20. (For its meaning, see the note on 2:8.)
   c. In 2:8 the false teaching is said to be based on 'the traditions of men'. A synonymous expression, 'based on the commands and teachings of men', is used in 2:22.

3. A possible summary statement. Less certain, but an attractive possibility, is that 2:23, the last verse of this section, is a final summary statement both of what the false teaching was and what Paul thought of it. If this is so, then it marks the end of the material dealing with the false teaching.

PROMINENCE AND THEME

The 2:8–23 section consists of three paragraphs, 2:8–15, 2:16–19, and 2:20–23. The first of these is a generic warning against being taken in by the false teaching; it also develops grounds for this warning in considerable detail. The other two paragraphs warn against various specific facets of this teaching. Hence, 2:8–15 is regarded as the nucleus in this section and consequently the theme of 2:8–15 is considered the theme also of 2:8–23.

SECTION CONSTITUENT 2:8–15 (Paragraph: Generic nucleus of 2:8–23)

THEME: Make sure that no one makes you become his disciples by teaching you a false religious philosophy, since you are spiritually complete because you are united to Christ.

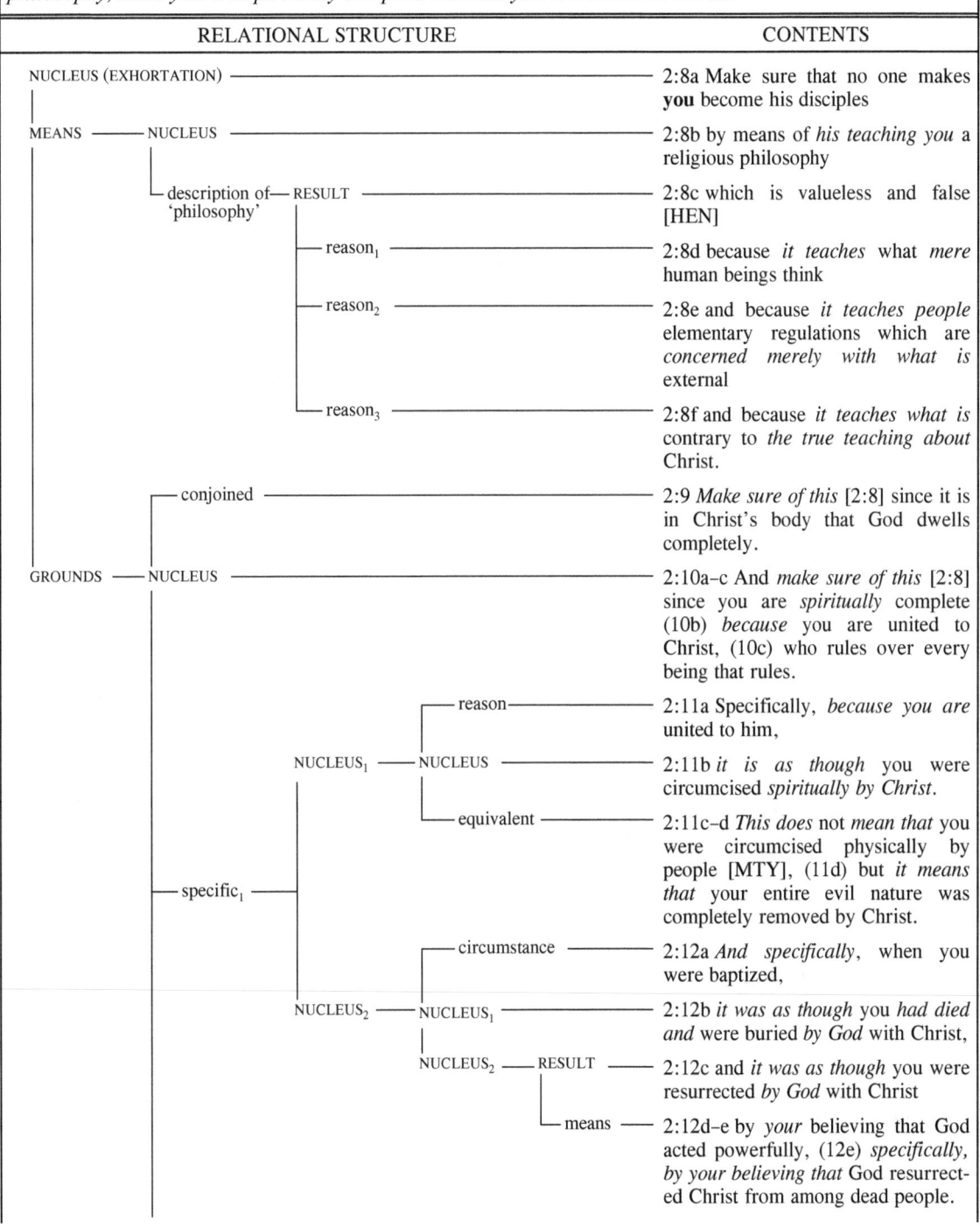

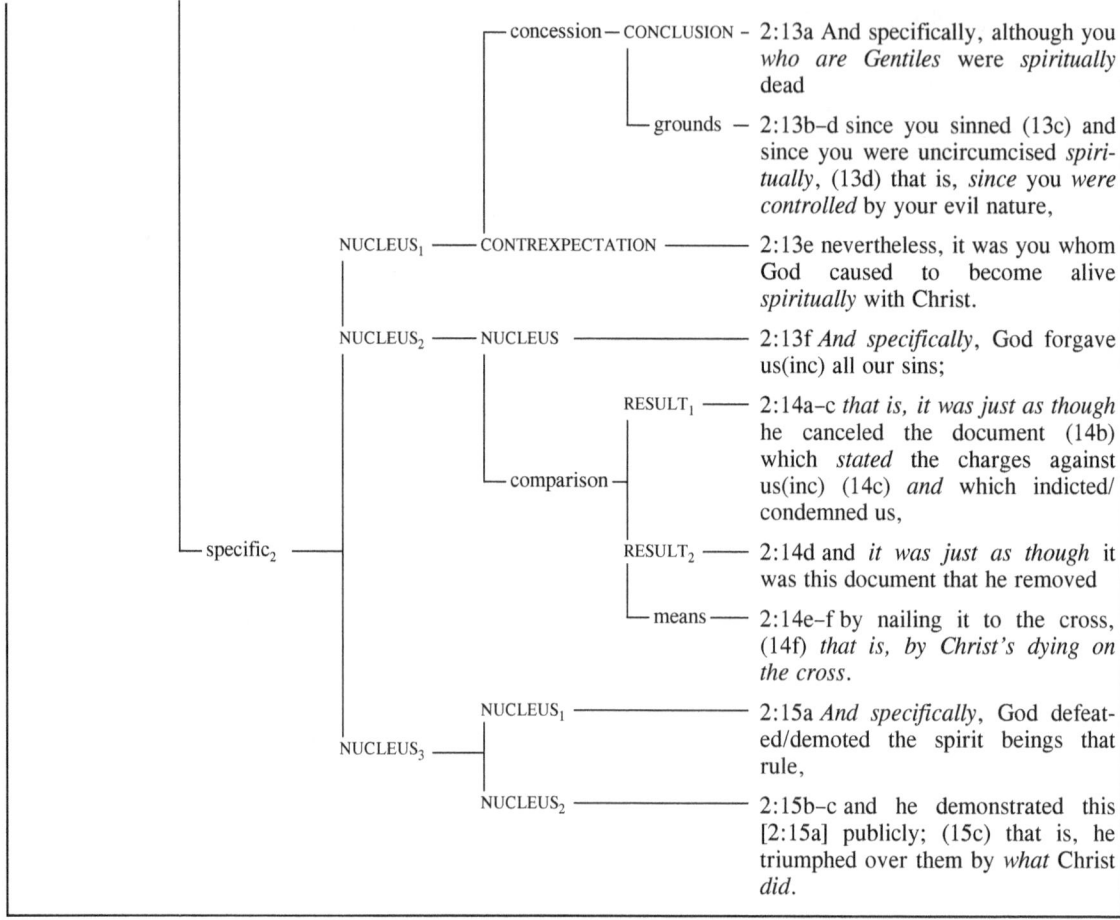

BOUNDARIES AND COHERENCE

The 2:8–15 paragraph opens with a warning to the Colossians against the dangers of being taken in by the false teaching current in their area. Verse 2:16 opens with a similar warning. The obvious parallel between 2:8 and 2:16 (even though 2:8 is formally a second person plural command and 2:16 is a third person singular command) indicates two related but distinct semantic units, so that 2:15 is the end of the first unit.

The 2:8–15 unit is very complex structurally. There are two distinct breaks within these verses, between vv. 9 and 10, and between vv. 12 and 13, as shown by the following evidence:

1. *Tail-head links*. Verse 2:9 has ἐν αὐτῷ 'in him' and πᾶν τὸ πλήρωμα 'all the fullness'; 2:10 has ἐν αὐτῷ and πεπληρωμένοι 'have become full'. Verse 2:12 has νεκρῶν '(the) dead'; 2:13 has νεκρούς (the same word but in a different case). Verse 2:12 has συνηγέρθητε 'you were co-raised (to life)'; 2:13 has the synonymous active form συνεζωοποίησεν ὑμᾶς 'he co-quickened-to-life you'.

2. *Change of person reference*. Although 2:8 opens with a second person plural verb, all the other verbs and participles in 2:8–9 have third person singular subjects or referents (ἔσται 'he will be', συλαγωγῶν '(he) capturing', κατοικεῖ '(it) dwells'). However, in 2:10 a second person plural verb ἐστέ 'you are' is used, and apart from two third-person singular verb forms in relative clauses, all the other verbs and participles in 2:10–12 are second person plural oriented. Thus, there is a change from third person singular forms to second person plural forms at 2:10.

In 2:13–15, however, there is a switch back to third person singular verb forms, with only the opening participle, ὄντας '(you) being', having a second person plural reference. In addition, after the two free pronoun references to 'you(pl)' in 2:13 (three in the UBS text), the free pronoun references switch to 'we(inc)'.

3. *Grammatical parallelism*. Verse 2:8 opens with an independent clause, without any formal link to the preceding material. Both 2:10 and 2:13 open with καί 'and' and a form of the verb 'to be'. Further, in 2:10 the full pronoun form ἐν αὐτῷ 'in him' is used, whereas in the other two clauses in 2:10-12 that have καί the dependent ἐν ᾧ 'in whom' is used, followed by καί 'also'. And 2:13, which starts with καὶ ὑμᾶς νεκροὺς ὄντας [ἐν] τοῖς παραπτώμασιν 'and you, dead being in trespasses' is very similar to 1:21, which starts with καὶ ὑμᾶς ποτε ὄντας . . . ἐχθροὺς . . . ἐν τοῖς ἔργοις τοῖς πονηροῖς 'and you formerly being . . . enemies . . . in evil deeds'. Verse 1:21, however, opens a new paragraph, which creates some precedence for 2:13 similarly opening a new paragraph, or at least signaling a major break within a unit.

This evidence, then, would indicate that there are three main constituents of 2:8-15, namely 2:8-9, 10-12, and 13-15.

But before a final conclusion about the structure of 2:8-15 can be reached, two other factors should be considered. First, a case can be made for a sandwich structure with parallels between 2:10 and 2:15 since both refer to 'principalities and powers'. The Greek words used are the same in both, although the singular form in 2:10 and plural in 2:15.

Second, the opening conjunction ὅτι 'because' in 2:9 is significant in view of its being the only subordinating conjunction in all of 2:8-15. Beekman argued that 2:10-15 constitutes a developed statement of grounds for 2:8, the command, and that 2:9 constitutes an undeveloped statement of grounds for 2:8. Since 2:10 is linked to 2:9 by καί 'and', he concluded that 2:9 should be given the same semantic relation as 2:10-15 yet with less prominence due to the extensive development of the point made in 2:10. Indeed, this seems the best analysis of 2:9.

The 2:8-15 paragraph can therefore be described as consisting of four main constituents: the nuclear command, 2:8; grounds$_1$, 2:9; and grounds$_2$, 2:10-15. This second grounds consists of its own nucleus, 2:10, and two specifics of that nucleus, 2:11-12 and 2:13-15.

But why call this one paragraph? Is it not structurally more like a group of paragraphs? It is true that it is structurally complex, but in function it parallels other semantic units that are unambiguously paragraphs. It is, in fact, technically a paragraph cluster, that is, a unit in which one or more constituents have a paragraph-like structure, but are in a close relationship to each other, and the unit parallels simple paragraphs in its distribution in a section.

Some of the evidence for the coherence of 2:8-15 has already been stated in discussing the complex structure. References to 'you(pl)' are found throughout, though in 2:13-14 this takes the form of 'we + you(pl)'. Also, there is constant reference to Christ throughout all of 2:8-13. At 2:13, there is a transition from 'Christ' to 'God the Father' (cf. 1:19 for a similar switch earlier), so that in 2:14-15 frequent references are made (though implicitly) to God the Father with only one (disputed) reference to Christ at the end of 2:15.

Formally, the main constituents are linked by ὅτι, καί, a relative clause, or asyndeton. Within the clause clusters, formal coherence is mainly indicated by participles that are dependent on a finite verb form.

PROMINENCE AND THEME

The 2:8-15 paragraph's main statement is in 2:8, with 2:8 being supported by 2:9-15 as grounds. However, 2:8 consists of a nucleus and a complex means. The nucleus is 'Make sure that no one makes you(pl) (emphatic) become his disciples'. This statement is very generic, with no indication given as to how someone might make the Colossian believers into his own disciples; hence, the nuclear proposition of the means is joined with the main proposition (2:8a), functioning something like an identification with a thing concept. The enlarged theme would be 'Make sure that no one makes you become his disciples by teaching you a religious philosophy'. The description of this philosophy as false is also included in the theme—it summarizes Paul's evaluation of it.

But there is also the question of the two grounds. Should either of them be included in the theme statement? In other words, is either of the grounds considered to be marked in any way as prominent? This was not at all easy to decide, but the decision to include 10a-b was based on the following considerations: First, 2:9, the first grounds, is undeveloped, whereas 2:10-15 is a fully developed grounds, so 2:9 is considered to be less prominent than 2:10-15 and is therefore not included in the theme. In contrast, the opening statement in 2:10-15 is quite distinctive. For one thing, it is in the form of a periphrastic perfect (ἐστὲ . . . πεπληρωμένοι 'you are . . . having-been-filled'), unlike any subsequent statement. Moreover, it is generic in content, whereas all the following statements are more specific. This opening statement is, therefore, considered to be the generic nucleus of all that follows, and 2:10–15 is considered to have marked prominence by virtue of its being fully developed. Hence, 10a and 10b are considered to constitute prominent grounds.

NOTES

2:8a Make sure that no one makes you become his disciples The words βλέπετε μή 'beware lest' constitute a warning to be careful, watchful, on one's guard. Rather than render this with the archaic 'beware lest' in the display, the positive form 'make sure that' is used. The words that follow, τις ὑμᾶς ἔσται ὁ συλαγωγῶν 'any of you there-be being-taken-captive' are considered to be a dead figure since there are no further allusions to it; hence the meaning is expressed nonfiguratively in the display: 'makes you become his disciples'. The position of ὑμᾶς 'you(pl)' gives it prominence. It was the Colossian church in particular that was threatened by this teaching, so it is they who are warned; this is not a general warning against a widespread heresy.

2:8b–c by means of *his teaching* you a religious philosophy which is valueless and false The term φιλοσοφία, rendered here as 'religious philosophy', was used of elaborate teachings which also served religious purposes, such as relating man to God and dealing with fleshly weaknesses. Put in another way, it was a system of thought directed towards religious ends, rather than, say, a theory of how the body works or what the nature of the universe is.

The primary meaning of κενός is 'empty', so in this context it conveys the idea that this system of thought had nothing of real value to offer its adherents; it did not provide the answers it claimed to provide. Hence, 'valueless' is used in the display. The abstract noun ἀπάτη 'deceit' represents the attribute 'false'.

The absence of διὰ τῆς 'by means of the' after καί 'and' shows that the φιλοσοφία is being described as valueless and false, rather than that a second means was being used to persuade people to believe the teaching. Because of this, 'false' is used in the display rather than a full proposition such as 'which deceives *people*'. The hendiadys here may be intended to give prominence to the description valueless and false.

2:8d because *it teaches* what *mere* human beings think The noun ἀνθρώπων refers to men in general, mankind, human beings. It is being used derogatively in this context, hence the addition of 'mere' in the display. It is an unfavorable contrast with the divinely revealed message about Christ which the Colossians had believed (2:6).

The word παράδοσις 'tradition' refers to ideas, teachings, and precepts passed on from one person to another. In the gospels, it is used to refer to the accumulated extrabiblical teachings upheld by the Pharisees, for slavish adherence to which Jesus condemned them. Paul, however, generally uses this word to refer to the body of Christian teaching transmitted by the Lord to the apostles, and by them to the churches. But here he qualifies it by τῶν ἀνθρώπων 'of men' to distinguish it from the true apostolic teaching.

The preposition κατά (with the accusative case, as here) has many meanings, but in most of the versions it is rendered with an expression equivalent to 'based on'. That is to say, this whole scheme derives its ideas, teachings, and precepts from human beings. This is expressed by 'it teaches what' in the display. Each κατά phrase is analyzed as giving a reason for Paul's description of this φιλοσοφία as 'valueless and false'. The first two κατά phrases explain why it is valueless, and the third why it is false.

2:8e and because *it teaches people* elementary regulations which are *concerned merely with what is* external The word στοιχεῖα, translated "elemental spirits" in the RSV, is given two different senses by the commentators. According to one view, it has the sense of 'elementary, rudimentary' (as in Heb. 5:12); according to the other, it refers to spirit beings, or angels, associated with the heavenly bodies, the sun, moon, stars, and planets. While it is not possible to give an exhaustive treatment of the meaning of στοιχεῖα τοῦ κόσμου here, the main arguments on both sides follow. (The commentaries of Hendriksen and Martin (1972:13–15) are very helpful; also see the article by Delling on στοιχεῖον, pp. 670–87.)

Note that the same expression is used again in Col. 2:20, where it is immediately followed by reference to certain prohibitions (2:20b–21), to man-originated teachings (2:22), and to ascetic practices (2:23). This would support the view that στοιχεῖα refers to an elementary form of religion, as is the emphasis on the necessity of observing rules and regulations. The subsequent genitive phrase, τοῦ κόσμου 'of the world' (used both here and in the Col. 2:20 context) adds the further information that this elementary form of religion expressed itself in outward forms such as prohibitions and asceticism. Again, there is a contrast with the inward spiritual nature of Christianity and its liberty from such rules and regulations.

The same phrase, στοιχεῖα τοῦ κόσμου, is also used in Gal. 4:3, where Paul says, 'Similarly we, when we were children, were enslaved by the στοιχεῖα τοῦ κόσμου'. The use of 'we', the following references to Christ's being born under the law and redeeming those under the law, and the illustration of an heir in his childhood being no better off than a slave would all indicate that Paul is describing the Old Testament religious system by this phrase, especially its many burdensome regulations and restrictions, which Peter referred to as a yoke (Acts 15:10). This interpretation fits the context of Col. 2:20 as well. Moreover, it is very difficult to conceive of Paul's saying that he (along with all his fellow-Jews) was ever in bondage to spirit beings, of whatever sort, under the Old Testament dispensation.

Paul refers again to στοιχεῖα in Gal. 4:9, and if 4:10 is taken as explanatory of 'you want to be slaves again to the στοιχεῖα', then the sense would be the same as in Gal. 4:3. The description in 4:9 of the στοιχεῖα as 'weak and poverty-stricken' may seem strong when referring back to the Old Testament system, but it was in the context of the contrast with the power and richness of the Christian faith, from which the Galatians were in danger of going back to Judaistic practices. If στοιχεῖα referred to spirit beings, then this would seem a strange description of them, far removed from the idea of 'principalities and powers', an expression used twice in Colossians in this context (2:10, 15). However, in Gal. 4:8, the verse preceding the reference to στοιχεῖα, Paul says, "Formerly, when you did not know God, you were in bondage to beings that by nature are no gods" (RSV), and those who advocate the meaning 'spirit beings' argue that στοιχεῖα is used synonymously with this preceding phrase.

It could also be argued that the genitive phrase τοῦ κόσμου, usually rendered 'of the world', seems somewhat anomalous when applied to beings associated with the heavenly bodies, nor do any of the quotations cited from the extrabiblical writings use this phrase. On the other hand, the twelve signs of the zodiac are called the twelve στοιχεῖα of heaven. The NEB, however, meets this objection by translating the phrase "the elemental spirits of the universe."

The main arguments of those favoring the meaning 'spirit beings' are twofold: First, it should be noted that in Colossians Paul refers to such beings several times: in 1:16, 2:10, 15, and 18. The first three references speak of ἀρχαί 'rulers' and ἐξουσίαι 'authorities' and these are generally understood as designations of angelic beings. The last reference speaks specifically of the worship of the angels. Hence, it is argued, this is what στοιχεῖα refers to. The juxtaposition of Gal. 4:8 and 4:9 is also said to support this interpretation. But is it not rather the φιλοσοφία being propagated that made much of angels, rather than that the word στοιχεῖα refers to them? The false teachers promoted the worship of angels, but when the phrase στοιχεῖα τοῦ κόσμου is used in Col. 2:8, it is a generic description of the whole system, parallel with the statement that it was human in origin. The second argument put forth in support of the meaning being 'spirit beings' is that extant astrological writings from this same era contain στοιχεῖα used in this sense in association with angel worship, asceticism, and the observance of special days astronomically determined. Hence, it is argued, since we find these same elements in Colossians, this makes the case for στοιχεῖα having the sense 'spirit beings' a very strong one.

However, the case probably is not so strong as it may seem. Much of the "evidence" is inferential. Moreover, there were quite a variety of mystical religions being propagated during this period which combined some or all of these elements. Hendriksen even questions whether this sense of στοιχεῖα had developed as early as the apostolic era. I have looked at the various citations, and indeed none are unambiguously B.C. in date. But some could be first century so that it does not seem possible to say an unequivocal yes or no to this question. However, it can be said that there is no unambiguous use of στοιχεῖα in the New Testament with the sense of 'angel beings', whereas it *is* used in the sense of 'the elements of which the world consists' in 2 Pet. 3:10 and 12, and in the sense of 'elementary, rudimentary' in Heb. 5:12.

In summary, the argument that in the New Testament τὰ στοιχεῖα 'the elements' refers to angelic beings associated with the heavenly bodies is ingenious and plausible, but not wholly convincing in its New Testament usage. On the other hand, the sense of 'elementary' or 'rudimentary' fits all the disputed contexts and is unambiguously attested in Heb. 5:12. Hence, it is followed in the display.

2:8f and because *it teaches what is* **contrary to** *the true teaching about* **Christ.** The Greek is καὶ οὐ κατὰ Χριστόν 'and not according to Christ'. In the context of a warning against a false religious philosophy, and in view of the emphasis in 2:6-7 on the (true) teaching the Colossians had already had, it seems best here to take οὐ κατὰ Χριστόν to mean 'not in accordance with *the true teaching about* Christ'. This is slightly simplified in the display with 'contrary to'.

2:9 *Make sure of this [2:8] since it is in Christ's body that God dwells completely.* This verse is very similar to 1:19. Note the following similarities:

1. The same verb is used in both verses: κατοικέω 'to dwell (permanently)'. Notice that in 1:19b the aorist infinitive is used, while here in 2:9 the present indicative is used.
2. In both verses ἐν αὐτῷ 'in him (i.e., Christ)' is in the emphatic forefronted position. (This emphasis is shown by the cleft construction 'it is in . . .'.)
3. In both verses, the subject of the verb κατοικέω 'dwell' is the expression πᾶν τὸ πλήρωμα 'all the fullness', but here in 2:9 it is further modified by the genitive phrase τῆς θεότητος 'of the Godhead'. As Arndt and Gingrich point out, θεότης is an "abstract noun for θεός [i.e., God]." Thus the expression here is more explicit than the one in 1:19, but it is semantically equivalent and is therefore represented here by 'God' and 'completely' just as in 1:19.

The difference between 1:19 and 2:9 is the addition in 2:9 of σωματικῶς 'bodily'. This is the adverb form corresponding to the adjective σωματικός, which means 'pertaining to the body'. The adjective is used only twice in the New Testament—once by Paul, in 1 Tim. 4:8, in the expression 'bodily/physical exercise' and once by Luke, in Luke 3:22, where he refers to the Holy Spirit's descending in a bodily form, as a dove. The adverb form here in 2:9 is the only occurrence of it in the New Testament, and commentators are divided as to its meaning. Some hold that it is essentially literal and others that it is nonliteral.

Those who take 'bodily' in the literal sense say that it means that all the fullness of God is in Christ's present, resurrected, glorified body—the present tense excludes any specific reference to the incarnation here (which some would nevertheless argue for). But those who hold to a nonliteral sense for 'bodily' suggest various senses depending on what it is contrasted with: It might mean (1) 'in reality' (as opposed to symbolically); (2) 'in actuality' (as opposed to apparently); or (3) 'as a complete whole' (as opposed to being distributed among various intermediary angelic beings).

To solve this type of exegetical problem, it seems best to choose an interpretation that suits the context of the epistle as a whole. This approach leads us to two possible interpretations:

1. That σωματικῶς is used literally, referring to Christ's resurrection body. In other words, all the fullness of the Godhead is to be found in Christ, the God-man. This would tie 2:9 closely to 1:19, with which it shares so much in common. The aorist tense in 1:19 may well refer to some historical moment, such as the baptism, when Jesus was anointed with the Holy Spirit without measure (cf. John 3:34 and Luke 4:1), whereas here in 2:9 the focus is on Christ's present state.
2. That σωματικῶς is used nonliterally as σῶμα is in 2:17, where it refers to what is real as opposed to temporary foreshadowings in the Old Testament era.

If the first of these views is followed, then the propositional statement takes the form 'it is in Christ's body that God dwells completely'. If the second is followed, then the propositional statement takes the form 'it is in Christ that God really dwells completely'. The first view is considered the better one and is given in the display, but either would be acceptable for translation.

2:10a-b And *make sure of this [2:8]* **since you are** *spiritually* **complete** *because* **you are united to Christ,** There is a tail-head link here with 2:9: ἐν αὐτῷ 'in him' occurs in both verses, and πλήρωμα 'fullness' in 2:9 and πεπληρωμένοι 'having been filled' in 2:10, both come from the same root, πληρόω 'to fill'. This is reflected in the display by 'completely' in 9 and 'complete' in 10a. The word 'spiritually' has been supplied in 10a because the context makes it clear that the Colossians' spiritual position in Christ is in view here. Beekman expressed the meaning as "you have no (spiritual) lack." This is a good way to express it in English, but because it is a litotes, I do not use it here.

It is uncertain whether the phrase ἐν αὐτῷ is forefronted or not, since it does not precede the finite verb ἐστέ 'you(pl) are'; it does, however, precede the perfect participle. (For clauses of a similar sort with a prominent genitive or dative phrase preceding the verb 'to be', see 1 Cor. 3:9 and Eph. 2:5 and 10.) As the commentators point out, two separate statements are fused together here: (1) ἐστὲ ἐν αὐτῷ 'you are in him'; and (2) ἐστὲ πεπληρωμένοι 'you have been filled' or 'you are full'. Two separate propositions are, therefore, used in the display. 'You are united to him' is considered to provide a reason for the main statement, 'you are complete'.

It is difficult to capture the force of the Greek periphrastic perfect that is used here, but one suggestion is 'You entered into a state/position of spiritual completeness and that is your state/position now'.

2:10c who rules over every being that rules. The nonfigurative equivalent of ἡ κεφαλή 'head' is 'rules over'. It is hard to say whether 'head' is a live or dead figure. Since there is no reference to a body, and such a comparison seems foreign to this context, it is probably best understood to be a dead metaphor, so no point of similarity is provided in the display.

There are two metonymies here: ἀρχή 'rule' and ἐξουσία 'authority'. What is being done (ruling, exercising authority) is put in place of the person who does it. It is generally agreed that the use of two synonyms together with πάσης 'every' is a way of referring to all beings who rule, whether supernatural or human (though the reference is probably primarily to the former). The complete supremacy of Christ is thus strongly asserted. In the display, this 10c statement is a description related to 'Christ' in 10b.

2:11a-b Specifically, *because you are* **united to him,** *it is as though* **you were circumcised** *spiritually by Christ.* The word 'circumcise' here is regarded as a live metaphor, since it is collocated with a series of associated lexical items: 'circumcision', 'not done by hands', 'putting off' (i.e., removing skin), 'body', and 'flesh'. Hence, the image of circumcision is retained in the display. The point of similarity is the removal of something from the person, but since this is part of the meaning of circumcise and since the nonfigurative meaning is given in 11d, the point of similarity is not supplied in 11b. Instead, περιετμήθητε 'you were circumcised' is treated as a simile: 'it is as though'.

Since περιετμήθητε 'you were circumcised' is a specific past event, with the verb in the aorist tense, it would be possible to interpret 'in him' as meaning not 'you *are* united to him', but 'you *became* united to him'. Throughout 2:11–15, Paul is emphasizing what has happened to the Colossians, or has been done on their behalf by God, so as to emphasize the spiritual privileges they now enjoy as believers. However, since (present) union with Christ has already been stated as grounds for their spiritual completeness in 2:10b, it seems most natural to regard 11a as a repetition, maintaining the logic of the argument. Further, if union with Christ is regarded as essentially eternal, outside the categories of time (cf. Eph. 1:4), then 11a would have to be 'since you are united to him'.

2:11c *This does* **not** *mean that* **you were circumcised physically by people,** The rest of 2:11 is a contrastive description, or rather an explanation, of what the figure of being circumcised means in this context. To make this connection clear, the implicit relator proposition 'this does not mean that' has been supplied.

Two negative facts about this circumcision are stated here in 11c, by means of metonymy: (1) it was not a physical circumcision, such as was still being carried out by the Jews; (2) it was not carried out by any human agent. The positive counterparts to these statements are found in 11d.

2:11d but *it means that* **your entire evil nature was completely removed by Christ.** This proposition gives the positive counterparts to 'not physical' and to 'not human agents'. The Greek is ἐν τῇ ἀπεκδύσει τοῦ σώματος τῆς σαρκός, ἐν τῇ περιτομῇ τοῦ Χριστοῦ 'in the putting off of the body of the flesh, in the circumcision of Christ'.

The simpler of the two Greek phrases is 'in the circumcision of Christ', which is understood to mean 'the (spiritual) circumcision which was carried out by Christ'. The genitive here states the source or origin of the event, which is a common use of the genitive. The whole phrase gives the contrast with the circumcision performed by people. The implication is that the spiritual circumcision is greatly superior because of the divine person who did it. It may also imply that the false teaching stressed the necessity of physical circumcision along with other outward observances referred to in later verses.

It is only fair to point out that some more recent commentators (e.g., Bruce 1957, Martin 1972, 1973) follow a quite different view of the phrase τῇ περιτομῇ τοῦ Χριστοῦ 'the circumcision of Christ'. Their view is that the phrase refers to a nonliteral circumcision that Christ personally underwent, reflecting another common use of the genitive construction. As to what that circumcision was, they hold that the triumphant death of Christ is in view, with which believers are identified in their own spiritual circumcision (cf. the imagery of the following verse). They base this view on the fact that the phrase τοῦ σώματος τῆς σαρκός 'the body of the flesh' that occurs here is also found in 1:22, where it refers to Christ's physical body, the context being his death on the cross. They also point out that the cognate verb ἀπεκδύομαι 'put off', which is a rare double compound, is found again a few verses later in 2:15, where Christ puts off the rulers and powers, the spirit beings arrayed against him, again a reference to his death.

Ingenious though this view is, it seems rather far-fetched to take 'circumcision' as figuratively referring to Christ's death. There is no suggestion of this in such passages as Rom. 2:28-29 or Phil. 3:3. And in the nearer context of Col. 2:15, it is not said that Christ put off his body of flesh, but rather the powers and authorities. Further, in chapter 3's ethical application of the teaching here, Paul, in 3:9, says that the Colossians have put off the old man with his (evil) deeds, a statement which is very similar to the one used here. Hence this view is rejected.

Now for the more difficult first phrase, 'in the putting off of the body of the flesh'. First it should be noted that 'putting off' is not used literally, but figuratively, and is regarded as part of the metaphor. It is generally agreed, based on the root's being a compound of two prepositions, ἀπ(ο) 'away from' and ἐκ 'out of', that the meaning is 'to remove completely', rather than simply 'to remove'.

It should also be noted that σαρκός 'flesh' is used here in the common Pauline ethical sense of 'evil nature', and the phrase τοῦ σώματος τῆς σαρκός 'the body of the flesh' is very similar in meaning to the expression 'the old man' used later in 3:9, which is also said to have been put off completely (cf. also 'the body of sin' in Rom. 6:6, where it is closely linked with 'the old man'). In the light of this, 'body' is understood as a figure signifying 'the whole of'; it is presumably used here because of its appropriateness to this context in which circumcision is the central image. The term 'body' may also imply a contrast with the foreskin, which is a very small part, again drawing attention to the superiority of their position as Christians to anything the false teaching could offer them.

In the propositional display, the meaning of the two Greek phrases is combined in a single nonfigurative proposition, since the phrase 'the circumcision of Christ' adds nothing more than the agent of the event, the event being the same.

This strong description of the spiritual position of the Colossians is not to be rejected because it was not true of their spiritual experience. It is their position in Christ that is being discussed (as also in Rom. 6, which gives rise to similar problems). The New Testament approach to Christian ethics is to state the facts of spiritual position or privilege and then urge believers to live accordingly. "Be what you are" is an excellent summary of this New Testament truth. In Col. 2:10-15 "what you are" is spelled out, and in Col. 3 "what you are to be in daily practice."

As pointed out in the discussion of the structure of this paragraph, 2:11 is regarded as a specific of the general statement in 10a. In other words, one aspect of the Colossians' spiritual completeness was that Christ had dealt with their sinful nature once and for all.

2:12a *And specifically,* when you were baptized, The textual variants here between βαπτίσματι and βαπτισμῷ need not concern the translator since both refer to baptism and there is no difference in meaning. Both are abstract nouns representing the event 'to baptize'. The construction ἐν + abstract noun could equally well represent the time or the means. Since there are considerable theological differences on how baptism is related to the spiritual events referred to here—whether symbolically, as a means of grace, or actually effecting what is described—the proposition is left as a statement of time.

2:12b *it was as though* you *had died and* were buried *by God* with Christ, In 2:12, Paul switches to a new set of related lexical terms—'buried', 'resurrected', 'the dead', and 'God's power at work'. As in the previous verse, this points to a live metaphor, so the images are retained in the display and should also be retained in translation.

The Colossians had not undergone physical burial or resurrection (see 12c), so these terms must have to do with their spiritual position, which conclusion is supported by the use of the aorist tense throughout 2:12 (as in 2:11). It seems reasonable to suppose that the meaning here is the same as in Rom. 6, where Paul says that our old man was crucified with Christ (6:6) and that we were buried with him by baptism into death (6:4) and that we have newness of life just as he has in his resurrection (6:4). Here in Colossians Paul uses 'we' for 'our old man'. In other words, our union with Christ is such that it means we are spiritually identified with Christ's death, burial, and resurrection. This imagery vividly portrays the radical break between the old life in Adam and the new life in Christ. It is thus not at all dissimilar to what 2:11 has already said, but with a new set of images here. In addition, it lays more stress on the positive side, our resurrection with Christ.

In the display, the same type of rendering, 'it was as though', is used as in 2:11 to indicate that these are images taken from the physical realm to describe spiritual realities. Further, since being buried implies having died first, 'you had died' is supplied as implicit information.

2:12c and *it was as though* you were resurrected *by God* with Christ The only question here is the referent of 'whom/which' in the phrase ἐν ᾧ 'in whom/which'. It could be Christ (cf. the meaning 'in Christ' elsewhere in this paragraph), or it could be baptism. The use of 'in Christ' earlier in this paragraph favors the first view; there is even an exact parallel between the beginning of 2:11, ἐν ᾧ καί + aorist verb, and this clause in 2:12, which also has ἐν ᾧ καί + aorist verb.

In favor of its meaning 'in baptism' it can be argued that:

1. The nearest appropriate antecedent to the relative pronoun is 'baptism'.
2. The conjunction καί 'and' more naturally links resurrection to burial than it links 2:12 to 2:11.
3. The verb here is 'co-raised' and it would be awkward to say 'raised with him in him'. In Greek there are two constructions that are used with 'co-' verbs, the second being far more common. In the first, the preposition σύν, rendered as 'co-', is repeated with the pronoun (the only example of this is in the next verse). In the second, the more common one, 'co-' is not repeated with the pronoun (or noun), which is in the dative case, the case that the preposition σύν 'with' takes. Hence, ἐν ᾧ here appears to be anomalous. Paul, in fact, seems to keep the two phrases separate: he does not mix 'in Christ' with 'with Christ'.

The view preferred here, therefore, is that ἐν ᾧ means the same as ἐν τῷ βαπτίσματι/-μῷ 'in the baptism' in the preceding clause. Since the two propositions, 12b and 12c, are joined by 'and', the identical 'when' proposition is not repeated. Rather, 12a is taken as stating the circumstances of the rest of this propositional cluster.

If ἐν ᾧ were taken as referring to union with Christ, then 12b–d would read as follows: '*it was as though* you *had died* and were buried with Christ. Since you are united to Christ, you were also raised with Christ . . .'.

2:12d by *your* believing that God acted powerfully, The Greek is διὰ τῆς πίστεως τῆς ἐνεργείας τοῦ θεοῦ 'through the faith of the inworking of the God'. This complex noun phrase has two abstract nouns, πίστις 'faith' and ἐνέργεια 'inworking', and is also a double genitive. The noun 'faith' refers to the event of believing, the Colossians' believing, since the Colossian believers are the only appropriate referent in the context.

When πίστις is followed by a genitive construction (thirty-six times in Paul's letters), there are three collocational patterns:

1. When the genitive is a reference to human beings, they are the ones doing the believing.
2. When the genitive is a reference to Christ, the faith is directed towards him.
3. When the genitive is a reference to something nonpersonal (e.g., 'gospel' in Phil. 1:27, 'truth' in 2 Thess. 2:13), it is the content of the faith—what was believed—that is in view.

In this particular clause, since ἐνεργείας 'inworking' refers to something nonpersonal, it is interpreted as the content of the believing, specifically, what the Colossians believed.

The gloss is given as 'inworking' in an attempt to indicate that the Greek word is not connected with the ordinary verb 'to work'. Arndt and Gingrich say it always has to do with supernatural beings. This being so, it is rendered here as 'powerfully' along with 'to act'. The genitive τοῦ θεοῦ 'of God' that follows ἐνεργείας indicates who it is that is acting powerfully.

2:12e *specifically, by your believing that* God resurrected Christ from among dead people. There is a minor textual matter here concerning whether the article should be included before νεκρῶν 'dead-ones' or not. But the meaning is the same for either variant.

The participial phrase here could be taken simply as a description of God, 'who raised Christ'. However, in this context, with its motif of death-burial-resurrection, a better alternative is to regard it as in apposition to the preceding genitive phrase (both being in the genitive). Thus regarded, the statement 'God resurrected Christ from among dead people' specifies more precisely what was believed about God's powerful acting. In other words, their faith in the fact that God had raised Christ was the means to their own spiritual resurrection with Christ.

2:13a And specifically, although you *who are Gentiles* were *spiritually* dead The pronoun ὑμᾶς 'you' is forefronted here, giving it prominence. Together with 2:13b and c, this prominence is evidently intended to convey the idea 'you of all people'. The Colossians were predominantly Gentiles, who previously were spiritually dead. The prominence is shown by putting 'it was you' at the beginning of the main proposition, 2:13e.

The conjunction καί 'and' could be taken as providing a link back to the previous proposition, 2:12d, which states that God raised Christ from among the dead. Its meaning in this case would be that God *also* raised you (he raised Christ, he raised you also). However, Christ was *physically* raised, whereas the Colossians were *spiritually* raised, which may be why Paul uses a different verb for the raising of the Colossians and the raising of Christ. (This latter verb is the usual one used for raising the dead.) Alternatively, καί may be linking this clause group (2:13) with the preceding ones, or it may be linking all of 2:13-15 with the preceding ones. In the light of the way these verses are linked, it seems most likely that καί is intended to link this new specific with the preceding ones.

The reason for supplying the words 'who are Gentiles' is explained in the note on 2:13c-d.

The word νεκρούς 'dead' is not used here in its primary physical sense; rather, it is used figuratively to refer to the spiritual realm. Since it follows so closely on 2:12 and is in the same context as 'made alive', it should be understood as a live metaphor. The point of similarity with the physical realm is the complete absence of life. In relation to the world of spiritual things, the Colossians were like dead men; they had no spiritual life, and they acted accordingly.

The semantic relation between 13a and the main proposition, 2:13e, could be simply that of time, but the lexical contrast between 'dead' and 'made alive' and the terminology relevant to Gentiles ('uncircumcision') make it more likely that the relation is one of concession. (When there is no formal marker of the relation, the preceding present participle seems often to be used for the concessive relation in New Testament Greek.)

2:13b since you sinned There is a minor textual variant here: ἐν 'in' is present in some manuscripts and absent in others, but this does not affect the meaning. The main question is the semantic relation between 13a and 13b. The choice is between reason and grounds. In other words, Paul is saying either that they were spiritually dead *because* they had sinned, or that the evidential proof of his assertion that they were spiritually dead is the fact that they had sinned. Both are theologically true and are acceptable alternatives. Possibly the use of an abstract noun, which draws attention to a state rather than an event, points to grounds—the state of constant sinning was the clear evidence of their state of spiritual death. Grounds is the label in the display, but either would be acceptable in a translation.

The noun παραπτώμασιν 'transgressions' is an abstract noun, representing the (continuous) event of sinning. It is not the usual word for sin, which is ἁμαρτία. Since 'transgressions' is repeated in 2:13f, it appears to have been a deliberate choice for this context. It could be that it is a term more appropriately collocated with the lexical items of 2:14. If that is so, the difference between it and the more generic ἁμαρτία may be that it represents sin as 'transgression of God's commands', which incurs the penalty of doing so. However, 'sinned' is used in the display since, if any distinction is intended, it is not well enough established to be certain.

2:13c–d and since you were uncircumcised *spiritually,* **that is,** *since* **you** *were controlled* **by your evil nature,** The Greek is καὶ τῇ ἀκροβυστίᾳ τῆς σαρκὸς ὑμῶν 'and in the uncircumcision of your flesh', which can be understood literally, meaning that they were Gentiles; or figuratively, meaning that they had not been spiritually circumcised as described in 2:11; or both. In view of its close link with 'in your transgressions' and the figurative use of 'circumcision' and 'flesh' in 2:11, I conclude that the main sense intended is the figurative one (referring to their spiritual state), and in this case 'the uncircumcision of your flesh' refers to the dominance or control of their evil nature. But the terms used are those that Paul tends to use of the Gentiles (cf. 1:21 and Eph. 2:11-12), and the emphatic initial καὶ ὑμᾶς 'and you(pl)' in 13a supports this. Hence, the implicit proposition 'who are Gentiles' has been attached to 'you' in 2:13a.

2:13e nevertheless, it was you whom God caused to become alive *spiritually* **with Christ.** Some manuscripts have ἡμᾶς 'us', others have ὑμᾶς 'you(pl)', and still others omit both. There seems little doubt that ὑμᾶς is the best reading, repeating the forefronted ὑμᾶς (see 2:13a). The manuscripts that omit ὑμᾶς probably reflect a more polished version, in which the object is stated only once; those with ἡμᾶς probably assimilated it to the first person plural pronouns in the following clause.

The only major issue here concerns the subject of this clause. Is the referent 'God the Father' or 'Christ'? Ellicott presents the arguments in favor of its being 'Christ' as follows:

1. It is unnatural to consider 'God' as subject based only on the oblique mention of 'God' at the end of 2:12.
2. 'Christ' is prominent throughout 2:9-12, and so should be here also.
3. The events referred to in 2:13-15, especially 2:14 and 15, are more naturally collocated with 'Christ' than with 'the Father'; in particular, it is Christ who deals with the rulers and authorities mentioned in 2:15.

These arguments can be answered as follows:

1. It is normal in Greek to use as subject a noun in an oblique case in a preceding clause.
2. Christ's prominence in 2:10-12 is mostly marked by prepositional phrases, such as 'in him' and '(with) him', not by being subject of the verbs. This is still the case in 2:13; and in 2:14 and 15 Christ is brought in indirectly via the cross.
3. The matter of natural collocation is not so difficult as it appears. In 2:14 forgiveness is expounded in some detail, and forgiveness is primarily associated with the Father, based on the Son's work. And while 2:15 is more problematic (see the notes on 2:15a–c), we observe that there is no overt change of subject in 2:14 and 15, and a change of subject should not be introduced simply because the exegesis is difficult.

In addition, 'Christ' is not the subject of the verbs in 2:10-12, which are passive. God the Father may well be understood as the unexpressed agent, since the events take place 'in Christ' or 'with Christ'. Also, it certainly sounds forced to say in 2:13, 'Christ made you alive with himself'.

In the display, then, the subject of the third person verbs and associated participles is taken to be 'God the Father' throughout 2:13-15.

2:13f *And specifically,* **God forgave us(inc) all our sins;** The meaning of this clause is straightforward, but it should be noted that the same word used for 'sins' in 2:13b is used here (παραπτώματα 'transgressions'); that the less common verb χαρίζομαι is used for 'to forgive'; and that the pronouns now switch to first person plurals, which are interpreted as 'we inclusive', since what is said applies to all Christians.

Once again, the difficult question is the semantic relation of this proposition with the preceding one (13e). As far as the sequence of the events in 13e and 13f, commentators are divided as to whether the forgiving (13f) preceded the making alive (13e) or was simultaneous with it. The use of the aorist participle would fit in with either of these views. Since there is no focus on the sequence of events—it is simply a description of what God has done—the relationship is taken to be simultaneous. In other words, Paul describes two of the things that God has done, but without precisely defining the relation.

As far as the more focal relationship, reason, grounds, specific, and circumstance are possible. But reason and grounds assume that the event of 13f preceded 13e in time, and this view has already been rejected. To take 'God forgave us' as a specific of 'God made you alive' is dubious; this would mean that 'made alive' has a generic sense, which it is does not seem to have (unlike the generic 'saved' or 'redeemed'). Circumstance would appear to be appropriate: its meaning is that God forgave as well as made alive, but with the forgiving backgrounded relative to the making alive. Support for this relation is that 'made alive' is represented by a finite verb and 'forgave' by a participle. However, 2:14 is a figurative description of forgiveness. That is, the statement about forgiveness is developed figuratively by 2:14 and thus the reference to forgiveness in 13e is part of a larger unit, 13e–14f, where forgiveness is the topic. This grouping in turn is regarded as yet another specific of the nucleus proposition, 2:10. Therefore, in such an analysis, 13e is not directly related to 13d, but they are related to each other only via their respective main propositions. It is a difficult decision, but the absence of any formal conjunction between 13d and 13e may be support for considering them conjoined specifics of the nucleus.

2:14a *that is, it was just as though* **he canceled the document** All of 2:14 is metaphorical; it centers on the image of χειρόγραφον '(written) debt'. This is generally regarded as referring to a written statement of indebtedness. The phrase καθ' ἡμῶν 'against us' implies that the debt had not yet been paid—it was still outstanding. The verb ἐξαλείφω 'wipe away' (of which ἐξαλείψας is the aorist participle referring back to 'he', i.e., God) is the appropriate one for canceling the debt by wiping the writing off a papyrus document or a clay tablet. (The phrase 'against us' is most naturally made part of the next proposition.)

2:14b which *stated* **the charges against us(inc)** The word δόγμα generally refers to official decrees, announcements, and regulations; Jewish writers used the word to refer to the Mosaic law and its individual commandments. In this particular context, δόγμα appears to refer to the written contents of the χειρόγραφον, as Arndt and Gingrich suggest. But it is the nonfigurative meaning of δόγμα that is in view: the law with its commands and prohibitions, which we have broken, incurring the penalty stated in the law. It seems best then not to interpret the word χειρόγραφον in 14a as the law (which has hardly been removed by nailing it to the cross), but as a document, drawn up, as it were, by God, listing the charges against us. It is a very serious document, because the penalty prescribed for these charges is death. Hence, in the display, χειρόγραφον is represented by 'document' (in 14a) and τοῖς δόγμασιν as an identification proposition, 'which stated the charges'.

2:14c *and* **which indicted/condemned us,** Here the sense of καθ' ἡμῶν 'against us' in 2:14a is repeated, presumably to give it greater prominence. However, this is not easily represented in the display. In both cases, it is stated that the document itself is 'against us', but this is no doubt a metonymy for the contents of the document. The expression 'to be against' is considered an idiom representing either of two events, 'to indict' or 'to condemn'.

2:14d and *it was just as though* **it was this document that he removed** The antecedent of the pronoun αὐτό 'it' is χειρόγραφον in 2:14a. This pronoun is probably slightly emphatic since it could have been omitted and since it precedes the verb (contrast this with the following clause). It is, therefore, rendered here with a cleft construction: 'it was this document that'.

The whole proposition represents an advance on propositions 14a–c, in that the condemning document is now removed altogether, rather than simply being canceled. Also the perfect tense is used to represent a past act whose consequences are still operative: it has been removed and it remains that way.

The phrase ἐκ τοῦ μέσου 'out of the middle' appears to refer to the document as a sort of barrier between God and us. This phrase is not represented separately in the display because 'removed' already expresses that idea.

2:14e–f by nailing it to the cross, *that is, by Christ's dying on the cross.* The Greek is figurative; no such document was actually nailed to the cross. It is a continuation of the figure of the document, stating the means by which the document was canceled and removed. The nonfigurative equivalent is given in 14f. The translator needs to decide, on the basis of receptor-language requirements, whether to include the nonfigurative statement or not.

2:15a *And specifically,* **God defeated/demoted the spirit beings that rule,** "In this difficult verse," says Peake, "the meaning of almost every word is disputed. It is therefore imperative to control the exegesis by strict regard to the context." Easier said than done!

One of the main problems in 2:15a is deciding what the referent of τὰς ἀρχὰς καὶ τὰς ἐξουσίας 'the rulers and the authorities' is. In 1:16 this phrase, together with 'thrones' and 'lordships', was interpreted as referring to all spirit beings that exercise authority, and in 2:10, earlier in this same paragraph, this expression was again interpreted as referring to all spirit beings that exercise authority (and possibly to human authorities as well). However, in 1 Cor. 15:24 and Eph. 6:12 the same combination refers to evil spirit beings, and in Tit. 3:1 to human authorities. It would seem, therefore, that the phrase itself simply refers to persons and spirit beings who rule, and the determination whether they are human or not, and whether they are evil or not, depends on the context.

Another problem is the meaning of ἀπεκδυσάμενος 'having put off'. Since this is an aorist participle in the nominative masculine singular form, it refers back to 'God the Father', the same subject as in 2:13 and 14. It is also in the middle voice, so a number of commentators insist that it must mean 'remove from oneself'. The same verb is used in 3:9, where it could mean 'you have put off, or removed, from yourself', the thing removed being 'the old man with his deeds'. The cognate noun occurs in 2:11 in the phrase 'in the putting off of the body of the flesh', but that was interpreted as meaning that Christ did it for them, or to them. With 'God the Father' as subject, it is much more likely that the verb is simply transitive, a view supported by Arndt and Gingrich, who suggest "disarm," and by Weigelt (p. 315), who takes it as referring to the known oriental custom of removing someone from office by stripping him of his official robes. Some of the versions agree, for example, Bruce's (1965) and Beck's rendering "He stripped . . . of their armor"; and Barclay is similar: "he stripped . . . of their power."

All these suggestions carry much the same idea of God's defeating, or greatly reducing in power, the rulers and authorities. The rulers and authorities could thus be regarded as enemies defeated by God, or as angels who had now been superceded by the divine mediator, the Son. Although most commentators take the former view, in some ways, this latter suggestion makes better contextual sense, since it seems apparent from Paul's references that the false teaching was unduly exalting angelic mediators, or intermediaries. He has already said they were created by Christ (1:16) and are ruled by him (2:10). Now he is saying that whatever importance they had before Christ's coming (and there are quite a few references in the Old Testament), this has been removed, so that Christ stands alone and supreme. This is not to say that angels have no part to play now (see Heb. 1:14), but it is a very subordinate part compared with the centrality and importance of the Redeemer himself. Hence, in the display, 'demoted' and 'defeated' are given as alternatives.

If 'demoted' is the correct meaning, then the phrase 'the rulers and authorities', as in its other two occurrences in Colossians, would refer to all spirit beings, good and bad, who exercise any sort of authority. But if 'defeated' is the correct meaning, then 'the rulers and authorities' would refer to evil spirits only.

2:15b and he demonstrated this [2:15a] publicly; Abbott points out that ἐδειγμάτισεν is "a rare word. . . . The idea involved . . . is . . . that of public exhibition," and although παρρησία normally means 'boldness of speech', it would seem that here it reinforces the idea 'publicly' or 'openly'. Following closely on 15a, this is a continuation of the picture of defeat in battle or demotion from office: the defeat or demotion is now made public.

Of course, 'he publicly exposed them' is clear enough, but what does it refer to? Most commentators see the answer to this question in the final clause (2:15c); that is, it was at the cross that the defeat or humiliation was publicly demonstrated. However, the defeat of God's enemies was *not* obvious at the cross—indeed, the opposite could be concluded. Rather, the resurrection, the ascension, and Christ's sitting down at God's right hand (referred to in 3:1) would seem much more appropriate as the referent for this. And to *whom* was this defeat or demotion made public? Probably it was to the inhabitants of the spiritual world, good and bad angels, and then by revelation to the apostles. However, few other Scriptures touch on this topic, so that it is not really clear just what Paul had in mind when he spoke of this public exposure.

2:15c that is, he triumphed over them by *what Christ did*. The verb θριαμβεύω usually means 'to lead in a triumphal procession', a custom of successful generals. The object of this verb is αὐτούς 'them', referring to 'rulers and authorities' in 15a. The gender is changed from feminine (strict concord) to masculine because Paul was thinking of them as persons. Following the pronoun 'them' is the phrase ἐν αὐτῷ 'in him/it'. This singular pronoun form is ambiguous and can either mean 'him' (i.e., Christ), or 'it' (i.e., the cross, referred to in 2:14e). There is a division of opinion among commentators and versions as to whether Christ or the cross is the appropriate referent, but the context here of public triumph would seem to suit Christ better. 'God' is still the subject and it was he who triumphed over these powers in Christ—not just at the cross, but throughout his life and in his death, resurrection, and ascension. However, the cross doubtless lies at the heart of the triumph, so an alternative rendering is provided below.

But first we have to decide what the relation of this proposition is to 15b. The two best choices are (1) that it is the means by which God demonstrated the defeat or demotion of the rulers and authorities, making the construction of 2:15 very much like that of 2:14; or (2) that it is equivalent to 15b, a restatement in other terms (i.e., the triumphal procession was the public exposure). Both of these make good sense. Interpretation 2 is what is in the display; interpretation 1 is propositionalized as follows:

2:15b he demonstrated this [2:15a] publicly,
2:15c by means of God's triumphing over them by *Christ's dying on* the cross.

SECTION CONSTITUENT 2:16–19 (Paragraph: Specific₁ of 2:8–15)

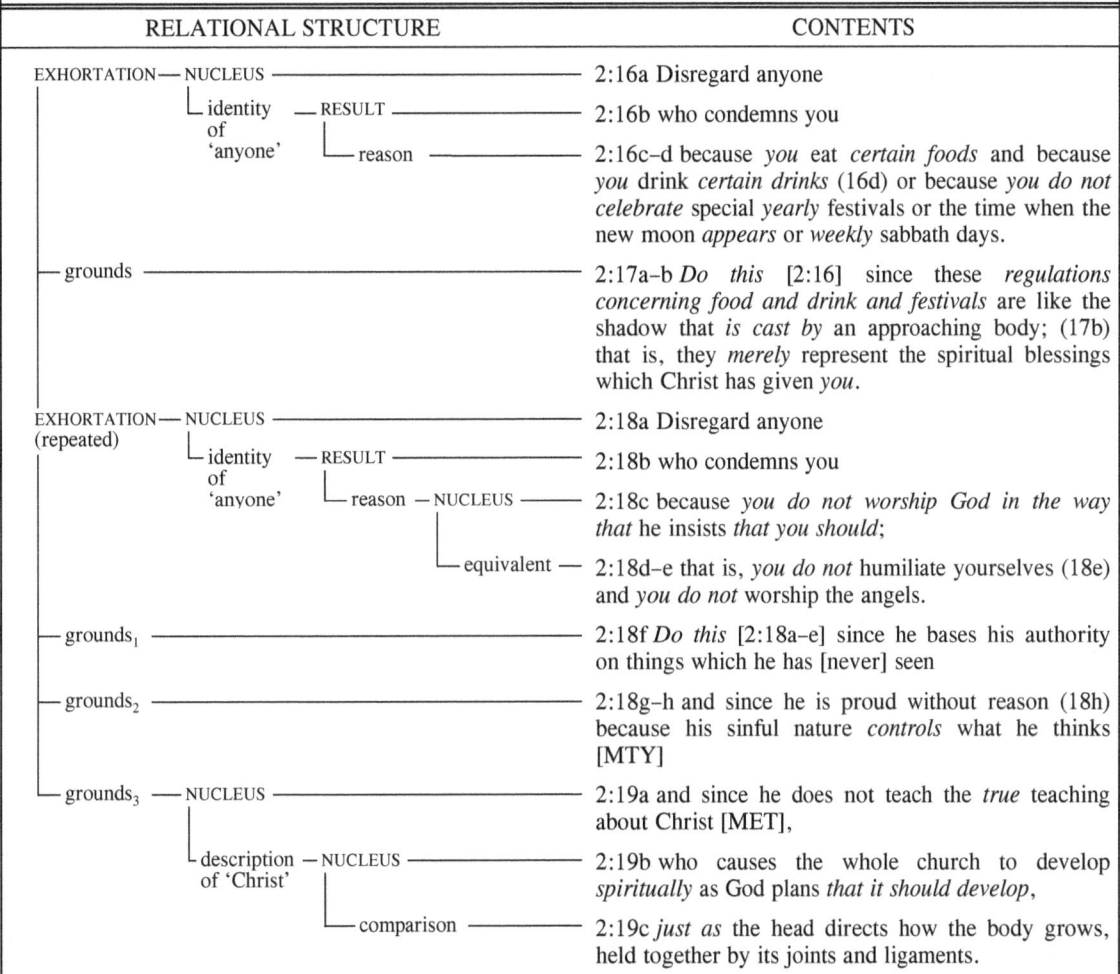

BOUNDARIES AND COHERENCE

The start of the 2:16–19 paragraph is marked by three features: the occurrence of the conjunction οὖν 'therefore' in 2:16; the change from aorist indicative verbs in 2:13–15 to a present imperative in 2:16; and the introduction of a new subject, τις 'someone', after a series of verb forms with the subject 'he', referring to God the Father.

Determining the closing boundary is more difficult. There is good evidence for its ending with 2:17 and also good evidence for its ending with 2:19. The features that favor its ending with 2:17 are that 2:18 closely parallels 2:16, so if 2:16 starts a paragraph, 2:18 should also. In addition, the reference to Christ at the end of 2:17 is characteristic of a paragraph ending in this part of the epistle (cf. 2:5, 15, 19; 3:4).

The reasons for the paragraph's *not* ending with 2:17 are as follows: (1) the two parallel commands in 2:16 and 18 are synonymous in their main statement (the support is different), which points to the second one being a repetition of the first within one unit, as in 3:1–4. (2) There is no obvious shift of subject between μή ... τις 'don't let anyone' and μηδείς 'let no one'. And (3) there is no οὖν in 2:18, though it is not certain just how significant this is since there is none in 2:20 either and 2:20 clearly starts a new paragraph.

While the decision regarding the paragraph's boundaries is not clear-cut, it seems that the evidence that favors treating 2:16–19 as one paragraph with two closely related halves is slightly better than the evidence for treating them as two separate paragraphs, although either approach would be acceptable in a translation.

There is surprisingly little obvious lexical coherence in this paragraph. What can be said is that much of the information falls within a semantic domain, that of the terms used by the false teaching—that is to say, terms referring to regulations dealing with such external matters as what is eaten or drunk, the observation of special days, and matters to do with worship, such as self-abasement and the worship of angels. In other words, Paul is taking up some of the matters emphasized in the false teaching and warning the Colossians against being taken in by them. In both halves of the paragraph there is also reference to Christ.

Grammatically, the paragraph consists of two parallel commands followed by a series of dependent constructions (either relative clauses or participial phrases) that support the two commands. Semantically, the two warnings are backed up by grounds for the commands, focusing on the temporary nature of such regulations and the unspiritual character of the false teacher himself.

PROMINENCE AND THEME

The main statement of the theme of the 2:16-19 paragraph is drawn from the two parallel warnings in 2:16a-b and 2:18a-b: 'Disregard anyone who condemns you'. Then, as usual, the question is whether more information than simply the command should be included in the theme, and if so, why. As the main statement stands, it lacks any definition of what sort of condemnation is being referred to—it could even have been a just condemnation. Hence, it seems necessary to add a generic summary of the reasons for the condemning given in 2:16c-d and 18c-e. In effect, these reasons have an identifying function with respect to the event 'condemns' and are an integral part of the theme.

NOTES

2:16a-b Disregard anyone who condemns you A fairly literal translation of the Greek here would be 'Don't let anybody judge you'. It seems clear from the context that this is not a command to stop people from judging them, which would hardly be possible, but to take no notice of such judgments. Their liberty as believers was not to be restricted by criticisms of this sort. Hence, the rendering in the display, 'Disregard anyone who . . .'. It is clear from the context that the judging referred to is adverse judgment, as in Matt. 7:1 and other New Testament passages. Since the English word *judge* is neutral, the word 'condemn' is used in the display; 'adversely criticize' would also do.

This verse is introduced by οὖν 'therefore', just as 2:6 is. In 2:6 οὖν is considered the marker of the beginning of the hortatory section of the epistle because it is the first occurrence of οὖν and it occurs only in the hortatory section.

Three suggestions can be made as to the function of οὖν here at the beginning of 2:16-19:

1. It marks an inference from the preceding material. Which particular preceding material depends, to some extent, on the exegesis one prefers. Many commentators refer it back to 2:15 (those who see angelic beings as the center of the heresy); others refer it back to 2:14 (those who link the regulations referred to in 2:16 with the interpretation of χειρόγραφον '(written) debt' as doing away with the regulations of the Mosaic law); still others refer it back to 2:10-15 as a whole; or, in the light of the analysis of the preceding paragraph, to 2:10, the nuclear statement of 2:10-15 (i.e., the statement, 'you are complete in him').

2. It marks the resumption of the theme-line. The thematic material in this hortatory section consists of the various commands. The last command was in 2:8, and this was followed by a lengthy exposition of the grounds for it. Now Paul returns to commands, and this return is marked by οὖν. Arndt and Gingrich say of οὖν, "inferential and then mainly a transitional conjunction," and under entry 2, "In historical narrative οὖν serves—a. to resume a subject once more after an interruption." This second alternative would then extend this view of οὖν in Arndt and Gingrich to epistolary, specifically hortatory, material. (It is only fair to add, however, that Arndt and Gingrich favor view 1 for this verse.)

3. It marks the surface paragraphs in the hortatory part of the epistle. This would mean that 2:6-3:17 would be divided into surface paragraphs as follows: 2:6-15; 2:16-23; 3:1-4; 3:5-11; and 3:12-17. However, it is an integral part of the semantic theory that underlies these displays that there is often a mismatch between the deep and surface structures; thus the surface and semantic boundaries would not necessarily have

to coincide. And it's true that Paul's surface paragraphs may consist of several semantic paragraphs. Their boundaries, however, rarely conflict. Each οὖν in Colossians does, in fact, coincide with the opening of a semantic paragraph, but there are more semantic paragraphs than there are occurrences of οὖν.

The first of the three preceding views is the common view, but its implication is that some or all of the material in 2:10-15 provides grounds for the warning in 2:16, and yet this warning carries its own grounds with it, so that this view is not convincing. The second one is certainly valid, but more research is needed before any accurate assessment of it can be made. More research is needed for the third as well. If in the receptor language there is some indicator of resumption of the hortatory themeline, however, it would be appropriate to use it here.

2:16c because *you* eat *certain foods* and because *you* drink *certain drinks* The text refers to condemnation concerning 'eating and drinking' but does not give any specifics at all—whether it was for eating certain foods or for not eating them, etc. However, the prohibitions in 2:21 and 22 concerning things that 'perish with use' and the mention of asceticism in 2:23 make it likely that the Colossian believers were being criticized because they ate and drank things prohibited by the false teacher. So far as the drinking is concerned, commentators generally agree that it was wine or strong drink that was forbidden, but it is not clear why, except that that would more readily link up with asceticism. One could ask what other drink there was to condemn people for drinking. However, because of the uncertainty, 'certain drinks' has been used in the display.

2:16d or because *you do not celebrate* special *yearly* festivals or the time when the new moon *appears* or *weekly* sabbath days. The noun ἑορτή 'festival', which is used to refer to major Jewish festivals such as Passover and Pentecost, is rendered here as 'special *yearly* festivals'. Commentators agree that, in this context, the festivals referred to were annual ones, in contrast with the monthly new moon feasts and the weekly sabbaths.

Both 16c and 16d are considered reasons for the condemnation: κρινέτω . . . ἐν means 'judge . . . with respect to', which more precisely is a reason relation. These propositions help to define 'anyone who condemns you' and so are part of the paragraph's first exhortation.

2:17a-b *Do this [2:16]* since these *regulations concerning food and drink and festivals* are like the shadow that *is cast by* an approaching body; that is, they *merely* represent the spiritual blessings which Christ has given *you*. The initial ἅ is a relative pronoun referring back to the preceding material. In gender it agrees with σαββάτων 'sabbaths', but there is no reason in the context to restrict its reference to this alone, so it is understood as referring back to all the matters mentioned—food, drink, festivals, etc.—which were the reasons the Colossians' behavior was being criticized. However, strictly speaking, what is in view here are the Jewish regulations concerning such matters as clean and unclean foods and observance of festivals that foreshadowed the Christian era; hence the implicit 'regulations concerning' is supplied.

The rest of 2:17 is figurative in the Greek: 'a shadow of the coming things, but the body (is) of Christ'. This is considered to be a live metaphor, since there are two interrelated images, a shadow and a body that casts a shadow. A very similar use of σκιά 'shadow' is in Heb. 8:5 and 10:1. Hebrew used *tsēl* 'shadow' figuratively, but not with this sense. It seems likely, then, that New Testament authors created this metaphor to express the relationship between the old and the new dispensations. As to its meaning, the phrase 'the coming things' refers to the Christian dispensation in contrast with the Old Testament. The various Old Testament regulations regarding clean and unclean foods, the special festivals in Jerusalem, and many other such matters were like the shadow cast by a body—they served to point forward to the spiritual and universal new dispensation. Hence σῶμα 'body' refers to the spiritual blessings that were prefigured—blessings which have now come with Christ.

The second half of 2:17, literally rendered, is 'the body is Christ's (or, of Christ)'. The genitive could mean that Christ is the source of the spiritual blessings, a common use of the genitive; or it could, in view of the constant emphasis in this epistle on the supremacy and all-sufficiency of Christ, mean 'centers in Christ', or even 'is Christ', although with this third interpretation one would have expected Χριστός 'Christ', in order to be in the same case as τὸ σῶμα 'the body' (i.e., the nominative case).

One question here is whether the two halves of 2:17 form a contrast. The relation of contrast has to have two points of difference one of which is negative-positive. There should also be a point of similarity. The two halves of 2:17 are as follows:

> these things are a shadow of the coming things
> of Christ (is) the body (of the coming things).

With this arrangement, it could be maintained that there are two points of difference, 'shadow' vs. 'body' and 'these things' vs. 'Christ', but neither is a negative-positive. I am inclined, therefore, to agree with Lenski that this is not a contrast. (Note that a number of versions do not use 'but' here.) In fact, 'the body' referred to is referentially the same as 'the coming things', but is expressed figuratively, rather than temporally. The second half of 2:17, therefore, elucidates these 'coming things' by relating them to Christ.

Verse 2:17 provides grounds for the warning in 2:16. In effect, Paul is saying, Disregard such criticisms—those who criticize you are basing their criticisms on the shadow, whereas you, as believers, already have the reality.

2:18a-b Disregard anyone who condemns you The Greek word in 2:16b that was rendered 'condemns' is a different one than is found here. What is here involves a simile: 'to pass (adverse) judgment like an umpire in the games'. However, as is well argued by Abbott, and supported by other commentators (Peake, Bruce 1957), the images of the games and the prize are not in focus here; in other words, it is a dead figure. The meaning is 'condemn', synonymous with the word for 'condemn' in 16b. Thus 18a-b is identical in meaning with 16a-b. One reason for the repetition is that though the warning has not changed, Paul has more to say in support of the warning, so he repeats it in order to attach further arguments to it. To have attached all he wished to say to one statement would have made for considerable complexity. (The 3:1-4 paragraph is handled in the same way.)

2:18c-d because *you do not worship God in the way that* he insists *that you should; that is, you do not* humiliate yourselves The present participle θέλων 'desiring', the first of four such participles in 2:18 and 19, refers back to the subject of the main verb, that is, to a false teacher. Normally, the verb θέλω means 'to desire (to), to wish (to), to will', but its collocation with ἐν 'in' is very unusual, and there are different opinions as to its meaning:

1. It is the primary meaning that is in focus, and there is an ellipsis: the whole would read 'who wants (to condemn you) with regard to . . .' (cf. the use of ἐν in 2:16).
2. It has an adverbial function and modifies 'condemn' so that the meaning is 'deliberately', 'voluntarily', or 'arbitrarily'.
3. It means 'delighting (in)'.
4. It means 'insisting (on)'.

It is very difficult to find objective reasons for choosing one view rather than another. Against the first view is the fact that it requires a supposed ellipsis, whereas the others do not. Also, it makes for an awkward sequence: Disregard anyone who condemns you, wanting to condemn you. Against the second view is the very different treatment of this first participle in contrast to the following three. Against the third view it is said that this is a Hebraism of the sort used in the Septuagint, and that Paul does not use this type of Hebraism. It is also said that ἐν in such a context is followed only by person referents, but Peake and Arndt and Gingrich (θέλω, 4.b) mention some collocations where this is not so. Arguments against the fourth view are much the same as against the third, that it is a Hebraism of a type not found in the New Testament.

However, when one looks at the verse as a whole, these different views of it do not really involve great differences. This verse either describes what the false teacher himself was doing, or else what he expected the Colossians to do and condemned them for not doing. Doubtless, what he did himself he taught others to do. It is helpful to note that, apart from the use of θέλων, the presentation of the warning and its supporting material is very similar to 2:16-17 and that it is therefore likely that Paul is here giving further reasons for the false teacher's criticisms of the Colossian believers. This view fits most readily with the fourth view, 'because he insists'.

It makes the argument clearer if an implicit proposition is supplied (18c) to the effect that the Colossians did not worship in the way that the false teacher wished and thus they incurred his condemnation.

The usual word for 'humility' is ταπεινοφροσύνη, but because here it is used to refer to some aspect of the false teaching, it seems likely that it is intended derogatorily. Hence, 'humiliate yourselves' is used in the display. Some commentators and translators use 'self-abasement', which also conveys the negative evaluation; it would be a good alternative here. A number of commentators also suggest that the close grammatical link with the following reference to the worship of angels may imply that the teacher claimed that it was a more humble approach to God to do so via angels.

2:18e and *you do not* worship the angels. The genitive construction θρησκεία τῶν ἀγγέλων 'worship of the angels' is formally ambiguous in that it may mean 'the angels worship' or 'worship the angels', although there is no reason to suppose the former was meant. The false teaching's emphasis on the place of angels is very likely to have gone hand in hand with a demotion of the importance of Christ, which the whole letter is directed against. The word for 'worship' here, θρησκεία, has a somewhat negative connotation. Paul does not use it of true worship at all, but uses it to refer to the Jewish religion in Acts 26:5. (James, however, does use it of true religion in James 1:27.) The negative connotation fits the present context well. The term carries overtones of the external forms of worship. Lightfoot says that in the Septuagint it is used for idolatry or false worship wherever collocated with θρησκεύω 'to perform religious observances' (a cognate form of θρησκεία not used in the New Testament).

2:18f *Do this [2:18a-e]* since he bases his authority on things which he has [never] seen With this statement, the grounds for the warning in 2:18 begin. In 2:17, the grounds consisted of a negative evaluation of the teaching; here the grounds are a negative evaluation of the teacher.

The meaning of the three (or four) Greek words here meet with considerable difference of opinion. There are two main issues: (1) the meaning of the verb ἐμβατεύω and (2) the text underlying proposition 18f. As to the first issue, the primary meaning of the verb ἐμβατεύω (which occurs rarely in Greek literature and only here in the New Testament) is 'to step on, to stand on'. From this it was extended to mean 'to dwell', 'to haunt', and 'to invade'. It then acquired the figurative sense of 'entering into' some subject. In this context it could mean 'examining' or 'investigating' what he has seen, or it could mean 'dwelling on', 'taking his stand on'. Modern commentators, such as Bruce (1957) and Martin (1972), mention that this verb has been found in a second-century inscription used "as a technical term for some act in a mystery ritual" (Bruce 1957) and thus may well have been a technical term from the false teaching Paul refers to here. Of all the suggested meanings, 'taking his stand on' fits this context at least as well and maybe better than any of the alternatives. However, 'taking his stand on' is a dead figure in English and so is rendered 'bases his authority on' here.

Most modern commentators prefer the text without the negative particle μή; it does not occur at all in the UBS text and the apparatus rates the text without the negative as B ("some degree of doubt"). If this text is followed, then the false teacher evidently claimed to have had visions and was basing his authority on them. This makes very good sense in this context and is a popular interpretation. But if the text with the negative particle included is preferred (and it is supported by most of the minuscules and many of the early translations), then the implication is that the false teacher was claiming knowledge of things (angels?) he had, in fact, never seen. The meaning of ἐμβατεύων is the same for either reading, the sense being 'basing his authority on things which he has never seen (or, has seen)'. Whatever it was that the false teacher claimed, Paul rejects it. (With the negative, ἐμβατεύων could mean 'investigating' or 'intruding into' as an alternative.) In the display, 'he bases his authority on' is used, and the negative is bracketed to indicate textual uncertainty at this point.

2:18g and since he is proud without reason The Greek word φυσιούμενος 'puffed up', is a dead metaphor rendered here as 'he is proud', the non-figurative equivalent.

In connection with the adverb εἰκῇ, usually rendered 'without reason' in this context, we need to ask if εἰκῇ goes with the participle that precedes it or the one that follows it. That is, does the clause boundary fall before or after εἰκῇ? Commentators point out that Paul always uses it preceding the verb form to which it is attached (Rom. 13:4; 1 Cor. 15:2; Gal. 4:11) except in Gal. 3:4, where it is in focus and follows the verb. Hence, it is considered better here to take it with the clause following it.

There is also a question concerning the meaning of εἰκῇ. In all the other Pauline usages it means 'to no purpose, in vain', but that meaning does not fit well here. However, in the other contexts, the verb is active, whereas here it is passive (and also represents a state proposition), which may account for the general acceptance of the meaning 'without reason'. Since εἰκῇ is an adverb, the adverbial phrase 'without reason' is used here. Spelled out, it would be 'even though he has no reason to be proud'.

2:18h because his sinful nature *controls* what he thinks The Greek is ὑπὸ τοῦ νοὸς τῆς σαρκὸς αὐτοῦ 'by the mind of the flesh of him'. In this phrase 'flesh' is understood as 'the evil/sinful nature' (Paul's common sense for it), and 'mind' is understood as a metonymy for what is done with the mind (i.e., think). The genitive 'the mind of the flesh' is taken to mean that the mind is controlled by the flesh (following Beekman). It may be that the word 'flesh' is intended as a contrast with the Colossian believers described in 2:11. A person who was proud and whose thinking was dominated by 'the flesh' was not the sort of person the Colossians should pay attention to.

2:19a–c and since he does not teach the *true* teaching about Christ, who causes the whole church to develop *spiritually* as God plans *that it should develop, just as* the head directs how the body grows, held together by its joints and ligaments. The first Greek verbal form here is the present participle of κρατέω. When used in the aorist tense, the primary sense of this verb is 'to take hold of', and it commonly occurs in this sense in the Gospels and Acts. When used in the present tense, it means 'to keep hold of' or 'to hold on to'. I can find only one example of it in the present tense where it is used in this primary sense: Acts 2:24, which says that it was not possible that Christ 'should be held on to' by death, as though death were a person holding on to or seizing someone else. It does occur elsewhere in the present tense, however, collocated with nonmaterial things, especially teaching or doctrine, and in such a context it has an extended sense: In Mark 7:3–8 reference is made three times to the Pharisees' holding on to the traditions of men. In 2 Thess. 2:15 believers are exhorted to 'hold on to' the Christian tradition, and in Heb. 4:14 to 'hold on to' our profession. In Rev. 2:13–14 the church at Pergamum is commended for 'holding on to' Jesus' name but is rebuked because some members of the church were 'holding to' the teaching of Balaam and of the Nicolaitans.

In view of this, what does 'not holding on to the head' mean here? Since the present tense form of κρατέω is commonly collocated with 'teaching', 'tradition', etc., and since the whole thrust of this subsection is a warning against being taken in by false teaching, and since Paul is constantly emphasizing the greatness of Christ in this epistle, it is best to understand this clause as referring to doctrinal aberration on the false teacher's part. This is supported by Paul's opening comment that the false φιλοσοφία was contrary to the true teaching about Christ (2:8). However, in v. 19 Christ is not referred to directly, but metaphorically, as 'the head', a live metaphor with the related images of a body, joints and ligaments, and growth. As in 1:18, 'head' is taken here to mean 'rules over', and the phrase πᾶν τὸ σῶμα 'all the body' later in v. 19 represents 'the whole church' over whom he rules. This being so, the best rendering of 'not holding on to the head' would seem to be 'not teaching the true teaching about Christ'.

Two points of similarity should be recognized in this live metaphor, based on the two main images. The point of similarity between Christ and a person's head is that both direct or control growth; the point of similarity between the church and a person's body is that both grow, one spiritually and the other physically. The primary thought here may be spiritual growth in the area of understanding so as not to be misled by false teaching; but also in view is a firm grasp of the truth, that is, stability, since stability is emphasized a number of times in this section of the epistle.

In the Greek, 19b continues on with the live metaphor, rendered nonfiguratively in the display. The phrase ἐξ οὗ 'from whom' is rendered 'causes', since 'from' indicates the source or cause of the growth. The figurative αὔξει τὴν αὔξησιν 'grows the growth' is rendered 'develop', its nonfigurative equivalent. The expression 'grows the growth' is attached to the genitive τοῦ θεοῦ 'of God', which commentators generally agree means that the growth comes from God, or that God bestows it. Another suggestion is that God looks after the growth, watches over it. Beekman suggested "growth of the kind God wants." This is a good suggestion, namely, that God plans the growth, but the growth is actually brought about by

Christ, the head. (This would agree with the general biblical representation of the relationship between the work of the Father and that of the Son.) Hence, 'of God' is propositionalized as 'as God plans *that it should develop*' (a comparison).

Proposition 19c is the image to which 19b is compared. However, the details are not entirely clear. It is generally agreed that the meaning of the two Greek nouns ἀφαί and σύνδεσμοι is 'joints' and 'ligaments', as in the RSV. It is also agreed that the second of the two verbs associated with these nouns means 'knit together', as in the RSV. But there is disagreement concerning the first of the two verbs, ἐπιχορηγέω: some take it to mean 'nourished, supplied, or provided (for)', the usual New Testament sense; others, 'supported (by), helped (by)'. Arndt and Gingrich, also Hendriksen, maintain that it has the latter sense. The problem with the former sense is essentially the result of a collocational clash. If it means 'nourished (by)', then it is not the joints and ligaments that do the nourishing; hence, the preference is for 'supported (by)'. If this latter view is correct, the two verbs are virtually synonymous in this context, hence rendered by only one verb in the display.

SECTION CONSTITUENT 2:20–23 (Paragraph: Specific₂ of 2:8–15)

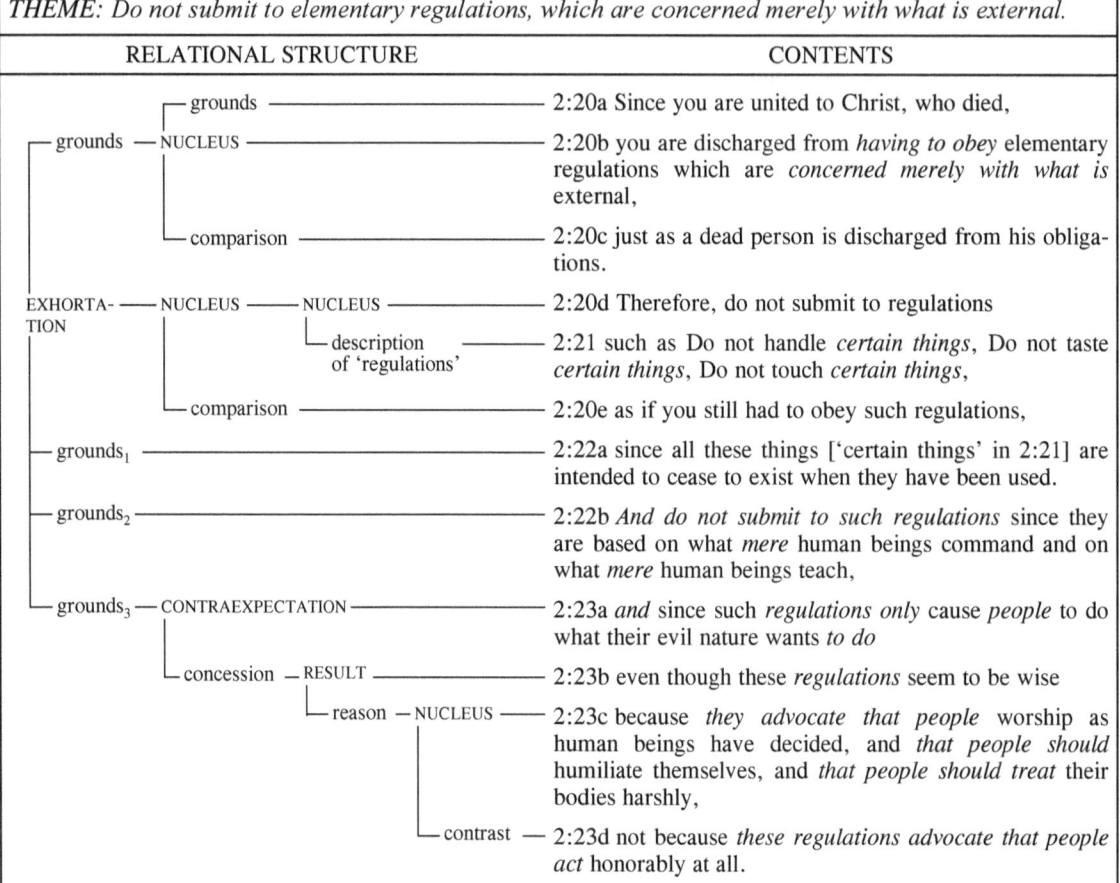

BOUNDARIES AND COHERENCE

The beginning of the 2:20–23 paragraph is clearly marked by the switch to second person plural forms after a succession of third person singular forms in 2:18 and 19, together with an initial aorist verb after a succession of present tense forms.

There are some striking parallels between 2:20 and 3:1. In both there is an initial 'if' clause, followed by the main clause, and in both the 'if' clause is in the aorist tense and the main clause in the present tense. Also, there are close lexical links: in both 2:20 and 3:1 the aorist verb refers to an action that took place *with* Christ, and is the lexical opposite of the other ('died' and 'rose'), though sequential in time. How is this parallelism to be interpreted? There are quite a number of examples of parallelism in this section and the next. (These are discussed in connection with the 2:6–3:17 division of the epistle.) Suffice to say that here, since the lexical information is contrastive, or antonymous, the two parallel 'if' clauses are regarded as initiating two separate paragraphs, not two parallel halves of the same paragraph, as is the case for the previous and following paragraphs. There is also a marked change of topic at 3:1, from the false teaching to Christian behavior. Thus, this paragraph is regarded as ending with 2:23.

Grammatically, 2:20–23 is one rather complicated sentence consisting of an independent clause preceded by an 'if' clause and followed by relative clauses. Lexically, it is like some of the preceding paragraphs in that its coherence is shown by lexical items related to the topic of the false teaching, a good number of these items having already been used in the earlier paragraphs of the section. (For details see the discussion of the 2:8–23 section.) Semantically, this paragraph, like the preceding paragraphs, consists of a command (though in the form of a rhetorical question) supported by propositions linked to it by the logical relation of grounds.

PROMINENCE AND THEME

As can be seen from the display, the 2:20-23 paragraph consists of a nuclear exhortation supported by four grounds. The theme of the unit consists of this command. The command involves a generic term, 'regulations', followed by specifics of the sort of regulations referred to. Beekman's theme for this paragraph was simply "Don't submit to rules," but some information from the paragraph needs to be added as to what sort of rules or regulations Paul had in mind. The best definition of these regulations is the one in 2:20b, 'elementary regulations which are concerned merely with what is external'. It is best because, for one thing, it is explicitly stated in the paragraph and also because it includes the specific examples given in 2:21.

NOTES

2:20a-c Since you are united to Christ, who died, you are discharged from *having to obey* **elementary regulations which are** *concerned merely with what is* **external, just as a dead person is discharged from his obligations.** Paul here takes up again the live metaphor used earlier in 2:12 (see 12b and 12c), where he describes the Colossians as those who had been 'buried with Christ' and 'resurrected with Christ'. (He continues it in 3:1, but there he is concerned with the implications of rising with Christ.) Proposition 20b gives the nonfigurative equivalent of the figure in 20c. It is generally agreed that the Greek phrase 'died from' means 'to be set free from (obligation to)', just as a person who has died is free from any legal or other claims on him, since he personally cannot be brought to trial. The difficult phrase τὰ στοιχεῖα τοῦ κόσμου 'the elements of the world' is interpreted in the same way as it was in 2:8.

Here εἰ 'if' does not indicate uncertainty, but a known truth from which a conclusion is drawn. It is rendered 'since' and the relation is labeled as grounds.

2:20d Therefore, do not submit to regulations The Greek has a rhetorical question here, the sense of which is a prohibition (see Beekman and Callow 1974:241-43). The earlier references to the stability and faith of the Colossians and the form of the warning in 2:8 would indicate that this rhetorical question is not a rebuke for something they were already doing, but a warning against something they might soon do. The sense of the verb δογματίζω when used in the middle voice, as it is here, is 'submit yourselves to regulations'. The rhetorical question is expressed in the display as the command 'do not submit'; it could also be expressed in the form 'you should not submit'.

2:21 such as Do not handle *certain things,* **Do not taste** *certain things,* **Do not touch** *certain things,* It will be noted that a slight departure from the Greek order is required here so that 21 can immediately follow 20d; 20e then follows 21.

The statements here are particular examples of the regulations referred to in 20b and d. It is likely that they are arranged climactically, progressing from a prohibition not to handle to a prohibition not even to touch. The most likely direct objects of the verbs are certain foods and drink (see Arndt and Gingrich, ἅπτω, 2.a; also Liddell and Scott). Proposition 22a makes it clear that these implied objects are such that they no longer exist once they have been used. However, the lack of any explicit direct objects in the text may indicate that while food and drink taboos were primary in Paul's mind, other taboos were not to be excluded. The polemic is against *all* rules and regulations based on externals.

2:20e as if you still had to obey such regulations, The phrase ἐν κόσμῳ 'in world' is not a reference to location—they *were* living in the world in the physical sense. Rather, it is a reference to their former condition with respect to which they had 'died with Christ'. (The use of κόσμος 'world' here is in keeping with its use elsewhere to describe such regulations and the condition of unbelievers.) What is in focus in this context is the obligation they used to be under to obey this type of regulation. The semantic relation is comparison, which is commonly introduced by ὡς 'as', as it is here.

2:22a since all these things ['certain things' in 2:21] are intended to cease to exist when they have been used. The Greek surface form is a relative clause descriptive of the forbidden things. However, in this context it is considered to be an argument supporting the main command; hence, in the display 22a is labeled as grounds.

The initial relative pronoun in v. 22 refers to the implicit objects in 21, the various foods and drinks. It is generally agreed that ἐστιν . . . εἰς 'are . . . for' indicates purpose (i.e., 'this is what these things were made for'). This purpose is expressed by means of two abstract nouns, φθοράν 'destruction' (or 'corruption') and ἀποχρήσει 'using-up', that is, 'being made use of'. In this particular context, destruction is not a suitable word since we do not speak of food's being destroyed as we eat it. Many versions use 'perish', but that is not really suitable either. The best English expression seems to be 'cease to exist'. Paul is saying that food and drink are physical objects that are inherently transitory and thus unrelated to spiritual matters, which have to do with the permanent and eternal.

The most natural way of connecting the 'using' to the 'ceasing to exist' is a time/circumstance relation, signaled by 'when'.

2:22b *And do not submit to such regulations* **since they are based on what** *mere* **human beings command and on what** *mere* **human beings teach,** This is another argument in support of the warning in 20d–21, but this time the argument relates back to the rules as such rather than the things the rules were concerned with. The preposition κατά 'according to' (used here with the accusative) is the same as is used three times in 2:8 to describe the false teacher's φιλοσοφία '(religious) philosophy' (see especially 2:8d).

The word 'mere' is supplied in order to convey the negative connotation of Paul's comments here. The word ἀνθρώπων does not mean 'men' as opposed to 'women', but 'human beings' as opposed to 'God', hence 'human beings' in the display.

2:23 In his comments on this verse, Moule (1957) opens with these words: "This verse is by common consent regarded as hopelessly obscure—either owing to corruption or because we have lost the clue." Caird says, "The Greek of the last clause is notoriously difficult." But there is no evidence of corruption of the text, so some clue needs to be sought. Hollenbach (n.d.) has made a very plausible suggestion as to what that clue is—namely, how the grammatical structure of this verse is to be understood. His arguments are summarized as follows:

1. The particle μέν occurs as the fourth word in this verse. But μέν always follows the first word of the grammatical unit to which it belongs, the rare exception being when it follows the first *two* words. In no case does it follow the first three words, as is assumed by many commentators and versions here. Hence, a comma needs to be placed after ἔστιν 'is/are'.
2. Hollenbach identifies the following five functions of μέν in the Pauline Epistles:

    a. to start a list;
    b. to mark a paragraph beginning;
    c. to emphasize a positive-negative lexical contrast;
    d. to mark a contrast (the other half of the contrast being marked by δέ); and
    e. to mark a concession (the contraexpectation being marked by δέ).

    Of these five possibilities, the fifth is the best in this context. Thus λόγον μέν ('appearance' + concession-marker) begins a concessive clause.
3. The next question is where the concessive clause ends. The grammar allows for only two possibilities: after σώματος 'of-body' and before οὐκ 'not' (as in the UBS text); or after τινι 'any' and before πρός 'toward'. Hollenbach rejects the first of these because it assumes a very unusual position for οὐκ 'not' (normally before the verb) and assumes an unproven meaning for τιμή: 'value, effectiveness'. This would point to the second possibility. This is supported by the use of the collocation ἔστιν πρός 'is toward' in John 11:4 and 1 Cor. 14:26, meaning 'have as an end result', which makes good sense here.
4. Hollenbach then goes on to explain the absence of δέ in the contraexpectation clause related to the concessive clause, saying that the appropriate part of the main clause precedes μέν in the concessive clause. He also defends the assumption of an embedded subordinate clause by referring to Philem. 9, and finally maintains that this analysis makes good sense in the context.

Based on Hollenbach's convincing analysis of the grammatical structure of v. 23, it is now possible to consider its individual propositions.

2:23a **and** *since such regulations only* **cause** *people* **to do what their evil nature wants** *to do* This is the main clause of 2:23: ἅτινά ἐστιν . . . πρὸς πλησμονὴν τῆς σαρκός 'such-things are . . . toward satisfaction of-the flesh'. It is presented first in the propositionalization of the verse.

As was pointed out earlier, ἔστιν πρός means 'have an end result'. The end result here is πλησμονὴν τῆς σαρκός. Arndt and Gingrich say of πλησμονή that it means "*satiety*, esp. w. food and drink." This is the meaning commentators generally advocate, rather than '(legitimate) satisfaction'. There is also widespread agreement that σάρξ 'flesh' is used here in its common Pauline sense, 'the sinful/evil nature' (cf. 2:18h). Thus the main clause of 2:23 means 'such things have as an end result the gratification/indulgence/satisfying of the flesh'. This provides a fourth grounds for the warning in 2:20d–21.

2:23b even though these *regulations* seem to be wise It is generally agreed that, in this context, λόγος means 'reputation', what people say about this religious philosophy. This meaning is represented in the display by 'seem to be'. The word σοφίας refers to what they seem to be, namely wise. The particle μέν shows that this clause stands in the relation of concession to the main one; hence, 23b is a concession to 23a. The particle ἔχοντα 'having' refers back to the opening ἅτινα 'such (regulations)', making it clear that it is these regulations which impress people.

2:23c because *they advocate that people* worship as human beings have decided, and *that people should* humiliate themselves, and *that people should treat* their bodies harshly, The Greek is ἐν ἐθελοθρησκίᾳ καὶ ταπεινοφροσύνῃ καὶ ἀφειδίᾳ σώματος 'in will-worship and humility and severity of-body'. This is a compound prepositional phrase governed by ἐν 'in'. The phrase is attached to the participle ἔχοντα 'having'. It gives three examples of the sort of thing that gave the impression that these rules and regulations were wise ones. The second of these examples was mentioned before, in 2:18d, where, because of the overall derogatory context, it was rendered 'humiliate yourselves'. The third, ἀφειδίᾳ σώματος, refers to harsh or severe treatment of the body.

As to the first word, ἐθελοθρησκίᾳ 'will-worship', it has been explained in a number of ways. Caird follows Moulton and Milligan (p. 181) in suggesting that Paul may have coined the word to describe what the false teaching was proposing, because the word has not been found elsewhere. Arndt and Gingrich suggest "self-made religion" or possibly "would-be religion"; Caird, however, says "the stress is . . . on the voluntary nature of the observances, or possibly on the tenacity with which they are maintained." Moule (1957) translates it "voluntary delight in religiousness." But Arndt and Gingrich's first suggestion, "self-made religion," is generally preferred; this is rendered in the display as 'worship as human beings have decided'. However, there are a number of words in which ἐθελω- occurs as part of a compound, and in these it has the sense of 'would be'. This would give 'because they claim to show how to worship *God but they do not*' as an alternative rendering.

Since people admired the sort of regulations advocated by the false teaching, the implicit information that these regulations 'advocate that people . . .' is supplied and the whole proposition is then treated as a reason for proposition 23b.

2:23d not because *these regulations advocate that people act* honorably at all. This phrase must be treated as part of the concessive clause, as Hollenbach shows.

For τιμή Arndt and Gingrich give two main senses: (1) price, value (in cash); and (2) honor, respect. Of this particular phrase in Col. 2:23 they say "[it] has not yet been adequately explained." In fact, it is generally agreed that the phrase is now obscure. Since there is nothing in the context about buying and selling, not even figurative, the second sense seems the likely one. Further, the regulations with which this religious system made a favorable impression are introduced by the preposition ἐν 'in' (in 23c), and this phrase in 23d also uses ἐν. This would point to a negative statement about these regulations. The force of this phrase, then, would seem to be that these regulations do not advocate anything worthwhile. In propositional form, it would be something like 'not because these regulations advocate that people act honorably at all' or 'which does not advocate that people act in any way to honor *God by what they do*'. The display has the former, but it is only a good guess.

In other words, Paul used the phrase οὐκ ἐν τιμῇ τινι to express his rejection of the actions that this false religion emphasized. In fact, with the final phrase πρὸς πλησμονὴν τῆς σαρκός 'to satisfaction of the flesh', he rejected the whole approach of rules and regulations of human origin.

It is possible that this last verse of the 2:8–23 section, introduced as it is by ἅτινα 'such things', which generalizes 'rules and regulations such as these', is Paul's final comment on this whole false system before he turns to the positive side of his exhortations. If this is so, then we can view the three areas specified in this verse—man-made religion, self-abasement, and ascetic practices—as a summary of the system's main tenets. The final comment, that such a system only leads to gratification of the flesh, denies what would appear to be one of the system's major claims—a higher spirituality—and at the same time leads naturally into Paul's positive exposition of true Christian holiness in the next section (3:1–16).

DIVISION CONSTITUENT 3:1–16 (Section: Specific₂ of 2:6–7)

THEME: *Be constantly wanting what is associated with heaven.*	
RELATIONAL STRUCTURE	CONTENTS
GENERIC	3:1–4 Be constantly wanting what is associated with heaven.
—specific₁	3:5–11 Do not do what is evil.
—specific₂	3:12–14 Do what is good; in particular, love one another.
—specific₃	3:15–16 Continue to be at peace with one another, be constantly thanking God, and continue getting to thoroughly know the message about Christ.

BOUNDARIES AND COHERENCE

As in 2:8–23, the previous section, the most obvious evidence for the 3:1–16 section's unity is the commonness of topic throughout: Every paragraph deals with ethical Christian behavior, whether good deeds to be done or evil deeds to be shunned. This implies that there is a change of topic from the previous section, and indeed there is, the previous section being concerned with warnings against the false teaching.

There do not seem to be any clear formal boundary markers as such in 3:1–16, but the opening verse has οὖν 'therefore', and 3:17 is a very generic command, like the one in 2:6 that opens the 2:6–3:17 division. In other words, 3:17 forms a sandwich structure with 2:6, marking the end of the 2:6–3:17 semantic unit. Further, 3:18 starts with a vocative, the first in this epistle, and is the beginning of a series of exhortations addressed to different subgroups in the congregation; so in that sense there is a shift of addressee beginning at 3:18.

There are two obvious features of coherence: (1) The Colossians are addressed throughout, so many of the verb forms are 'you(pl)' oriented, even those that are third person singular imperatives formally. (2) The lexicon is drawn from the semantic sets of vices and virtues; this is especially so in the two central paragraphs, 3:5–11 and 3:12–14.

There are other lexical features that lend coherence besides the one relating to the topic. The associated live metaphors of death and resurrection in the first paragraph (3:1, 3) are picked up again at the beginning of the second paragraph with 'put to death' in 3:5. Then 'put to death' is paralleled by the dead metaphor 'put off' in 3:8 in the same paragraph, and there is a contrast with 'put off' later in the paragraph, namely 'put on' in 3:10. This, in turn, is picked up again at the beginning of the third paragraph in 3:12. Notice, too, the contrast in the first paragraph between 'the things above' (3:1–2) and 'the things on the earth' (3:2); this latter is then repeated at the beginning of the second paragraph in 3:5. These are lexical threads, as it were, running through the section for shorter or longer stretches.

There are also certain structural parallelisms. The first and second paragraphs have the similar structure of two halves, each opening with synonymous commands. The second and third paragraphs each open with a command clause, followed by five noun phrases that are the objects, in list form, of the opening verb. In the fourth paragraph there are parallel third person commands: both have the subject preceding the verb, and both are followed by a prepositional phrase referring to 'you(pl)' by means of a pronoun.

PROMINENCE AND THEME

The 3:1–16 section consists of four paragraphs, of which the first (3:1–4) is clearly generic in content; the others are specifics. Since, apart from special prominence features, a generic paragraph ranks higher than a series of specifics, the theme statement for the section is the same as that for the opening paragraph.

SECTION CONSTITUENT 3:1-4 (Paragraph: Generic nucleus of 3:5-16)

THEME: *Be constantly wanting what is associated with heaven.*	
RELATIONAL STRUCTURE	CONTENTS
NUCLEUS — grounds	3:1a-b Since you were caused to live spiritually *by God*, (1b) *just like* you were resurrected together with Christ *by God*,
NUCLEUS — EXHORTATION	3:1c-e be constantly wanting what *is associated with* heaven [MTY], (1d) where Christ is, (1e) who has been given supreme authority and the highest honor *by God*.
amplification — EXHORTATION — A NUCLEUS	3:2a Be constantly wanting what *is associated with* heaven;
B contrast	3:2b do not *be constantly wanting to do* the *evil* deeds *that are done by* people on earth [MTY]
grounds₁ — B' NUCLEUS₁	3:3a-b since you have ceased to behave as you formerly did, (3b) *like* a person who has died.
A' NUCLEUS₂	3:3c-d And *be doing this* [3:2] since you *now* live *spiritually* together with Christ in *the presence of* God; (3d) *and this* [3:3c] cannot be seen *by people*.
grounds₂ — time	3:4a When Christ, who causes you/us(inc) to live *spiritually*, is revealed publicly *by God*,
NUCLEUS	3:4b-c then you also will be revealed publicly *by God* together with Christ (4c) *and you together with Christ will be* glorious.

BOUNDARIES AND COHERENCE

In the discussion of the boundaries of 2:20-23, the previous paragraph, the formal parallelism between its opening clause and the opening clause of the 3:1-4 paragraph was noted; and it was concluded that this parallelism pointed to separate units because the content was antonymous: 'rose again' (3:1) as opposed to 'died' (2:20). In addition to this, 3:1 has the conjunction οὖν, which occurs only paragraph initial in the hortatory part of this epistle, and there is also an obvious change of topic from warnings against the false teaching to exhortations to righteous conduct. Hence 3:5 is considered to begin a new paragraph. The indicators can be summarized as follows:

1. The occurrence of οὖν 'therefore'.
2. The switch from the present tense imperatives of 3:1-2 to the aorist imperative of 3:5.
3. The switch from the generic expression τὰ ἄνω 'the things above' to specifics, and these are negative (i.e., vices), not positive.

The reference to 'you(pl)' throughout is also significant. Apart from the relative clause in 3:1, every clause contains a reference to 'you', either in the verb itself or in the expressed subject of the verb (in apposition to the subject in 4a). In addition, there is an apparent progression through the paragraph: in 3:1 the Colossians are said to have been raised from death, in 3:3 their life is hidden with Christ in God, and in 3:4 they will be revealed. In other words, there is a past event of resurrection with Christ ('died' is mentioned in 3:3, but not in sequence); a present state of hiddenness; and a future event of being revealed with him. In association with this sequence, there are three lexical groupings:

 a. 'resurrected' (1), 'died' (3), 'life' (3, 4)
 b. 'above' (1, 2), 'the right hand of God' (1), 'in God' (3), 'in glory' (4), 'earth' (2)
 c. 'hidden' (3), 'revealed' (4)

PROMINENCE AND THEME

In the 3:1-4 paragraph there are two independent commands, τὰ ἄνω ζητεῖτε 'seek the things above' (3:1) and τὰ ἄνω φρονεῖτε 'set your minds on the things above' (3:2). These commands are regarded as synonymous, or near-synonymous, in this paragraph; and so they are given the same propositional form. Consequently, the theme of this paragraph is the propositional representation of these two commands.

NOTES

3:1a–b Since you were caused to live spiritually *by God, just like* you were resurrected together with Christ *by God,* The initial οὖν 'therefore' here is considered either to mark the resumption of the positives of the 3:1–16 section theme line (the negative theme line having been developed in the 2:8–23 section) or to mark the beginning of the 3:1–4 paragraph.

The verb συνηγέρθητε means 'you were jointly resurrected'. This figure echoes 2:12, where the same figure was interpreted as a live one. It is taken as a live one here also, since it refers back to a live figure and also since it occurs here associated with a related figure, 'you died', as well as with 'your life' (v. 3). In the display the nonfigurative meaning is given in 3:1a and the image 'resurrected' in 1b, with 'just like' used to indicate the comparison. It is assumed that the implicit agent is God the Father, since the event is resurrection together with Christ.

3:1c be constantly wanting what *is associated with* heaven, For the meaning of ζητεῖτε 'be seeking' Arndt and Gingrich give two senses: (a) "try to obtain, desire to possess" (sense 2a); and (b) "strive for, aim (at), desire, wish" (sense 2b). The word has to do with the aim of one's life: "all your aims must centre in heaven" (Lightfoot). Greeven (p. 893) is probably correct when he says "the orientation of [man's] will." It is very difficult to find a nonfigurative equivalent in English. The continuous form 'be constantly wanting' in the display reflects the significance of the Greek present imperative here.

As to the meaning of τὰ ἄνω 'the things above', the commentators express it in different ways: "heavenly, spiritual things" (Alford); "all the great and blessed, truly spiritual things" (Lenski); "the spiritual values embedded in the heart of the exalted Mediator" (Hendriksen). But basically it refers to spiritual values or ethical standards characteristic of heaven and its inhabitants. It is a very generic form to cover the virtues of the Christian life that are dealt with in detail in subsequent paragraphs. But it is important to retain the reference to heaven here because of the statements about Christ. In other words, ἄνω 'above' is a metonymy for heaven, the direction being used for what is located in that direction.

In the display the term 'heaven' is used for the first time in the epistle. It is difficult to know how to link the '(spiritual) things' they should be wanting with 'heaven'. Possible links are 'are associated with', 'are characteristic of', even 'are found in'. The first of these is used in the display, but the translator should remember when translating this that 'things' is generic and abstract and here refers to principles, values, and standards— not material things.

3:1d where Christ is, The main question here is whether there is one clause or two. Is it 'where Christ is sitting' or 'where Christ is, who sits'? The commentators who discuss this seem agreed that the latter is preferable, hence the two propositions (1d and 1e) in the display. However, this conclusion needs verification. (According to our present research into such periphrastic clauses, if οὗ ὁ Χριστός ἐστιν 'where the Christ is' is *not* periphrastic, then ὁ Χριστός 'the Christ' is in a prominent position before the copula ἐστιν 'is' in a relative clause.)

3:1e who has been given supreme authority and the highest honor *by God*. The phrase ἐν δεξιᾷ τοῦ θεοῦ 'on the right of God' is a dead figure referring to the place of highest honor and supreme power. In different passages one or the other of these ideas is put into prominence, but often both ideas, honor and power (or authority), are present without being sharply distinguished. Both seem relevant in the larger context here, since the false teachers were depreciating Christ in regard to both. The immediate context does not seem to require giving prominence to one aspect or the other. God is considered the agent, the one who has given this high place to Christ.

3:2–3 It would appear that the four semantic constituents of these verses (2a, 2b, 3a–b, and 3c–d) are arranged in the chiastic pattern A, B, B', A', as indicated in the display. A and A' give the positive command and its positive grounds, while B and B' give the negative command (prohibition) and its negative grounds. The grouping of A with B and of B' with A' reflects the grouping signaled in the Greek by γάρ (indicating grounds), which introduces both B' and A'.

3:2a Be constantly wanting what *is associated with* heaven; The command of 3:1c is repeated here in a somewhat similar form. The RSV has "set your minds on." Arndt and Gingrich point to "thinking" as the central component, though some commentators make suggestions such as "devote ourselves to" (Lenski) and "ponder and yearn for" (Hendriksen). The force of the present imperative is 'have your minds occupied with', 'keep thinking about'. It is difficult to be sure whether the two commands are intended to be completely synonymous in this context. For the display it is assumed that they are, since the object of the verb in each case is identical and the grounds given are very similar in content. If there is a distinction, it would be that ζητεῖτε 'seek' in 3:1c expresses 'the set of the will' while φρονεῖτε 'think' in 3:2a expresses 'the set of the mind', the inner attitudes which lead to the set of the will.

3:2b do not *be constantly wanting to do* **the** *evil* **deeds** *that are done by* **people on earth** Proposition 2b is in contrast with 2a, so 'things on the earth' seems best interpreted as having a morally bad sense—worldly, unspiritual, evil things—rather than a morally neutral sense ('don't be preoccupied with earthly matters such as food and clothing, etc.').

3:3a-b since you have ceased to behave as you formally did, *like a* **person who has died.** This proposition, which is introduced by γάρ, is the grounds for the command in 3:2. It is the fourth segment in a chiastic structure of grounds-command-command-grounds; that is, the grounds for the command in 3:1 are given in 3:1a and the grounds for the command in 3:2 are given in 3:3. The two grounds propositions are complementary in that the first one refers to resurrection ('with Christ'), the second one to death ('with Christ' being clearly implied).

'You died' repeats, in minimal form, the statement in 2:20, which, in turn, goes back to 2:12. As in those cases, it is regarded as a live metaphor. Spelled out fully, it would be 'You have made a complete break with your former life, just as a person who has died has made a complete break with his former life'. In other words, death severs the connection with (the old) life. In the display, the nonfigurative meaning is given in 3a, and the image in 3b.

3:3c-d And *be doing this [3:2]* **since you** *now* **live** *spiritually* **together with Christ** *in the presence of* **God;** *and this [3:3c]* **cannot be seen** *by people.* A rather complex clause underlies 3:3c-d. First is the abstract noun ζωή 'life', which refers to the event of living. It is the life mentioned in 3:1a, the spiritual, resurrection life that has replaced the old life to which the Colossians had died.

The next problem is the meaning of κέκρυπται 'is hidden' here. This depends on whether it is to be understood figuratively (i.e., 'protected') or literally (i.e., 'concealed from view'). Only Barnes and Arndt and Gingrich support the figurative sense. However, Arndt and Gingrich (under sense 2) say "*hide* in a safe place" and they do not italicize "in a safe place"; moreover, there is nothing in the context to suggest the need for protection. On the other side, the following considerations favor the literal meaning: (1) This life is hidden 'with Christ', and the sense of protection is irrelevant to Christ, who has just been described as having supreme authority. (2) In 3:4 'Christ' is collocated with φανερόω, an antonym of 'hidden'; it means 'to bring out into the open, make visible'. This is clearly literal, referring to the return of Christ. (3) Also in 3:4 it is said that just as the Colossians' (spiritual) life was hidden with Christ, so they would be made visible with Christ (again φανερόω), and this is also literal.

As to the meaning of σὺν τῷ Χριστῷ 'with Christ' it has the normal sense here that what is true of Christ is also true of the Colossian believers. (This is also its meaning in 3:4.) Christ is hidden in God and so are they; he will be made publicly visible and so will they. In other words, σύν 'with' has the sense of 'in association with', 'in company with', 'together with'.

The unusual collocation ἐν τῷ θεῷ 'in God' is difficult to interpret and difficult to express propositionally. The basic statement 'Christ is hidden in God' seems most likely to mean 'hidden from human sight and in the presence of God' in keeping with phrases such as 'at the right hand of God' and 'above', which focus on the location of Christ at the present time.

The question has been asked why Paul would say that both Christ and the Colossians' spiritual life are hidden from view. In view of the situational context, it is probably because the false teacher was stressing the outward, the visible, the external. To counteract this, Paul stresses the hidden nature of the spiritual life of the Colossians. However, he is quick to assert that (1) although hidden, it is with God that their spiritual life is hidden; and (2) it is only hidden temporarily, for the time is coming when both Christ and the Colossian believers would be publicly visible (φανερόω) in glory (ἐν δόξῃ). So they were not to be taken in by the outward show of the false teaching—*their* "outward show" was coming and would be incomparably greater than anything the false teacher was offering.

3:4a When Christ, who causes you/us(inc) to live *spiritually*, is revealed publicly *by God*, The textual evidence is divided between 'the life of you' and 'the life of us'. The UBS text has the former, and this seems the best choice for the following contextual reasons:

1. There is no reference to 'we' anywhere in this paragraph, nor in the contiguous paragraphs.
2. The phrase ἡ ζωὴ ὑμῶν 'the life of-you' is used in the preceding verse, and there is no overt reason for a change.
3. The participants in 3:4 are 'Christ' and 'you'. The Greek word order has 'Christ' and 'you' forefronted in the two clauses of this verse, thereby emphasizing the participants. To introduce 'we' would mar this parallelism.

Moreover, the textual evidence for 'you' is stronger according to Metzger: "the Committee was impressed by the considerably stronger manuscript evidence which supports ὑμῶν, including p⁴⁶ and good representatives of both the Alexandrian and the Western text-types" (p.624). While there is good minuscule support for ἡμῶν 'us', and it is not at all uncommon for Paul to switch from 'you' to 'us' (e.g., in this epistle 1:13 and the end of 2:13), in such cases Paul always continues with 'we', which is not the case here in 3:4. So, all in all, 'you' seems preferable.

The next question is the meaning of 'the life of you' here, where it is in apposition to 'Christ'. The commentators generally say that this phrase refers to our union with Christ: we live in him, and he in us. The identical phrase was used in the preceding verse, and was interpreted there as meaning 'you live spiritually'. The most natural connection, therefore, when this statement is linked to Christ, is to say that he is the source of that spiritual life or, put in propositional form, 'who causes you to live spiritually'. But it is not clear what this statement contributes to the statements in the surrounding propositions. Possibly the idea is that without the life which Christ gives, there is no question of appearing publicly with him in glory. The glory presupposes the life.

3:4b–c then you also will be revealed publicly *by God together with Christ, and you together with Christ will* be glorious. The problem in this verse is the meaning of the phrase ἐν δόξῃ 'in glory' and how it is to be connected with the rest of the verse. The choices would seem to be either that it can describe the manner of the event of revealing, meaning 'in a glorious manner', or it can describe the state of those who are being revealed, 'in a glorious state'. With the emphasis in the preceding verse on being hidden (from view) and being with Christ in heaven, the second alternative seems slightly preferable. Note that 'glorious' is a technical Christian term, meaning 'in that state that results from being glorified', where 'glorified' refers to the resurrection of the body, its perfection, and the perfection of holiness of character of those who are glorified.

SECTION CONSTITUENT 3:5–11 (Paragraph: Specific₁ of 3:1–4)

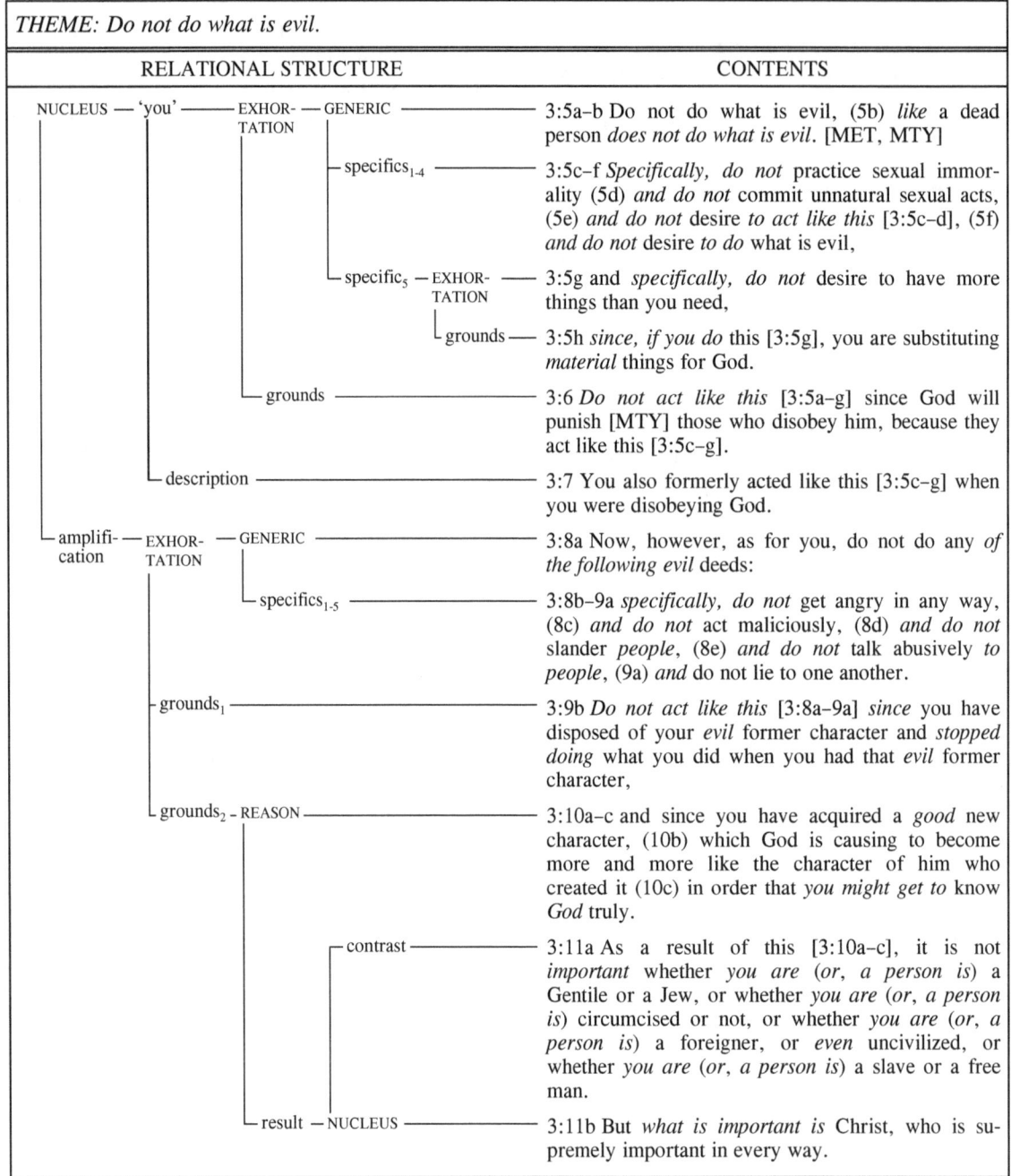

BOUNDARIES AND COHERENCE

Verse 3:5 is considered to be the beginning of a new paragraph because of the occurrence of οὖν 'therefore', the switch to an aorist imperative after present tense imperatives, and the change of subject matter from 'the things above' to various vices, referred to figuratively as 'the members which are on the earth'. So far as boundaries are concerned, the 3:5–11 paragraph raises very similar issues as the previous one—a parallel command in 3:8 which is not considered as starting a new paragraph, and a later command in 3:12 which is.

The evidence for a new paragraph beginning at 3:12 is much the same as that for a new paragraph beginning at 3:5—the use of οὖν and a switch of subject matter, in this case from (forbidden) vices, to (exhorted) virtues. In addition, 3:11 ends with reference to Christ, the only one in 3:5–11, and

3:11 is a very generic statement of the kind that occasionally terminates paragraphs elsewhere (as short doxologies often do).

The reasons 3:8 is not regarded as starting a new paragraph are that (1) there is no change of topic—vices are still being listed and forbidden; and (2) this command is synonymous with the opening command, so there is no change of theme either; and (3) this verse is closely linked with the previous verse by contrastive features—νυνί 'now' as opposed to ποτε 'formerly' and the particle δέ, marking a contrast. However, 3:8 does initiate a distinct second half of the paragraph; thus, the paragraph is in two halves as was the preceding one.

Apart from 3:6 and 11, every verse in the 3:5-11 paragraph is strongly 'you' oriented, primarily by means of finite verbs and participles; also there are three occurrences of the pronoun, once in 3:7 and twice in 3:8. The paragraph's two halves have strong internal relational coherence. In the first half (3:5-7) the opening phrase τὰ μέλη τὰ ἐπὶ τῆς γῆς 'the members upon the earth' is neuter plural, and this is picked up again in 3:6 with δι' ἅ 'because of which', and in 3:7 with ἐν οἷς 'in which'. In the second half, the finite verb in 3:8 is followed by two dependent participles, in turn followed by a relative clause introduced by ὅπου 'where/in which'. The second half is also tied together lexically by the use of two different verbs meaning 'to put off', followed by one meaning 'to put on'; and by the lexical contrast of new versus old in 3:9 and 10. In 3:9 and 10 there is also a choice of lexical items calling the creation account to mind—'man', 'image', and 'created'.

PROMINENCE AND THEME

As discussed under boundaries and coherence, the 3:5-11 paragraph consists of two major constituents, each of which opens with the same command, 'Do not do what is evil', and each of which is supported by specifics and grounds. Consequently, this command is considered the theme for this paragraph.

NOTES

3:5a-b Do not do what is evil, *like* **a dead person** *does not do what is evil.* The figurative language of the previous paragraph is continued in this verse with νεκρώσατε 'put to death', continuing the live metaphor of death, resurrection, and life. For that reason, 'put to death' is regarded as a live metaphor, even though the figure is not again referred to in this paragraph, and even though ἀπόθεσθε 'put off', which parallels it in 3:8, is regarded as a dead metaphor. Proposition 5a gives the nonfigurative meaning, and 5b retains the image of a dead person. The phrase τὰ μέλη 'the members' (i.e., of the body) is regarded as a metonymy, the parts of the body being put for what is done with them (cf. Mark 9:33-37 for a similar metonymy). The phrase τὰ ἐπὶ τῆς γῆς 'those on the earth' here occurred also in 3:2; it has the same sense here that it has there, namely what is morally and ethically evil. The nonfigurative meaning of the proposition is 'Do not do what is evil'.

The occurrence of οὖν 'therefore' in this clause is regarded as primarily marking the hortatory theme line, but that does not rule out the possibility that there is also an inference from 'you died' in 3:3, especially since Paul picks up the same metaphoric language.

The question can be asked whether the use of the article τά in the command is equivalent to 'the following' in English. (The same question can also be asked about 3:8.) The answer to this question is not known. Against it would be the generic use of τὰ ἐπὶ τῆς γῆς 'the things on the earth' in 2:2 and possibly the absence of the article in the list of vices.

3:5c-f *Specifically,* **do not practice sexual immorality,** *and do not* **commit unnatural sexual acts,** *and do not* **desire** *to act like this [3:5c-d], and do not* **desire** *to do* **what is evil,** The main question here is whether the first three terms are to be distinguished in meaning or regarded as synonymous, with the repetition being an emphatic device. All three refer primarily to sexual sins, so the second of these views would be equivalent to the meaning 'all forms of sexual sin'. However, Arndt and Gingrich do not treat these three nouns as synonymous with overlapping glosses. The first word, πορνεία, refers to all forms of illicit sexual intercourse; the second, ἀκαθαρσία, emphasizes the sense of perverted and unnatural sexual activities; the third, πάθος, emphasizes the powerful desires, or lusts, from which the preceding evil practices spring. These distinctions are reflected in the display. (The distinctions are based on Arndt and Gingrich, but it should be noted that there is very little consensus as to the precise distinctions.) These are all abstract nouns representing events, so each vice is cast in the form of a separate proposition, a negative command.

The final noun phrase ἐπιθυμίαν κακήν 'evil desire' (5f) is not primarily concerned with sexual sin, but like πάθος 'passion' it focuses on the inner desires from which the outward deeds spring. The Greek ἐπιθυμία is a stronger word than the English *desire*—it means 'strong desire', 'longing', 'craving'. It is, however, neutral as to the type of desire, so κακήν 'evil' is added in the Greek text of this verse.

3:5g and *specifically, do not* desire to have more things than you need, The word πλεονεξία here can be translated by 'greed' or 'covetousness' (Arndt and Gingrich). The basic idea is wanting more than you need. However, two commentators, Moule (1957) and Caird, take a somewhat different view. According to Moule, "the evidence points to πλεονεξία meaning 'ruthless and aggressive self-seeking'"; Caird states that "πλεονεξία is more than *covetousness*; it is the arrogant and ruthless assumption that all other persons and things exist for one's own benefit." If these lexical comments are correct, then it is not surprising that Paul added the further comment 'which is idolatry' (see 5h).

This fifth vice is preceded by καί 'and' and has the article. Blass and Debrunner (p. 134) take it as emphatic and Vincent translates it as "and *especially*," but others (e.g., Meyer) explain καί as introducing the last item in the list, and the article as necessitated by the following relative clause. This latter view is followed in the display, since there is nothing else in the context to give prominence to this particular vice.

3:5h *since if you do* this [3:5g], you are substituting *material* things for God. The meaning of ἐστίν 'is' is a question here. Should it be interpreted as 'is like', 'is equivalent to', 'is a form of', or 'is an example of'? Probably the underlying thought goes back to Jesus' own words, 'You cannot serve God and Mammon' (Matt. 6:24). Another god has been, in effect, chosen, the god of material gain. However, the word 'idolatry' is not intended in the strictly literal sense of worshiping a physical form of some sort, since the covetous or greedy or self-absorbed person is not offering worship to the things desired. Rather, it is disobeying the commandment 'You are not to have any other gods before me'. This being so, 5h is put in the form 'you are substituting *material* things for God' (cf. Rom. 1:23, 25).

Although this is a relative clause in the Greek, it is interpreted as grounds for the preceding prohibition. Paul is doing more than simply describing covetousness; he gives grounds why the Colossian believers should shun this particular sin.

3:6 *Do not act like this [3:5a-g]* since God will punish those who disobey him, because they act like this [3:5c-g]. The antecedent of the clause-initial δι' ἅ 'because of which things' is τὰ μέλη τὰ ἐπὶ τῆς γῆς 'the members upon the earth', which is a metonymy signifying the evil deeds done by these 'members' (see the note on 3:5a-b); 'because of' indicates that it is the doing of these evil deeds that is the reason for God's anger and punishment.

The verb ἔρχεται 'comes' (in 'God's wrath comes') is in the present tense but probably has a future reference as in Eph. 5:6 and 1 Thess. 1:10 and, by implication, in Rev. 6:17 and 11:18, where the aorist is used. (All these references refer to the coming day of judgment when God's wrath will be shown in punishing sinners.) The word 'wrath' here is a metonymy that means 'punish', the cause being put for the effect; thus, the core of this proposition is the assertion that God will punish. (In Rom. 1:18, where reference is made to God's wrath operating in time, it is not the verb 'to come' that is used, but the verb 'to reveal'.)

The words 'ἐπὶ τοὺς υἱοὺς τῆς ἀπειθείας 'upon the sons of disobedience' appear in brackets in the UBS Greek text; they are classified as D in the UBS textual apparatus, indicating "a very high degree of doubt" concerning its inclusion. However, the arguments of Abbott and also Metzger would seem to support its retention. There are two main arguments: (1) The use of καὶ ὑμεῖς 'and you(pl)' in the following verse (preceding the verb) is a construction which usually implies the mention of some group of people to whom ὑμεῖς 'you(pl)' can be related either as part of the group or as a parallel group. If the phrase in question here is omitted, καὶ ὑμεῖς is left dangling. (2) There is "very widespread testimony supporting the longer reading" (Metzger, p. 6 24). One reason for its genuineness to be doubted is that it is omitted from two manuscripts, but the main reason is that the identical phrase occurs in Eph. 5:6, which lends itself to the theory that scribes added the phrase here to produce a consistent parallelism. But this is no more than an assumption, as over against the considerably more objective evidence of the grammar and the manuscripts.

The phrase 'upon the sons of disobedience' refers to those who will be punished. 'Sons of' is a common Hebrew idiom meaning 'those characterized by . . .'. What is disobeyed is either God himself or his laws. The former is given in the display.

3:7 You also formerly acted like this [3:5c–g] when you were disobeying God. There are two ambiguous back-reference forms in this verse. The first is the opening relative phrase ἐν οἷς 'in which'—it could refer back to the 'sons of disobedience' just mentioned, in which case it would mean 'among whom', or it could refer back to the evil deeds listed and commented on in v. 6, in which case it would mean 'in which (you walked)'. The second ambiguous form is the final τούτοις 'these' (or αὐτοῖς 'them'), which could refer back to either of the same two referents. (Whether the choice of reading here makes any difference to the meaning is not known. Modern editors prefer τούτοις; it is not discussed in the UBS text. The Textus Receptus reading is αὐτοῖς, which has the support of the majority of the minuscules as well as some uncials, but the earlier uncials support τούτοις.)

With the words καὶ ὑμεῖς 'also you' a parallel is drawn between the Colossian believers and the 'sons of disobedience', but with the difference that the sons of disobedience are still doing these evil deeds, whereas the believers, who did them formerly, no longer do so. This parallel makes it more natural to take ἐν οἷς at the beginning to refer to the evil deeds in which the sons of disobedience are still walking. Also, since the evil deeds are the topic of the whole paragraph, they would have the preference in this main clause. Moreover, apart from 2 Thess. 3:11, where the verb περιπατέω 'walk' is collocated with ἐν and people, it is always collocated with abstract nouns of various sorts, which makes that the more likely collocation here.

As to the referent of the final ἐν τούτοις/αὐτοῖς 'in these/them', Abbott states that "ζῆν ἐν is never used in the N.T. of living amongst persons, while it is frequently used with things." While this is true as it stands, Paul does speak in Gal. 2:20 of Christ's 'living in me' (ζῇ ἐν ἐμοί), and in Acts 17:28 Luke quotes Paul as saying 'we live in him (God)' (ἐν αὐτῷ ζῶμεν). Hence, in this context, it does not seem unreasonable to take τούτοις/αὐτοῖς as referring to the 'sons of disobedience', especially since ζῆν 'to live' is commonly used of 'being alive'. However, they were still living among the disobedient, so the collocation here must mean 'living as one of their number'. Hence, 'when you were disobeying God' is used in the display, and περιπατέω 'to walk' is considered to have its usual Pauline sense of 'to behave, conduct oneself'.

3:8a Now, however, as for you, do not do any *of the following evil* deeds: The opening νυνὶ δέ 'but now' stands in contrast to the ποτέ 'formerly' of 3:7. Previously, they had behaved in a certain (evil) way; now, by way of contrast, they were to behave in a certain (good) way.

The dead metaphor 'put off' (as one puts off clothing) is semantically equivalent to 'put to death' in 3:5. Both are rendered the same in the display.

Note that in this verse the words καὶ ὑμεῖς 'and/also you' follow the verb in the normal position, whereas in 3:7 the same words precede the verb, showing that a parallel is being drawn. Here καί probably signals a return to the theme line after the discussion in 3:6 and 7—'I am now addressing you again directly'. On the other hand, the repeated synonymous command in 3:2 did not use a free subject, even though there had been some comments about Christ. It is quite likely, therefore, that there is emphasis as well, possibly contrastive, since there is already a contrast with respect to time in this same proposition. Hence the word 'you' (referring to the Colossian believers) is in contrast to 'the sons of disobedience' who are not putting off evil deeds.

The phrase τὰ πάντα 'all the things' could be taken as referring back to what Paul has already said about vices or as anticipating the list of vices that follows. Since that list follows immediately, I agree with the view of Moule (1957): "More probably it refers *forward*, introducing a new group of sins. . . ." Hence, in the display 'any of the following' is supplied as implicit information.

3:8b–9a *specifically, do not* get angry in any way, *and do not* act maliciously, *and do not* slander *people, and do not* talk abusively *to people, and* do not lie to one another. There does not appear to be any clearly established distinction between the two nouns ὀργή and θυμός. Arndt and Gingrich use the glosses 'anger, wrath' for them both. Consequently, they are regarded as a doublet, with some emphasis, probably meaning 'any sort of anger'. This is also Moore's view (p. 25). If a distinction is intended, then ὀργή is a more settled form of anger, whereas θυμός is an angry outburst.

The words 'act maliciously' in 8c are a rendering of κακία 'maliciousness'. It is action aimed deliberately at producing evil results—and anger can readily lead to it. The word 'slander' (βλασφημία) in 8d refers to deliberately spreading false information *about* others behind their backs; 'talk abusively' (αἰσχρολογία) in 8e refers to speaking in an abusive, rude, insulting manner directly *to* people. These last two terms could be regarded as specific instances of κακία, but without knowing the exact components of each word, this is probably a bit too precise or overrefined.

Verse 8's final phrase ἐκ τοῦ στόματος ὑμῶν 'out of your mouth', is connected either with the preceding noun only, or the two preceding nouns (as closely similar). It emphasizes the activity of speaking. It seems likely that sins of speech were prevalent in pagan communities and had carried over into the Christian congregation.

In 9a another sin of speech is prohibited, but as a verb, not a noun: μὴ ψεύδεσθε can mean either 'stop lying' (assuming they were in the habit of lying) or 'do not tell lies' (no assumptions). The latter view seems preferable since the overall context does not suggest that these vices were prominent at Colosse.

3:9b Do not act like this [3:8a–9a] since you have disposed of your *evil* former character and *stopped doing* what you did when you had that *evil* former character, The aorist participle ἀπεκδυσάμενοι 'having put off' is figurative, but it is regarded as a dead metaphor just as ἀπόθεσθε 'put off' in 3:8. (Similarly, the contrastive 'put on' in 3:10 is regarded as a dead metaphor.)

There are two main questions in connection with this clause. The first is the relation of 'having put off' to the preceding list of sins. Grammatically, it could be considered either a command ('put off') or grounds ('since you have put off'). There are several reasons for taking it as grounds in this context: First, that is how Paul has already argued in 2:11 and 3:3. Second, it seems somewhat anomalous to introduce generic commands when he has already done this in 3:1–4 and has now shifted to specific commands dealing with specific vices. Third, considering it as grounds for the command in 3:8a makes the second half of the 3:5–11 paragraph parallel with the first, in that both follow the same pattern, command plus specifics plus grounds. Note that it is better to take the grounds as referring back to proposition 8a rather than to the command not to tell lies, which is simply the last item in the list of sins.

The second question that must be settled here concerns the meaning of the phrase τὸν παλαιὸν ἄνθρωπον 'the old person'. This is regarded as figurative language because no actual person is involved. It seems to be used to signify 'what you were in your entirety'. It does not refer just to certain bad habits or a way of life, but what they were in their unregenerate state, as pagans. The adjective 'old' refers both to time, 'former', and to character, 'evil'. RSV, NEB, and Phillips translate it "the/your old nature"; JB, NIV, and TEV translate it "the/your old self." It is not easy to represent the idea propositionally, but 'character' is reasonably satisfactory and is used in the display.

3:10a and since you have acquired a *good* new character, The terms here are antonyms of the terms in 3:9b: 'put on' is the opposite of 'put off'; 'new' is the opposite of 'old'. As so often, it is not easy to find good English nonfigurative equivalents. Following Beekman, 'you have acquired' is used for 'having put on', and the meaning of 'new' is considered to be new in time and good in character.

3:10b-c which God is causing to become more and more like the character of him who created it in order that *you might get to* know *God* truly. The initial article of 10b, τόν 'the-one', and the final pronoun of 10c, αὐτόν 'him', both refer back to 'the new man' in 10a. Thus 10b-c is basically a description of the 'new man' or 'new character'.

There are two different Greek roots in v. 10 that are generally rendered 'new' and 'renew', respectively. In the 10a participial phrase is 'the new man', which is based on the root νεο 'new (recent)'; in the next participial phrase is 'the one being renewed in knowledge', which is based on καινο 'new, different'. These two roots are distinguished in Greek, but Moule, both in his commentary and in his 1973 article, suggests that in this context the usual distinction is not being maintained but that the interchange of the two roots is stylistic. In support of this he points to Eph. 4:23–24, where very similar ideas are expressed, but the root καινο is used in 'the new man' and νεο in the verb 'renewed'. This seems a reasonable argument here. But what does 'the new man is being renewed' actually mean? This is explained by the two following prepositional phrases. The first, the εἰς 'toward' phrase, gives the goal of the renewal; the second, the κατά 'according to' phrase, gives the standard being aimed at. These show that 'being renewed' is a figurative way of indicating that this new man is being constantly changed, or transformed (cf. 2 Cor. 3:18 and Rom. 12:2 for similar ideas). Expressed propositionally, this is 'causing to become more and more'.

The final phrase of v. 10, κατ' εἰκόνα τοῦ κτίσαντος αὐτόν 'according to the image of the one who created him', states what the new character is becoming more and more like. The language is strongly reminiscent of the Genesis 1 creation account, in which man was made in the image of God; that is to say, the new character is being made more and more like God. It should be remembered that in 1:15 the Son was said to be the image of the invisible God, so that likeness to God is equally likeness to Christ; it seems unlikely, however, that Christ is directly referred to here by the expression 'the image of the one who created him' because of its association with the creation account.

The abstract noun ἐπίγνωσιν 'knowledge' represents a transitive event; the object of this knowledge is most simply supposed to be God. (In 1:9 its object is 'the will of God'; in 1:10 its object is 'God'; in 2:2 its object is 'the mystery of God'.) The one who comes to know is the new man, strictly speaking, but in the overall context this is 'you'. The compound form ἐπίγνωσις is taken to mean 'know truly'.

The preposition εἰς can signal either result or purpose. As is so often the case, either makes good sense in the context, but God's *purpose* in the renewal process seems collocationally preferable: in order that you might regain the knowledge of God that was lost in the fall.

3:11a As a result of this [3:10a–c], it is not *important whether you are (or, a person is)* a Gentile or a Jew, or whether *you are (or, a person is)* circumcised or not, or whether *you are (or, a person is)* a foreigner or *even* uncivilized, or whether *you are (or, a person is)* a slave or a free man. The first word in v. 11 is ὅπου 'where', yet no location has been mentioned for it to refer back to. It is probably more or less equivalent to ἐν ᾧ 'in which',

referring back to 'the new man' (see Arndt and Gingrich under ὅπου).

The rather unusual form ἔνι here is regarded as a short form of ἔνεστι 'is in, is located in, is contained in'. A paraphrase of 11a would be, No such distinctions as Jew and Gentile, etc., are to be found in the new man (i.e., in the new character). To propositionalize this idea is difficult. After considerable consultation, 'it is not important' was arrived at as the best suggestion. Paul is not saying that such distinctions do not exist among the believers; in fact, later in this same letter he addresses slaves and masters separately. Rather, he is saying that these distinctions no longer have any importance for the new character—what I am myself, or what others are, does not affect or influence my attitude to them.

Another difficulty here is how the statements in 3:11 relate to the preceding information. The reasoning seems to be that the creation of the new man has abolished the ethnic, social, and other distinctions characteristic of the old man. Hence the connection is one of reason-result, 3:10 giving the (complex) reason, and 3:11 the result. An alternative would be to regard 3:11 as a conclusion drawn from the statements in 3:10. The first alternative is probably the better one— ὅπου οὐκ ἔνι seems to emphasize the facts as they are. In either case, it is necessary to refer back to propositions 10a–c in order to attach 3:11—the ὅπου is a shorthand way, in the surface structure, of referring back to the statement in v. 10.

The first distinction here is Ἕλλην καὶ Ἰουδαῖος 'Gentile and Jew', Ἕλλην 'Greek' being taken in its broader sense of 'Gentile', see Arndt and Gingrich, 2.a. This is an ethnic distinction looked at religiously as brought out by the next pair of contrasts: περιτομὴ καὶ ἀκροβυστία 'circumcision and uncircumcision'. Circumcision is the distinctive mark of the Jewish religion.

The next two pairs of terms occur without a conjunction. The term βάρβαρος 'foreigner' was used by Greek speakers to refer to those who did not speak Greek. Later the Romans identified themselves with the Greeks, so that a βάρβαρος was a foreigner, outsider, with the implication of being uncultured. The term Σκύθης 'Scythian' was used of a fierce group of tribes from the Russian steppes who had invaded part of the Roman Empire before the Christian era. It was used to refer to peoples considered to be savage and uncivilized. Quite possibly the sequence βάρβαρος, Σκύθης, is climactic in force. The last pair, 'slave, freeman', involve a social distinction, as opposed to ethnic, religious, or cultural. The eight terms in 11a are probably intended to cover all such distinctions, since they overlap. (A Scythian could also be a slave; a Jew, a free man or a slave; etc.)

3:11b but *what is important is* Christ, who is supremely important in every way. The conjunction ἀλλά 'but' here introduces what is important in contrast to what is not. 'Christ is all things' is equivalent to 'Christ is supremely important'.

The phrase ἐν πᾶσιν 'in all' is gender-ambiguous; 'all' could be masculine or neuter. In other words, 'all' could refer to people, or 'in all' could be an adverbial phrase. If the former is intended, it would mean 'Christ is in all'. There are two reasons to favor this view: (1) If it were adverbial, it would mean the same as the opening τὰ πάντα 'all things', adding emphasis to it, but when it is used in this way, καί 'and' is not used and there is an explicit verb (see 1 Cor. 15:28; Eph. 1:23). And (2) καί is best considered as introducing a separate idea (cf. Moule 1959:160), namely 'Christ is in all believers'. This statement would collocate well with the negative statements preceding it.

However, it is abrupt and unexpected to refer here to Christ's being in all believers, and more appropriate to the context to emphasize Christ's supreme importance. It is because he is so important that all the previously important distinctions fade into insignificance. Hence, καὶ ἐν πᾶσιν 'and in all' is here considered to reinforce the preceding τὰ πάντα and the sentence-final Χριστός 'Christ' in this position is considered to be an emphatic device. This is brought out in the propositionalization by the cleft construction: 'what is important is Christ' (cf. Alford).

SECTION CONSTITUENT 3:12–14 (Paragraph: Specific₂ of 3:1–4)

THEME: *Do what is good; in particular, love one another.*	
RELATIONAL STRUCTURE	CONTENTS
┌─ grounds	3:12a-c Since you *have been* chosen *by God*, (12b) and since you *have been* reserved *by God* for himself, (12c) and since you are loved *by God*,
│ EXHORTATIONS₁₋₆	3:12d-13a be compassionate *to one another*, (12e) and be kind *to one another*, (12f) and be humble, (12g) and be meek/considerate *toward one another*, (12h) and be patient *with one another*, (13a) and tolerate one another.
│ EXHORTA- ─ NUCLEUS	3:13b-c And forgive one another, (13c) if one *of you* has a grievance/grudge against another.
│ TION₇ └─ comparison	3:13d Just as Christ (*or*, the Lord *Jesus*) *freely* forgave you, you, too, *freely forgive one another*.
│ EXHORTA- ─ EXHORTATION	3:14a It is more important than all of these [3:12d-13d] that you love *one another*,
└ TION₈ (marked) └─ grounds	3:14b *since* by loving one another you will be perfectly united together.

BOUNDARIES AND COHERENCE

A new semantic unit is marked at 3:12 by οὖν 'therefore', by the second person plural aorist imperative ἐνδύσασθε 'put on', and by the change of subject matter from vices to be got rid of to virtues to be acquired. That 3:12 is parallel to 3:5 is obvious: 3:12 is the positive development of the generic commands in 3:1–4.

More difficult than the question of where the 3:12–14 paragraph begins is where it ends. There are four possible answers:

1. It ends with 3:17. Here the instructions to the whole congregation, without any sort of distinctions drawn, come to an end, and 3:18 starts a series of commands addressed to particular subgroups of the congregation. A number of the versions take 3:12–17 to be a single paragraph—RSV, NEB, TEV, for example. (Out of twenty-six versions consulted, seventeen took 3:12–17 as one paragraph.) However, as will be argued later, 3:17 is a separate semantic unit that terminates the division.

2. It ends with 3:14. In 3:14 the verb ἐνδύσασθε is assumed from 3:12, so it cannot be separated from 3:12. Moreover, 3:14 is expressed climactically—'above all'. The lexical link between ἠγαπημένοι 'beloved' in 3:12 and ἀγάπην 'love' in 3:14 could be considered a sandwich structure. Analyzed thus, 3:12–14 would clearly parallel either half of the 3:5–11 paragraph, because the verb is followed by a string of five nouns or noun phrases. The NIV, Phillips, and Beck have a paragraph break at the end of 3:14.

3. It ends with 3:15. This view accepts the arguments concerning the unity of 3:12–14, but brings out several other factors:

   a. Both of the commands in 3:15 are introduced by καί 'and', but the command in 3:16 is not.
   b. The second of the two commands in 3:15 is a command to be thankful, and reference to thankfulness is a closure at certain points in this epistle (see 1:12; 3:17; cf. also 3:16).
   c. There is a change of subject matter at 3:16. Verses 3:12–14 deal with the virtues of the individual Christian, such as kindness, patience, forgiveness, and love; 3:15 also deals with two such virtues—peace with one another and gratitude to God. In 3:16, however, the command has to do with the 'message of Christ' and the emphasis is more on congregational activities. The JB has a paragraph break after 3:15. Meyer comments, "The series of exhortations begun in ver. 12 is now closed, and Paul proceeds to give . . . an encouraging allusion to the *Christian means of grace* for furthering the common life of piety. . . ." (Six of twenty-six versions have a paragraph break after 3:15.)

4. It ends with 3:16. This view draws attention to the structural parallelism between 3:15 and 16. Both are third person singular present tense commands, with the noun phrase subject preceding the verb and itself a genitive construction. In both cases, the verb is followed

by a prepositional phrase introduced by ἐν 'in' and referring to 'you(pl)'. It is argued that such an obvious formal parallelism points to treating both of these *verses* in the same way. Following this line of argument, however, would appear to lead to two main alternatives:

a. If 3:15 is not regarded as part of the paragraph beginning at 3:12, then 3:16 should not be either.
b. If 3:15 is regarded as part of the paragraph beginning at 3:12, then 3:16 should be included in it.

Note that if view a is followed, 3:15 and 16 could either be grouped together to form a single paragraph or could be considered separate constituents of the section. Interestingly enough, none of the twenty-six versions referred to had a paragraph break after 3:16.

Beekman concluded that 3:12–17 consisted of four paragraphs; 3:12–14, 15, 16, and 17. I have modified this slightly, grouping 3:15 and 16 into one paragraph on the grounds of the strong structural parallelism between them. Also, it is noted that καί introduces 3:17, a separate unit; thus it seems likely that the presence of the initial καί in 3:15, but not in 3:16, indicates that these two verses constitute a unit.

There is clear relational coherence in this paragraph in that all the information is tied back to the opening verb either by case (accusative), or by participle (nominative case, masculine plural), or by clauses attached to the accusative nouns or the participles. As is to be expected in hortatory material, the majority of the verb forms are second person plural. There are also three occurrences of second person plural pronouns. Lexically, much of the vocabulary is drawn from the semantic domain of virtues.

PROMINENCE AND THEME

Deriving a theme for the 3:12–14 paragraph is somewhat more difficult than for the preceding paragraphs. Here, there is no generic command, but only a series of specifics. However, the paragraph stands in overall contrast lexically with the preceding one, the theme of which is 'Do not do what is evil'. Hence, a good generic theme for this paragraph would be 'Do what is good'. However, in 3:14 a prominence device singles out the command to love one another. No other command seems to be marked in any way, so this command is regarded as having marked prominence and hence is thematic.

NOTES

3:12a–c Since you *have been chosen* by God, and since you *have been* reserved *by God* for himself, and since you are loved *by God*, The verb in the opening command, ἐνδύσασθε 'put on', is the same verb as was used in 3:10, and the antonym of the one in 3:8. It is considered a dead metaphor, as in the earlier instances. There is no generic expression following the command as its grammatical object, as there was in 3:5 and 3:8. Consequently, the command is taken with the individual abstract nouns as equivalent to "do this," so has no separate representation. Also, this means that the first specific command is found in 12d.

Three descriptions of the Colossians are given following ὡς 'like'. The second one is ἅγιοι, usually translated 'holy' or 'saints', but in this context its other sense, 'separated out', seems better, since the other two descriptions clearly refer to what God had done to them. Only the first description is followed by 'of God'; however, it should probably be understood as applying to all three; it states who does the choosing, the separating, and the loving.

As to the relation of these three descriptions to the commands expressed in 3:12d–14b, the clue is their introducer, ὡς. The normal function of ὡς is to compare: 'behave *like* (in the same way as) those who are elect'. However, Arndt and Gingrich do say that "ὡς with the participle gives the reason for an action" and reason and grounds are very similar. Further, it could be argued that there is an ellipsed participle (ὄντες 'being') following the ὡς. Since we see a consistent pattern of command supported by grounds throughout the hortatory part of this epistle, this is taken to be the pattern here also.

The use of adjectives, rather than participles, in the first two descriptions draws attention to the present state of the Colossians, rather than a past act that brought them into that state. The third description, the perfect participle ἠγαπημένοι 'loved', functions similarly, although it does point to a past act also. To convey these nuances in English the perfect tense is used with the first two and the present tense with the third.

3:12d–13a be compassionate *to one another,* **and be kind** *to one another,* **and be humble, and be meek/considerate** *toward one another,* **and be patient** *with one another,* **and tolerate one another.** The only question here is the best way to express these five nouns or noun phrase in English. The first, σπλάγχνα οἰκτιρμοῦ 'compassion', is a response to the need of others, a concern for the needy and a readiness to meet it. The second, χρηστότητα 'kindness', is similar; it represents an attitude to others that is the opposite of bitterness, envy, or despising them. The third, ταπεινοφροσύνην 'humility', is one's attitude to oneself of a true, not inflated, estimate of one's own character and gifts. The fourth, πραΰτητα, is particularly difficult to translate. It seems to have two components: consideration for others (an ability to see things from the other's point of view) and willingness to waive legitimate rights (Martin 1972), "the willingness rather to *suffer* injury than to *inflict* it" (Hendriksen). There does not seem to be any one English word that covers these senses, so both *meek* and *considerate* are given as alternatives in the display. (There is no contextual reason to choose one rather than the other.) The fifth word is μακροθυμίαν 'patience', which is not so much endurance under persecution (ὑπομονή), but patience toward fellow believers who annoy or rub us the wrong way.

Following this list, Paul goes on to list more virtues with verb constructions. The first of these verbs is ἀνέχομαι, which has the sense of putting up with, enduring, bearing with the things in others that would naturally produce reactions such as anger or resentment. It is very similar to 'patience', the last of the nouns, or even the last two nouns, 'consideration/meekness' and 'patience'. Thus it would be possible to take this verb and the verb 'forgive', which follows it, as restatements of the nouns, with the relation of equivalence. Meyer even suggests that they are the *result* of putting on the last two virtues. Alternatively, they may be regarded simply as two more virtues, coordinate with the preceding five.

The use of ἀγάπην 'love' in 3:14, assuming ἐνδύσασθε 'put on' from 3:12, may indicate that the list is continued in 3:14 with 3:13 simply clarifying and expanding on part of the list. However, to posit such relations is probably overdoing the analysis; so this proposition and the next are treated simply as conjoined to the preceding ones; that is, they continue the list of virtues.

3:13b–c And forgive one another, if one *of you* **has a grievance/grudge against another.** The word ἑαυτοῖς here is rendered 'one another'. In 13a the word ἀλλήλων is also rendered 'one another'. Strictly speaking, ἀλλήλων means 'one another' and ἑαυτοῖς 'yourselves', but of course 'forgiving yourselves' can only mean 'forgiving one another'. The reason different terms are used is probably to avoid repetitiousness, rather than make some subtle distinction. Moule (1959:120) says, "In Col. iii.13 it [ἑαυτοῖς] seems to be used as a synonym for the reciprocal ἀλλήλους." Turner (1963:43–44) and Robertson (1919:690) are similar.

The verb translated 'to forgive' in this verse is the same one as in 2:13. It is confined to the writings of Luke and Paul. Paul, in fact, does not use the other verb, ἀφίημι 'remit', at all in the sense 'to forgive' except in quoting the Old Testament in Rom. 4:7. There does not appear to be any semantic distinction between the two verbs. This is the only place in the New Testament in which μομφή 'complaint' is used. Probably 'grudge' or 'grievance' would be better English renderings, but there seems to be no way in English to avoid the use of *has* plus the noun, whichever word is chosen.

3:13d Just as Christ (*or,* **the Lord** *Jesus*) *freely* **forgave you, you, too,** *freely forgive one another.* The only question here is the best text. Was the original ὁ κύριος 'the Lord' or ὁ Χριστός 'the Christ'? Semantically, it probably makes no difference, as most agree that ὁ κύριος here means 'the Lord Jesus'. Metzger (p. 625) suggests that Χριστός 'Christ' was substituted for the more ambiguous κύριος 'Lord'. Both are well supported by uncials, but Χριστός has better support in early translations, in the Fathers, and in the minuscules. However, κύριος is supported by p[46], one of the earliest papyri (second or third century), though Pickering (1977b, p. 119) quotes from the textual scholars Zuntz and Hoskier to the effect that p[46] is marred by many errors. All in all it seems best if the translator translates this phrase as unambiguously referring to the Lord Jesus.

While 3:13d is clearly a comparison, it can be asked in *what way* the forgiveness exercised by the Colossians is to resemble that shown by the Lord. The answer would appear to be that his forgiveness was given freely, that is, unconditionally, without limit; hence 'freely' is supplied here.

3:14a It is more important than all of these [3:12d–13d] that you love *one another*, The opening phrase in this verse is ἐπὶ πᾶσιν 'in addition to all'. One question is the force of ἐπί here. Many commentators consider 'put on' in 3:12 to be a live figure and see the figurative language of 3:12 continued here. Love is the outer garment, so that ἐπί means 'on top of' but with the idea of 'most important' or 'supremely'. Meyer and also Arndt and Gingrich take ἐπί as meaning 'in addition to'. However, the presence of δέ would suggest a climax rather than simply the end of a list. It is not necessary to assume a live figure for this phrase to mean 'most important'. The comment in 3:14b supports this view, as well as the supreme place assigned to love in 1 Corinthians 13.

The noun 'love' is in the accusative case, showing that it is the object of the verb ἐνδύσασθε 'put on' in 3:12. When combined with this verb, the meaning is a command, 'love (one another)'.

3:14b *since* by loving one another you will be perfectly united together. The genitive construction σύνδεσμος τῆς τελειότητος 'a bond of perfection' is subject to many interpretations. But before considering them, it is necessary to look at the textual question as it relates to the opening relative pronoun. All modern editors have the neuter pronoun, ὅ 'which', while the Textus Receptus has ἥτις 'which', the feminine form. It is generally assumed that ἥτις was substituted for ὅ by later copyists so that there would be concord of gender with ἀγάπη, a feminine noun. There can be lack of concord between the noun and the relative pronoun for various reasons. When the neuter is used, it almost invariably means 'that is to say', 'what I mean is'; and as Abbott points out, if that were the function of the neuter here, then the phrases should be the other way around: 'put on the bond of perfection, that is to say, love'. In fact, Turner (1963:317) says, "Such a solecism appears nowhere else in the Paulines." In the light of the grammatical problems, the widespread support in the minuscules for ἥτις, and the fact that the pronoun refers back to τὴν ἀγάπην 'the love' (no other satisfactory alternative has been found), it would seem that ἥτις has as good a claim to be original, if not better, than ὅ has. In either case, the referent of the relative pronoun is 'love'.

There are two basic problems to be resolved in connection with the phrase σύνδεσμος τῆς τελειότητος 'a bond of perfection'. First, what is bound together? Second, what is the relation intended by the genitive here?

To answer the first question there are two possibilities: the preceding list of Christian virtues or the Christian congregation, the believers themselves. Either is contextually appropriate. The virtues have just been referred to by τούτοις 'these' in the preceding clause; and the congregation has been referred to as well, by ἀλλήλων 'one another' and ἑαυτοῖς 'yourselves' in the previous verse. Besides, the virtues themselves are those that are especially relevant to relations between members of a group.

To answer the second question there are more possibilities. Ellicott alone discusses four. Also tied up with this question is the matter of what τελειότητος 'perfection' refers to. An abstract noun, τελειότητος represents either the attribute 'perfect' (referring to things) or 'perfectly' (referring to an event, presumably, in this case, that of σύνδεσμος 'binding together').

Suggestions for the thing to which the attribute 'perfect' is related are as follows:

1. It is the believer or the group of believers. If the believer loves, then he will be perfect (i.e., fully mature, what he ought to be). Some who hold this view emphasize the plural; they speak more of the group of believers as a whole. Meyer adopts the singular view. Hendriksen, Lenski, and Martin 1972 (partially) take the plural view. Perfection is usually seen as the goal. This view goes with either view of the meaning of 'bond'. It may be the believers, as a group, moving towards perfection; or it may be the virtues, united by the virtue of love, which yields the perfect believer.

2. The reference of 'perfect' is to the attribute itself: 'unity' or 'harmony' or 'whole'. This view fits either view of the meaning of 'bond'. Either the Christians are bound together in perfect harmony or unity, or the virtues themselves are (see Abbott, Lightfoot, Bruce 1957, and Arndt and Gingrich). This view is based on the figurative sense of 'bond', which is taken to mean 'binds into harmony, unity, wholeness', and the quality of perfection is then applied to that.

Complex though these different views seem the basic choice is between the view that the virtues mentioned are bound together into a unified whole, or that the believers are. There does not seem much in the context to lead to a choice, but since all these virtues have to do with interpersonal relations, it is perhaps better to give the preference to the view that it is the group of believers at Colosse that are to be knit together by putting on love. This would yield a proposition such as 'which unites all of you perfectly', using the nonfigurative meaning of 'binds together'. However, the collocation of 'love' with 'unites' is a personification of 'love'. In the display this problem is addressed by rewording it as 'by loving one another you will be perfectly united together' (cf. 2:2b–c for a similar statement). The implication of 'perfectly' here is that the other virtues mentioned, such as patience, unite only imperfectly without love. Love alone can completely or perfectly unite believers. Some commentators (e.g., Hendriksen and Lenski) take the word 'perfection' here to be the goal of the unity. The view that love binds the other virtues into unity or harmony seems obscure, at best. It seems more likely that Paul's concern is with the congregation than with relationships between the virtues. In other words, in the context of a series of exhortations to a Christian congregation, it seems much more likely that his concern was that they be bound together by love rather than with abstract statements concerning the virtues he has mentioned.

SECTION CONSTITUENT 3:15–16 (Paragraph: Specific₃ of 3:1–4)

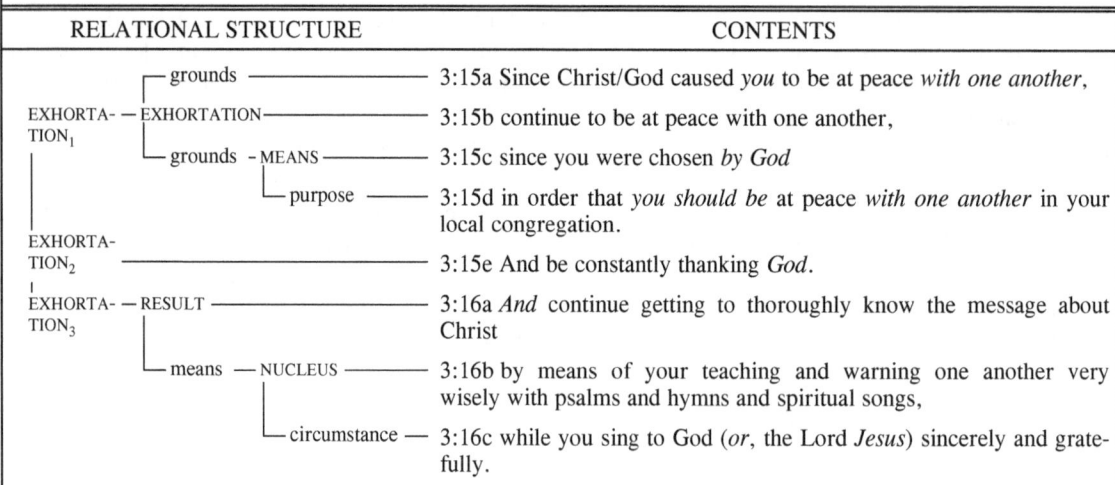

BOUNDARIES AND COHERENCE

The initial boundary of the 3:15–16 paragraph was already discussed in connection with the boundaries of the preceding paragraph, 3:12–14. The issue that needs to be discussed at this point is whether there is a boundary after 3:16 or after 3:17. In other words, does this unit consist of 3:15–16 or 3:15–17?

The best analysis is to recognize 3:17 as the final constituent of the 2:6–3:17 division, rather than as a part of the 3:15–16 paragraph or as a part of the 3:1–16 section. Although it is the final command in the series of commands starting at 3:12, as shown by the absence of any change in the subject matter, that is to say, the positive side of Christian behavior, it is not only the final command but is so generically expressed that it is semantically equivalent to the generic command in 2:6, 'walk in him', which opens the hortatory division, 2:6–3:17. Thus, in 3:17, 'all' (πᾶν, πάντα) is used twice.

A number of commentators support this analysis. Alford describes 3:17 as a "*general exhortation*, comprehending all the preceding spiritual ones"; F. F. Bruce (1957) says that "these general injunctions are summed up in an exhortation of universal scope"; and Hendriksen says that it "summarizes and climaxes." In addition, the accompanying reference to giving thanks, expressed in a full form with both the object of the thanks and the mediator through whom the thanks are offered being explicit, makes for an even closer parallel with 2:6–7.

Therefore, 3:16 is treated as forming a paragraph with 3:15, and 3:17 as a separate constituent of the whole division.

Every clause in 3:15 and 16 makes reference to 'you(pl)' by pronouns, verb ending, or nominative plural participles. Although the finite verbs in the two opening clauses are formally third person singular, they are semantically equivalent to second person plural commands, as is shown in 3:16 by the three following participles, which are nominative plural referring to the Colossians (every grammar consulted confirms this) and as shown in 3:15 by the second person plural finite verb ἐκλήθητε 'you were called'.

PROMINENCE AND THEME

The 3:15–16 paragraph is built around three independent imperative verbs representing three independent hortatory propositions (3:15b, 15e, and 16a). The paragraph's theme can either be abstracted from the three as a generic, or the three can be stated in the form of a compound sentence. Since positive generic commands are already clearly thematic in 3:1–4 and 3:12–14, abstracting a third generic command would not be as communicative of the theme as presenting the three commands as specifics of 3:1–4.

NOTES

3:15a–b Since Christ/God caused *you* to be at peace *with one another,* continue to be at peace with one another, There is a textual problem here, the variants being 'Christ' and 'God'. The variant Χριστοῦ 'of Christ' is better supported in the uncials, θεοῦ 'of God' in the (later) minuscules. At this point, where no grammatical or semantic considerations affect the choice, the choice depends on the textual theory one espouses. Until that is more settled, the translator may choose either reading. For convenience, however, the text will be referred to in the following notes as if Χριστοῦ were the only reading, so as to avoid stating both alternatives, 'Christ/God', each time a reference is made. (This is done without prejudice to the textual reading.)

The verse begins (after καί) with ἡ εἰρήνη τοῦ Χριστοῦ 'the peace of Christ'. All authorities agree that the genitive phrase here means, essentially, 'the peace which Christ has given'. This phrase is the subject of the verb βραβευέτω 'let-it-arbitrate'. If this verb represents a live figure, then its meaning is 'award a prize (at the games)'; if not, then it has the more generic sense of 'judge, decide' or 'control, rule'. Most commentators agree that the more generic sense is to be preferred. (Cf. the nonfigurative use of the compound κατα-βραβεύω 'give judgment against' in 2:18a.) Whatever the sense chosen, a personification is involved in which 'peace' is spoken of as if it were a person who could perform such actions as judging or controlling.

This raises the question of the meaning underlying this personification—what is the nonfigurative equivalent? One possibility is that it is a person doing the action and peace is the means used in connection with the action. In this view the person would be either Christ himself or the believer.

In semantic theory, 'peace' is not a thing, but an attribute, and the thing this attribute qualifies is 'hearts' (i.e., the center of the personality). In other words, Christ causes the center of the personality to be peaceful, in a state of peace. However, it may be that 'hearts' here is a synecdoche meaning 'you'; in this case, 'in your hearts' could mean 'among you'. This may seem farfetched, but the statement that follows makes more sense if 'peace' is seen as peace among the believers rather than *within* each of them individually.

The form of the verb is third person present imperative: βραβευέτω 'let it be controlling, ruling'. Semantically, this presumably means 'submit to the control of', being a second person imperative directed to the Colossians.

All these factors combine to make it very difficult indeed to arrive at a nonfigurative propositionalization of this command. But the emphasis on mutual relationships in the preceding paragraph (3:12–14) and on mutual ministry in 3:16 creates a strong contextual preference for understanding the peace referred to as peace among the believers in the local congregation at Colosse. Hence, one way in which the opening clause in 3:15 could be expressed propositionally would be 'Since Christ has caused *you* to be at peace *with one another*, continue to be at peace with one another', as in the display. In other words, the blessing of peace that they now had as believers was to be carefully maintained.

3:15c–d since you were chosen *by God* in order that *you should be* at peace *with one another* in your local congregation. This clause opens with εἰς ἥν 'to which', 'which' referring back to εἰρήνη 'peace' in the preceding clause. This phrase expresses the purpose of God's call, 'to which you were called'. The verb καλέω is commonly translated 'to call' in English versions, but by 'to choose' in propositionalization. Theologians often express this as the effectual call, the action in time corresponding to the choosing before time. It is only in the Gospels that 'called' and 'chosen' are contrasted; in the Epistles, if you are called, you are also chosen. (See Lightfoot's discussion of 3:12, echoed in Abbott; see also Arndt and Gingrich under καλέω, 2: "in the usage of the NT, as well as that of the LXX, of the choice of pers[ons] for salvation.")

The main question in 15c–d is how ἐν ἑνὶ σώματι 'in one body' relates to the rest of the clause. Three different views are given in the commentaries:

1. One body is the result of the calling. That is, they are now in one body (Abbott, Meyer, Peake, and possibly Lenski and Moule 1957).
2. 'In one body' refers to "the sphere and element in which that peace . . . was to be carried on and realized" (Alford).
3. As members of one body (Hendriksen, Lightfoot).

It is difficult to see ἐν 'in' as signaling a result. That is usually signaled by εἰς if a preposition is used. It is also difficult to attach a purpose and a result naturally to 'you were called'. For this reason, the second and third views are to be preferred. View 2 treats the ἐν phrase as a location—it is *in* one body that the peace is to be expressed. View 3 treats the ἐν phrase as a grounds: 'since you are members in one body'. View 2 assumes a common and well-established use of ἐν, whereas 1 and 3 do not. And against 3 it can also be argued that the relative clause has a grounds function already, so a further grounds combined with it is unnecessarily complex. Hence, view 2 is chosen here: that the peace to which they were called was to be expressed in one body.

However, there is a further question: Does σώματι 'body' refer to the Colossian congregation or the church as a whole? The latter is already referred to by the image of σῶμα 'body' in 1:18 and 2:19. Since the vices and virtues referred to in this chapter have much to do with harmony between Christians, and since there is no article with σώματι (as there is in 1:18 and 2:19), it seems better to take 'one body' as referring to the congregation of believers at Colosse.

It is not clear just what the function of καί 'and, also' in this relative clause is. The verb here is ἐκλήθητε 'you were called', which is generally used in connection with 'salvation' ('called to salvation'), and it may be that καί is used to suggest that they were called to peace as well as to salvation.

3:15e And be constantly thanking *God*. The verb γίνομαι normally represents a change of state; its use here could imply that the Colossians had hitherto been unthankful. But since this is one item in a series of ethical exhortations, there is no need to make such an inference. Arndt and Gingrich say that γίνομαι with an adjective can "paraphrase the passive" (γίνομαι, 4b) and also that it can substitute for the verb 'to be' (II.1). Probably γίνομαι is used here to avoid a second person plural imperative of the verb 'to be' (εἶναι). The implied object of 'thanking' is 'God'.

3:16a *And* continue getting to thoroughly know the message about Christ The phrase ὁ λόγος τοῦ Χριστοῦ 'the word of Christ' is very widely interpreted as meaning 'the word which Christ taught, or gave, or which came from him' as opposed to 'the message about Christ'. But there is little real difference. The message which came from Christ is also extensively concerned with him, as has already been evident in the earlier parts of this epistle. This latter consideration points to the meaning 'the message about Christ', which was the answer to the heretical teaching they were being confronted with.

This command is parallel in form to 3:15, which begins with the figure of personification, and there is a personification here also. The 'word of Christ' refers to a message, to teaching, but it 'indwells'. The verb for 'dwell' is ἐνοικέω (not identical with that used in 1:19 and 2:9, which is κατοικέω, but there seems little difference in meaning). Used only by Paul (including a quotation from the Old Testament), ἐνοικέω occurs only six times in the New Testament, including this one in Col. 3:16. The quotation from the Old Testament refers to God's dwelling among (or in) his people (2 Cor. 6:16). In Rom. 8:11 and 2 Tim. 1:14 the reference is to the Spirit's indwelling believers. The remaining two references are personifications analogous to God and the Spirit's dwelling in people: In Rom. 7:17 Paul speaks of being indwelt by sin, and in 2 Tim. 1:5 of Timothy's mother and grandmother's being indwelt by faith.

As to the nonfigurative meaning of 'Let the word of Christ dwell in you richly', Beekman took it to be "Always respond to the message which Christ gave (us)." However, 'respond to' refers not to the actual indwelling, but to the response to the indwelling. Both Meyer and Lenski suggest that believers (collectively or individually) are being compared to a house where the word dwells, working within them and ruling them. Hendriksen speaks of the word's "bearing sway," the only nonfigurative rendering I could find. So the question remains, What exactly were the Colossians being asked to do? It would seem they were being asked to meditate on the word, think about it, memorize it, absorb its truths and principles, so that what they spoke to one another, or sang, all that they expressed in words, was in conformity with the message about Christ. However, meditation, memorization, etc., all were means to the end of *knowledge* of the message, and knowledge was the means to the end that all they did—speaking, singing, whatever—was to be in conformity with the message they had received about Christ. The adverb 'richly' intensifies the verbal idea. (According to Meyer its final position is for emphasis.) It is rendered "in ample measure" by Meyer, "in abundance and fulness" by Alford, and "a large and liberal occupancy" by Eadie. Since the third person command here is considered to be semantically equivalent to a second person command, and since a nonfigurative equivalent of 'indwelling' is 'get to know', this command is propositionalized as

'Continue getting to thoroughly know the message about Christ'.

3:16b by means of your teaching and warning one another very wisely with psalms and hymns and spiritual songs, The first question to answer here is, How are the various phrases attached to the (four) different verb forms? To answer this, several factors need to be considered:

1. Various commentators argue that the ἐν phrases, ἐν πάσῃ σοφίᾳ 'in all wisdom' and ἐν χάριτι 'in grace/thanks', should be handled in a parallel manner. This means, in practice, that they may be attached to either the preceding clause or the following clause in each case; so this view does not resolve the problem.
2. In 1:28 Paul has already said 'warning every man and teaching every man in all wisdom' using the same two verbs and the same prepositional phrase, ἐν πάσῃ σοφίᾳ 'in all wisdom'. This provides good collocational evidence for taking 'in all wisdom' with the two following participles (which are closely linked by καί 'and'). If the parallelism suggested in point 1 is granted, then 'in grace/thanks' would go with ᾄδοντες 'singing'.
3. If the suggestion in point 2 is not followed, the sequence of prepositional phrase + adverb + prepositional phrase would result, and this is a rare order. A more normal order should be given preference, namely the order that results from attaching the second prepositional phrase to the following participle(s), as suggested in point 2.
4. It is also interesting that in 1:10–11 Paul uses an almost identical construction: ἐν-phrase + participle + καί + participle + dative phrase, ἐν-phrase + participle. . . .

Thus, it is preferable both collocationally and grammatically to take the two ἐν phrases under consideration with the participles that follow them, as do most of the commentators.

Another question is whether ψαλμοῖς ὕμνοις ᾠδαῖς πνευματικαῖς 'psalms, hymns, spiritual songs' is attached to the preceding participles, διδάσκοντες καὶ νουθετοῦντες 'teaching and warning', or the following one, ᾄδοντες 'singing'? The arguments in favor of attaching it to the preceding participles are as follows:

1. If the parallel ἐν phrases are considered to initiate their clauses, as argued above, then this phrase would have to belong to the preceding clause.
2. The participle ᾄδοντες 'singing' already has two modifying prepositional phrases and a dative phrase, so a fourth modifying phrase is of low statistical probability.
3. In the parallel passage, Eph. 5:19, it is very likely that the corresponding phrase goes with 'speaking to one another' rather than with 'singing and making melody'; otherwise, Paul is understood to be urging the Ephesians to speak to one another!
4. If this phrase is attached to the following clause, then the word order is unusual, with a dative phrase preceding a prepositional phrase, both before the verb. If it is attached to the preceding clause, its order is normal.
5. If this phrase is attached to ᾄδοντες, it would be accusative (being what was sung); no examples of what was sung have been found in the dative case, which is the case here.

The only argument against attaching it to the preceding clause(s) is the collocational one, that it seems much more natural to collocate 'psalms, hymns, spiritual songs' with 'singing' than with 'teaching and warning'. However, the cumulative force of the preceding arguments is considerable, especially the last one. A decision is not at all easy, but on the whole I am inclined to agree with the older commentators and put this phrase with the preceding participles rather than with the following one, even though the collocation seems rather unnatural.

The second question that must be addressed is, What semantic relation do the participial clauses have to the command indicated by the imperative verb? Three quite different views can be found. Meyer and Alford suggest that the indwelling of the word of Christ is the means leading to the result of teaching.

Beekman had another view: he took the participles as semantically equivalent to commands (so also Lightfoot), labeling them as specifics of the opening command. The same conclusion would be reached by recognizing that the various activities referred to by the participles can be considered specific activities related to the generic command concerning the word of Christ, to be carried out by the congregation as a whole. Since they are specific activities of a generic command, they function semantically as specific commands (cf. 1:9–12 for a parallel paragraph, where the series of present participles are specific purposes related to a generic purpose). In other words, they are not specifics because they are commands; they are commands because they are specifics.

The third view is the reverse of the first, in which the participles are considered to be the means. As each specific means is carried out, the generic command is fulfilled, which would make the command the result. The second and third views are, in fact, very similar, as, in either case, the carrying out of the participial commands would entail the fulfilling of the main command.

However, in either of these two, it is not at all obvious how 'singing to God' would promote knowledge of the message about Christ. For this reason singing to God is best understood as a simultaneous activity: while they were singing to God, they were at the same time to be teaching and warning one another by means of the contents of their various sung items. Consequently, 'teaching and warning' are seen as means to the end of the main command, while 'singing' is what was going on at the same time (i.e., circumstance).

For the meaning of νουθετέω 'to admonish, warn', the second verb in 3:16b, see the note on 1:28b.

Much space could be devoted to the three terms translated 'psalms', 'hymns', and 'spiritual songs'. Commentators generally do not see them as distinct types of song. Lightfoot says, "It was quite possible for the same song to be at once ψαλμός, ὕμνος, and ᾠδή." Peake says, "The precise distinctions intended are not certain, and perhaps they should not be sharply drawn. The meaning is, whatever kind of song it may be, let it be made the vehicle of religious instruction and admonition." Others tend to agree (e.g., Martin 1972, 1973, also Bruce 1957). This does not mean that the terms are used synonymously, however, but rather that they cover the whole semantic field of songs that the Colossian Christians were singing in their public meetings (for that is the context).

While this is all no doubt true, still there are clues as to what the individual terms might mean. The word ψαλμός 'psalm' is used in Luke 20:42, 24:44, Acts 1:20, and 13:33 to refer to the Book of Psalms, or an individual psalm, and is the Greek term used in the Septuagint to translate the Hebrew word *mizmōr*, which only occurs in titles to psalms (fifty-seven in all). It seems very unlikely, therefore, to a New Testament Christian, using the Septuagint as his Old Testament and taught mostly by Jewish Christians, that ψαλμός meant anything other than an Old Testament psalm.

The word ὕμνος 'hymn' is much more difficult. It occurs only here and in Eph. 5:19, the parallel passage. The corresponding verb, however, is used of Jesus and the disciples at the Last Supper (Matt. 26:30; Mark 14:26), and it is commonly suggested that they sang Psalms 115–118. The verb is also used of Paul and Silas singing in prison (Acts 16:25).

The word ᾠδή 'song' is a generic term; the addition of πνευματικός 'spiritual' distinguishes these songs from the secular songs of the day. It is the term used of the songs mentioned in Rev. 5:9, 14:3, and 15:3.

While certainty is not possible, a good suggestion is to translate the word 'psalm' here as for any reference to an Old Testament psalm. The word 'song' here can be translated with a generic word for any song, and 'hymn' can be translated by the idea of praise, since this Greek word was used in the Septuagint to translate a Hebrew word meaning 'praise' (from the same verb as 'hallelujah'). In the light of modern experiences, 'spiritual songs' may mean songs given (immediately) by the Holy Spirit, and 'hymns' may have been longer-established compositions, perhaps ones that congregations shared. (Because there is no historical evidence for this, certainty is not possible.)

3:16c while you sing to God (*or*, the Lord *Jesus*) sincerely and gratefully. The Greek is ἐν [τῇ] χάριτι ᾄδοντες ἐν τῇ/ταῖς καρδίᾳ/καρδίαις ὑμῶν τῷ θεῷ/κυρίῳ 'in [the] grace/thanks singing in the heart/hearts of-you to-the God/Lord'. There are some textual variants here, but it is generally agreed that the meaning is unaffected by the choice between any except the last: θεῷ 'God' and κυρίῳ 'Lord'. Since the choice depends solely on what theory of textual criticism is followed, the translator is free to choose either 'God' or 'the Lord'.

The phrase ἐν τῇ/ταῖς καρδίᾳ/καρδίαις 'in the heart(s)' almost certainly, in this context, does not refer to singing "inwardly" (whatever that might mean). Rather, it means singing sincerely or genuinely. Both the Old Testament and the New Testament strongly condemn outward religion in which religious observances are adhered to while the heart is far from God. This then is a warning against outward singing that is not sincerely meant. Other such uses of either ἐν τῇ καρδίᾳ 'in the heart' or simply τῇ καρδίᾳ 'the heart (dative)' are in Rom. 9:2, 10:9; 2 Cor. 8:16; and the parallel Eph. 5:19. (The phrase ἐκ τῆς καρδίας 'from the heart' means 'wholeheartedly, enthusiastically', and is a different idiom.)

A further question is the meaning of χάριτι. Either 'grace' or 'gratitude' is quite possible, and the commentators are divided. One factor affecting the choice is that gratitude is mentioned at the end of the previous verse and again at the end of the next one, so that here, it is argued, it seems rather redundant. The other factor is textual—is the text with the article (ἐν τῇ χάριτι) better than the text without it (ἐν χάριτι)? The former would favor 'grace' more than the latter, it is argued, but neither the text nor the conclusions drawn from it are certain. A third factor, not suggested by the commentators, is that in all the other references to thanksgiving in this epistle Paul uses the stem εὐχαριστ- (verb, noun, and adjective forms). A fourth factor is the possible parallelism (see the note on 3:16b) of ἐν πάσῃ σοφίᾳ 'in all wisdom' in 3:16b and ἐν χάριτι 'in grace' here in 3:16c: ἐν πάσῃ σοφίᾳ is a prepositional phrase that functions as an adverb, 'very wisely', and modifies 'teaching and warning', so if ἐν χάριτι is parallel with it, it is adverbial and would most likely mean 'gratefully' or 'beautifully'. But χάρις is not used with this latter meaning in the New Testament except in connection with speech, twice, in Col. 4:6 and Luke 4:22. Although this use of ἐν χάριτι later in Colossians could favor the same sense here, this, like the other factors, is not definitive; therefore 'gratefully' and 'graciously' (i.e., 'in a manner appropriate to those in a state of grace') are both good alternatives.

DIVISION CONSTITUENT 3:17 (Propositional Cluster: Equivalent of 2:6–7)

THEME: Do everything in the manner that those should do who are the people of the Lord Jesus.

RELATIONAL STRUCTURE	CONTENTS
NUCLEUS (EXHORTATION) — NUCLEUS ┬ identity of 'all'	3:17a Whatever you say and whatever you do,
	3:17b do all *of this* [3:17a] in the manner that those who are subject to the Lord Jesus *should do*,
└ circumstance	3:17c while you constantly thank God our(inc) Father by means of the Lord Jesus' *mediating between God and you*.

BOUNDARIES AND COHERENCE

The boundaries of the 3:17 unit have already been discussed in connection with the boundaries of 3:15–16.

As to the coherence of the 3:17 unit, all the verb forms, including the clearly ellipsed one, ποιεῖτε 'do', are 'you(pl)' oriented. Further, the singular πᾶν 'everything' in the first clause is repeated in the plural (πάντα 'all things') in the second clause and the reference to the Lord Jesus in the second clause is repeated with a pronominal reference in the third clause. Grammatically, there is one finite verb clause (with an ellipsed verb, 'do') preceded by a noun phrase with an embedded relative clause functioning as the object of the main clause and followed by a dependent participial phrase.

Structurally 3:17 is considered to be a propositional cluster, related directly to 2:6–7, the nucleus paragraph of the 2:6–3:17 division. Its relation is that of equivalence since it restates the command in 2:6 in synonymous terms.

PROMINENCE AND THEME

The theme of the 3:17 unit corresponds to the unit's main proposition. Within this main proposition is an embedded manner proposition whose semantic function in relation to the verb is like the function of an identification proposition in relation to a thing; it is, therefore, also included in the theme.

NOTES

3:17a Whatever you say and whatever you do, The Greek 'whatever you do in word or in deed' is a circumlocution. It means 'whatever you say and whatever you do'. The periphrastic form is effective in that it uses the same verb, 'do', that is understood in the command clause; thus 'in speech' and 'in deed' are two specifics that represent the whole field of outward action, concerning which Paul is giving instructions.

3:17b do all *of this [3:17a]* in the manner that those who are subject to the Lord Jesus *should do*, There is no explicit verb in this clause, but it is readily supplied from the preceding one, ποιεῖτε 'do', the present plural imperative.

The phrase ἐν ὀνόματι κυρίου Ἰησοῦ 'in (the) name of (the) Lord Jesus' is variously interpreted. The problem is that the phrase is generic, and any particular interpretation chooses a more specific sense of the phrase, but there is little in such a generic context to favor one specific sense over another. The main suggestions are: (1) under the lordship/authority of the Lord Jesus; (2) in accordance with the revealed truth about the Lord Jesus; (3) called by name of the Lord Jesus; and (4) as representatives of the Lord Jesus. Suggestions 1, 3, and 4 all say, from different perspectives, 'belonging to the Lord Jesus' (i.e., 'the people of the Lord Jesus'). The command that opened the hortatory part of this epistle, 'walk in him', was rather similar in that it means walk as those who are his people, united to him by faith. (Note that suggestion 2 presupposes 1, 3, and 4, for it is only those who belong to the Savior who are concerned to act in accordance with the truth about him.) Suggestions 1, 3, and 4 also fit in with the other contextually similar uses of this phrase in Paul's letters (1 Cor. 5:4 and 2 Thess. 3:6). In other words, as some of the commentators say, there is very little difference, if any, between 'in the name of the Lord Jesus' and the simpler 'in the Lord' used later in this same epistle. For the display, it is suggestion 1 that is chosen: 'those who are subject to the Lord Jesus'.

3:17c while you constantly thank God our(inc) Father by means of the Lord Jesus' *mediating between God and you*. The first question here is the semantic relation of the thanking to the doing (i.e., between 17c and 17b). The relation would appear to be circumstance (both are present tense): the thanking is to accompany the doing.

The second question is the referent of the phrase δι' αὐτοῦ 'through him'. It refers to the Savior as the Mediator between his people and God the Father. It is he who takes our thanks and presents them to the Father. Such is the theological understanding. It is expressed by supplying the implicit information 'mediating between God and you'.

The third question has to do with the textual variant. Does καί 'and' occur between θεῷ 'God' and πατρί 'Father'? The UBS editors think not; they assume that καί was inserted later to bring what would otherwise be a "very unusual collocation" (so Metzger, p. 626) into conformity with the general New Testament pattern. As so often, there is extensive minuscule support for the presence of καί, but probably stronger uncial support for its omission. In either case, πατρί identifies God as God the Father (i.e., our Father), so there is no semantic difference.

PART CONSTITUENT 3:18–4:6
(Division: Conjoined (secondary matters) to 1:13–3:17)

THEME: Act as believers should toward those of their household. Pray persistently, and act wisely toward unbelievers.

RELATIONAL STRUCTURE	CONTENTS
NUCLEUS$_1$	3:18–4:1 Be subject to those in authority at home; and if you have authority, exercise it as those who believe in the Lord Jesus should do.
NUCLEUS$_2$	4:2–6 Pray to God persistently and pray for me. Also, always speak wisely and graciously toward those who do not believe in the Lord Jesus.

BOUNDARIES AND COHERENCE

The end of the 2:6–3:17 division was clearly marked by the rhetorical bracketing of a very generic command together with reference to thanksgiving. The beginning of this new division, 3:18–4:6, is marked by a switch from commands addressed to the Colossian congregation as a whole to commands addressed to groups within the congregation, together with the only use in the epistle of vocatives. Its end coincides with the end of the hortatory genre at 4:6 and a return to nonhortatory genre at 4:7, where indicative verbs mark the beginning of the epistle closing. Thus 3:18–4:6 is seen as constituting the last division of the 1:3–4:6 body (see the display of the whole epistle).

This division has certain particular characteristics. One is that it is marked by parallelisms. The body's introduction, 1:3–12, and the hortatory division of the primary matters, 2:6–3:17, are similarly characterized by parallelisms, but the parallelisms in 3:18–4:6 are not the same in form as those found previously. It is interesting, though, that the parallelisms here are more like those in 1:3–12 than in 2:6–3:17 in view of the fact that 1:3–12 begins the body and this unit closes it.

The parallelisms in 3:18–4:6 are parallelisms of form. In the first constituent (3:18–4:1) they consist of clause-initial plural vocatives followed by present tense plural imperatives. There are six such parallelisms, in 3:18, 19, 20, 21, 22, and 4:1. In the second constituent (4:2–6), the parallelisms are quite different in form. The two paragraphs of this section open with a forefronted noun phrase with the noun in the dative case followed by a second person plural imperative verb. There is also semantic parallelism: both commands have to do with the manner in which the event is to be carried out and are followed by a related specific command.

Also particular to this division, but found only in the first constituent, is the use of the phrase ἐν κυρίῳ 'in the Lord', in 3:18 and 20, together with very frequent references simply to 'the Lord' ([ὁ] κύριος).

PROMINENCE AND THEME

The 3:18–4:6 division consists of two constituents, 3:18–4:1 and 4:2–6. Although they are both hortatory in genre, they are quite independent of each other, and it is difficult to determine a theme for the division. Beekman suggested "Fulfill your obligations to others." Broadly speaking, this does cover the constituents' themes, but much of the previous division could also be summarized in the same way. One might even summarize the whole of Christian ethics this way, 'Fulfill your obligations to God and to your fellow men'. In other words, it is too generic a theme. Therefore the theme here is derived by abbreviating the two constituent themes and conjoining them.

DIVISION CONSTITUENT 3:18–4:1 (Section: Nucleus₁ of 3:18–4:6)

THEME: Be subject to those in authority at home; and if you have authority, exercise it as those who believe in the Lord Jesus should do.

RELATIONAL STRUCTURE	CONTENTS
NUCLEUS₁	3:18–19 Wives, be subject to your husbands; husbands, love your wives.
NUCLEUS₂	3:20–21 Children, obey your parents in every circumstance; parents, do not overcorrect your children
NUCLEUS₃	3:22–4:1 Slaves, obey your masters in every circumstance sincerely and wholeheartedly; masters, provide for your slaves justly and fairly.

BOUNDARIES AND COHERENCE

The most obvious characteristic of the 3:18–4:1 section is parallelism. There are six vocative phrases, all in the same form: article + plural noun. Each of these phrases occurs clause initial and "clause cluster" initial. (Vocatives can also be clause medial and clause final in the New Testament.) Further, each vocative is followed in the same clause by a present imperative verb in the second person plural. And each command is supported by other statements, though these vary considerably.

There is frequent use of (ὁ) κύριος '(the) Lord' throughout this material (in 3:18, 20, 22 [twice], 23, 24 [twice], and 4:1 [twice]). This is not a characteristic of the preceding paragraphs (there are references in 3:13 and 17 only), nor the following ones. Some of the references are to the Lord Jesus, some to earthly masters. It is the presence of this lexical thread in these verses and its absence in the surrounding ones that indicate that these verses constitute a semantic unit.

The strong formal parallelism could reasonably be considered to point to six semantic units in 3:18–4:1, especially since there are no formal links between any of the six. However, there is a noticeable reciprocity between successive pairs of clause clusters. For example, the first such cluster is addressed to wives and gives a command relating to their husbands; the second is addressed to husbands and gives a command relating to their wives; similarly with the second and third pairs. This evidence can be considered as indicating that there are three semantic units, each consisting of a lexically reciprocal pair of constituents. This means, in effect, that each paragraph is in two halves, as has been observed a number of times in the hortatory paragraphs of this epistle. The main propositions of each half, however, are not synonymous, as was the case in the preceding paragraphs, but rather, in a general sense, reciprocal.

PROMINENCE AND THEME

The 3:18–4:1 section consists of three paragraphs, and there are no formal grounds for ranking one paragraph above another. Thus the theme for 3:18–4:1 may be a generic abstraction of the themes of the three, or it may be simply a conjoining of the themes of the three. Beekman suggested as an abstraction "Fulfill obligations to those in your household." Commentaries and versions that give headings are generally similar: JB has "The morals of the home and household" and the NIV has "Rules for Christian Households."

While recognizing the difficulty of abstracting a theme accurately, it seems to me that such expressions as "obligations," "morals," and "rules" are too generic for the specific commands in these verses. These commands refer to a relatively narrow area of behavior, namely interpersonal relations between what might be called reciprocal parties. My suggestion is that what the commands in this section have in common is the matter of authority. Three of the groups addressed are under authority (wives, children, slaves) and the other three are exercising authority (husbands, parents/fathers, masters); the commands have to do with either submission to or exercise of authority. Also, there is frequent reference to the Lord, the supreme authority. It is very interesting that it is almost exclusively to those under authority that statements are made involving reference to the Lord. His authority is what makes it possible to accept authority in a Christian way.

The words 'at home' are included in the theme because the commands involving families evidently have their application in the home. While it is possible that masters and slaves might be involved in businesses outside the home, it is more likely that Paul was thinking of the Christian home here, and not the employment of slaves in business. In the case of four of the groups addressed, appeal is made to their relationship to the Lord Jesus, although this is expressed in a variety of ways—'in the Lord' (3:18, 20), 'fearing the Lord' (3:22), 'being slaves of the Lord' (3:24), and 'having a Lord in heaven' (4:1). In other words, it is because they are believers that Paul expects them to act in the ways commanded, and this fact is reflected in the wording of the theme.

SECTION CONSTITUENT 3:18–19 (Paragraph: Nucleus₁ of 3:18–4:1)

THEME: Wives, be subject to your husbands; husbands, love your wives.

RELATIONAL STRUCTURE	CONTENTS
NUCLEUS₁ — EXHORTATION	3:18a Wives, be subject to your husbands,
└─ grounds	3:18b-c since that is what *you* should do (18c) since *you are* united to the Lord *Jesus*.
NUCLEUS₂ — GENERIC (EXHORTATION)	3:19a Husbands, love your wives;
└─ negative specific	3:19b in particular, do not be harsh with them.

BOUNDARIES AND COHERENCE

See the discussion of the boundaries and coherence of 3:18–4:1.

PROMINENCE AND THEME

Each half of the 3:18–19 paragraph contains a single positive command expressed in the form of a finite imperative verb, so this is considered to constitute the thematic material. Proposition 19b is a negative command; as a single specific of a generic command, it would normally be considered to be more prominent than the generic command, but since it is negative, and the command is positive, this is not the case here. The theme, therefore, consists of the two positive commands conjoined, together with a vocative reference to those addressed.

NOTES

3:18a Wives, be subject to your husbands, The verb ὑποτάσσεσθε is here rendered 'be subject to'. This is the rendering given by Beekman and the RSV and NEB. The 1966 TEV has "be obedient to"; the NIV, LB, and the 1976 TEV have "submit to"; Phillips has "adapt to"; JB has "give way to."

The question is how ὑποτάσσω differs from ὑπακούετε 'obey' in 3:20 and 22. A study of the approximately forty occurrences of ὑποτάσσω in the New Testament suggests that it means 'to accept/recognize the authority of another'. Caird says, "The wife is to respect her husband's position as head of the household." Martin puts it this way: "[they] are summoned to accept their place in the divine ordering of family life." Thus it differs significantly from 'obey'. Though husband and wife are in the unique relationship of being "one flesh," God has appointed the husband as the head in this relationship; and ὑποτάσσομαι expresses the wife's recognition and acceptance of his headship. Obedience will flow from this acceptance, but the command here is 'accept', not 'obey'. The command is in the present tense, as are all others in the paragraph. This probably gives the force of 'constantly, always'—implying that the acceptance is to be characteristic of their conduct.

3:18b-c since that is what *you* should do since *you are* united to the Lord *Jesus*. The clause ὡς ἀνῆκεν ἐν κυρίῳ, literally 'as it was fitting in the Lord', presents some difficulties. Some of the commentators interpret the imperfect tense of ἀνῆκεν to mean that, to some extent at least, the Christian wives at Colosse had failed in this duty. But Turner says (1963:90–91), "It is not suggested that the past obligation was not lived up to; it is simply a present obligation expressed for some reason in the imperfect. The reason may be . . . simply because the obligation logically conceived is anterior to the implied fulfilment of the obligation." Note that English translations use the present tense.

Grammatically, the phrase ἐν κυρίῳ 'in the Lord' is to be connected with 'as was fitting', not with the main command. But what does it mean, and how is it related? The phrase ἐν κυρίῳ seems approximately equivalent to *as Christians* in English. That is how the TEV translates it; NEB and Phillips use the expression "your Christian duty." However, the term 'Christian' is very rare in the New Testament, and to use it as a rendering of 'in the Lord' distorts the historical setting. The commonest way to refer to Christians in the New Testament is probably ἐν Χριστῷ 'in Christ', generally understood to mean 'united to Christ', and it is assumed that ἐν κυρίῳ 'in the Lord' is an alternative way of referring to union with Christ. However, since the phrase is 'in the Lord' rather than 'in Christ', the phrase could be expanded as 'you believe in the Lord' or 'you belong to the

Lord'. Paul may have used ἐν κυρίῳ rather than ἐν Χριστῷ because he is dealing with questions of authority in the Christian community here.

The impersonal verb ἀνῆκεν can be translated as 'it is fitting, proper, appropriate, or right'. But is it *socially* fitting or *divinely* fitting (i.e., according to God's will, pleasing to him)? It seems unlikely that Paul would have backed up a command to do what was socially acceptable with an appeal to their union with the Lord. Rather, this is the divine will for the relationship of wives to their husbands, and hence it is to be obeyed by those who belong to the Lord.

Beekman so phrased it that ἐν κυρίῳ came out as "who belong to the Lord," identifying the wives. But identification is essentially contrastive and would imply that some did not belong to the Lord and thus accepting their husbands' authority did not apply to them. Paul makes it clear throughout the letter, however, that he is addressing Christians. Hence, ἐν κυρίῳ is represented in the display as 'since you are united to the Lord *Jesus*'; their Christian standing is both assumed and appealed to.

The supporting clause here is introduced by the conjunction ὡς. This conjunction commonly indicates a comparison, but when supporting a command, it can signal the grounds for that command. In this case, the use of ἀνῆκεν strengthens the case for grounds, since it refers to what is appropriate or right.

3:19a Husbands, love your wives; It should be noted that in the Greek here, as well as in 3:18a, there is no distinction between 'men' and 'husbands' (both are ἄνδρες) nor between 'women' and 'wives' (both are γυναῖκες). It is the context of the paragraph as a whole, and what is said, that decides the meaning 'husbands' and 'wives', rather than 'men' and 'women'.

3:19b in particular, do not be harsh with them. The words μὴ πικραίνεσθε 'do not be bitter' are usually translated "do not be harsh" (RSV, and similarly in most versions). Given the context, it seems very likely that the abuse of the authority vested in the husbands is in Paul's mind with this negative command—the husband is not to be a petty tyrant. Lenski, Hendriksen, and also the JB see the double negative as a litotes; the JB renders it "treat them with gentleness." But the positive command to love them covers such specific attitudes as gentleness, patience, and forbearance (see 1 Corinthians 13), so it seems preferable to take the negative command as a warning against a misuse of their God-given authority.

The command not to be harsh is a negative specific of the generic command to love. Since this one specific is singled out, it is introduced in the display by 'in particular'.

SECTION CONSTITUENT 3:20–21 (Paragraph: Nucleus₂ of 3:18–4:1)

THEME: Children, obey your parents in every circumstance; parents, do not overcorrect your children.

RELATIONAL STRUCTURE	CONTENTS
NUCLEUS₁ — EXHORTATION	3:20a Children, obey your parents in every circumstance,
└ grounds	3:20b since *God* is pleased when you *who are* united to the Lord *Jesus* do this [3:20a].
NUCLEUS₂ — MEANS (EXHORTATION)	3:21a Parents/Fathers, do not overcorrect your children,
└ purpose	3:21b in order that they not become discouraged.

BOUNDARIES AND COHERENCE

See the discussion of the boundaries and coherence of 3:18–4:1.

PROMINENCE AND THEME

As in 3:18–19, there are two finite imperative clauses here, with supporting subordinate clauses. Thus the theme of 3:20–21 is the two commands.

NOTES

3:20a Children, obey your parents in every circumstance, In this command, the verb is ὑπακούετε 'obey'. The authority relationship is not the same as that between husbands and wives. The phrase κατὰ πάντα 'according to all things' defines the scope of this obedience and states it to be universal.

3:20b since *God* is pleased when you *who are* united to the Lord *Jesus* do this [3:20a]. The neuter demonstrative τοῦτο 'this' refers back to the preceding command 'obey your parents'. As to εὐάρεστον, opinion is divided as to whether it means 'pleasing to God' or 'pleasing to people generally' (i.e., socially approved and acceptable). The argument given in connection with 3:18b is appropriate here as well, namely, that the appeal to their Christian standing ('in the Lord') is too strong if only socially acceptable conduct were intended. Obedience to parents is one of the Ten Commandments and is thus clearly God's will and pleasing to him.

The phrase ἐν κυρίῳ 'in (the) Lord' is handled in the same way as in 3:18c. The commentaries point out that ἐν κυρίῳ does not mean 'pleasing to the Lord', because this is expressed by a different construction (the simple dative). The parallel with 3:18 supports this interpretation.

The grounds constituent, therefore, has two factors acting as support for the command: (1) the command is an action pleasing to God, and (2) it is an action appropriate to those who are Christians, committed to obeying the Lord's commands and pleasing him.

3:21a Parents/Fathers, do not overcorrect your children, The first question here is whether this command is addressed to fathers or both parents. The word πατέρες, literally 'fathers', can have either of these senses (as well as others, such as 'forefathers'). In favor of the meaning 'parents' is the reciprocal nature of each pair of commands: 'parents' would correspond to 'children' in 3:20. In favor of the meaning 'fathers' is the fact that the word for parents has just been used (γονεῦσιν in 3:20a), that πατέρες rarely means 'parents' in the New Testament (Heb. 11:23 is the only unambiguous example), and that this is a command much more relevant to fathers than to mothers. Because of the uncertainty of interpretation here, both are used in the display, but 'parents' is slightly preferable.

The meaning of ἐρεθίζετε is also a problem. It has been variously rendered as 'provoke', 'irritate', 'exasperate', 'overcorrect', 'scold', 'embitter'. Moreover, it is by no means certain whether the best text is ἐρεθίζετε or παροργίζετε (the verb used in Eph. 6:4). Lightfoot says that the latter "has higher support, but is doubtless taken from the parallel passage," and Abbott says that it is "very strongly supported." The meaning of παροργίζω is specifically 'to make someone angry', while ἐρεθίζω has the sense of 'provoking someone, stirring them up either to good or bad reactions'—if to anger, then it would be synonymous with παροργίζω. It is helpful to see here a warning against the abuse of authority. Children are commanded to obey their parents, but this does not mean that the parents can exercise that authority in a wrong manner. Alford describes it well in his note on the parallel passage in Eph. 6:4: "provoking by vexatious commands, and unreasonable blame, and uncertain temper." Beekman gave two alternatives, 'exasperate' and 'overcorrect'. In view of the context perhaps preference should be given to the latter.

3:21b in order that they not become discouraged. The most common rendering of ἀθυμῶσιν is 'they become discouraged'. Other renderings are 'grow disheartened', 'feel frustrated', 'lose heart'. It is generally agreed that excessive strictness on the part of parents/fathers may, in the long run, cause children to give up trying to obey. Such parental demands can never really be satisfied no matter how hard the children try. Hence, 'become discouraged' or 'become disheartened' are good renderings.

Purpose clauses may often be transformed into grounds propositions, though to do so here an implied conditional clause needs to be added:

Do not overcorrect your children
since, if you do, they will become discouraged.

However, with ἵνα μή the focus is on the parent's responsibility to avoid the possible consequences of overcorrection. Thus the phrase 'in order that . . . not' is used in the display. Of course, 'lest' would be simpler, but 'in order that . . . not' coveys an unambiguously negative purpose.

SECTION CONSTITUENT 3:22–4:1 (Paragraph: Nucleus₃ of 3:18–4:1)

THEME: Slaves, obey your masters in every circumstance sincerely and wholeheartedly; masters, provide for your slaves justly and fairly.

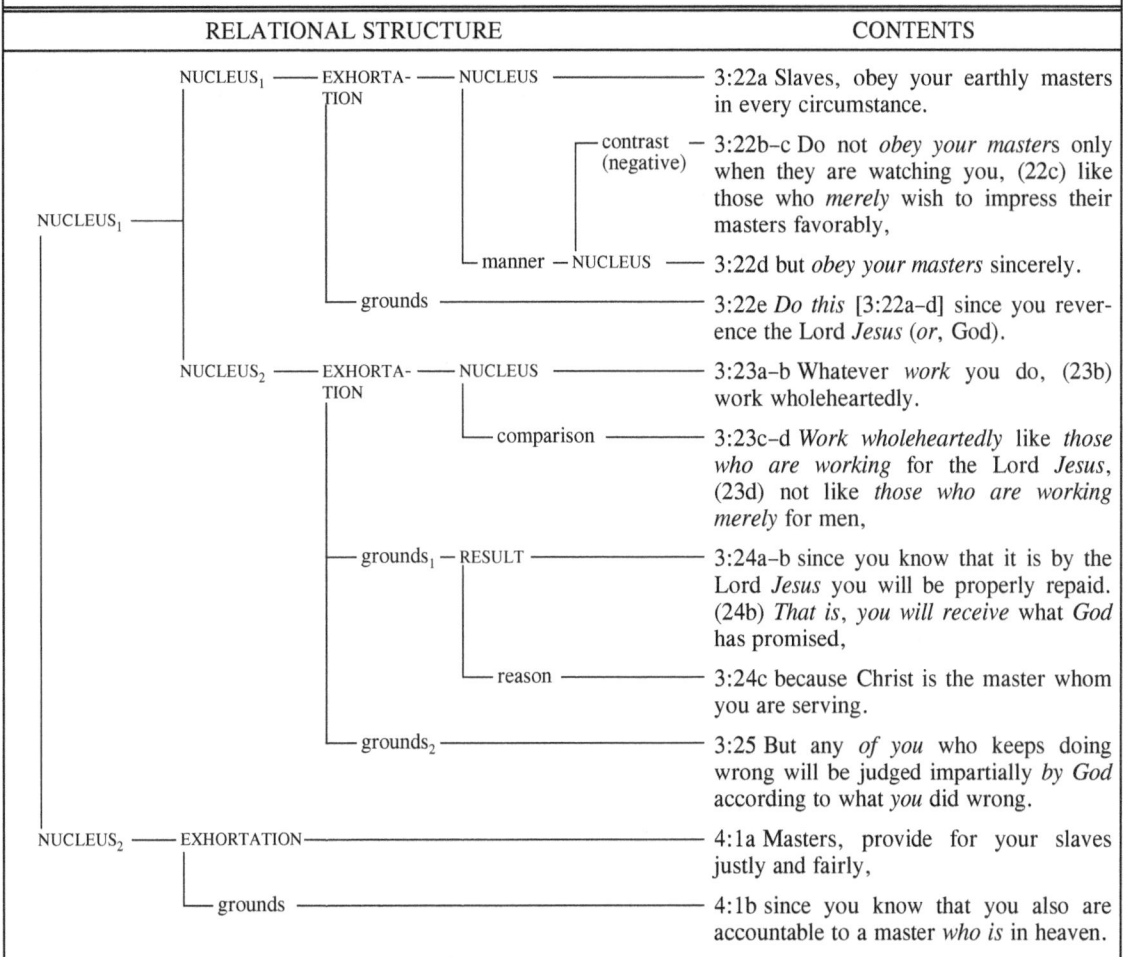

BOUNDARIES AND COHERENCE

See the discussion of the boundaries and coherence of 3:18–4:1.

PROMINENCE AND THEME

As with the two preceding paragraphs, the prominent information in the 3:22–4:1 paragraph consists of the commands addressed to the two related parties, here the slaves and their masters. However, the establishing of the content of the command addressed to the slaves is not straightforward. This longer constituent (3:22–25) contains two commands, 3:22a and 23b. As is argued in the notes, the two propositional clusters of which these are the main propositions are related by conjoining. However, in the context of the whole constituent, 3:22–25, proposition 3:23b, 'work wholeheartedly', is regarded as broadly synonymous with proposition 3:22a, 'Slaves, obey your earthly masters in every circumstance sincerely'. That is to say, the command 'work' is addressed to the slaves; it is earthly masters they are working for; and 3:23a, 'whatever *work* you do', is equivalent to 'in every circumstance'. The obedience is in the realm of work done for their masters; that is 'obey' is equivalent to 'do the work you are told to do'. Hence, 3:23b is considered to add to 3:22a only the manner concept 'wholeheartedly'. In other words, the prominent information of 3:22–25 is the same as that of 3:22a with the addition of 'wholeheartedly'.

NOTES

3:22a Slaves, obey your earthly masters in every circumstance. This command is closely parallel to the command in 3:20a. The phrase κατὰ σάρκα 'according to flesh' describes the masters in order to contrast them with the heavenly Master or Lord. The Greek word for 'master' is the same in this paragraph as for 'Lord', so if no qualifying phrase is used, the reader has to decide who the referent is based on the context.

3:22b–d Do not *obey your masters* **only when they are watching you, like those who** *merely* **wish to impress their masters favorably, but** *obey your masters* **sincerely.** The Greek is μὴ ἐν ὀφθαλμοδουλίᾳ ὡς ἀνθρωπάρεσκοι ἀλλ᾽ ἐν ἁπλότητι καρδίας 'not in eye-service, like men-pleasers, but in singleness of-heart'. From the standpoint of semantic analysis, these three phrases are somewhat difficult. Basically, they represent a contrast of manner, referring back to the main verb 'obey'. Slaves are first told how *not* to obey, then how they *should* obey. Hence, semantically, these phrases are part of the main proposition, embedded in it, like propositions with the relation of description or identification. In the display, therefore, the main verb is repeated in 22b and 22d (but not in 22c, which is a comparison used to explain 22b).

The first noun, ὀφθαλμοδουλία 'eye-service', may be in the plural; there is considerable manuscript support for this. While its being plural or singular does not affect the basic meaning, the plural tends to draw attention to the multiple acts of eye-service being carried out. As to its meaning, there is some difference of opinion about whether it refers to doing good work only while being watched, or to doing only work that could be seen (hence, no sweeping behind the furniture). Since it seems likely that the two events of working as a slave and being watched occur at the same time as the work itself, this is rendered in the display 'do not obey your masters only when they are watching you'.

Similarly, ἀνθρωπάρεσκοι, an adjective that functions as a complex noun here, means 'those whose aim is to *merely* please men'. In other words, such an aim is not to please God, nor is it to do a good job, but simply to do enough to be acceptable to the master.

The third phrase, ἐν ἁπλότητι καρδίας 'in singleness of heart', is a Greek idiom for the opposite of the sort of conduct that has just been described, as is shown by the contrastive conjunction ἀλλά, that is to say, conduct that is genuinely motivated, sincere. This is represented in the display by 'sincerely', attached to a partial repetition of the main proposition, 3:22a.

3:22e *Do this [3:22a–d]* **since you reverence the Lord** *Jesus (or,* **God).** Some manuscripts have φοβούμενοι τὸν κύριον 'fearing the Lord', while others have φοβούμενοι τὸν θεόν 'fearing God'. This is a further example in this epistle of where the choice of manuscript reading reflects one's theory of manuscript transmission. Hence, until a definitive theory of manuscript transmission is established, the translator is free to choose either of these variants. If the former is chosen, it is likely that the referent of τὸν κύριον 'the Lord' is the Lord Jesus, not the Lord God, since that is how κύριος in the singular is used throughout this section. (In the plural, it refers to earthly masters.) The word φοβούμενοι 'fearing' is used in a specific sense: 'showing respect for, reverence for' or 'standing in awe of'.

Some commentators dispute whether 3:22e is related to 22d, the immediately preceding proposition, or 22a, the main proposition. However, as was pointed out in the note on 22b–d, propositions 22b and 22d state the manner of the obedience enjoined in 22a, the main proposition, and thus, technically speaking, are embedded in it, delimiting the main verb, 'obey'. If 3:22d were written out fully, it would be 'obey your earthly masters in every circumstance sincerely', which is exactly the same as 3:22a with the new information 'sincerely' being added. Hence, from a semantic standpoint, 22e's being related to 22a is effectively the same thing as being related to 22d.

Beekman gave two relations between 3:22e and 22a as alternatives, manner or grounds. But it is not easy to conceive of 3:22e as delimiting the command 'obey', and the manner of the main event is already described in 3:22b–d. Furthermore, it seems likely that 'fearing the Lord' is the equivalent, in these rather more detailed instructions to slaves, to the phrase 'in the Lord' in 3:18 and 20. Again, Paul appeals to their Christian standing as the grounds, the true motivation, for genuine obedience. Hence, 22e is labeled as grounds for the command in 22a.

3:23a–b Whatever *work* **you do, work wholeheartedly.** Verse 3:22 is very similar to 3:18 and 20. Verses 3:23 and 24, however, have no parallels, but are an expansion and clarification of 3:22.

The Greek underlying 3:23a is very similar to that underlying 3:17a. (Some manuscripts have ὅ τι ἐὰν ποιῆτε making it even closer.) In the display, therefore, it is handled in a parallel way to 3:17a as 'whatever *work* you(pl) do'. In this context, the implicit 'work' is the work that slaves do for their masters. That Paul has this in mind here is shown by the following command. (In 3:17a it was without restriction.)

The phrase ἐκ ψυχῆς 'out of soul' is an idiom meaning 'wholeheartedly' or 'genuinely' (or possibly 'enthusiastically'). While this idea is similar to 'sincerely', the idea of expressed in 3:22d, and both describe the manner in which the slave is to obey or work, it is considered to express a conjoined but different manner. (The same idiom is used in Eph. 6:6.)

Proposition 23b is the main proposition in 3:23–25 (i.e., the rest of the instructions addressed to slaves), which is the second of the two constituents that make up 3:23–25, the first being 3:22. The relation between these two constituents is not an easy question, because on the one hand 23b, a second command, adds more information to the command in 22a, which would point to the relation of conjoining. On the other hand, the two commands of the main propositions are so expressed that they can be regarded as synonymous in this context, which would point to contraction-amplification. But the relation of conjoining is considered better here, since Paul is not really clarifying what he has just said, but going on to develop it with a number of new ideas (see the discussion of the theme for 3:22–4:1).

3:23c–d Work wholeheartedly like *those who are working* for the Lord *Jesus*, not like *those who are working merely* for men, The grammars agree that there is an ellipsis here of the participle 'working'. This points to the relation of manner. More precisely, these propositions clarify the manner adverb 'wholeheartedly' by means of a comparison. The comparisons can be filled out to give 'work wholeheartedly, like those who are working for the Lord; do not work like those who are working merely for men'. In the long run the work done by a Christian is done for the Lord, even though also done for an earthly master or employer. As the grammars say (Blass and Debrunner, p. 219; Turner, 1963:158), ὡς 'like' introduces the subjective motivation for wholeheartedly working.

Some commentators take ὡς in 23c to mean 'as if' or 'as though', but others reject this interpretation since it weakens the statement so that it can hardly be considered to be a motive at all. Also, if interpreted like this, 3:23 would not connect well with 3:24 and the promise of a reward from the Lord: If they were not *really* working for the Lord, on what basis would he reward them?

A third possible interpretation is to treat propositions 23c and d as contrasting grounds for the command 'Work wholeheartedly'. To render it 'Work wholeheartedly since you are working for the Lord and not merely for men' makes it more forceful. Nevertheless, this interpretation is rejected in favor of the comparison relation for three reasons: (1) an unambiguous grounds follows in 3:24; (2) taking it as comparison means that 3:23 and 24 follow the same pattern of relations as 3:22 (i.e., manner/comparison followed by grounds); and (3) the use of ὡς to introduce a comparison is well established, but to introduce grounds considerably less so.

3:24a–b since you know that it is by the Lord Jesus you will be properly repaid. *That is, you will receive* **what** *God* **has promised** The participle εἰδότες 'knowing' is taken as introducing the grounds for the command in 3:23b (so NIV and Barclay). Having told the slaves at Colosse *how* they should work, Paul now tells them *why* they should work like that.

The genitive in τὴν ἀνταπόδοσιν τῆς κληρονομίας 'the repayment of the inheritance' is appositional: the repayment *is* the inheritance. The term 'inheritance' means 'the Lord will give you what he has promised'. Most of the versions translate the noun ἀνταπόδοσις as 'reward', but this is not really supported by the lexicons. Abbott-Smith does not suggest this sense. Arndt and Gingrich give it only for this verse; they have "give back, repay, return" for the related verb ἀνταποδίδωμι, and "paymaster" for ἀνταποδότης, one of its noun forms. The basic idea seems to be 'to pay you what you deserve, good or bad', and so another noun, ἀνταπόδομα, is mostly used in the Septuagint for 'retribution', also in Rom 11:9. Paul here chooses a term appropriate to the context of slaves being paid by their masters. He has just said (at the end of 3:23) that they are really working for their heavenly master; now he asserts that that same heavenly master will pay them properly, what they deserve, or perhaps, as some suggest, pay them fully. The implication is that it was unlikely that their earthly masters would do so. The expression 'receive the repayment' is the reciprocal of 'give the repayment' and so functions as a passive here, keeping 'you' as the subject, and the repayer in a prepositional phrase.

The phrase ἀπὸ κυρίου 'from (the) Lord' is prominent by virtue of its being forefronted in its clause. This is represented in the display by a cleft construction, 'it is by the Lord'.

3:24c because Christ is the master whom you are serving. The textual tradition divides on whether the conjunction γάρ is to be included in this clause or not, and, so far as the manuscript evidence is concerned, the decision will depend on what theory is followed, as elsewhere in this chapter. Its inclusion or omission affects the meaning of this clause.

Another problem here is that the verb form δουλεύετε is formally ambiguous: it could be either imperative, 'serve!', or indicative, 'you serve'. The two main arguments are:

1. All the commands throughout this section have been reciprocal: to wives with regard to their husbands, to husbands with regard to their wives, etc. The same is true of the slaves—they have been commanded to obey their masters in 3:22, and to work for them wholeheartedly in 3:23—and to take this clause as an imperative would run counter to the whole pattern of the section. Generally speaking, only those commentators who omit γάρ suggest that δουλεύετε is a command; almost no versions do so, because the resulting sequence of thought would be rather difficult to render.
2. If δουλεύετε is taken as an indicative, then it fits in most naturally as a final confirmatory statement supporting what has just been said about the Lord repaying those servants of his who were slaves. He is the one they are really serving as slaves, and so it is appropriate that he should repay them properly. With this approach, γάρ would be implicit, so it seems preferable to follow those manuscripts which include it. It also makes it natural that the phrase τῷ κυρίῳ Χριστῷ 'the Lord Christ' should be forefronted, as there is an implicit contrast with their earthly masters, whom they serve on earth, but who are not their ultimate masters.

So far as I am aware, the phrase τῷ κυρίῳ Χριστῷ that occurs here is unique in terms of its constituents and order. It is forefronted, hence prominent. This prominence is reflected in almost all the English versions, RSV and Phillips being two exceptions. In this phrase Χριστῷ is in apposition to κυρίῳ, as Lightfoot and Abbott point out. Examples of similar constructions are found in 1 Cor. 12:3 and Phil. 2:11: In 1 Cor. 12:3 is the phrase ἀνάθεμα Ἰησοῦς 'a curse (is/be) Jesus'. This is followed by κύριος Ἰησοῦς 'Lord Jesus', meaning 'Jesus is Lord'. In Phil. 2:11 is κύριος Ἰησοῦς Χριστός 'Lord Jesus Christ', meaning 'Jesus Christ is Lord'. In each case, the complement or predicate precedes the subject. Here in Col. 3:24c the complement is 'Lord', and 'Christ' is the subject. This is most naturally expressed in the display by 'Christ is the Lord/master whom you are serving'.

3:25 But any *of you* who keeps doing wrong will be judged impartially *by God* according to what *you* did wrong. There is a textual variant for the conjunction here: Some manuscripts have γάρ 'for', others δέ 'but'. Modern editors of the text prefer γάρ, but commentators find it difficult to see how γάρ can fit in here. It is noticeable that the versions, if they follow a text with γάρ, tend to avoid translating it as "for" or "because" (NEB, NIV, and JB use no English conjunction at all; TEV has "and"; Phillips has "but"). The usual solution proposed by the commentators is that the wrongdoer referred to is the master, and the statement is an encouragement to the slaves. But there are objections to this view. One is that Paul is not aiming so much at encouraging them as telling them how to behave as Christian slaves; the other is that it is an obscure way to suddenly refer to the master—the context points to its being the slaves who are addressed and referred to if there is no evidence to the contrary. In the light of these considerations, the text with δέ is followed in the display, and 'wrongdoer' is taken to refer to any of the slaves addressed.

An alternative to taking δέ as the original text is to follow Hendriksen's suggestion that, as often is the case, there is an ellipsed clause preceding the clause introduced by γάρ: 'you should obey the above instructions, *for* wrongdoers will be judged'. The heavenly rewarder is also the heavenly judge.

The use of the present participle ἀδικῶν 'doing wrong' makes it likely that Paul is referring to a regular practice of wrongdoing rather than an occasional lapse. In this case, the significance of δέ would be to add a warning to the previous glowing statements about their future inheritance: receiving the heavenly inheritance and constant misconduct are incompatible. The verb κομίσεται 'will be requited' tends to draw attention to the punishment matching the evil that was done; it paves the way for the statement in the second half of the verse.

So far as the semantic relation of 3:25 is concerned, it is seen as a further grounds for 3:23a-b, in addition to 3:24a-c. The latter presents a positive encouragement to wholehearted service, namely, a proper repayment by their heavenly master, while 3:25 presents a negative warning against bad behavior as a slave.

will be judged impartially *by God* The Greek is a negative existential: καὶ οὐκ ἔστιν προσωπολημψία 'and partiality does not exist'. In the context, it is clear that Paul means that partiality does not exist with God—the full form is given in Rom. 2:11. The abstract noun προσωπολημψία 'partiality' together with the negative particle represents the attribute 'impartially'; the propositonal form is '*God* judges *all* impartially'.

The only other question is what relation καί signals here. In most versions it is rendered "and"; the 1976 TEV has "because." Beekman labeled it manner of 3:25a. But if it is asked why an attribute of manner should be expressed with a full clause and introduced by 'and', there are at least two possible answers. One is that it is a convenient way to avoid using the word 'to judge' and being passive (i.e., to avoid saying 'and he will be judged impartially'); the other is that it gives prominence to the concept of 'impartially'; or quite possibly both answers are correct. There seems no way of deciding, so the adverb 'impartially' is used in the display to represent this clause.

4:1a Masters, provide for your slaves justly and fairly, In 4:1 there is a return to the pattern of vocative and command.

One question here is whether there is a distinction between τὸ δίκαιον 'the righteous-thing' and τὴν ἰσότητα 'the equality' in this context. Hendriksen says he is inclined to regard them as synonyms. Arndt and Gingrich describe the use of the neuter form of the adjective δίκαιος 'righteous' (the form used here) as "that which is obligatory in view of certain requirements of justice"; they give the meaning of ἰσότης as "fairness." It seems unlikely that there were any legal requirements about wages and working conditions for slaves (no commentator suggests that there were), so that τὸ δίκαιον here, where Christian masters are in view, probably means 'what is right in God's sight', 'what a master would not be ashamed of as a Christian master'. It may be, then, that ἡ ἰσότης means 'fair' or 'reasonable' in the circumstances; experience and reliability, for example, would merit more pay than inexperience or unreliability. Since the words are similar, but not synonyms, both are therefore represented in the display, treated as abstract nouns with the function of attributes. This agrees with Moore for Col. 4:1 (p. 25); he calls these words "near synonyms."

Another question is the meaning of παρέχεσθε 'grant'. The verb is in the middle voice and has essentially the same meaning in the active voice. (Arndt and Gingrich have "grant" for both.) The older commentators interpreted the use of the middle to mean 'grant, on your part', 'supply, on your side'. In other words, the middle voice could have the extra nuance of "correspondingness" (so Lightfoot): sincere, wholehearted work on the part of the slave should be matched by reasonable treatment on the master's part. A number of versions render παρέχεσθε as 'treat', but some English speakers feel that this word excludes the idea of payment. In the display it is rendered 'provide for', as it was by Beekman.

4:1b since you know that you also are accountable to a master who is in heaven. The participle εἰδότες 'knowing' is used here in the same way as it was used in 3:24a, and is again interpreted as giving grounds for the commands.

The words καὶ ὑμεῖς 'also you' echo the statement in 3:24c addressed to slaves. Slaves have a master in heaven, and earthly masters also have a master in heaven.

Beekman gave a good rendering for ἔχετε 'you have': "you are responsible to." It is not simply that they have a heavenly master, but that they are answerable to him for how they treat their slaves. In the display here, 'responsible to' is strengthened to 'accountable to'.

DIVISION CONSTITUENT 4:2–6 (Section: Nucleus₂ of 3:18–4:6)

THEME: Pray to God persistently and pray for me. Also, always speak wisely and graciously toward those who do not believe in the Lord Jesus.

RELATIONAL STRUCTURE	CONTENTS
NUCLEUS₁	4:2–4 Pray to God persistently. And pray that God will give me opportunities to declare the secret-message about Christ.
NUCLEUS₂	4:5–6 Always speak wisely and graciously to those who do not believe in the Lord Jesus.

BOUNDARIES AND COHERENCE

Verses 4:2–6 are sandwiched between two different types of material, which shows that these verses form a unit. The preceding unit is a highly structured set of commands to reciprocal groups in the congregation. The following material, beginning at 4:7, is no longer hortatory, but has to do with greetings and information. Thus, this section is the last section to consist of hortatory material. Like much of the hortatory part of this epistle, it is addressed to all of the Colossian Christians without distinction.

Within these verses, we once again see the phenomenon of parallelism. Both 4:2 and 4:5 begin with a noun in the dative case followed by a second person plural present-tense verb. (The noun phrases are not absolutely parallel in that one has an article and the other is without an article and is preceded by the preposition ἐν.) The commands that these parallel structures express are not, however, synonymous, so 4:2 and 4:5 are considered the beginning of two separate paragraphs within the 4:2–6 section.

The main evidence of coherence is references to the Colossians with second person plural forms throughout these verses, except in the latter half of 4:3 and in 4:4, where there is a switch to first person temporarily. The two paragraphs 4:2–4 and 4:5–6 each show their own internal coherence (see the discussion of coherence under the respective displays that follow). In addition, both paragraphs deal with Christian behavior.

Further evidence for the unity of the 4:2–6 section can be drawn from the fact that the two paragraphs are parallel semantically as well as in their opening formal structures. Both open with a generic command; and both emphasize the manner in which that generic command is to be carried out. The first emphasizes persistence in prayer; the second, wisdom in behavior towards those who are not believers.

PROMINENCE AND THEME

The 4:2–4 and 4:5–6 paragraphs deal with different topics (prayer in the first, and behavior towards unbelievers in the second) and they lack any formal connection between them. Hence, they are treated as conjoined paragraphs and the theme of this section is simply the conjoined themes of the two paragraphs. However, the second half of the 4:2–4 theme is reduced to 'and pray for me' at this higher level of the discourse.

SECTION CONSTITUENT 4:2–4 (Paragraph: Nucleus₁ of 4:2–6)

THEME: Pray to God persistently. And pray that God will give me opportunities to declare the secret-message about Christ.

RELATIONAL STRUCTURE	CONTENTS
NUCLEUS₁ (EXHORTATION)	4:2 Pray *to God* persistently, and at the same time be alert and be thanking *God*.
NUCLEUS₂ — NUCLEUS — EXHORTATION	4:3a–c Pray also for me (3b) that God will give me opportunities to speak (3c) in order that I might declare the secret-message about Christ,
grounds₁	4:3d–e since I am in prison (3e) because *I declared* it.
restatement — EXHORTATION	4:4a *That is, pray for me that God will give me opportunities to speak* in order that I may make it known publicly
grounds₂	4:4b since I am obliged to declare *it*.

BOUNDARIES AND COHERENCE

The initial boundary of the 4:2–4 paragraph has already been discussed under the boundaries of the 4:2–6 section. The closing boundary of 4:2–4 is considered to be at 4:4 for the following reasons:

1. There is a change of topic from prayer in 4:2–4 to wise behavior in 4:5–6.
2. Verses 4:2–4 are all one sentence in Greek; 4:5 is the start of a new sentence.
3. There is a switch from the first person references of 4:3–4 to second person plural references in 4:5.

Grammatically, 4:2–4 constitutes one sentence, with one finite independent clause to which the other clauses are related by means of participles, an infinitival clause, ἵνα 'that' clauses, a ὡς 'as' clause, and a relative clause. Semantically, it consists of a generic command concerning prayer followed by Paul's request for prayer for himself. Lexically, 4:2 and 3 are linked by a common reference to prayer (προσευχῇ, προσευχόμενοι). Verses 4:3 and 4 are linked by a number of references (pronoun and verb) to the first person, some plural, some singular; by references to the content of the spoken ministry (λόγος 'message', μυστήριον 'mystery'); and by verbs referring to that spoken ministry (λαλέω 'to speak' and φανερόω 'to make evident').

PROMINENCE AND THEME

The 4:2–4 paragraph comprises two constituents: the command in 4:2 and the specific request in 4:3, which is elaborated in 4:4. There are no grounds stated for what is semantically the generic command ('pray'), but it is further modified by an attribute with the role of manner ('persistently'), which is in the form of a finite verb in the Greek text, in fact, *the* independent finite verb of this paragraph, so this attribute is considered to be marked for prominence, hence included in the theme.

The request expressed in 4:3–4 is considered to be a second nucleus for two reasons: (1) it is introduced by a verb form of the event 'to pray' (in the main command it is a noun form); and (2) the request is considerably developed relative to the main command, which is hardly developed at all. The theme consists of these two commands, the second being expressed in a slightly abbreviated version of the full propositional form of the nucleus.

NOTES

4:2 Pray *to God* persistently, and at the same time be alert and be thanking *God*. The Greek for the initial part of this verse is τῇ προσευχῇ προσκαρτερεῖτε 'in prayer be-persevering'. The event 'pray' is expressed in the form of an abstract noun and the attribute modifying it is in the form of a verb. This mismatch is resolved in the display, where the command is 'pray' modified by the attribute 'persistently'. (Alternatively the modifier could be 'steadfastly' or 'perseveringly'.) It seems likely, as with previous examples, that the mismatch gives prominence to the attribute. There is no easy way, however, to render this in English so as to show this prominence.

Note that 'persistently' or 'perseveringly' is a strengthened form of 'continue at', which is a modal concept delimiting the event 'to pray'.

The forefronting of the abstract noun serves to topicalize it—to show that the topic of this paragraph is prayer, as vv. 3 and 4 bear out.

The participle γρηγοροῦντες 'watching' is considered to be figurative: the meaning is 'keeping alert', 'being vigilant', 'not being lethargic'.

The most interesting question here is the semantic relation between 'keeping alert' and 'pray'. The same question applies to 'thanksgiving'. Note that because these events of keeping alert and thanking God are attached to the command, they are also commanded. It seems best, then, to understand the relation between 'pray' and these other two events as a simultaneous one.

4:3a Pray also for me Paul now moves from a general command to keep praying to a specific request that they should pray for him. As to the adverb ἅμα 'together', its meaning is that while praying as commanded, they would, along with other matters, pray for him.

As in 3:16, the Greek participle here is representing a command, since it is dependent on a command. For the interpretation of ἡμῶν 'us' as referring only to Paul himself, see the note on 4:4a.

4:3b-c that God will give me opportunities to speak in order that I might declare the secret-message about Christ, As elsewhere (e.g., 1:9), ἵνα here introduces the content of the prayer. Although ἀνοίξῃ θύραν 'open a door' is figurative, it is probably a dead figure: Martin says that "the metaphor . . . is found in the Jewish rabbinic writings"; Hendriksen says that Paul here is "using an idiom that may have belonged to the common speech of that day." Its meaning is 'give an opportunity'. (The same expression is also found in Acts 14:27, 1 Cor. 16:9, and 2 Cor. 2:12.) The opportunity is given 'to us' (ἡμῖν), that is, to Paul; and it is 'for the message' (τοῦ λόγου), that is, 'to speak the message', explained more precisely as τὸ μυστήριον τοῦ Χριστοῦ 'the secret of Christ', meaning 'the now-revealed truths about Christ' (see the notes on μυστήριον in 1:26-27). The genitive is the genitive of reference: the secret is about Christ, not the secret Christ has revealed. The Father is always represented as doing the revealing.

The verb λαλέω 'to speak', which is used here in the infinitive form, quite often refers to public speaking as well as private speaking (see Arndt and Gingrich, λαλέω, 2b). So it is represented in the display by 'declare', following Beekman. The aorist infinitive signals the relation of purpose here—opportunities were desired in order that he might declare the secret-message.

4:3d-e since I am in prison because *I declared* it. The relative ὅ 'which' most likely refers back to 'the secret', in which case Paul is saying that he is in prison because of the secret (elliptical for 'because I declared the secret-message'). Alternatively, ὅ could be taken as referring to the preceding clause, 'to speak the secret of Christ'. In either case, however, the meaning would be the same.

The word δέδεμαι 'I have been bound', rendered here as 'I am in prison', can be regarded either as figurative, meaning Paul was in prison (a metonymy), or as literal and elliptic for 'I am bound here in prison'. In either case, the meaning is essentially the same. As to the relation of 'I am in prison' with the surrounding propositions, one commentator, Meyer, suggests that it gives grounds for Paul's request for them to pray for him. This makes good sense in the overall context (see the note on 4:4a), so this suggestion is followed in the display. An alternative would be to regard it as a description of Paul, and nothing more.

4:4a *That is, pray for me that God will give me opportunities to speak* in order that I may make it known publicly Here αὐτό 'it' refers back to 'the secret'. But the difficult question here is just what the ἵνα clause (i.e., the purpose clause) relates back to. It is an important question, as the answer calls for exegetical decisions at various points throughout vv. 3 and 4. The significant factors in reaching a decision are as follows:

1. According to Hollenbach's (n.d.) theory of subordination in complex sentences, the finite clause here would not be subordinate to the preceding infinitive λαλῆσαι 'to speak' in 4:3b. It could, however, be subordinate to the first ἵνα 'that' (at the beginning of 3b) or to the original request to pray in 3a. (This was the view taken by Beekman.) This gives two alternatives: it is either the purpose of 3b or the content of 3a.

2. In the Greek underlying 4:3a-c, the first person references are plural—the change to singular occurs in 3d. If 4a is related to either 3a or 3b,

it would seem strange for Paul to ask prayer that 'we' have opportunities to declare the message, but that only 'I' would have the purpose of revealing it. Hence, it is concluded that the plural forms underlying 3a and 3b are singular in reference—it is for himself that Paul is asking prayer at this point, since he is the one in prison and needing such opportunities.

3. Another factor is the meaning of the verb φανερόω here. It is most often rendered "make clear" (RSV; cf. JB, NIV, TEV) or "make plain" (NEB, Phillips), implying that the secret-message was obscure, difficult to understand. With such a rendering Paul is asking prayer that he might make this obscure secret-message plain to understand, that he might declare it clearly, not in an obscure manner. But it doubtful that φανερόω means this. It has already been used twice, in 1:26 and 3:4, where the context is contrastive (the opposite of 'hidden'). In 1:26 it is used of the secret-message itself, hidden in the sense of not having been revealed to former generations; in 3:4 it is used of Christ and believers, whose true glory is hidden now but will be revealed when Christ returns. (These two occurrences seem typical of the verb's meaning elsewhere in the New Testament.) In both 1:26 and 3:4 it means 'make publicly evident', 'make known publicly', 'show people what they could not see or did not know before'.

4. If, now, the 4:3c and 4:4a clauses in the Greek are compared, it will be seen that they hardly differ at all. The former is λαλῆσαι τὸ μυστήριον τοῦ Χριστοῦ 'to speak the secret of the Christ', and the latter is ἵνα φανερώσω αὐτό. The pronoun αὐτό 'it' refers back to τὸ μυστήριον τοῦ Χριστοῦ, and so is semantically identical. In this context, as has been argued, λαλῆσαι refers to public proclamation, and so does φανερώσω; hence they are synonyms or near synonyms. Finally, λαλῆσαι is an infinitive of purpose (it states the purpose of the opportunities that were sought) and ἵνα is the purpose conjunction. It seems reasonable to conclude, therefore, that 4a is a restatement of 3c.

This conclusion is in accord with the first alternative arising from Hollenbach's theory, which is described under the first of these four considerations. The fourth one points to the further conclusion that 4:4a is in the relation of equivalence to 4:3c. While the relation of equivalence generally has the function of highlighting the first of two equivalent propositions, here it seems better to say that the information in 4:3c is repeated, not to show prominence, but simply to add the further supporting information of 4:4b to the nucleus. Hence, 4:4a is considered to be a recapitulation of 4:3c. But since 3c is dependent on 3a and 3b, 4a recapitulates 3c explicitly in the display and 3a–b implicitly.

4:4b since I am obliged to declare *it*. There are two possible interpretations here. Either Paul is describing the manner in which he is to make known the secret—'in the manner that I ought to declare it'—or he is describing the constraint that he was under to declare it as he says in 1 Cor. 9:16, 'Woe to me if I do not preach the gospel!' In the light of the use of the strong word δεῖ 'it is necessary' and of φανερόω 'to make manifest' (discussed in point 3 of the note on 4:4a), preference is given to the second of these alternatives in the display. The first would be quite acceptable, however, especially as it means ὡς would be interpreted in its more usual function of introducing a manner proposition.

SECTION CONSTITUENT 4:5–6 (Paragraph: Nucleus₂ of 4:2–6)

THEME: *Always speak wisely and graciously to those who do not believe in the Lord Jesus.*		
RELATIONAL STRUCTURE		**CONTENTS**
EXHORTATION (generic) — GENERIC —		4:5a Act wisely towards those who do not *believe in the Lord Jesus* [MTY];
└ specific —		4:5b use every opportunity to do this [4:5a].
EXHORTATION (SPECIFIC) — REASON —		4:6a *In particular*, always speak graciously *to those who do not believe in the Lord Jesus.*
└ result —		4:6b As a result, you will come to know in what manner you should answer each one *of them*.

BOUNDARIES AND COHERENCE

The initial boundary of the 4:5–6 paragraph has already been discussed in connection with the preceding paragraph. Its final boundary coincides both with the end of section 4:2–6 and of division 3:18–4:6 (see the discussions of the boundaries of these larger units). In other words, this is the last paragraph of the body of the Epistle, closing the secondary matters.

The most obvious evidence for the paragraph's coherence is the constant reference, explicit or implicit, to the Colossians by the second person plural forms in each clause. In addition, in 4:6, the opening λόγος 'word' and the final ἀποκρίνεσθαι 'to answer' are both lexical items drawn from the domain of speech. Semantically, there is a generic command in 4:5 with a specific command in 4:6.

PROMINENCE AND THEME

In 4:5a there is a generic command to behave wisely towards unbelievers; in 4:6a the focus is on gracious speech to unbelievers. When a generic proposition is followed by a single specific proposition like this, it is the latter that is naturally prominent. The absence of any finite verb in 4:6a might seem to argue against its being considered the more prominent constituent; yet in 3:17 there is such a construction and no one disputes its being more prominent there, and here it is only the verb 'to be' that is omitted. In view of these things, 6a is treated as more prominent; and since ἐν σοφίᾳ 'wisely' is prominent in 5a, this attribute is included in the theme as well. The suggestion is that 'act wisely' includes 'speak wisely'.

NOTES

4:5a Act wisely towards those who do not *believe in the Lord Jesus*; The construction ἐν + abstract noun often has an adverbial function in New Testament Greek. The initial position of this construction here ('in wisdom') gives it prominence, though this is not shown in the display. The verb form περιπατεῖτε 'walk' is a present tense command and refers to behavior at any time. The phrase τοὺς ἔξω 'those outside' is a metonymy (place for relationship) meaning unbelievers, those who do not belong to the local Christian congregation. This is represented in the display by 'those who do not believe', which is a common New Testament way of referring to non-Christians. Since the word 'Christian' is rare in the New Testament, it seems better not to introduce it here.

4:5b use every opportunity to do this [4:5a]. In Greek there are two words that are rendered 'time' in English, χρόνος and καιρός. It is καιρός that is used here. The two words are not always distinguished and sometimes occur together. Here, however, there is widespread agreement that καιρός has the sense of 'opportunity', that is, particular occasions or times that come to a believer. In the context, it is understood as special opportunities to act wisely toward nonbelievers.

The verb ἐξαγοραζόμενοι 'buying up' is used figuratively; its nonfigurative meaning is 'use to the full', 'make the most of', as in many versions. It was difficult to find a good nonidiomatic equivalent in English; the rendering in the display is idiomatic and includes an abstract noun, 'opportunity'. While 'Whenever you can' would get near to the meaning, it suggests the idea of acting wisely only whenever you can and not at other times.

The relationship between 4:5b and 5a is not easy to determine. Beekman suggested that 5b is a specific of 5a, which is essentially right. However, in 5a the topic is 'walking' and the comment on that topic is 'wisely', forefronted for emphasis. In other words, 5b draws attention to a particular aspect of 'wisely', namely, 'using every opportunity to the full'. No new event is involved; the specific meaning of the generic 'wisely' is described in connection with the opportunities believers have with their non-Christian contacts. Hence, while specific is indeed right, it is a specific of the prominent manner adverb; and this in turn is a concept within the discourse concept 'act wisely'. So, viewing 4:5b as a specific of 'wisely' or as a specific of 'act wisely' is much the same thing.

4:6a *In particular,* **always speak graciously** *to those who do not believe in the Lord Jesus.* The abstract noun λόγος 'word' represents an event, 'to speak' and it is widely agreed that, in this hortatory context, the absence of any overt verb makes it equivalent to an imperative. In other words, the nominalized topic 'speech' is, in a hortatory paragraph, semantically equivalent to a command about speaking.

The prepositional phrase ἐν χάριτι 'in grace' has an adverbial function as the noun is abstract. It is difficult to know whether 'grace' is used here in its theological sense or the more colloquial sense, 'favorably', 'attractively', 'with the purpose of creating a good impression'. Probably it is the colloquial sense, in view of the appositional phrase 'seasoned with salt', which has a similar meaning.

The phrase ἄλατι ἠρτυμένος 'seasoned with salt' is a dead metaphor, an idiom. All sorts of suggestions are made as to what it might mean—exciting, stimulating, fresh, vitally brisk, giving flavor to what is said, pleasant, attractive, interesting, fruitful. Evidently, the precise meaning of this idiom is no longer known. But it seems likely that it refers to the manner of the speaking, since (1) it is in apposition to a phrase that does certainly describe manner and (2) since manner is being emphasized in this paragraph—manner of conduct in general and of speech in particular—and (3) since πῶς 'how' in the following clause is more likely to refer to the reply's manner than its content (Robertson 1919:1045). If this argument is correct, then 'seasoned with salt' is not likely to mean 'good' or 'worthwhile', which words describe the content of what is said. Rather, if it refers to the manner of speaking, the most plausible hypothesis is that it defines ἐν χάριτι more precisely (so Meyer). But even so, it is far from clear how this should be rendered so as to accurately convey the meaning. Until more light is available, the two phrases are represented by the one word 'graciously', which is intended to convey the ideas of 'courteously', 'wisely', and 'thoughtfully'.

Proposition 6a is regarded as a specific example of 5a. As is argued in the discussion of the paragraph's prominence and theme, speaking is a specific type of behavior, and 'graciously' is a particular expression of 'wisely'.

4:6b As a result, you will come to know in what manner you should answer each one *of them.* This clause, in the Greek, bears a marked resemblance to the 4:4b clause.

(6b) **πῶς** δεῖ ὑμᾶς ἑνὶ ἑκάστῳ ἀποκρίνεσθαι

(4b) **ὡς** δεῖ με λαλῆσαι

The word πῶς in 6b is the question word corresponding to ὡς; the latter means 'in the manner that', while πῶς 'in what manner?' is a type of question. The only other difference is that in 4b Paul is concerned with his public proclamation of the gospel whereas in 6b he is concerned with how the Colossians will reply to those who question or challenge them, presumably concerning their beliefs or behavior. The phrase ἑνὶ ἑκάστῳ is equivalent to 'each individual'.

The problem here is how 6b relates to 6a. It is generally translated as a command: "and learn/know how. . ." (e.g., in Phillips and TEV; NEB omits "and" and renders it "study how best . . ."). The grammars, however, uniformly reject the interpretation of 6b as a command; rather, they treat εἰδέναι 'to know' as an infinitive of result. The argument appears to be that, if the Colossian Christians constantly speak graciously ('to unbelievers' is implied), they will learn by experience how to respond to anyone who challenges or questions them. The emphasis is not on learning *what* to say to such outsiders, but the *manner* in which to say it. The content may or may not offend, depending on how the hearer reacts to the truths of the gospel; but the manner in which the truth is presented ought not offend in any way. The emphasis on 'each individual' shows that Paul had in mind anyone from a neighbor to a high-ranking official such as a pro-consul or even a governor.

EPISTLE CONSTITUENT 4:7–18 (Section: Closing of the Epistle)

THEME: As for all that has been happening to me Tychicus will tell you. My fellow workers here greet you. Obey these instructions. I, Paul, am penning this final greeting myself in order that you may know that this letter was truly sent by me. Remember to pray about the fact that I am in prison.

RELATIONAL STRUCTURE	CONTENTS
NUCLEUS$_1$	4:7–9 As for all that has been happening to me Tychicus will tell you.
NUCLEUS$_2$	4:10–14 My fellow workers here greet you.
NUCLEUS$_3$	4:15–17 Obey these instructions.
NUCLEUS$_4$	4:18 I, Paul, am penning this final greeting myself in order that you may know that this letter was sent by me. Remember to pray about the fact that I am in prison.

BOUNDARIES AND COHERENCE

At 4:7 there is an obvious change from the hortatory genre, with its finite verbs in the imperative mood, to nonhortatory genre—in the 4:7–18 section the finite verbs are in the indicative mood. There is also a marked change of topic from the doctrine and exhortations characteristic of the body of the letter to such matters as news about Paul, greetings from his co-workers, some final instructions, and his final signature and benediction.

It is equally obvious that the close of the section as well as the close of the letter is at 4:18. Paul is here writing his greetings and closing with the benediction 'grace be with you', with which he closes all his letters in some form or other. Like the opening two verses in the epistle, 4:18 is characterized by verbless clauses (two out of the three clauses in that verse omit the verb).

But are there not internal points at which the unit opening at 4:7 might be considered to end? Two observations answer that question:

1. There are constant references to Paul directly, or indirectly, throughout this material. He is referred to directly (by pronoun, verb ending, or personal name) in 4:7, 8, 10, 11, 13, and 18; and he is referred to indirectly in a number of ways. Thus, when he calls Tychicus 'beloved' in 4:7, or Luke in 4:14, he is referring to his own love for these fellow believers; when he speaks of Tychicus as a fellow slave in 4:7 and Aristarchus, Mark, and Jesus Justus as fellow workers in 4:11, he means together with himself, *his* fellows. Similarly, when in 4:11 he describes these last three men as 'from the circumcision' (i.e., Jews), there is the implication that he also is a Jew. And the commands to the Colossians in 4:15–17 are commands from Paul to them. (The reference to 'the letter' in those commands is to the letter that he has written to them.) This thread of references to Paul is in marked contrast with the hortatory part of the epistle (2:6–4:6) where Paul does not mention himself at all, except for a request to pray for him right at the very end (4:3–4).

2. There are indeed a number of points within 4:7–18 where clear breaks can be identified—at 4:9, 14, 17, and 18. But only 4:18 shows any evidence for a final break. This is confirmed, of course, by the fact that the whole letter ends at that point.

In the light of these observations, 4:17–18 is taken as the final section of the epistle. It consists of four constituent paragraphs (4:7–9, 10–14, 15–17, and 18).

PROMINENCE AND THEME

Section 4:7–18 consists of four paragraphs. As is characteristic of the end of an epistle, Paul deals with four separate matters here. They are related to each other only in that they are appropriate to the end of a letter. Hence, it would be difficult to abstract any sort of generic theme. All that can be done to indicate the content communicated in the ending is to conjoin the four paragraph themes.

SECTION CONSTITUENT 4:7–9 (Paragraph: Nucleus₁ of 4:7–18)

THEME: *As for all that has been happening to me Tychicus will tell you.*	
RELATIONAL STRUCTURE	CONTENTS
NUCLEUS — NUCLEUS	4:7a–b As for all that *has been happening* to me, (7b) Tychicus, who is a brother whom *I/we(exc)* love and who helps me faithfully and who serves the Lord *Jesus* together with *me*, will tell you.
NUCLEUS₁ — MEANS	4:8a I am sending Tychicus to you for this very purpose:
PURPOSE	4:8b–c in order that he might know how you are (8c) and in order that he might strengthen you. (*Or*, (8b) in order that you might know about us(exc) (8c) and in order that he might comfort you.)
amplification — NUCLEUS₂	4:9a–c *I am sending him to you* with Onesimus, (9b) who is a faithful brother whom *I/we(exc)* love (9c) and who is your fellow townsman.
summary	4:9d They will tell you about all that *has been happening* here.

BOUNDARIES AND COHERENCE

The initial boundary of the 4:7–9 paragraph coincides with the start of the closing of the epistle, as is shown by the change of genre from hortatory to nonhortatory. There is also a switch from the 'I/you'-orientation of the preceding paragraphs to a 'he-they/you'-orientation in this paragraph.

The following evidence shows that the end of the paragraph is at 4:9:

1. There is rhetorical bracketing of the unit's first and last clauses.

    (4:7a) τὰ κατ' ἐμὲ πάντα γνωρίσει ὑμῖν Τύχικος
    'the-things concerning me all will-make-known to-you Tychicus'

    (4:9) πάντα ὑμῖν γνωρίσουσιν τὰ ὧδε
    'all to-you they-will-make-known the-things here'.

    The only differences here, apart from order, are that 'the things concerning me' has been generalized to 'the things here' in 4:9 and 'Tychicus' has been expanded to 'they', that is, Tychicus and Onesimus.

2. The main finite verbs in 4:7–9 are future tense; then in 4:10 there is a switch to the present tense.

3. There is a change of participants from Tychicus and Onesimus in 4:7–9 to Aristarchus, Mark, Jesus Justus, and others in 4:10ff.

4. There is a change of theme from news about Paul to greetings from his associates.

In these three verses there are no less than five (or six depending on the text followed for 4:8) second person plural pronouns in oblique cases (cases other than nominative and vocative). Thus the paragraph is clearly 'you'-oriented throughout. The three closely related phrases τὰ κατ' ἐμέ 'the things concerning me', τὰ περὶ ὑμῶν/ἡμῶν 'the things concerning you/us', and τὰ ὧδε 'the things here' occur one in each of the three verses. Further, this paragraph centers around two persons, Tychicus and Onesimus, who are both described and who are also the subjects of verbs in each of the three verses.

Grammatically, this paragraph is one long sentence, in which the final clause repeats the first clause. Semantically, it consists of an opening statement with an amplification of it, followed by a closing summary.

PROMINENCE AND THEME

There are only two independent clauses in the paragraph, the first and the last, the same two that were compared above. The opening one is expanded by the rest of 4:7–9, with the exception of the final independent clause. This clause summarizes the information given in 4:7–9. Hence, the paragraph is analyzed as a nucleus (4:7a–9c) followed by a summary (4:9d). With such a structure, the summary functions as a closing recapitulation and is considered to be of less prominence than what it summarizes. Hence, the theme is taken from the nucleus, 4:7a–9c, that is, the information communicated in 4:7a–b apart from the descriptions of Tychicus.

NOTES

4:7a–d As for all that *has been happening* to me, Tychicus, who is a brother whom *I/we(exc)* love and who helps me faithfully and who serves the Lord *Jesus* together with *me*, will tell you. The opening phrase is τὰ κατ' ἐμέ, an idiom meaning 'what concerns me', 'my affairs', 'what has been happening to me'. Its initial position in the Greek clause marks it as the topic of this paragraph.

The description of Tychicus raises some questions:

1. Does πιστός 'faithful' refer only to διάκονος 'helper' or also to σύνδουλος 'fellow slave'?
2. Similarly, how far back does the phrase ἐν κυρίῳ 'in Lord' refer—just to σύνδουλος, or to διάκονος as well? (It seems generally agreed that ἀδελφός 'brother' does not occur with this phrase in the New Testament; the only possible exception is Phil. 1:14 and there it is uncertain which phrase 'in the Lord' is attached to.)
3. What does διάκονος mean here?
4. Who are the implicit participants in such events as 'love', 'help', and 'serve'?

Although it is difficult to find objective criteria that could help us decide on the scope of an adjective like πιστός 'faithful', the symmetrical structure of the three parts of this compound phrase makes it likely that each adjective is related to its own noun only, and that ἐν κυρίῳ 'in Lord' fulfills an equivalent role for σύνδουλος 'fellow slave'.

Commentators generally agree that διάκονος does not mean 'deacon' here, nor 'helper' in a general sense, but rather it means that Tychicus was an official assistant to Paul at this time. In Eph. 6:21–22, which is almost identical with Col. 4:7–8, it is clear that Tychicus was being entrusted with the letter to Ephesus as well as the one to Colosse, and that he was accompanying Onesimus, the runaway slave, on the journey to Colosse. However, it is difficult to assess how significant such information is, so in the display διάκονος is rendered by its usual meaning, 'one who helps'.

The question of participants is more difficult. Beekman argued for 'us(inc)' in 4:7b and c on two grounds: no pronouns are used in the original so a general sense should be followed, and Tychicus was going to exercise a ministry to the Colossians so they should be included in the referents of the pronoun. Against this view it can be argued that Paul appears to be introducing and commending Tychicus to the Colossians, who was probably not known to them personally. This makes it more likely that the participants are either simply 'I' or 'we(exc)' ('we' being those associated with Paul at the time of writing). Since the appellation 'beloved brother' is equally true of Tychicus in relation to Paul or in relation to Paul and his associates, both alternatives, 'I' or 'we(exc)', are in the display. As διάκονος, however, Tychicus was Paul's helper, so the singular is used in this part of the description. And, similarly, the noun σύνδουλος 'fellow slave' is much more likely to mean 'a slave together with me' rather than 'with us', since Paul uses the συν- prefix elsewhere to identify himself with someone, as in 4:10 (συναιχμάλωτος 'fellow prisoner'), 4:11 (συνεργοί 'fellow workers'), and 1:7 (where σύνδουλος is used of Epaphras.)

Beekman regarded the phrase ἐν κυρίῳ as the grounds for "who is a servant (of the Lord) with (us excl.)," noting that the same phrase was analyzed as grounds in 3:18 and 20. However, in those contexts, Paul was commanding a certain type of behavior because the addressees were Christians, that is, ἐν κυρίῳ. Here, he is simply describing Tychicus, and ἐν κυρίῳ indicates the type of σύνδουλος he was, a Christian one. The simplest rendering of this is 'who serves the Lord together with *me*'.

Note that the use of noun phrases in the Greek indicates that these phrases most likely represent state propositions. In 4:7b, the state proposition 'who is my faithful helper' would be an acceptable alternative to the rendering in the display, and 'who is a brother' is a state proposition. A state alternative is not given for 'fellow slave', however, since the statement 'who is a fellow slave' is open to misunderstanding. It may seem to imply that both Tychicus and Paul were actually slaves, whereas Paul, at least, was a free man and a Roman citizen. In fact, δοῦλος 'slave' is being used figuratively here, not literally, and so is better represented by 'serves' in English.

4:8a I am sending Tychicus to you for this very purpose: The relative pronoun ὅν refers back to Tychicus. Both commentaries and grammars agree that ἔπεμψα 'I sent' is an epistolary aorist; that is, it is used in letters to refer to an action about to take place from the point of view of the writer, but which, from the standpoint of the recipients, was now past. Paul is about to send Tychicus with this letter, but by the time Tychicus reaches the Colossians with it, the sending will be a past event. The most natural English equivalent is the present continuous 'I am sending', though strictly speaking the meaning is 'I am about to send'.

The phrase εἰς αὐτὸ τοῦτο 'for this very thing' refers forward to the clauses introduced by ἵνα 'that'. Hale in his study of the similar phrase διὰ τοῦτο 'because of this' considers whether it refers backward (anaphoric) or forward (cataphoric): "The other eleven occurrences of διὰ τοῦτο . . . have forward references and are all followed by constructions that explain the meaning" (p. 2). The same is also true for εἰς τοῦτο 'for this', and here in 4:8a the ἵνα clauses explain what τοῦτο is referring to. The addition of αὐτό makes it emphatic, 'for this very purpose'. The use of εἰς τοῦτο preceding ἵνα is probably another prominence device highlighting the double purpose, so it is given equal rank with the 4:8a MEANS proposition.

The semantic relationship between 4:8a and 4:7a–b is a particularly difficult question. Beekman labeled this relation a comment on Tychicus (i.e., a description of Tychicus), thus making it a continuation of the descriptions already given in 4:7. But in his notes he pointed out that, although there is a relative clause in the Greek, it is really introducing a minor break or switch, as elsewhere in Colossians. The information provided in 4:8a is closely related to the main information in 4:7. In 4:7, Paul says that Tychicus will tell the Colossians all about Paul himself; in 4:8a, Paul says that he is sending Tychicus to them for certain purposes. It is presupposed in 4:7 that Paul is sending Tychicus to Colosse; otherwise Tychicus could not have passed on the news to the Colossians. In other words, 8a is making explicit what is implicit in 7. In addition, two purposes of Paul's sending Tychicus are given in 8b and 8c. One of these may or may not be the same as given in 7, but the second is certainly new. Further, in 4:9a, the information is added that Tychicus will be accompanied by Onesimus. It seems best, therefore, to regard 8a–9c as a cluster that functions to enlarge on the more condensed statement. Hence, the relation of 8a–9c to 7a–b is amplification.

4:8b in order that he might know how you are This is the first of the two purpose clauses mentioned in the note on 4:8a. The only question here is what the best text is. Was Paul saying that he was sending Tychicus so that the Colossians might have news about Paul (repeating what he has already said in 4:7), or so that he, Tychicus, might find out how the Colossians were doing? Either makes good sense in the context, but the former is the most widely preferred. It is generally assumed that εἰς αὐτὸ τοῦτο 'for this very thing' is drawing attention to the (implied) purpose in proposition 4:7, and so 8b is regarded as a restatement of 7a, but put in a reciprocal form. It is argued, therefore, that to introduce a new purpose here would be to dislocate the sequence of thought.

However, it can be pointed out that there is no need for Paul to immediately repeat what he has just said. (He will, in fact, repeat it again at the end of 4:9.) Further, much of the epistle is in response to Epaphras's report of the arrival of false teaching in Colosse. Hence, Paul, being concerned for how things have been going since Epaphras left Colosse, sends Tychicus, probably a more experienced worker, to find out. Also, the second half of the purpose does state unambiguously what Tychicus will do, so it is not unreasonable to take the view that the first half of the purpose also does. In other words, there is really only one purpose, namely, help for the Colossians in their present circumstances. Further, it seems clear from all the references to Tychicus in the New Testament (Acts 20:4, Eph. 6:21, 2 Tim. 4:12, Tit. 3:12) that he was part of Paul's team over a period of years, so it is more likely that Paul was entrusting him with the responsibility of returning with an up-to-date report on the situation. Thus, based on the context, a definitive decision one way or the other cannot be made; however, the second alternative seems slightly preferable. In any case, it should be remembered that this is essentially a textual matter and the choice of text depends on one's textual theory. Until the matter of which is the better text here is settled, the translator is free to choose to follow either text. (If the first view is preferred, then ἡμῶν 'us' refers to Paul and the others who were with him.)

4:8c and in order that he might strengthen you. This clause gives Paul's second purpose in sending Tychicus to Colosse. As in 2:2, τὰς καρδίας ὑμῶν 'your hearts' is considered to be a synecdoche for 'you'. The verb παρακαλέω 'to comfort' is difficult to translate into English. In particular, was Tychicus going to *comfort* the Colossians (assuming they were unhappy or discouraged or worried) or *strengthen* them (assuming they were in danger of succumbing to temptation, persecution, or the false teaching)? It is hard to say—either would be possible here. In the context of the whole epistle, 'strengthen' would seem best because they were beset by false teaching. In the immediate context, with its several references to the affairs of Paul and the others with him, comfort seems more likely, as Paul was in prison (so also was Aristarchus) and might well be facing death. It thus depends to some extent on the view taken of proposition 8b. If 8b refers to the Colossians' hearing about Paul, then 'comfort' seems best; if it refers to Tychicus's finding out how the Colossians were, then 'strengthen' would be preferable.

4:9a *I am sending him to you* with Onesimus, In the Greek this is a continuation of the relative clause begun in 4:8. It is necessary to repeat 8a here so as to add 'with Onesimus' to it. But how are 9a and 8a related? Since 9a is a continuation of 8a, 'with Onesimus' should have been included, strictly speaking, in 8a. But this would have been confusing, so the contents of 8a are repeated in 9a and the relation regarded as conjoining. Note, however, that 4:9a–c simply continues 4:8a and completes it.

4:9b who is a faithful brother whom *I/we(exc)* love The only question here is the same one that was raised in connection with 4:7b, namely, who is doing the loving? As there, there is a choice between 'I' and 'we(exc)' and both are given in the display.

4:9c and who is your fellow townsman. Onesimus is identified here as a Colossian: 'who is one of you'. Assuming that this is the Onesimus about whom Paul wrote to Philemon, this is generally regarded as a tactful comment on Paul's part making it easier for the Colossian believers to welcome him in spite of his disreputable past. (Tychicus, it is generally thought, was not a Colossian. Possibly he was an Ephesian.)

4:9d They will tell you about all that *has been happening* here. This is essentially a restatement of 4:7a, but there are some interesting, though minor, differences:

1. In v. 7 the first words are τὰ κατ' ἐμέ 'the things concerning me'. This phrase is restated at the end of v. 9 as τὰ ὧδε 'the things here', broadening it from news of Paul personally to news about the state of affairs where he was.
2. In 9d the subject is plural: Onesimus, as well as Tychicus, will tell the Colossians the news. This is generally regarded as another tactful remark on Paul's part.
3. The pronoun ὑμῖν 'to you(pl)' in v. 9 is front shifted, giving it more emphasis than in v. 7.
4. In 9d πάντα 'all' precedes the verb, as it also does in 7a, but in 9d it is clause-initial as well, which is probably a bit more emphatic.

SECTION CONSTITUENT 4:10–14 (Paragraph: Nucleus₂ of 4:7–18)

THEME: My fellow workers here greet you.

RELATIONAL STRUCTURE	CONTENTS
NUCLEUS₁ — NUCLEUS₁	4:10a Aristarchus, who is in prison with me, greets you.
NUCLEUS₂ — NUCLEUS	4:10b Mark, who is Barnabas's cousin, also *greets you*.
parenthesis — EXHORTATION — grounds	4:10c *Since* you have been instructed *by me* about Mark,
condition	4:10d if he comes to you,
CONSEQUENCE	4:10e welcome him.
NUCLEUS₃	4:11a Jesus, who is *also* called Justus, also *greets you*.
description of 'Aris., Mark, and Jesus J.' — NUCLEUS₁ — MEANS	4:11:b These *three men* are the only Jewish [SYN] *believers* who are working with me
purpose	4:11c in order that *people would submit to* God as their king.
NUCLEUS₂	4:11d They have comforted me.
NUCLEUS₂ — 'Epaphras'	4:12a Epaphras, who is your fellow townsman and who serves Christ *Jesus*, greets you.
description — RESULT	4:12b–d Epaphras prays earnestly for you very often, (12c) that you might be *spiritually* mature (12d) and that you might be fully convinced about all that God wills,
reason — NUCLEUS	4:13a because Epaphras is deeply concerned for you and for those *who are/live* in Laodicea *town* and for those *who are/live* in Hierapolis *town*;
orienter (evaluative)	4:13b I can vouch for this [4:13a].
NUCLEUS₃	4:14 Luke, the doctor, whom *I/we(exc)* love, and Demas greet you.

BOUNDARIES AND COHERENCE

Paragraph 4:10–14 contains three parallel independent clauses: 4:10, 12, and 14. The verb is identical in each, ἀσπάζεται 'he greets', a third person singular present middle indicative.

This paragraph is distinct from the preceding and following material both in content and by virtue of the formal parallelism of the three independent clauses. While the verbs of the preceding unit are also third person singular, they are future tense; and the unit following 4:10–14 is built around second person plural commands. The content of 4:10–14 is greetings from various colleagues of Paul, whereas 4:7–9 has to do with news about Paul and others, and 4:15–17 consists of instructions from Paul to the Colossians and other Christians.

Since each of the first two constituents of 4:10–14 consists of more than one propositional cluster and a theme could be stated for each of these parts, each could be considered as constituting a paragraph structurally. However, since they form a unit that is distinct from 4:7–9 and 4:15–17, they are not treated simply as three independent paragraphs within the epistle closing. Instead, they are considered a paragraph, a constituent of the 4:7–18 section. Of course, it is a compound paragraph, that is, one that consists of three independent constituents linked by the relation of conjoining, and functioning as a single unit within the section.

Alternatively, 4:10-14 could be seen as a paragraph cluster, with the first two constituents (4:10-11 and 12-13) each being a paragraph in composition.

The coherence of the paragraph is shown in a variety of ways, one being the parallelism already noted: ἀσπάζεται ὑμᾶς X ὁ . . . , 'X, the . . . , greets you' (in 4:10, 12, 14). There is reference to the Colossians (i.e., 'you(pl)') in every verse except 4:11. There are also references to Paul (first person singular) in 4:10, 11, and 13. Within each clause, there is a back reference to the greeter by means of an article, relative clauses, the deictic οὗτοι 'these', and a nominative participle. Within the constituents the names of the persons sending greetings are linked by καί 'and'.

PROMINENCE AND THEME

The 4:10-14 paragraph consists of three main constituents, related to each other by conjoining. There is nothing formal to give prominence to any one of these three parts, unless length is considered, but this is not a useful criterion in this instance. Hence, a generic theme has to be abstracted from the content of the three parts, as represented by their themes, which are the following:

> Aristarchus, Mark, and Jesus Justus greet you.
>
> Epaphras greets you.
>
> Luke and Demas greet you.

Beekman's theme was "These friends greet you." Since, however, Paul is writing the letter and comments on five of these six in terms of their work, relation to himself, etc., it seems preferable to modify this slightly to 'My fellow workers here greet you'. Or, if it is assumed that there were others who did not send greetings, then the two suggestions could be combined to 'Some of my fellow workers here greet you'. But it is perhaps better to assume that they all sent greetings, and where there was nothing to say specifically about them, as in the case of Demas, only the name was included.

NOTES

4:10a Aristarchus, who is in prison with me, greets you. The question here is whether Paul, when he refers to Aristarchus as his 'fellow prisoner', intends it to be understood literally or not. Is this figurative, like 'fellow slave' in 4:7 and 'fellow soldier' (συστρατιώτης) in Phil. 2:25 and Philem. 2? But we note that here 'fellow prisoner' lacks any qualifying phrase such as 'of the Lord', so it would be taken as literal, especially since Paul was writing from prison and it would be natural to understand it literally unless clearly indicated otherwise.

On the other hand, some argue that 'fellow prisoner' cannot be literal, because in Philem. 23-24, where Aristarchus is called a 'fellow worker' of Paul, Epaphras is called a 'fellow prisoner' whereas in Colossians Epaphras is not called a 'fellow prisoner' in the references to him there (in 1:7-8 and in 4:12-13). Since it is generally agreed that Colossians and Philemon were written at much the same time—as evidenced by references to the same people, in particular Onesimus, the topic of the letter to Philemon—it seems very unlikely that Aristarchus and Epaphras would have changed roles in such a brief time. They could not have been in and out of prison that quickly. (To answer this, various commentators offer the suggestion that Aristarchus and Epaphras possibly took turns in some voluntary form of imprisonment with Paul, living in prison with him.)

In the light of these pro's and con's it is difficult to reach a decision. However, since a number of other Christians are mentioned, but only Aristarchus is called a 'fellow prisoner', yet all of them must have been in reasonably close contact with Paul to be sending greetings to the Colossians, it seems preferable to take the phrase literally. Whether Aristarchus was imprisoned by the Roman authorities or was a voluntary prisoner we cannot know, but in either of these cases it is the literal sense that is intended, not a figurative one.

Note that the word refers to a prisoner taken in war, not someone in prison for wrongdoing.

4:10b Mark, who is Barnabas's cousin, also greets you. The name 'Mark' is linked with 'Aristarchus' by καί 'and'. Both men are sending greetings to the Colossians. Note that ἀνεψιός is 'cousin' and not 'sister's son' as in the KJV.

4:10c *Since* you have been instructed *by me* about Mark, The relative pronoun οὗ 'whom' refers to Mark, not to Barnabas. (In most English versions the rendering is ambiguous.) The Greek 'you received commands' is semantically equivalent to the passive 'you were commanded' or 'you were instructed'. (Most versions have "instruction.") Since Paul evidently considers the instructions to be still in force in that they are not yet carried out, the rendering in the display is 'you have been instructed'. There is no hint as to who had given these instructions to the Colossians, so if an agent has to be stated in translation, it seems best to assume that Paul himself had given the instructions rather than that he was referring to someone else's instructions. Hence, 'by me' is supplied as implicit information.

The most difficult question here is the semantic relationship of this statement to the surrounding ones. According to Beekman, "these propositions are parenthetical," and in numerous versions, such as the RSV, TEV, NEB, and NIV, the second half of 4:10 is indeed in parentheses. (JB uses dashes.) But what, from a semantic point of view, *is* a parenthesis in a letter? Tentatively, I would say that it is information that is lexically, but not logically, connected with the surrounding information, and with a switch of persons at the interpersonal level within the same paragraph. All of these criteria apply here: the second half of 4:10 (i.e., 10c-e) is lexically connected with the first half (both refer to Mark), but not logically; and it switches from a third person orientation ('Mark *greets you*') to a second person orientation ('you welcome Mark'). Therefore in the display 10c-e is labeled a parenthesis. Note that this material has its own set of internal relations and its own main proposition.

4:10d-e if he comes to you, welcome him. The best translation of δέξασθε seems to be 'welcome'. Meyer has "of *hospitable* reception, as often in the N. T."

The only question here is whether 10d and e are the content of the 'instructions' referred to in 10c. Beekman argued against this, saying that if they were the content, ἐντολάς 'instructions' would either be preceded by the article τάς or followed by ἵνα 'that', or both; also, he said, the term 'instructions' seems a rather grandiose way to refer to the simple command 'welcome him'. Hence, 10d and e are not regarded as the content of 'instructed' in 10c. Another possibility is to treat 10c as generic, and 10e as specific. Still another possibility is to treat 10c as grounds for the command in 10e. This latter seems preferable, as it would seem somewhat anomalous semantically to relate a generic statement to a specific command. For these reasons, 10c is labeled in the display as grounds for 10e.

4:11a Jesus, who is *also* called Justus, also *greets you*. As in 10b, καί 'and' links 'Jesus' with 'Mark' and 'Aristarchus' in sending greetings to the Colossians.

In the TEV Ἰησοῦς is here rendered 'Joshua'. While Ἰησοῦς is the New Testament equivalent of the Old Testament 'Joshua', it is probably better to stick to 'Jesus' here, as almost all the versions do.

4:11b-c These *three men* are the only Jewish believers who are working with me in order that *people would submit* to God as their king. In the commentaries and grammars there is considerable discussion of the grammar of theses two clauses and how they should be punctuated. But however the clauses are punctuated and related to one another formally, the meaning in the overall context is clear. These three men just named, Aristarchus, Mark, and Jesus Justus, were Jews. The phrase ἐκ περιτομῆς 'out of circumcision' refers to their origin; 'circumcision' here is a synecdoche for the person who was circumcised. They alone, out of the Jewish Christians, were active co-workers with Paul at this point. It is clearly implied that they were believers, since Paul calls them fellow workers.

The phrase 'the kingdom of God' is preceded by εἰς, which commonly signals purpose (see the note on 4:8a) whether it is followed by a noun (usually abstract) or an infinitive phrase. A comparison of this abbreviated phrase with Phil. 1:12-13 and Col. 1:6-7 suggests the implicit event 'with the purpose of spreading/extending the kingdom of God' (see Beekman).

The word βασιλεία 'kingdom' is generally regarded as an abstract noun referring to the event of 'ruling', and the genitive construction τοῦ θεοῦ 'of God' indicates who does the ruling. If, however, εἰς τὴν βασιλείαν τοῦ θεοῦ is propositionalized as 'in order that God might rule people', there is a theological problem: God already rules the whole universe by Jesus, the Lord of Lords and King of Kings. The meaning here is rather that sinners might come to accept and submit to God's rule willingly and openly acknowledge that Jesus is Lord. The rendering in the display is an attempt to avoid denying God's universal kingship.

4:11d They have comforted me. The abstract noun παρηγορία 'comfort', which occurs only here in the New Testament, represents the event 'to comfort', and μοι 'to me' shows that it was Paul who was comforted. The relative pronoun οἵτινες 'who' refers back to the three men mentioned earlier in this paragraph.

The verb γίνομαι generally has the sense of 'to become', but as Arndt and Gingrich suggest, it can be used as a substitute for forms of εἰμί, the verb 'to be'. This may well be so here, especially as it is in the aorist tense, a tense not exhibited by the verb 'to be' in Greek. As to why Paul chose the aorist of γίνομαι here, the implication may be that, at some point in the past, probably while he was in prison, these men joined up with him and helped him in the work of the kingdom and that their coming and help were a great comfort to him. Whether this is so or not, the best English rendering seems to be 'they have comforted me', implying a past event with present implications. Most versions have "they have been . . . ," which likewise implies a past start with present effects.

4:12a Epaphras, who is your fellow townsman and who serves Christ *Jesus*, greets you. Epaphras, referred to by name in 1:7, is again named here. His name is followed by ὁ ἐξ ὑμῶν 'the one out of you', the same idiomatic construction as underlies 4:9c (see the note there).

Epaphras is called δοῦλος 'slave', but this is figurative, being collocated with 'Christ (Jesus)'. That is, Epaphras was not an actual slave, but served the Lord Jesus as a slave serves his master. The same figure was used in 4:7b.

Note the textual variants here: some texts have the full form 'Christ Jesus', while others have 'Christ' only. Translators may choose one or the other depending on the theoretical approach they prefer.

4:12b Epaphras prays earnestly for you very often, Here an abstract noun, 'prayers', represents the event; and a verb, 'strive', represents the attribute modifying that event. What Epaphras was doing was praying, and ἀγωνιζόμενος 'striving' describes the manner of his praying. The semantic mismatch gives prominence to the manner.

The same participle, ἀγωνιζόμενος, is used in 1:29c; its cognate noun ἀγών is used in 2:1b. In both cases, it means the expending of considerable effort. In the display this idea is represented by 'earnestly'. Other possibilities are 'fervently' and 'energetically'.

4:12c-d that you might be *spiritually* mature and that you might be fully convinced about all that God wills, Here ἵνα introduces the content of Epaphras's prayers, but there is considerable discussion as to what that content actually is. Note that the Greek manuscripts are divided between σταθῆτε and στῆτε for the second word, but both forms, according to Turner (1963:57), have the same active meaning, even though the first is a passive and the second active. There are two interrelated questions here: What does the perfect passive participle πεπληροφορημένοι mean? And with what is the final prepositional phrase connected?

Lightfoot gives three meanings for the verb πληροφορέω, from which the participle here is formed: (1) 'to fulfill, accomplish' (e.g., Luke 1:1; 2 Tim. 4:5, 17); (2) 'to persuade fully, to convince' (e.g., Rom. 4:21; 14:5); and (3) 'to fill' (Rom. 15:13 may be an example, though it seems likely that the simple verb πληρόω 'to fill' is used there). Neither the first nor third meaning seems to make much sense here: In each of the examples of the first, something is clearly referred to as accomplished or fulfilled; as to the third, it is doubtful that this sense even occurs in the New Testament. Hence, the second sense is the one preferred by most exegetes. This is confirmed by the fact that it was Epaphras who brought the report to Paul of the Colossians' situation, and, in particular, of the false teaching which had arrived in their area. Given this sense, Epaphras would indeed be praying that the Colossians would be fully convinced of the truth of the gospel. Also, the cognate noun πληροφορία 'full assurance' is used in 2:2 in connection with understanding.

As to what the final prepositional phrase is connected with, it could be either with the immediately preceding participle 'fully convinced' or with the verb 'you might stand'. The two main views are (1) that it should be linked with the participle πεπληροφορημένοι 'having been fully convinced' because it is contiguous (this is the predominant view) and (2) that it should be linked with the verb 'you might stand' because the sequence στήκω/ἵστημι + ἐν 'stand' + 'in' occurs a number of times in the New Testament, and so is a natural collocation and should be preferred over the more doubtful collocation 'fully convinced in'.

The grammar allows for either of these views, so it seems to be essentially a question of collocation. Lightfoot gives several examples of 'being fully convinced' followed by ἐν in the writings of Ignatius, a bishop martyred in the early part of the second century. In two of these, the collocation means 'fully convinced about', which would make good sense here in Colossians, since the whole letter has been concerned with the problem caused by the rise of heretical teaching. If this view is followed, then σταθῆτε/στῆτε could mean 'you remain' (i.e., assuming that the Colossians already were mature and convinced) or 'you be', which does not carry any implications with it except that this is what Epaphras wanted them to be. The more neutral 'be' is in the display.

The adjective τέλειοι means 'mature'; here the meaning is 'spiritually mature'. In other words, Epaphras was concerned both that they would be mature in character and firmly convinced in doctrine so that the false teacher could not unsettle them because of weakness of character or because of doctrinal wavering.

If the other view is followed and the verb σταθῆτε is connected with the prepositional phrase, it is not clear what 'stand (firm) in all God's will' might mean. Although there are six or seven occurrences of this collocation ('stand in') in the Pauline letters, they either have the sense of 'stand firm' (as in 1 Cor. 16:13; Phil. 1:27; 4:1; 1 Thess. 3:8) or 'you have come to stand' (Rom. 5:2 and 1 Cor. 15:1, where the perfect tense is used), meaning 'you are now in the permanent position'. Neither of these senses collocates well with 'in God's will'. Hence, the prepositional phrase is here seen as being connected with πεπληροφορημένοι.

Whether σταθῆτε/στῆτε is taken to mean 'remain' or 'be', there are two petitions joined by καί 'and'. Therefore in the display the contents of the praying are conjoined.

4:13a–b because Epaphras is deeply concerned for you and for those *who are/live* in Laodicea *town* and for those *who are/live* in Hierapolis *town*; I can vouch for this [4:13a]. The first problem here is to determine what relation γάρ signals at the beginning of 13a. Commentators such as Meyer and Lenski refer to it as "confirmatory," that is, confirming the truth of what Paul has just said about Epaphras, especially his earnest praying for the Colossians. The construction μαρτυρῶ αὐτῷ 'I testify to-him' at the beginning of the verse is an orienter, and γάρ is linked to the content of the orienter. This means that γάρ introduces the deep concern Epaphras had for the Colossians and the other believers mentioned, and that this concern is expressed in his earnest prayers for them. In the display, this relationship is communicated more clearly by placing the orienter *after* the content, not before it as in the Greek. In this context the verb μαρτυρῶ is best translated 'I can vouch for'—it is his concern that is being vouched for.

There is a question here concerning the text. Is it πολὺν πόνον 'great toil' or ζῆλον πολύν 'great zeal'? Again, as so often in Colossians, the choice of text is a matter of which theory you follow. Fortunately, in this case, the difference semantically is relatively slight.

The second question is, If the first of these variants is followed, what does πόνος mean in this particular context? The commentators make two points here: (1) The word πόνος collocates naturally with ἀγωνιζόμενος 'striving' in the previous verse (see 4:12b), as both have to do with battle and strife: ἀγωνίζομαι is the strife itself, πόνος the effort put into it or the pain and distress resulting from that strenuous effort. (2) In this context, πόνος is essentially figurative; it is applied to the spiritual realm, being mental, not physical, effort.

In trying to decide the meaning of πόνος here, it should be borne in mind that it confirms or supports what Paul has already said about Epaphras's earnest praying. Most versions render it "work"; and prayer, presumably, would be a particular example of the sort of work meant. But Phillips has "he has a real passion for your welfare," and Hendriksen, "he has put himself to much trouble." Weymouth speaks of "the deep interest he takes in you," and Goodspeed, "how anxious he is." These seem better. They point to the underlying attitude that gave rise to the earnest praying. In the display 'concerned' is used in the sense of awareness of a difficult situation plus showing interest. If rendered 'distressed' or 'anxious', that would make it sound as if Epaphras were afraid that the Colossians would succumb, or had already succumbed, to the false teaching, and this is not implied here or anywhere in the epistle.

As to the textual variant ζῆλον πολύν, the word ζῆλος means 'zeal'. However, 'zeal' generally refers to enthusiasm or eagerness and modifies activities, rather than people. That is, one is zealous to do things, not zealous for people. But 'zeal on behalf of' is what Paul has here, and this zeal issues in earnest praying. So, in this context, 'zeal' seems equivalent to 'deep concern for', a concern that expresses itself in prayer; and the rendering 'deeply concerned' would cover either πόνος or ζῆλος in this particular context.

Laodicea and Hierapolis were two towns in the same river valley as Colosse. They were quite possibly visited and evangelized by Epaphras, and potentially threatened by the same heretical teaching.

4:14 Luke, the doctor, whom *I/we(exc)* love, and Demas greet you. For a discussion of the agent of the event 'to love', see 4:7b. Here again the agent is either Paul himself or those associated with him.

SECTION CONSTITUENT 4:15–17 (Paragraph: Nucleus₃ of 4:7–18)

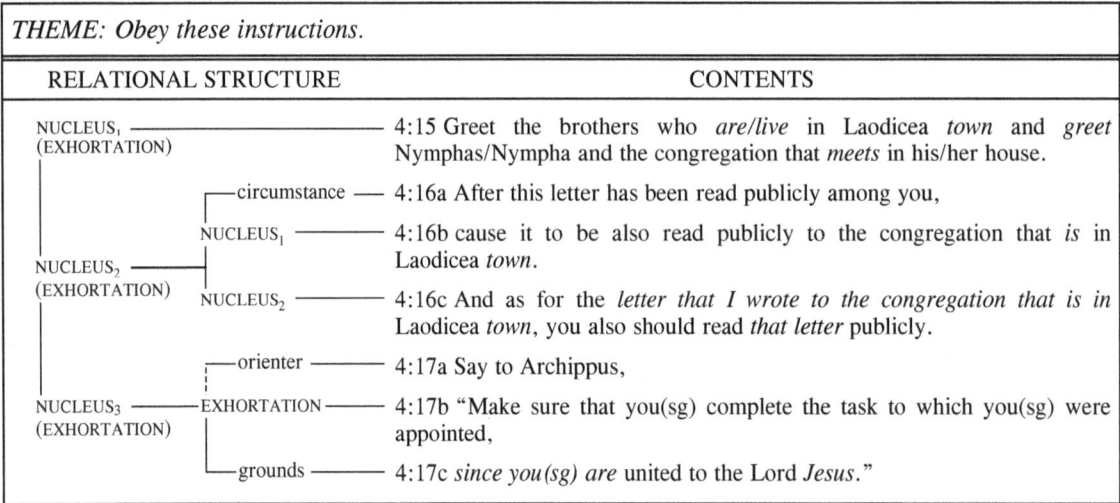

BOUNDARIES AND COHERENCE

Verses 4:15–17 are distinguished from the preceding paragraph by the fact that their main clauses are second person plural commands, not third person singular greetings. Further, 4:10–14 centers on Paul and his co-workers, whereas 4:15–17 is concerned with the believers at Colosse and the neighboring town of Laodicea. It is also distinct from the following unit, 4:18, which is the formal "sign-off" of the letter and has two verbless clauses. Hence, 4:15–17 forms a separate unit.

There are three second person plural commands in 4:15–17, one in each verse, and all of them in the aorist tense. They are linked by καί 'and' but have very little content in common except that they are directed to the Colossian Christians. Thus, they form three separate units. Unlike the constituents of the preceding unit, these are not like paragraphs in structure. Rather, they are propositional clusters. Thus the 4:15–17 paragraph is seen as comprising three conjoined constituents.

The main evidence for the coherence of this paragraph is, in fact, the parallelism of the three aorist commands directed to the same group of people and linked by καί 'and'. There are also two second person plural pronouns, referring to the Colossians, in 4:16. The first two commands contain references to the believers in Laodicea.

PROMINENCE AND THEME

Since the 4:15–17 paragraph is made up of three independent constituents, the theme either has to be abstracted from them in some generic way or else the three constituent themes be conjoined. The former is preferred, since the latter would simply repeat almost the whole paragraph. However, it is rather difficult to abstract a generic theme: the three commands have very little in common, the first being Paul's greetings to individual believers; the second, instructions to read the letter publicly and send it on to Laodicea; and the third, instructions for Archippus, one of the believers. Beekman suggested the theme "Do these things that I ask." This has been shortened here to 'Obey these instructions', in order to avoid 'things', which is very generic.

NOTES

4:15 Greet the brothers who *are/live* in Laodicea town and *greet* Nymphas/Nympha and the congregation that *meets* in his/her house. There is a question here as to the best text to follow. Commentators disagree, although the modern versions all tend to follow the text with αὐτῆς 'her (house)'. There does not even seem to be agreement as to which choice is the best supported. The problem is that the proper name Νύμφαν in the Greek is in the accusative case of either Νυμφᾶς, a masculine name, or Νύμφα, a feminine name. And although these two names have different accent marks in later Greek, the early manuscripts did not use these marks, so they were spelled identically. The ambiguity in the accusative form of the name would be resolved by the pronoun following οἶκον 'house'; but unfortunately manuscripts differ as to whether that pronoun is αὐτοῦ 'of him' or αὐτῆς 'of her'. Moreover, scholars disagree as to which of these is better supported. Modern editors tend to prefer the feminine form, while earlier commentators tend to prefer the masculine or, in some cases, another variant altogether, the plural αὐτῶν 'of them'.

In terms of internal considerations (i.e., other than manuscript factors), the following points can be made:

1. Either of the singular forms makes good sense and is quite acceptable. The plural does not really make sense, although some of the older commentators took it to mean 'Nymphas and his family's house'. But this is not normal Greek, nor plausible. Nympha(s) was quite sufficient to identify the house in question.
2. If the original was feminine in case, then, it is suggested, it may have been changed to masculine, as the copyists may have thought it inappropriate for the church to meet in a lady's house. (But there is nothing in the New Testament against such a possibility, so it would have to be a later prejudice.)
3. If the original was masculine in case, it is suggested that scribes were misled by the form Νύμφαν and thought it was feminine, since -αν is a common feminine accusative ending. Then they used αὐτῆς to agree.
4. If Νύμφαν is feminine, then the nominative form would be Νύμφα. Some of the commentators point out that this is a Doric form of the name, unlikely to be met with in Colosse, where Νύμφη would be the norm.

In view of the uncertainty surrounding the correct text, the display has both alternatives. (For languages that distinguish between masculine and feminine gender, it should be noted that Nymphas is the masculine form of the name, Nympha the feminine.)

The word ἐκκλησία, which is very commonly translated 'church', is here translated 'congregation'. This is unambiguous, unlike the English *church*, the primary sense of which is the building in which a congregation meets.

4:16a After this letter has been read publicly among you, Commentators agree that 'the letter' is equivalent to 'this letter', so in the display the deictic 'this' is used.

The phrase παρ' ὑμῖν 'with you' seems to be a way of referring to the congregation as a whole. The letter was to be read publicly to the assembled congregation.

The verb is a passive; the subject of the verb is ἡ ἐπιστολή 'the letter'. The clause-final position of ἡ ἐπιστολή is unusual and may indicate that this is a new (minor) topic, a view that may be supported by the position of τὴν ἐκ Λαοδικείας 'the one from Laodicea' preceding the conjunction ἵνα in 4:16c. Paul is now giving instructions about his letters.

The passive is retained in the display rendering, and 'this letter' is the subject. However, 'read to you' in English would suggest that someone from outside the congregation was reading the letter to them. Since this is not the implication, 'among you' is used.

4:16b cause it to be also read publicly to the congregation that *is* in Laodicea town. The main verb ποιήσατε 'do' is translated in various ways in English versions: "have (it read)," "see (that it is read)," "send it on (to be read)," "make sure (that it is read)." But here in the display a more neutral word, 'cause', is used since it was the responsibility of the Colossian Christians to see that it was done.

4:16c And as for the *letter that I wrote to the congregation that is in* Laodicea *town*, you also should read *that letter* publicly. The article τήν refers to 'the letter', which is further described as 'from Laodicea'. Most commentators agree that this is a shortened form of expression for 'the letter that is at Laodicea and is to be fetched from there'. It is not a letter written by the Laodiceans, nor one written by Paul while at Laodicea. The parallelism of content, along with καὶ ὑμεῖς 'also you(pl)', makes it clear that there was to be reciprocal activity: the Colossians were to make sure that their letter would be read at Laodicea, and that they themselves read the one to the Laodiceans. (Much ink has been used in discussing what this letter to the Laodiceans was and what happened to it, but fortunately for the translator, such discussions do not affect the translation.)

The forefronting of τὴν ἐκ Λαοδικείας 'the (one) from Laodicea' (it occurs before ἵνα 'that') puts emphasis on the phrase; in the display this emphasis is conveyed by the forefronted phrase beginning 'as for'. Just when this letter was written to the Laodiceans is not clear. The general presumption is that it had reached Laodicea before the Colossians received their letter, so the implicit information supplied is 'that I wrote'.

There is also some discussion in the grammars and commentaries on the force of ἵνα in 4:16c. Three suggestions are made: (1) It is dependent on ποιήσατε as is the preceding ἵνα in 4:16b. (2) It assumes an ellipsed verb, such as βλέπετε 'see (that)'. (3) It is an example of an imperatival ἵνα, that is, ἵνα introducing a command. Semantically, the difference between these three is slight: 'cause that you read it', 'see that you read it', and 'read it' each convey much the same sense as the other—a command to read the letter. The rendering in the display is based on a neutral position among these three alternatives.

4:17a Say to Archippus, The third of Paul's instructions is introduced by καί 'and'. There are various conjectures as to why this message to Archippus (who is mentioned also in Philem. 2) is transmitted via the believers at Colosse, but none of these affect the rendering.

4:17b–c "Make sure that you(sg) complete the task to which you(sg) were appointed, *since you(sg) are* united to the Lord *Jesus*." Commentators concentrate on the question of what this service might have been, but for a semantic analysis there are other problems. The abstract noun phrase τὴν διακονίαν 'the service' represents the event 'to serve/work'. The verb παρέλαβες 'you(sg) received' is the equivalent of a passive here: 'to which you were appointed' or 'which was committed to you'. As is widely agreed, πληρόω means 'to fulfill, complete, finish' when collocated with "an obligation, . . . a duty" (Arndt and Gingrich, entry 4). The verb βλέπε 'see' is closely linked to the ἵνα clause, ἵνα αὐτὴν πληροῖς 'that you(sg) fulfill it', and so, as in some of the versions, is best translated by such expressions as "see to it that" (NIV), "be sure to/that" (TEV, LB), "see that you" (RSV, Phillips). It is a prominence orienter. Paul could have said simply 'fulfill the ministry', but the initial βλέπε 'see' draws attention to the command. The implication is probably that Archippus was giving evidence that he was less than likely to fulfill this particular responsibility. However, when the verb 'to complete' is used as a rendering of πληρόω, it requires a noun as its object, hence 'the task'.

The main question in connection with the phrase ἐν κυρίῳ 'in (the) Lord' is what it is attached to—the immediately preceding verb παρέλαβες 'you received' or βλέπε 'make sure'? In 3:18 and 20 ἐν κυρίῳ was part of the grounds for commands addressed to the wives and the children, and in 4:7 it was part of the description of Tychicus. Assuming that ἐν κυρίῳ is used consistently in this epistle, it would refer to Archippus's union with Christ, the Lord (i.e., to the fact that he was a believer). If, then, this phrase is attached to παρέλαβες 'you received', it would mean either 'while you were a believer' or 'since you are a believer'. If it is attached to βλέπε 'make sure', it would presumably be grounds: 'do what I am telling you, since you are a believer'. Grounds, then, fits with both alternatives and so is preferable.

SECTION CONSTITUENT 4:18 (Paragraph: Nucleus₄ of 4:7–18)

THEME: I, Paul, am penning this final greeting myself in order that you may know that this letter was sent by me. Remember to pray about the fact that I am in prison.

RELATIONAL STRUCTURE	CONTENTS
NUCLEUS₁ —MEANS	4:18a–b *I, Paul, greet you.* (18b) *I myself am penning this* [4:18]
└─purpose	4:18c *in order that you may know that this letter was truly sent by me.*
NUCLEUS₂ (EXHORTATION)	4:18d *Remember to pray about the fact that I am in prison* [MTY].
└─conjoined	4:18e *I/we(exc) pray that our(inc) Lord Jesus Christ would act graciously towards you.*

BOUNDARIES AND COHERENCE

The 4:18 paragraph is distinguished from the preceding instructions in that although there is a request that the Colossians remember (probably in prayer) that Paul is in prison, it conveys Paul's own greetings to the Colossians and his final benediction on them. It is also distinguished formally: two of the three clauses are without verbs.

The first two clauses overtly refer to Paul himself, both by name and with first person singular pronouns or adjectives. The third clause is probably covertly a wish or prayer on Paul's part for the Colossians. However, there are no formal links between the parts.

PROMINENCE AND THEME

Here in 4:18, as in the two previous paragraphs, there are three independent main constituents, with very little in common among them except the references to Paul himself. What Paul is doing is closing off the letter. The final clause, in some form or other, closes all of Paul's letters; and his own personal greeting, written in his own hand, is found associated with the final benediction in 1 Cor. 16:21 and 2 Thess. 3:17. The fact that Paul took up the pen himself indicates that the letter has come to its end. Hence, one possible theme would be 'I, Paul, am penning this final greeting myself in order that I close this letter'. However, as the notes on 18a–c suggest, Paul's main purpose in writing with his own hand was to guarantee the authenticity of the letter, since spurious letters were already beginning to appear. Hence, a better theme would be, 'I, Paul, am penning this final greeting myself in order that you may know that this letter was sent by me'. This reflects a more significant purpose than the first alternative and is therefore used as the theme in the display. 'Final greeting' is added to 'this' since otherwise 'this' would have no clear reference in the higher-level displays. In addition, the request to be remembered, presumably in prayer, in 4:18d, is treated as thematic since it repeats a similar request in 4:3–4 and occurs right at the end of the letter, giving it prominence.

NOTES

4:18a–c *I, Paul, greet you.* **I myself am penning this [4:18]** *in order that you may know that this letter was truly sent by me.* It is widely agreed that 'the greeting by my hand' means that Paul wrote this last verse with his own hand, having dictated the rest of the letter. And it is also generally agreed that he did this so that the readers would know that the letter was genuine and came from him: there were evidently already spurious letters in circulation, claiming to be written by Paul (cf. 2 Thess. 3:17 and Col. 2:2). Thus there is a considerable amount of implied information here, as is supplied in 18c. The translator will have to judge how much of this implicit information is needed in a given translation.

The word 'penning' is used to make it unambiguously clear that Paul actually wrote this himself with a pen or stylus.

The abstract noun ἀσπασμός 'greeting' here represents the event of Paul's greeting the Colossian believers. In 4:10–14 are the greetings his colleagues had sent, and in 4:15 are Paul's greetings to the congregation at Laodicea. Now, Paul greets the Colossians.

The construction τῇ ἐμῇ χειρί 'by the my hand' is an article + possessive pronoun + noun, which is considered to be "very emphatic" (Turner, 1963:189). That is, the possessive pronoun 'my' is very emphatic. In the display this emphasis is shown by using 'I, Paul' in 18a and 'I . . . myself' in 18b.

4:18d Remember *to pray about the fact* that I am in prison. As previously, δεσμῶν 'bonds' is taken as a metonymy for 'imprisoned'. Various suggestions are given as to why this was said by Paul at this point, but the most likely is that he wanted them to pray for him (as already expressed more fully in 4:3-4). Beekman's propositional form is used here: 'Remember *to pray about the fact* that I am in prison'. In some languages it may also be necessary to repeat from 4:3 the information that Paul was in prison because he preached about Christ.

4:18e *I/We(exc) pray that our(inc) Lord Jesus Christ would* act graciously towards you. This is the shortest form of the final greeting that Paul uses—it is the same as in 1 Tim. 6:21 and 2 Tim. 4:22. (In Tit. 3:15 it is also the same except that 'all' is added.)

The word χάρις 'grace' is a particularly difficult concept to render propositionally; it is not really clear whether it is an event or an attribute. In either case, participants are needed for the event, yet collocations in this area of meaning are problematic in English. Beekman has "(act in) grace," Blight's "Literary-Semantic Analysis of Paul's First Discourse to Timothy" has "be given grace," and Beekman and Smith's *Literary-Semantic Analysis of Second Timothy* has "bless." Perhaps the best that can be managed in English is 'act graciously', with 'graciously' being a technical term.

But who is acting graciously? In some versions it is 'God' and a number of commentaries support this; the display for 1 Tim. 6:21 (see Blight) also uses 'God'. But Lightfoot correctly points out that in all the longer forms of this final greeting Paul adds all or some of the phrase 'the/our Lord Jesus Christ'. Hence, 'the Lord Jesus (Christ)' is taken as the agent in this rather specialized context. This final benediction is regarded as a prayer. It seems more likely that, in this verse, where the references are to Paul himself, exclusive of Timothy, that the form of the orienter should be 'I pray'. However, 'we(exc) pray' is quite acceptable.

BIBLIOGRAPHY

Greek Texts and English Versions

Aland, Kurt, Matthew Black, Bruce M. Metzger, and Allen Wikgren, eds. 1966 and 1975. *The Greek New Testament*. New York: United Bible Societies.

Barclay, William, tr. 1969. *The New Testament: A new translation*. New York: Collins.

Beck, William F., tr. 1963. *The New Testament in the language of today*. St. Louis: Concordia.

Bruce, F. F., tr. 1965. *The letters of Paul*. Grand Rapids: Eerdmans.

Good News Bible: The Bible in today's English version. 1976. New York: American Bible Society.

Good News for modern man: The New Testament in today's English version. 1966. New York: ABS.

Goodspeed, J. Edgar, tr. 1923. *The New Testament: An American translation*. Chicago: University of Chicago Press.

The Holy Bible: Authorized (or King James) version. 1611.

The Holy Bible: (English) Revised version. 1885.

The Holy Bible: New international version. 1978. Grand Rapids: Zondervan.

The Holy Bible: Revised standard version. 1952. New York: Thomas Nelson.

The Holy Bible: The Berkeley version in modern English. 1958/59. Tr. Gerrit Verkuyl. Grand Rapids: Zondervan.

The Jerusalem Bible. 1966. Garden City, N.Y.: Doubleday.

Kleist, James A., and Joseph L. Lilly, trs. 1956. *The New Testament*. Milwaukee: Bruce.

Knox, Ronald, tr. 1954. *The Holy Bible*. New York: Sheed and Ward.

The living Bible. 1971. Tr. Kenneth N. Taylor. Wheaton, Ill.: Tyndale.

Montgomery, Helen Barrett, tr. 1924. *The New Testament in modern English: Centenary translation*. Philadelphia: Judson.

The new American Bible. 1971. New York: Catholic Press Publishers.

New American standard Bible. 1973. Anaheim, Calif.: Foundation Press.

The new English Bible: New Testament. 1970. 2d edition. Oxford: Oxford University Press; Cambridge: Cambridge University Press.

Norlie, Olaf M., tr. 1961. *The New Testament: A new translation in modern English for today's reader*. Grand Rapids: Zondervan.

Phillips, J. B., tr. 1953. *The New Testament in modern English*. New York: Macmillan.

Saint Joseph edition of the Holy Bible. 1963. Confraternity version. New York: Catholic Book Publishing Co.

The twentieth century New Testament. [1904] 1945. New York: Revell.

Weymouth, Richard Francis, tr. [1908] 1929. *The New Testament in modern speech*. 5th edition (1st American edition) revised by J. A. Robertson. Boston: Pilgrim Press; London: James Clarke.

Williams, Charles Kingsley, tr. 1952. *The New Testament: A new translation in plain English*. London: S.P.C.K. and Longmans, Green.

Commentaries, Lexicons, and Other General References

Abbott, T. K. 1897. *A critical and exegetical commentary on the Epistles to the Ephesians and to the Colossians*. International Critical Commentary. Edinburgh: T. and T. Clark.

Abbott-Smith, G. 1956. *Manual Greek lexicon of the New Testament*. Edinburgh: T. and T. Clark.

Alford, Henry. 1880. *The Greek New Testament,* vol. 3. London: Rivingtons.

Arndt, William F., and F. Wilbur Gingrich. 1957. *A Greek-English lexicon of the New Testament and other early Christian literature*. Chicago: University of Chicago Press.

Barnes, Albert. 1962. *Barnes' notes on the New Testament*. First American reprint edition. Grand Rapids: Kregel.

Beare, Francis W., and G. Preston MacLeod. 1955. The Epistle to the Colossians. In *The interpreter's Bible,* vol. 11, 132–241. Nashville, Tenn.: Abingdon.

Beekman, John. 1974. An analysis of the semantic structure of the Epistle to the Colossians. Prepublication draft prepared in consultation with international translation consultants of Wycliffe Bible Translators. Dallas: SIL.

Beekman, John, and John Callow. 1974. *Translating the Word of God*. Grand Rapids: Zondervan.
Beekman, John, John Callow, and Michael F. Kopesec. 1981. The semantic structure of written communication. Prepublication Draft. Dallas: SIL.
Beekman, John, and Robert E. Smith. 1981. *A literary-semantic analysis of Second Timothy*. Dallas: SIL.
Blass, F., and A. Debrunner. 1961. *A Greek grammar of the New Testament*. A translation and revision of the ninth-tenth German edition by Robert W. Funk. Chicago: University of Chicago Press.
Blight, Richard. 1977. A literary-semantic analysis of Paul's first discourse to Timothy. Prepublication draft. Dallas: SIL.
Bruce, F. F. 1957. Commentary on the Epistle to the Colossians. In *Commentary on the Epistle to the Ephesians and to the Colossians,* 159-313. The New International Commentary on the New Testament. Grand Rapids: Eerdmans.
Bullinger, E. W. 1898. *Figures of speech used in the Bible*. London: Eyre and Spottiswoode.
Caird, G. B. 1976. *Paul's letters from prison: Ephesians, Philippians, Colossians, Philemon, in the revised standard version*. The New Clarendon Bible, ed. H. F. D. Sparks. London: Oxford University Press.
Callow, John. 1978. To what do *touto* and *tauta* refer in Paul's letters? *Notes on Translation* 70:2-8.
Callow, Kathleen. 1974. *Discourse considerations in translating the Word of God*. Grand Rapids: Zondervan.
Carson, Herbert M. 1960. *The Epistles of Paul to the Colossians and to Philemon*. The Tyndale New Testament Commentaries. Grand Rapids: Eerdmans.
Delling, Gerhard. 1971. στοιχεῖον. In *Theological dictionary of the New Testament*, ed. Gerhard Friedrich, tr. Geoffrey W. Bromiley, vol. 7, 670-87. Grand Rapids: Eerdmans.
Deer, Donald S. 1973. More about the imperatival *hina*. *The Bible Translator* 24:328-29.
Eadie, John. [1884] 1979. *Commentary on the Greek text of the Epistle of Paul to the Colossians*. John Eadie Greek Text Commentaries, vol. 4. Reprint. Grand Rapids: Baker.
Ellicott, Charles J. 1865. *A critical and grammatical commentary on St. Paul's Epistles to the Philippians, Colossians, and to Philemon*. New York: Hurd and Houghton.
Erdman, Charles R. 1933. *The Epistles of Paul to the Colossians and to Philemon*. Philadelphia: Westminster.
Findlay, G. G. 1950. Colossians. In *Galatians, Ephesians, Philippians, Colossians*, i-247. The Pulpit Commentary, vol. 20, ed. H. D. M. Spence and Joseph S. Exell. Reprint. Grand Rapids: Eerdmans.
Foerster, Werner. 1965. κλῆρος. In *Theological dictionary of the New Testament*, ed. Gerhard Kittel, tr. Geoffrey W. Bromiley, vol. 3, 758-64. Grand Rapids: Eerdmans.
Friberg, Timothy. 1982. New Testament Greek word order in light of discourse considerations. Ph.D. diss., Minneapolis: University of Minnesota.
Greenlee, Harold. 1982. A note on 'knowledge'. *Selected Technical Articles Related to Translation* 6:30-31. (Dallas: SIL.)
Greeven, Heinrich. 1964. ζητέω. In *Theological dictionary of the New Testament*, ed. Gerhard Kittel, tr. Geoffrey W. Bromiley, vol. 2, 892-93. Grand Rapids: Eerdmans.
Hale, Clarence B. 1975. Paul's use of *dia touto*. *Notes on Translation* 57:2-4. (Dallas: SIL.)
Hendricks, William L. 1973. All in all: Theological themes in Colossians. *Southwest Journal of Theology* 16:1:23-35.
Hendricksen, William. 1964. *Exposition of Colossians and Philemon*. New Testament Commentary. Grand Rapids: Baker.
Hollenbach, Bruce E. n.d. Two constraints on subordination in Koine Greek. Mexico, D.F.: SIL.
———. 1979. Col. 2:23: Which things lead to the fulfillment of the flesh. *New Testament Studies* 25:2:254-61.
Keach, Benjamin. 1856. *Tropologia: A key to open Scripture metaphors*. London: William Hill Collingridge.
Lamarche, Paul. 1975. Structure de l'épitre aux Colossiens. *Biblica* 56:453-63.
Lenski, R. C. H. 1937. *The interpretation of St. Paul's Epistles to the Colossians, to the Thessalonians, to Timothy, to Titus, and to Philemon*. Columbus, Ohio: Wartburg.

Liddell, Henry G., and Robert Scott. 1972. *A lexicon, abridged from Liddell and Scott's Greek-English lexicon*. Oxford: Clarendon.

Lightfoot, J. B. 1961. *St. Paul's Epistles to the Colossians and to Philemon*. Reprinted from the revised 1879 edition. Grand Rapids: Zondervan.

Martin, Ralph P. 1972. *Colossians: The Church's Lord and the Christian's liberty*. Exeter: Paternoster.

———. 1973. *Colossians and Philemon*. New Century Bible Commentary. Grand Rapids: Eerdmans.

Metzger, Bruce M. 1971. *A textual commentary on the Greek New Testament*. London and New York: United Bible Societies.

Meyer, H. A. W. 1875. *Critical and exegetical hand-book to the Epistles to the Philippians and Colossians*. Edinburgh: T. and T. Clark.

Michaelis, Wilhelm. 1968. πρωτεύω. In *Theological dictionary of the New Testament*, ed. Gerhard Friedrich, tr. Geoffrey W. Bromiley, vol. 6, 881–82. Grand Rapids: Eerdmans.

Moore, Bruce R. 1972. *Doublets. Notes on Translation* 43.

Morris, Leon. 1959. *The First and Second Epistles to the Thessalonians*. The New International Commentary on the New Testament. Grand Rapids: Eerdmans.

Moule, C. F. D. 1957. *The Epistles of Paul the Apostle to the Colossians and to Philemon*. The Cambridge Greek Testament Commentary. Cambridge University Press.

———. 1959. *An idiom-book of New Testament Greek*. 2d ed. Cambridge University Press.

———. 1973. 'The new life' in Colossians 3:1–17. *Review and Expositor* 70:4:481–93.

Moulton, James Hope, and George Milligan. 1972. *The vocabulary of the Greek Testament*. Reprinted from the 1930 edition. Grand Rapids: Eerdmans.

Moulton, W. F., and A. S. Geden. 1926. *Concordance to the Greek Testament*. 3d ed. Edinburgh: T. and T. Clark.

Peake, A. S. 1961. The Epistle to the Colossians. *The expositor's Greek Testament*, vol. 3. Reprinted from the 1898 edition. Grand Rapids: Eerdmans.

Pickering, Wilbur N. 1977a. A framework for discourse analysis. Ph.D. diss., University of Toronto.

———. 1977b. *The identity of the New Testament text*. New York: Thomas Nelson.

Robertson, A. T. 1919. *A grammar of the Greek New Testament in the light of historical research*. London: Hodder and Stoughton.

———. 1931. *Word pictures in the New Testament*, vol. 4. Nashville, Tenn.: Broadman.

Robertson, A. T., and W. Hersey Davis. 1933. *A new short grammar of the Greek Testament*. New York: Harper.

Sanders, Jack T. 1962. The transition from opening epistolary thanksgiving to body in the letters of the Pauline corpus. *Journal of Biblical Literature* 18:4:348–62.

Scott, E. F. 1930. *The Epistles of Paul to the Colossians, to Philemon and to the Ephesians*. The Moffatt New Testament Commentary. New York: Harper and Row.

Turner, Nigel. 1963. *Syntax. A grammar of New Testament Greek,* vol. 3. Edinburgh: T. and T. Clark.

———. 1965. *Grammatical insights into the New Testament*. Edinburgh: T. and T. Clark.

Vincent, Marvin R. 1946. *Word studies in the New Testament*, vol. 3. Reprinted from the 1890 edition. Chicago: Moody.

White, John Lee. 1972. *The form and function of the body of the Greek letter*. 2d ed., corrected. Society of Biblical Literature Dissertation Series, 2. Missoula, Mont.: Scholars Press.

Weigelt, Horst. 1975. δύω (ἀπεκδύομαι). In *The new international dictionary of New Testament theology*, ed. Colin Brown, vol. 1, 314–16. Grand Rapids: Zondervan.

Winer, G. B. 1882. *A treatise on the grammar of New Testament Greek*. Edinburgh: T and T. Clark.

www.ingramcontent.com/pod-product-compliance
Lightning Source LLC
Chambersburg PA
CBHW081147230426
43664CB00018B/2840